N. Gittfried G. Lienke F. Seiferlein
J. Leiendecker B. Gehra K. Hefter
F. Hildebrand (eds.)

# Non-financial Risk Management in the Financial Industry

## A Target Operating Model

Frankfurt School
Forum

**Bibliographic information from the German National Library**
The German National Library lists this publication in the German National Bibliography.
Detailed bibliographic data is available online at https://dnb.dnb.de.

Visit us online: https://www.fsforum.de/.



ISBN (print): 978-3-95647-237-4
ISBN (epub): 978-3-95647-238-1
ISBN (pdf): 978-3-95647-239-8

Second, revised and extended edition 2025

# Table of contents


Table of contents . . . . . . . . . . III
Editors . . . . . . . . . . XXI
Contributors . . . . . . . . . . XXII
Foreword . . . . . . . . . . XXV

**1 Introduction: Rising to the Challenges of Non-Financial Risk Management . . . . . . . . . . 1**
*Dr. Bernhard Gehra, Jannik Leiendecker, Dr. Georg Lienke*
1.1 New risks and challenges . . . . . . . . . . 2
1.2 A forward-looking solution for non-financial risk management in the financial industry . . . . . . . . . . 3
1.3 Defining and aligning non-financial risk categories . . . . . . . . . . 3
1.4 Establishing a non-financial risk appetite framework to prevent an undesirable risk-taking . . . . . . . . . . 4
1.5 Building key governance and organizational pillars for non-financial risk management . . . . . . . . . . 4
1.6 Generating excellence in the non-financial risk management lifecycle 5
1.7 Using data, IT and artificial intelligence and staying cyber resilient . . 6
1.8 Putting conduct and ethics at the center of sustainable non-financial risk management . . . . . . . . . . 7
1.9 A holistic approach to Sustainability Risk Management in Financial Institutions . . . . . . . . . . 8

**2 Definition of Non-Financial Risk in Financial Institutions . . . . . . . . . . 11**
*Dr. Julia Gebhardt, Dr. Katharina Hefter, Jennifer Rabener, Dr. Carsten Wiegand*
2.1 Introduction . . . . . . . . . . 11
2.2 History of non-financial risk and specifications by key regulators . . . 13
2.2.1 A short history of non-financial risk . . . . . . . . . . 14
2.2.2 Existing non-financial risk specifications by key global and regional regulators and associations . . . . . . . . . . 17
2.3 Differentiation of financial and non-financial risk . . . . . . . . . . 18
2.3.1 Financial risk definition . . . . . . . . . . 19
2.3.2 Non-financial risk definition . . . . . . . . . . 20

2.4 Specific clusters of non-financial risk .......................... 20
2.4.1 Operational risk ........................................ 23
2.4.1.1 Financial crime risk ............................ 23
2.4.1.1.1 Money-laundering/terrorist financing risk 24
2.4.1.1.2 Sanctions and embargoes risk .......... 24
2.4.1.1.3 Bribery and corruption risk ............ 25
2.4.1.1.4 Facilitation of tax evasion .............. 25
2.4.1.2 Conduct risk ................................. 26
2.4.1.2.1 Market conduct risk .................. 26
2.4.1.2.2 Client conduct risk ................... 27
2.4.1.2.3 Employee conduct risk ................ 27
2.4.1.3 Regulatory compliance risk ..................... 27
2.4.1.4 Fraud risk ...................................... 28
2.4.1.4.1 Account-opening fraud risk ............ 29
2.4.1.4.2 Debt/credit card fraud risk ............. 29
2.4.1.4.3 Fraudulent paper-based payment transactions risk ...................... 30
2.4.1.4.4 Online banking fraud risk ............. 30
2.4.1.4.5 Credit fraud risk ..................... 30
2.4.1.4.6 Theft risk ........................... 30
2.4.1.4.7 Embezzlement/breach of trust risk ...... 30
2.4.1.4.8 Antitrust violation risk ................ 30
2.4.1.4.9 Balance sheet manipulation ........... 31
2.4.1.5 Information, Communication & Technology (ICT) and cyber risk .................................. 31
2.4.1.5.1 Data confidentiality risk ............... 33
2.4.1.5.2 Data availability risk .................. 33
2.4.1.5.3 Data integrity risk .................... 34
2.4.1.5.4 Information security risk .............. 34
2.4.1.6 Data privacy and bank secrecy risk .............. 34
2.4.1.6.1 Data privacy risk ..................... 35
2.4.1.6.2 Bank secrecy risk ..................... 35
2.4.1.7 Resilience risk ............................... 35
2.4.1.8 Outsourcing and vendor risk .................... 37
2.4.1.8.1 Intragroup outsourcing risk ............ 38
2.4.1.8.2 External outsourcing risk .............. 38
2.4.1.8.3 Vendor risk ........................ 38
2.4.1.9 Tax reporting risk ............................ 38
2.4.1.10 Other operational risk ........................ 39
2.4.1.10.1 Human resources risk ................ 39
2.4.1.10.2 Legal risk ......................... 39
2.4.1.10.3 Physical damage risk ................. 40
2.4.1.10.4 Execution, delivery and process risk ..... 40
2.4.1.10.5 Reporting risk ...................... 40
2.4.1.10.6 Accounting risk ...................... 40

2.4.1.10.7 Project risk . . . . . . . . . . 40
2.4.1.10.8 Competition law risk . . . . . . . . . . 41
2.4.1.10.9 Model risk . . . . . . . . . . 41
2.4.2 Strategic risk . . . . . . . . . . 41
2.4.2.1 Reputational risk . . . . . . . . . . 41
2.4.2.2 Sustainability risk . . . . . . . . . . 42
2.4.2.2.1 Climate change risk . . . . . . . . . . 42
2.4.2.2.2 Human rights risk . . . . . . . . . . 43
2.4.2.3 Business risk . . . . . . . . . . 44
2.4.2.3.1 Forecasting risk . . . . . . . . . . 44
2.4.2.3.2 Inorganic growth risk . . . . . . . . . . 44
2.4.2.3.3 New business risk . . . . . . . . . . 44
2.4.2.3.4 Investor relations risk . . . . . . . . . . 44
2.5 Conclusion and outlook . . . . . . . . . . 45

**3 Risk Boundaries – Setting an Analytical Risk Appetite Framework for Non-Financial Risks . . . . . . . . . . 47**
*Federico Truffelli, Dr. Ulrich Göres, Lorenzo Fantini, Michele Rigoni, Luca Rancan*
3.1 Introduction . . . . . . . . . . 47
3.1.1 Regulatory requirements . . . . . . . . . . 47
3.1.2 RAF in practice . . . . . . . . . . 49
3.2 RAF level 1: overall risk appetite statement . . . . . . . . . . 51
3.2.1 Overall statement . . . . . . . . . . 51
3.2.2 Prohibited activities . . . . . . . . . . 53
3.3 RAF level 2: risk appetite metrics . . . . . . . . . . 53
3.3.1 Defining appropriate metrics . . . . . . . . . . 53
3.3.2 Metrics: setting the thresholds . . . . . . . . . . 54
3.3.2.1 Thresholds based on benchmark and historical internal loss data for a metric based on operational losses . . . . . . . . . . 55
3.3.2.2 Thresholds based on residual risk levels for a metric based on risk assessment . . . . . . . . . . 56
3.4 RAF level 3: Key Risk Indicators . . . . . . . . . . 57
3.4.1 Selecting KRIs . . . . . . . . . . 57
3.4.1.1 Candidate indicators identification . . . . . . . . . . 58
3.4.1.2 Appetite tracking suitability . . . . . . . . . . 58
3.4.1.3 Expert judgement . . . . . . . . . . 58
3.4.2 KRIs: setting and calibrating the thresholds . . . . . . . . . . 62
3.4.2.1 Threshold calibration based on historical data analysis and percentiles . . . . . . . . . . 62
3.4.2.2 Threshold fine-tuning based on benchmarking and backtesting . . . . . . . . . . 64

3.5 RAF governance ........ 65
3.5.1 RAF design and update ........ 66
3.5.2 RAF monitoring and reporting ........ 67
3.5.3 RAF threshold breaches and escalation ........ 68
3.5.4 Action plan definition ........ 70

**4 The Three Lines of Defence Model: Key Success Factors for Effective Risk Management ........ 73**
*Dr. Georg Lienke, Dr. Oliver Engels, Marc Peter Klein, Peter Gürtlschmidt, Rei Tanaka*
4.1 Introduction ........ 73
4.2 Regulatory framework in selected key jurisdictions ........ 74
4.2.1 European Union ........ 74
4.2.2 United States of America ........ 75
4.2.3 Hong Kong ........ 75
4.2.4 Singapore ........ 76
4.2.5 Risk-type-specific qualifications of the 3LoD model: financial crime prevention ........ 76
4.2.5.1 EU: remaining country-specific variation in 1st and 2nd LoD mandate ........ 76
4.2.5.2 United States of America: BSA Compliance Officer . 77
4.2.5.3 Hong Kong: Money Laundering Reporting Officer and Compliance Officer ........ 77
4.3 Key roles and responsibilities of 1st, 2nd and 3rd LoD ........ 77
4.3.1 The first line of defence: risk owner ........ 78
4.3.1.1 Scope of 1st LoD mandate ........ 78
4.3.1.1.1 Risk ownership ........ 78
4.3.1.1.2 Implementation and execution of 1st LoD controls ........ 79
4.3.1.2 Allocation of 1st LoD responsibility ........ 79
4.3.1.3 1st LoD risk-coordinating function (1.5th LoD) ..... 79
4.3.1.3.1 Coordination of risk management activities ........ 79
4.3.1.3.2 Interface to 2nd LoD ........ 80
4.3.1.3.3 Regulatory advisor ........ 80
4.3.2 The second line of defence: internal control functions ....... 80
4.3.2.1 Scope of 2nd LoD mandate ........ 81
4.3.2.1.1 Standard setting ........ 81
4.3.2.1.2 Testing of 1st LoD controls ........ 81
4.3.2.1.3 Risk assessment ........ 81
4.3.2.1.4 Training and advisory ........ 82
4.3.2.2 Risk materiality and corresponding intensity of 2nd LoD risk oversight ........ 82

4.3.2.3 Independence of 2nd LoD risk oversight ........... 82
4.3.2.3.1 Organisational independence .......... 82
4.3.2.3.2 Functional independence .............. 83
4.3.2.3.3 Internal control functions performing 1st LoD activities ..................... 83
4.3.2.4 Key success factors for effective 2nd LoD risk oversight ..................................... 84
4.3.2.4.1 Methodology consistency across 2nd LoD functions ........................... 84
4.3.2.4.2 Bodies and committees: adequate 2nd LoD participation and information sharing ... 86
4.3.2.4.3 Appointment of primus inter pares non-financial risk governance function ...... 87
4.3.3 The third line of defence: internal audit as provider of independent assurance ................................. 87
4.3.3.1 Independent assurance ......................... 87
4.3.3.1.1 Adequacy of risk management framework 87
4.3.3.1.2 Design and operating effectiveness ...... 88
4.3.3.1.3 Compliance with regulatory requirements and internal standards ................ 88
4.3.3.2 Advising the board of directors .................. 88
4.4 Common pitfalls of the 3LoD model and precautionary measures .. 89
4.4.1 Insufficient risk ownership by 1st LoD ................... 89
4.4.2 Lack of 2nd LoD expertise ............................ 89
4.4.3 Inadequate assurance by 3rd LoD ........................ 90
4.5 Conclusion ............................................ 90

**5 Global Functional Lead in Non-Financial Risk Management: Ensuring Consistency and Integration in Complex Organisations .... 91**
*Ulrike Brouzi, Dr. Michael Lange, P. Robert Mieszkowski, Jannik Leiendecker, Dr. Georg Lienke, Florian Seiferlein, Norbert Gittfried, Rei Tanaka*
5.1 Introduction ........................................... 91
5.2 Regulatory framework in select key markets ................... 93
5.2.1 European Union ..................................... 93
5.2.2 United States of America ............................. 93
5.2.3 Hong Kong .......................................... 94
5.2.4 Singapore ........................................... 94
5.3 Global functional lead: individual corporate parameters to consider . 94
5.3.1 Corporate culture .................................... 94
5.3.2 Organisation's complexity ............................. 95
5.3.3 IT landscape ......................................... 95
5.3.4 Geographical footprint ................................ 95

5.4 Major components of global functional lead in non-financial risk management .......... 95
5.4.1 Operating model: striking a balance between global standards and regional execution .......... 96
5.4.1.1 Regulatory horizon screening .......... 97
5.4.1.2 Setting of risk-specific standards .......... 98
5.4.1.3 Training and advisory .......... 99
5.4.1.4 Controls by the 1st and 2nd line of defence .......... 99
5.4.1.5 Non-financial risk assessment .......... 100
5.4.1.6 Non-financial risk reporting .......... 101
5.4.1.7 Group risk oversight .......... 101
5.4.2 Reporting lines: establishing implementation accountability in vertical functions .......... 102
5.4.2.1 Solid reporting lines into local legal entity and branch 102
5.4.2.2 Dotted reporting lines into global risk management organisation .......... 103
5.4.3 Meeting governance: supporting effective management of a global risk function .......... 103
5.5 Conclusion .......... 104

**6 Policies and Procedures: Framework and Governance Requirements in the Financial Sector .......... 107**
*Dr. Erasmus Faber, Björn Stauber, Dr. Georg Lienke*
6.1 Introduction .......... 107
6.2 Regulatory framework in selected key jurisdictions .......... 107
6.2.1 European Banking Authority (EBA) .......... 108
6.2.2 US regulators .......... 109
6.2.2.1 The Federal Reserve .......... 109
6.2.2.2 Office of the Comptroller of the Currency .......... 109
6.2.3 Hong Kong Monetary Authority .......... 110
6.2.4 Monetary Authority of Singapore .......... 111
6.3 Policy framework: key implications for a target concept .......... 111
6.3.1 Status quo: need for structured approach .......... 111
6.3.1.1 Lack of a harmonised approach .......... 111
6.3.1.2 Policy gaps and redundancies .......... 112
6.3.2 Policy framework: design concept and hierarchies .......... 112
6.3.2.1 Design concept: key hypotheses for an effective policy framework .......... 112
6.3.2.1.1 Harmonised design approach .......... 112
6.3.2.1.2 Completeness .......... 113
6.3.2.1.3 Uniform naming convention .......... 113
6.3.2.1.4 Precise wording .......... 113
6.3.2.1.5 Assignment of responsibilities .......... 113
6.3.2.1.6 Governance rules .......... 113
6.3.2.1.7 Linkage to internal processes and controls 113

6.3.2.2 Suggested hierarchy levels: key criteria and examples 114
6.3.2.3 Level one: overarching risk strategies, policies and documents – risk and business segment agnostic .... 114
6.3.2.3.1 Key criteria .... 114
6.3.2.3.2 Key risk type and business segment agnostic topics .... 115
6.3.2.4 Level two: risk-type-specific policies and procedures 115
6.3.2.4.1 Key criteria .... 115
6.3.2.4.2 Risk-type-specific documents .... 116
6.3.2.5 Level three: customer-related and business-specific policies and procedures .... 117
6.3.2.5.1 Key criteria .... 117
6.3.2.5.2 Customer-related and business-specific topics .... 117
6.3.2.6 Level four: policies and procedures in international locations .... 118
6.3.2.6.1 Scope of applicability: subsidiary companies and branch offices .... 118
6.3.2.6.2 Key criteria .... 118
6.4 Policy governance, repository and workflow tool .... 119
6.4.1 Approval of policies and procedures .... 119
6.4.1.1 Level one: board of directors .... 119
6.4.1.2 Level two: responsible board member .... 120
6.4.1.3 Level three: senior management on N-1 level .... 120
6.4.1.4 Level four: general manager or 2nd LoD N-1 .... 120
6.4.2 Authorship, ownership, creation as well as update of policies and procedures .... 120
6.4.2.1 Document authorship .... 120
6.4.2.2 Document ownership .... 121
6.4.2.3 Document creation process .... 121
6.4.2.4 Stringent management of update process .... 121
6.4.2.4.1 Regular validation based on time intervals 121
6.4.2.4.2 Ad hoc updates .... 122
6.4.3 Policy repository, including workflow tool: centralised management of policies and procedures .... 122
6.4.3.1 Facilitation of access .... 122
6.4.3.2 Document lifecycle management .... 123
6.4.3.2.1 Regular validation of documents .... 123
6.4.3.2.2 Ad hoc updates .... 123
6.4.3.2.2.1 Changes in business and operating model .... 123
6.4.3.2.2.2 Changes in regulatory framework .... 123
6.4.3.3 Audit-proof change log .... 124
6.5 Conclusion .... 124

7 **Top-Down Risk and Control Assessment: A Forward-Looking Approach to Evaluate Company-Wide Non-Financial Risk Exposure** .......... **125**
*Hurdogan Irmak, Burcu Nasuhoglu, Dr. Erasmus Faber, Lorenzo Fantini, Benedetta Testino, Jannik Leiendecker, Barbara Fojcik, Dr. Georg Lienke*
7.1 Introduction .......... 125
7.2 Top-down vs. bottom-up: different approaches based on desired outcomes .......... 126
7.2.1 Approaches: risk-specific focus vs. overarching non-financial risk coverage .......... 126
7.2.1.1 Bottom-up approach: risk-specific, granular focus .. 127
7.2.1.2 Top-down approach: overarching, holistic non-financial risk coverage .......... 127
7.2.2 Potential outcomes: different scope of risk-coverage and level of granularity .......... 128
7.3 Key success factors: maximising the effectiveness of top-down risk and control assessments .......... 128
7.4 Regulatory framework, best practice and standard setter guidelines .. 129
7.4.1 COSO ERM framework .......... 129
7.4.2 Bank for International Settlements .......... 130
7.4.3 EBA and ECB .......... 130
7.5 Methodology of top-down risk and control assessment: evaluation of inherent risk, control adequacy and residual risk .......... 131
7.5.1 Non-financial risk taxonomy as a starting point .......... 131
7.5.2 Measurement of inherent risk .......... 131
7.5.2.1 Calculation of severity .......... 132
7.5.2.1.1 Organisation-specific risk indicators .... 132
7.5.2.1.2 Industry adjustments .......... 134
7.5.2.1.3 Weighting of risk indicators based on data source reliability .......... 135
7.5.2.2 Calculation of likelihood .......... 135
7.5.2.3 Inherent risk matrix .......... 136
7.5.3 Measurement of internal control adequacy .......... 136
7.5.3.1 Control indicators .......... 137
7.5.3.2 Weighting of control indicators .......... 138
7.5.3.3 Control rating .......... 138
7.5.4 Determination of residual risk .......... 139
7.6 Breakout: building an institution-wide internal control system ...... 140
7.6.1 Introduction .......... 140
7.6.2 Alternative path to building an internal control framework: top-down, risk-based approach .......... 140
7.6.3 Five-step approach: building an internal control framework .. 141
7.6.3.1 Step 1: determination of NFR criticality .......... 141
7.6.3.2 Step 2: mapping of key risks to process landscape ... 141
7.6.3.3 Step 3: definition of control objectives, key controls and control repository .......... 142

7.6.3.4 Step 4: assessment of controls .................. 142
7.6.3.5 Step 5: design NFR control report .............. 143
7.7 Approach to handling residual risk ........................... 143
7.7.1 High residual risk: project and investment imperative to mitigating residual risk ............................... 144
7.7.2 Medium-high residual risk: action plan to reduce inherent risk exposure ........................................ 144
7.7.3 Medium-low residual risk: continuous control testing and selected action requested .............................. 144
7.7.4 Low residual risk: periodic, risk-based controls ............ 144
7.8 Integrated process to perform annual top-down risk and control assessment ............................................... 145
7.8.1 Phase 1: pre-assessment by control functions .............. 145
7.8.2 Phase 2: assessment by business senior management ........ 146
7.8.3 Phase 3: validation and reporting ....................... 146

**8 A Top-Down Approach to Non-Financial Risk Reporting: Collaboration Across Risk Types for Sustainable Risk Steering ....... 147**

*Valérie Villafranca, Dr. Georg Lienke, Florian Seiferlein, Kai Gammelin, Dr. Katharina Hefter, Norbert Gittfried*

8.1 Introduction: the imperative of top-down non-financial risk reporting ................................................ 147
8.2 Regulatory framework in selected key markets .................. 148
8.2.1 European Union ...................................... 148
8.2.2 United States ........................................ 149
8.2.3 Hong Kong ........................................... 149
8.2.4 Singapore ........................................... 150
8.3 Current state of non-financial risk reporting: formats with inconsistent scopes and methodologies .......................... 150
8.3.1 Operational risk reports .............................. 150
8.3.2 Additional 2nd LoD reports on specific non-financial risk types ................................................. 151
8.3.3 Reports on internal control system ..................... 152
8.4 Key parameters of top-down non-financial risk reporting: methodology, required input and results ....................... 152
8.4.1 Identification and evaluation of key risk indicators ......... 153
8.4.1.1 Determination of key risk indicators, thresholds and potential input sources ........................ 153
8.4.1.1.1 Step 1: understand risk factors ......... 153
8.4.1.1.2 Step 2: identify key risk indicators ...... 153
8.4.1.1.3 Step 3: derive institution-specific thresholds ......................... 153

8.4.1.2 Example KRI's: financial crime risk, outsourcing risk and human resources risk ..... 154
8.4.1.2.1 Key risk indicators for financial crime risk 155
8.4.1.2.2 Key risk indicators for outsourcing risk .. 156
8.4.1.2.3 Key risk indicators for human resources risk ..... 157
8.4.1.3 Evaluation of key risk indicators ..... 157
8.4.2 Assessment of key controls as risk-mitigating measures ..... 159
8.4.2.1 Step 1: capturing and allocation of controls ..... 159
8.4.2.2 Step 2: assessment of controls ..... 160
8.4.3 Determination of residual risk and required risk-mitigating actions ..... 162
8.4.3.1 High level of residual risk ..... 162
8.4.3.2 Medium level of residual risk ..... 162
8.4.3.3 Low level of residual risk ..... 163
8.5 Reporting process and governance ..... 163
8.5.1 Governance arrangements ..... 163
8.5.1.1 Board of directors ..... 163
8.5.1.2 Chairman of the supervisory board ..... 163
8.5.1.3 Central reporting unit ..... 164
8.5.1.4 2nd LoD control functions ..... 164
8.5.1.5 Operational risk department ..... 164
8.5.2 Reporting process ..... 164
8.6 Conclusion ..... 165

**9 Internal Investigations into Corporate Misconduct: Applying an Investigative Approach to Enable Proactive Risk Oversight ..... 167**
*Lora von Ploetz, Florian Seiferlein*
9.1 Introduction ..... 167
9.2 Selected laws, regulations and standards ..... 168
9.2.1 Supervisory sanction relief based on voluntary investigation and cooperation ..... 170
9.2.1.1 Jurisdictions potentially reducing sanctions and enforcement actions due to effective investigation and cooperation ..... 171
9.2.1.2 Jurisdictions not explicitly providing a bonus for self-disclosure and cooperation ..... 172
9.2.1.3 Jurisdictions where investigations and cooperation do not change assessment of law enforcement ..... 173
9.2.2 Statutory disclosure requirements ..... 173
9.2.3 Investigation standards and requirements ..... 174

9.3 Concept for proactive risk oversight using an investigative approach 175
9.3.1 Investigation process 176
9.3.1.1 Proactive risk management 177
9.3.1.2 Strategic and tactical investigations 179
9.3.1.3 Example: sanctions-driven investigations 180
9.3.2 Information sharing and global risk management 183
9.3.2.1 How to connect needles in the same haystack (in a financial institution) 183
9.3.2.2 How to connect needles in different haystacks (between different financial institutions) 184
9.4 Success factors and common pitfalls 186

**10 Technical Application and Data Architecture for Non-Financial Risk Management 189**
*Kai Gammelin, Björn Stauber, Dr. Christian N. Schmid, Dr. Jan-Oliver Fröhlich, Annika Melchert, Daniel Wagner*
10.1 Introduction 189
10.1.1 A fragmented ICT landscape 190
10.1.2 ICT's impact on data availability 190
10.1.3 Data availability across borders 192
10.1.4 Additional challenges associated with group companies 192
10.2 Regulatory requirements 193
10.3 Seven challenges in NFR management and reporting 193
10.3.1 Challenge 1: the lack of a defined NFR-ICT strategy 194
10.3.2 Challenge 2: responsibility for and execution of NFR reporting-related activities (operational unit vs. NFR management) 195
10.3.3 Challenge 3: consistency and transparency of ICT architecture 196
10.3.4 Challenge 4: alignment of data architecture for transparency on data lineage 197
10.3.5 Challenge 5: implementing a solid ICT target architecture 198
10.3.6 Challenge 6: cost-benefit considerations 198
10.3.7 Challenge 7: "make-or-buy" decision 199
10.4 A target ICT architecture for NFR 199
10.4.1 The NFR architecture ecosystem 201
10.4.2 Dashboards and reporting 201
10.4.3 Other key enabling technologies 202

**11 Data Governance in Non-Financial Risk Management 205**
*Björn Stauber, Dr. Christian N. Schmid, Dr. Jan-Oliver Fröhlich, Annika Melchert, Daniel Wagner*
11.1 Introduction 205
11.2 Regulatory requirements 206

11.3 Data governance to support NFR management ... 207
11.3.1 Data structures and description ... 208
11.3.2 Data governance and policies ... 208
11.3.3 Data governance tools and automation ... 209
11.3.4 Data organisation and target operating model ... 210
11.4 Scaling up state-of-the-art NFR data governance ... 211
11.4.1 Specific roles and responsibilities ... 212
11.4.2 Tool optimisation ... 213
11.5 Conclusion ... 213

**12 Optimizing Effectiveness and Efficiency: Deployment of Artificial Intelligence in Non-Financial Risk Management ... 215**
*Dr. Jochen Papenbrock, Dr. John Ashley, Dr. Georg Lienke, Florian Seiferlein, Norbert Gittfried, Dr. Stiene Riemer, Hanjo Seibert*
12.1 Introduction ... 215
12.2 The transformative journey of AI: from rule-based systems to advanced analytics, machine learning and generative AI ... 217
12.2.1 Classical AI: rule-based systems and early automation ... 217
12.2.2 Advanced analytics: from description to prediction ... 218
12.2.3 Machine learning & deep learning: from pattern recognition to adaptive decision-making ... 219
12.2.4 Generative AI (GenAI): transforming risk intelligence and compliance ... 220
12.3 Global approaches to AI regulation ... 221
12.3.1 The need for AI regulation in financial services ... 222
12.3.2 European Union: the AI Act and its impact on financial institutions ... 222
12.3.3 United States: recent shift to AI innovation and deregulation . 222
12.3.4 China: AI regulation, cybersecurity, and data sovereignty ... 223
12.4 Deep dive: AI-driven prevention of financial crime ... 224
12.4.1 Overall challenges in financial crime prevention ... 224
12.4.1.1 Enhancing detection accuracy in complex risk environments ... 224
12.4.1.2 Reducing manual burden in compliance operations . 225
12.4.1.3 Ensuring data availability, quality, and consistency .. 225
12.4.2 Case studies: deployment of AI in financial crime prevention 225
12.4.2.1 Case study 1: using digital fingerprinting and synthetic identity coherence to prevent application fraud ... 226
12.4.2.1.1 Starting position & specific challenges ... 226
12.4.2.1.2 Solution: applying digital fingerprinting & synthetic identity coherence analysis ... 226
12.4.2.1.3 Benefits for financial institutions ... 228

12.4.2.2 Case study 2: automating KYC file creation and maintenance ... 228
12.4.2.2.1 Starting position & specific challenges ... 229
12.4.2.2.2 Solution: modernizing KYC documentation with AI ... 229
12.4.2.2.3 Benefits for financial institutions ... 231
12.4.2.3 Case study 3: optimizing transaction monitoring E2E ... 231
12.4.2.3.1 Starting position & specific challenges ... 231
12.4.2.3.2 Solution: AI-powered holistic optimization of TM ... 232
12.4.2.3.3 Benefits for financial institutions ... 234
12.4.2.4 Case study 4: enhancing sanctions screening with AI-powered intelligence ... 234
12.4.2.4.1 Starting position & specific challenges ... 234
12.4.2.4.2 Solution: AI-augmented sanctions screening framework ... 235
12.4.2.4.3 Benefits for financial institutions ... 237
12.5 Responsible AI: addressing key challenges in AI deployment ... 238
12.5.1 Responsible AI frameworks ... 238
12.5.2 Deep dive: implementing effective AI risk management ... 239
12.5.2.1 Managing AI model risk ... 240
12.5.2.1.1 Governing AI models to ensure reliability and compliance ... 240
12.5.2.1.2 Approach to managing AI model risks ... 240
12.5.2.2 Bias detection and fairness monitoring ... 241
12.5.2.2.1 Preventing discriminatory AI-driven decisions ... 241
12.5.2.2.2 Approach to bias detection and fairness monitoring ... 242
12.5.2.3 Scenario stress testing and AI model validation ... 242
12.5.2.3.1 Ensuring AI models perform under varying market conditions ... 242
12.5.2.3.2 Approach to AI stress testing and AI model validation ... 243
12.5.3 Deep dive: sovereign AI and infrastructure – control, compliance, and capability ... 243
12.6 Conclusions and key takeaways ... 244

**13 Enhancing the Cyber Resilience of Financial Institutions ............ 247**
*Anna Streuli, Dr. Roman Schnalle, Felix Hildebrand, Dr. Georg Lienke*
13.1 Introduction ........................................ 247
13.1.1 Focus of this chapter ................................ 247
13.1.2 Magnitude of the cyber threat ........................... 248
13.1.3 Urgency of the issue: digital transformation, cyber threats, and third-party risks .................................. 248
13.1.4 Impact on financial institutions .......................... 249
13.2 Regulatory requirements and oversight: strengthening cyber resilience ................................................ 249
13.2.1 Regulatory frameworks ............................... 249
13.2.1.1 European Union: Digital Operational Resilience Act (DORA) and NIS2 ......................... 250
13.2.1.2 United States: New York Department of Financial Services Cybersecurity Regulation and U.S. SEC Cybersecurity Disclosure Rule .................. 251
13.2.1.3 Asia-Pacific: Singapore's Cybersecurity Act and Hong Kong's Cybersecurity Measures ............ 252
13.2.2 Regulatory oversight ................................ 253
13.2.2.1 Supervision and enforcement .................... 253
13.2.2.2 Incident reporting and management ............. 253
13.2.2.3 Third-party provider oversight .................. 253
13.2.2.4 Stress testing and audits ...................... 254
13.3 Industry frameworks for cyber resilience ...................... 254
13.3.1 Overview of NIST CSF and ISO/IEC 27001 .............. 255
13.3.2 Comparison of NIST CSF and ISO/IEC 27001 ............ 255
13.3.2.1 Scope and focus ............................. 255
13.3.2.2 Implementation approach ...................... 255
13.3.2.3 Typical use cases ............................ 256
13.4 The six functions of NIST CSF ............................. 256
13.4.1 Function 1: Govern ................................. 257
13.4.1.1 Organizational context ........................ 257
13.4.1.2 Risk management strategy ..................... 258
13.4.1.3 Roles, responsibilities, and authorities ........... 258
13.4.1.4 Policy ..................................... 258
13.4.1.5 Oversight .................................. 258
13.4.1.6 Cybersecurity supply chain risk management ...... 260
13.4.2 Function 2: Identify ................................. 262
13.4.2.1 Asset management ........................... 262
13.4.2.2 Risk assessment ............................. 262
13.4.2.3 Improvement ................................ 263

13.4.3 Function 3: Protect ... 263
13.4.3.1 Identity management, authentication, and access control ... 263
13.4.3.2 Awareness and training ... 263
13.4.3.3 Data security ... 265
13.4.3.4 Platform security ... 265
13.4.3.5 Technology infrastructure resilience ... 265
13.4.4 Function 4: Detect ... 266
13.4.4.1 Continuous security monitoring ... 266
13.4.4.2 Anomalies and events ... 266
13.4.5 Function 5: Respond ... 267
13.4.5.1 Incident management ... 267
13.4.5.2 Incident analysis ... 268
13.4.5.3 Incident response reporting and communication ... 268
13.4.5.4 Incident mitigation ... 268
13.4.6 Function 6: Recover ... 269
13.4.6.1 Incident recovery plan execution ... 269
13.4.6.2 Incident recovery communication ... 269
13.5 Emerging challenges and adaptation strategies in cyber resilience ... 270
13.5.1 Emerging technologies: impact on cybersecurity ... 270
13.5.1.1 Artificial Intelligence (AI): enhancing security and enabling sophisticated attacks ... 270
13.5.1.2 Cloud and API security: securing financial infrastructure in a digital world ... 271
13.5.1.3 Digital identity and authentication security: strengthening fraud prevention ... 271
13.5.1.4 Quantum computing: a future threat to encryption standards ... 272
13.5.2 Adaptation strategies: adapting to evolving cyber threats ... 272
13.6 Four strategic recommendations for strengthening cyber resilience ... 273
13.6.1 Strengthen cybersecurity governance and leadership ... 273
13.6.2 Implement comprehensive cybersecurity ... 273
13.6.3 Perform rigorous third-party oversight ... 274
13.6.4 Strategic technology adoption ... 274

**14 Core Elements of Conduct and Ethics in the Context of Non-Financial Risk ... 275**
*Dr. Barbara Roth, Dr. Erasmus Faber, Dr. Julia Gebhardt, Dr. Katharina Hefter, Constanze Westwood*
14.1 Conduct risk: definitions, characteristics and regulatory landscape ... 275
14.1.1 Conduct and compliance, ethics versus integrity ... 275
14.1.1.1 Finding common ground: definition of key terms ... 275
14.1.1.2 Conduct-based versus integrity-based ethics ... 277
14.1.1.3 An integrative approach for synthesising conduct-/compliance-based and integrity-based ethics ... 278

14.1.2 What is meant when we talk about conduct risk? ........... 280
14.1.2.1 No universal definition ......................... 280
14.1.2.2 Three key topics: market, client and employee conduct risk ................................. 281
14.1.3 Conduct risk in the NFR taxonomy .................... 283
14.2 Regulatory landscape ........................................ 284
14.2.1 European perspective .................................. 287
14.2.1.1 European/UK regulators ....................... 287
14.2.1.2 Other European countries ...................... 293
14.2.2 US perspective ........................................ 296
14.2.3 Asia-Pacific perspective .............................. 298
14.3 Why conduct risk matters .................................... 302
14.3.1 Increased regulatory scrutiny ......................... 302
14.3.1.1 Focus on regulatory oversight ................... 302
14.3.1.2 Frequency of regulatory actions ................ 303
14.3.2 Supervisory and legal actions ......................... 304
14.3.2.1 Actions against firms .......................... 304
14.3.2.2 Actions against individuals ...................... 305

**15 Managing Conduct Risk: Framework and Perspectives .............. 309**
*Prof. Dr. Martin Schulz, Dr. Julia Gebhardt, Dr. Katharina Hefter, Constanze Westwood*
15.1 Trends and perspectives in respect of conduct risk in the regulatory context ...................................................... 309
15.1.1 Treating Customers Fairly (TCF) ........................ 309
15.1.2 Senior management regimes as emerging global trends in conduct risk ............................................ 311
15.1.2.1 UK ............................................ 312
15.1.2.2 Hong Kong and Singapore ..................... 313
15.1.2.3 Malaysia ...................................... 314
15.1.2.4 Australia ...................................... 314
15.2 Conduct risk management as an integral part of sustainability ...... 315
15.2.1 Governance and conduct in a sustainability context ......... 315
15.2.2 New legislative focus and recent regulatory developments ... 316
15.3 Managing conduct risk ....................................... 319
15.3.1 The Conduct Risk House .............................. 319
15.3.2 Building a conduct risk framework ..................... 320

**16 A Holistic Approach to Sustainability Risk Management in Financial Institutions – A Global Perspective ............................... 323**
*Oliver Engels, Jannik Leiendecker, Larissa Pilz, Aytech Pseunokov, Benedetta Testino, Anita Varshney*
16.1 Introduction ............................................. 323
16.2 Regulatory frameworks in selected key jurisdictions .............. 326
16.2.1 EBA Guidelines on ESG Risk Management (EU – Banks) ... 326
16.2.2 OCC/Federal Reserve/FDIC Climate Risk Management Principles (US – Banks) ............................... 327
16.2.3 PRA Supervisory Statement on Climate Risk (UK – Banks & Insurers) ........................................... 327
16.2.4 MAS Environmental Risk Management Guidelines (Singapore – Banks, Insurers, Asset Managers) ........... 328
16.2.5 HKMA Supervisory Policy Manual GS-1 Climate Risk Management (Hong Kong – Authorized Institutions) ...... 329
16.3 Sustainability risk management: upcoming challenges for FIs ...... 330
16.4 Target picture: effective management of sustainability risk drivers .. 332
16.4.1 Sustainability strategy ................................ 333
16.4.2 Sustainability governance and organization ............... 334
16.4.3 Sustainability risk steering ............................ 335
16.4.4 Identification of enabling factors ....................... 337
16.5 Conclusion ............................................... 338

Bibliography ................................................... 341

# Editors

**Norbert Gittfried** is a Partner and Director at Boston Consulting Group. As topic coordinator for Compliance & Regulation, he advises large financial institutions worldwide on complex compliance transformations and the development of overarching non-financial risk (NFR) steering approaches. His focus lies both on establishing effective Compliance and NFR management systems, on digitising those functions and making them more efficient. Prior to joining BCG 15 years ago, he was Senior Manager at a Big 4 Company. He is a lecturer at Goethe Business School and a permanent representative in various industry bodies for FI.

**Dr. Georg Lienke** is a lawyer and Associate Director at Boston Consulting Group focusing on non-financial risk management and Compliance. Georg regularly publishes on non-financial risk topics. He holds a Ph.D. in law from the Technical University Dresden and an LL.M. in Corporate and Financial Law from the University of Hong Kong. Prior to joining BCG, Georg worked at a Big 4 Company, a global bank and an international law firm.

**Florian Seiferlein** is a former Partner at Boston Consulting Group. For more than a decade, he advised leading Financial Institutions on Strategy, Finance and Risk Management. He managed large-scale transformations, implementations of digitalized End-to-End Target Operating Models as well as regulatory assessments in Europe, North America and Africa, and he was also a part of US Monitor teams. After BCG, a Big4 and another management consulting firm, he moved into a leading role in the financial industry. Florian holds a Master of Science in business engineering (Karlsruhe Institute of Technology).

**Jannik Leiendecker** is a Partner and Associate Director at Boston Consulting Group. He is co-leading BCG's Center for Sustainability Policy and Regulation and is also a member of EFRAG's Sustainability Reporting Technical Expert Group. Over the last 15 years, his work has been focused on Non-Financial Risk Management and Sustainability-related topics especially within the Financial Services Industry. He is a regular guest lecturer and has published intensively on the subject.

**Dr. Bernhard Gehra** is a Managing Director and Senior Partner at Boston Consulting Group, based in New York City. With more than 20 years of experience, he specializes in Risk, Compliance, and Technology, advising global organizations on complex challenges in these domains. In the past decade, he has led large-scale, international programs with a particular focus on Risk and Non-Financial Risk management. At BCG, Bernhard holds multiple leadership roles within the firm's Risk & Compliance practice, including heading the North America branch. Prior to joining BCG, he worked for a leading global securities services provider. He holds a Ph.D. in Information Science.

**Dr. Katharina Hefter** is a Managing Director and Partner at Boston Consulting Group. With more than 15 years of experience, she specializes on Compliance, Risk, and Ethics supporting clients in preventive transformative programs as well as remediation efforts. She leads complex, international programs in Non-Financial Risk Management for Banks, Payment Providers and Insurance Companies. Furthermore, Katharina holds several leadership roles within BCG and is BCG's Global Lead for Compliance and Crisis Management. Katharina holds a Ph.D. in international management from ESCP Europe.

**Felix Hildebrand** is a Managing Director & Partner at Boston Consulting Group, where he leads the firm's Compliance business for financial institutions across Central & Northern Europe. With roughly 15 years of experience in the industry, his work focuses on the design and transformation of Compliance and Non-Financial Risk functions. He has led numerous large-scale engagements related to risk governance, operational resilience, and regulatory-driven change. Felix regularly publishes on compliance & non-financial risk topics, and actively drives the agenda of several think tanks.

## Contributors

Dr. John Ashley, Director, Global Public Sector Solutions Architecture & NVIDIA AI Technology Centers, NVIDIA, Los Angeles

Ulrike Brouzi, Member of the Board of Managing Directors, DZ BANK AG, Frankfurt

Dr. Oliver Engels, Senior expert in the field of integrated governance, risk and compliance as well as sustainability, process improvement and operations in the financial service industry, Frankfurt

Dr. Erasmus Faber, Managing Director, Chief Compliance Officer, Twelve Securis, Munich

Lorenzo Fantini, Managing Director & Partner, Boston Consulting Group, Milan

Barbara Fojcik, Senior Strategist, Group Strategy & Impact, Allianz SE, Munich

Dr. Jan-Oliver Fröhlich, Associate Director, Boston Consulting Group, Hamburg

Kai Gammelin, Senior expert of governance, risk management and compliance in a leading position in the financial industry, Bludenz

Dr. Julia Gebhardt, Managing Director & Partner, Boston Consulting Group, Munich

Dr. Ulrich Göres, Frankfurt

Peter Gürtlschmidt, Mag. MA, Director, Head BLAFC Corporate Bank BizBanking Germany, Deutsche Bank AG, Frankfurt

Hurdogan Irmak, Head of Risk Management, Isbank, Istanbul

Marc Peter Klein, Ass. jur., Managing Director, Group Chief Compliance Officer & Chief Human Rights Officer, Deutsche Börse AG, Eschborn

Dr. Michael Lange, Managing Director, Divisional Head Compliance, DZ BANK AG, Frankfurt

Annika Melchert, Principal, BCG Platinion, Dubai

P. Robert Mieszkowski, DZ BANK AG, Frankfurt

Burcu Nasuhoglu, Head of Operational Risk Management, Isbank, Istanbul

Dr. Jochen Papenbrock, EMEA Head of Financial Technology, NVIDIA, Frankfurt

Larissa Pilz, Manager (VP), Chief Risk Office, Deutsche Börse AG, Frankfurt

Aytech Pseunokov, Project Leader, Boston Consulting Group, Dubai

Jennifer Rabener, Compliance Specialist, Green Climate Fund, Seoul

Luca Rancan, Chief Executive Officer, Gratitude Holding, Milan

Dr. Stiene Riemer, Managing Director and Partner, Boston Consulting Group, Munich

Michele Rigoni, Partner and Associate Director, Boston Consulting Group, Milan

Dr. Barbara Roth, LL.M., Chief Administration Officer, Executive Board Member, State Street Bank International GmbH, München

Dr. Christian N. Schmid., Managing Director & Partner, Boston Consulting Group, Munich

Dr. Roman Schnalle, Executive Director, Chief Information Security Officer, Helaba Landesbank Hessen-Thüringen, Frankfurt

Prof. Dr. Martin Schulz, Attorney at law, Counsel, CMS Hasche Sigle, Frankfurt, Professor of Business Law, IU International University of Applied Sciences, Erfurt

Hanjo Seibert, Managing Director and Partner, Boston Consulting Group, Washington D.C.

Björn Stauber, M.Sc., First Vice President Compliance, KfW Bankengruppe, Frankfurt

Anna Streuli, Managing Director, Head Chief Risk Office, Helaba Landesbank Hessen-Thüringen, Frankfurt

Rei Tanaka, Senior risk management expert in the financial services consulting sector, Tokyo

Benedetta Testino, Associate Director, Boston Consulting Group, Milan

Federico Truffelli, Deputy Head of Group Anti-Financial Crime, Group Head of AML/FS Monitoring Strategy, UniCredit Group, Milan

Anita Varshney, Global Vice President, Strategic Customer Engagements, SAP Sustainability, Singapore

Valérie Villafranca, Managing Director, Group Head of ESG Transformation, Société Générale, Paris

Lora von Ploetz, LL.M. Law, LL.M. Finance, Senior financial crime and compliance expert with expertise in regulatory supervision, investigative strategy and global compliance frameworks, Frankfurt

Daniel Wagner, Delivery Executive, Google, Frankfurt

Constanze Westwood, Partner, Boston Consulting Group, Munich

Dr. Carsten Wiegand, Director, Boston Consulting Group, Frankfurt

# Foreword

The world of non-financial risk management has not stood still; in fact, it has accelerated, fractured, and expanded in ways few could have predicted when the first edition of this handbook was published in 2022. The financial industry continues to face immense pressure to adapt – driven not only by the regulatory transformation but increasingly by exponential technological change, deepening geopolitical complexity, and a rapidly evolving threat landscape. In this second edition, we aim to reflect that new reality.

Artificial intelligence has morphed from niche technology to foundational element of financial services. Institutions are no longer experimenting with small-scale pilots – instead, many now rely on machine learning models in core processes like fraud detection, credit underwriting, compliance monitoring, and customer due diligence. At the same time, generative AI is unlocking entirely new opportunities – and entirely new risks. Issues like model transparency, data provenance, algorithmic bias, and explainability are no longer academic – they are central to regulatory scrutiny and reputational risk. The intersection of AI with non-financial risk management is no longer optional, it is essential.

Cyber risk, too, has taken on a new dimension. Threat actors are becoming more sophisticated, leveraging advanced technologies, geopolitical tensions, and systemic interdependencies to exploit vulnerabilities at scale. Attacks on third parties, critical infrastructure, and cloud-based services now pose real-time threats to operational resilience and trust. As the digital transformation accelerates, the industry must rethink its risk architecture to manage not just technological failure, but adversarial intent.

There has also been notable progress on considering sustainability as an increasingly important factor for policymakers, businesses, and financial institutions. Growing regulatory expectations towards risk management from banking regulators are calling banks and financial institutions for a better integration of sustainability into strategy, controls, and risk reporting.

Compounding these developments is a backdrop of growing geopolitical volatility. The Russian war in Ukraine, tensions in the Indo-Pacific, the weaponization of economic policy, and shifting global alliances all impact the financial sector's risk exposure. Whether through supply chains, regulatory divergence, sanctions regimes, or market fragmentation, the geopolitical environment now plays a direct role in shaping non-financial risk.

Against this background, the rationale for a second edition of this handbook is clear. Financial institutions require up-to-date guidance to navigate an increasingly complex, digital, and interconnected risk environment. This edition significantly updates and deepens the original content, with fully revamped chapters on artificial intelligence and sustainability – reflecting the scale and speed of developments in these areas. It also introduces a new chapter on cyber resilience, addressing the growing relevance of cyber threats, third-party risk, and operational continuity in an increasingly digitized landscape.

All other chapters have been carefully reviewed and updated to reflect the latest regulatory developments, supervisory expectations, and market trends. While continuing to build on the foundational concepts of risk appetite, governance, control frameworks, and risk assessment, this edition now places a greater emphasis on integration, scalability, and practical implementation in today's fast-changing environment.

The editors are once again grateful to the contributors – leading practitioners and experts who are deeply engaged in building the next generation of non-financial risk management. Their insights offer not only technical depth but a shared commitment to helping the industry move forward with resilience, integrity, and purpose.

Frankfurt, Munich, and Berlin, August 2025

The editors Norbert Gittfried, Dr. Georg Lienke, Florian Seiferlein, Jannik Leiendecker, Dr. Bernhard Gehra, Dr. Katharina Hefter and Felix Hildebrand

# 1 Introduction: Rising to the Challenges of Non-Financial Risk Management

*Dr. Bernhard Gehra, Jannik Leiendecker, Dr. Georg Lienke*

Historically, financial institutions have concentrated their risk management efforts on financial exposures directly linked to core business activities. In recent years, however, non-financial risk (NFR) management has gained prominence – driven by a rapidly evolving mix of regulatory expectations, societal pressures, and emerging technological as well as geopolitical risks. New rules on responsible AI, heightened scrutiny of data protection and cyber resilience, and the operational risks linked to cloud adoption and third-party dependencies are reshaping the institutions' obligations to monitor, mitigate, and manage risk. At the same time, tightened regulatory expectations towards management of sustainability risks – such as the latest guidance from the European Banking Authority (EBA) – are urging banks and financial institutions to take action and recognize sustainability-related risks in their risk management processes.

The need for a robust and adaptable NFR framework becomes particularly evident in times of systemic disruption. This was clearly demonstrated during the Russia–Ukraine conflict, when an unprecedented wave of sanctions required financial institutions to react rapidly and decisively across jurisdictions. In today's environment, cyber threats and AI-related vulnerabilities represent similar systemic challenges: They evolve rapidly, cut across organizational boundaries, and often require cross-functional crisis response. In parallel, regulatory enforcement has intensified. Fines for failures in anti-money laundering (AML) and related compliance areas have exceeded $300 billion globally between 2013 and 2023, particularly impacting North American and European institutions.[1] Effective non-financial risk management is no longer just a support function – it is a strategic capability and a prerequisite for institutional resilience.

This handbook explores the key success factors for mastering the evolving demands of non-financial risk management. It introduces an institution-specific target operating model (TOM) that integrates all essential components – strategy, governance, risk management, information and communication technology, data architecture, digitization, artificial intelligence, and ethics – into a cohesive framework. Authored by senior experts in NFR, compliance, and sustainability from Europe, North America, and Asia, this book provides practitioners with the practical guidance needed to navigate today's increasingly complex risk environment. Each chapter combines a clear overview of regula-

[1] BCG 2025.

tory expectations with actionable insights, implementation challenges, and real-world examples from across the financial sector.

## 1.1 New risks and challenges

The non-financial risk landscape has evolved dramatically in recent years. Financial institutions now face a diverse and growing array of external and internal risk drivers – from geopolitical instability and climate regulation to reputational exposure, cybersecurity threats, and responsible AI. These developments are mirrored by an increasingly complex regulatory environment, including new and far-reaching obligations such as the Digital Operational Resilience Act (DORA), and AI-specific legislation. As a result, non-financial risks are no longer confined to specialist teams; instead, they are becoming central to strategic decision-making processes, regulatory compliance, and stakeholder trust.

According to a recent BCG report, three issues stand out as particularly pressing: the rising importance of emissions reporting, the growing threat of reputational damage through adverse media coverage, and the emergence of responsible AI and data protection as core compliance concerns. These trends reflect the extent to which new risk types are rapidly gaining relevance – and in many cases overtaking traditional compliance topics in respect to their urgency.[2]

Many institutions have responded to these developments with isolated, reactive measures – layering new controls and reporting mechanisms onto legacy frameworks without stepping back to assess overall coherence. This often leads to fragmentation, duplicative assurance efforts, and an escalating complexity – particularly as internal compliance demands increasingly match or even exceed those from external regulators. Ambiguities in governance, inconsistent risk definitions, and siloed responsibilities inhibit the ability to manage non-financial risks transparently and effectively.

Despite the potential of advanced technologies to support risk management, adoption remains narrow. AI, for instance, is frequently applied to administrative tasks, while its strategic potential – and its corresponding risks – is still insufficiently explored. The growing mismatch between risk complexity and organizational readiness is compounded by regional divergence in regulatory priorities and expectations, placing a particular strain on global financial institutions.

[2] BCG 2024.

In this environment, the traditional models of non-financial risk management are reaching their limits. Institutions must rethink their definition, organization, and prioritization of risks – not only to remain compliant but to stay resilient. This calls for a shift toward holistic, adaptive frameworks that balance resilience with simplicity, and regulatory fulfilment with operational focus.

## 1.2 A forward-looking solution for non-financial risk management in the financial industry

To continue to thrive in an increasingly challenging risk environment, financial institutions need to develop a sophisticated approach to non-financial risk management. This can be done by establishing an institution-specific non-financial risk TOM, which will subsequently allow for a proper definition of risks, creating an integrated view of the 3LoD and building an effective internal control system – informing a sensible executive decision-making that can prevent inevitable risks getting out of control.

This handbook outlines the key ingredients of a non-financial risk TOM for financial institutions. The book sections follow a consistent structure: chapters start with an individual introduction to the topic at hand, followed by a summary of key regulatory expectations across the EU, the US and Asia. Each chapter assesses operational challenges and complexities, and it delivers approaches to define solutions based on industry success factors. Chapters are augmented by practical, hands-on examples from seasoned practitioners. They conclude with the summaries of key takeaways.

## 1.3 Defining and aligning non-financial risk categories

Risks are inherent to every business model, so that a zero-risk tolerance approach is in fact counter-intuitive. Historically, financial institutions have focused their attention on financial risks, including credit risk, market risk, liquidity risk and funding risks, aggregating the remainder under a category most often labelled as operational risk. Recently, non-financial risks have evolved as an independent category for risk management, allowing for a more tailored approach to management of individual non-financial risks. *Chapter 2* provides a general definition of non-financial risk, delineates non-financial risk from financial risk, and provides definitions for categories and types of non-financial risk for financial institutions.

## 1.4 Establishing a non-financial risk appetite framework to prevent an undesirable risk-taking

Following the definition of non-financial risk, *chapter 3* provides a holistic approach to defining a non-financial risk appetite framework for financial institutions across three levels. This includes qualitative risk appetite statements for individual non-financial risk categories, outlining the level and types of risk that the financial institution is willing to take on in order to achieve its strategic objectives and business plan (level 1). Qualitative risk appetite statements are broken down into risk appetite metrics and corresponding thresholds, enabling institutions to set quantifiable tolerance levels for non-financial risk and underlying operational activities (level 2). Level 3 cascades the risk appetite framework to business lines and entity levels via pre-defined key risk indicators, facilitating the early detection of potential deviations from risk appetite objectives and potentially triggering timely interventions. The chapter also draws an outline of the corresponding governance that is required to operate a risk appetite framework.

## 1.5 Building key governance and organizational pillars for non-financial risk management

Three chapters outline the governance and organizational structures required for sustainable non-financial risk management, standing on three major pillars. The three lines of defense (LoD) model (*chapter 4*) defines the roles and responsibilities of the first LoD (front, middle and back office), the second LoD (risk control functions) and the third LoD (internal audit). The chapter focuses on the independence of second-LoD control functions and describes the concept of risk coordinating functions in the first LoD as a regulatory competence center, coordination unit and interface to the second LoD.

'Global functional lead' (*chapter 5*) stands for a combination of strategic, governance and risk management elements defined by an institution that aim to enable a consistent execution of risk management activities across complex organizations. It comprises the central setting of global risk management standards by horizontal risk management functions and their execution by vertical product- or region-focused functions, with direct or indirect reporting lines into horizontal functions. A policy and procedure framework (*chapter 6*) intends to ensure that standards are met in the execution of an institution's business and operational activities. It builds a structural policy hierarchy, allocating the financial institution's documents including board directives, policies and procedures to different hierarchical levels. It structures them by risk types, business segments and relevant geographies.

## 1.6 Generating excellence in the non-financial risk management lifecycle

Three chapters describe the most essential components of a financial institution's non-financial risk management lifecycle.

Sophisticated institutions apply a top-down approach to non-financial risk assessment, using risk-type agnostic criteria to evaluate their exposure to non-financial risks and derive the proper implications for bank-wide risk management. Chapter 7 elaborates on the methodology for a top-down non-financial risk assessment. A key element of effective risk mitigation is the underlying internal control framework. Controls can take a variety of forms, ranging from automated/manual process controls to the conduct of training sessions and the definition of internal policies and requirements. A comprehensive internal control framework needs to combine a top-down approach (focusing on controls addressing the most relevant risk types) with a bottom-up approach (whereby individual risks and controls are identified based on a detailed review of the underlying processes). *Chapter 7* comprises a deep dive on the top-down approach for the creation of an internal control framework.

Financial institutions are confronted with non-financial risks that are increasing both in number and severity, and they face non-financial risk exposure in almost every area of activity. In many institutions, this has resulted in a heterogenous reporting landscape for non-financial risks, with a variety of bottom-up, risk-specific reports from different functions and often diverging criteria for the measurement of risk. Hence, financial institutions are in an ever-stronger need of an overall non-financial risk reporting approach, spanning across risk types and consolidating the measurement of risk and the adequacy assessment of risk-mitigating controls. Only such a top-down report can give executive management the fact base and insights necessary to steer an institution effectively. *Chapter 8* describes an approach to risk-agnostic non-financial risk reporting.

*Chapter 9* is a deep dive into investigation capabilities, combined with root cause analysis. Alongside the on-going harmonisation of European corporate law, individual jurisdictions are increasingly requesting the strengthening of investigative capabilities to better understand root causes of corporate misconduct. This includes the establishment of risk oversight and reporting capabilities, the establishment of a dedicated organisational unit as well as of processes and methods, alongside communication with stakeholders. Particular emphasis is put on the root cause analysis to determine the underlying reasons for misconduct. These insights are then used to identify corresponding lessons learned.

## 1.7 Using data, IT and artificial intelligence and staying cyber resilient

Today, excellent non-financial risk management is heavily supported by an adequate data and IT architecture. *Chapter 10* starts with an outline of the associated challenges, ranging from heterogeneous (and partially unavailable) non-financial risk data and fragmented responsibilities to partially-integrated IT applications. These challenges can be addressed by defining a comprehensive strategy, creating full transparency of the IT architecture and aligning with the required data architecture. This can subsequently be translated into a short- and long-term roadmap towards a more public cloud-based or on-premises data platform.

*Chapter 11* describes the data governance required to facilitate an effective NFR management. Historically, data governance has focused on "financial risk" thereby often leaving non-financial risk aside. Yet, an effective non-financial risk data governance system can be established by leveraging existing data governance frameworks. This will entail a clear assignment of roles and responsibilities (including non-financial risk data officers, data owners, stewards and custodians), implementing concrete use cases, scaling-up as well as defining a comprehensive data catalogue and supporting technologies. The resulting data governance should subsequently be integrated into existing governance structures on both entity and group levels.

Since the publication of the first edition in 2022, the field of artificial intelligence has advanced at remarkable speed – both in terms of technological capability and its application across the financial industry. The emergence of generative AI, regulatory developments such as the EU AI Act, and a widespread adoption of machine learning and natural language processing in compliance and risk functions have fundamentally reshaped the AI landscape. Reflecting this momentum, the AI chapter has been fully overhauled for this second edition to capture the scale of change, the latest use cases, and the implications for non-financial risk management. Chapter 12 now provides a comprehensive overview of AI's evolution, from classical automation to predictive and generative intelligence, and highlights its integration into core compliance workflows. Real-world examples – from AI-enabled fraud detection and KYC file automation to optimized transaction monitoring and sanctions screening – illustrate how institutions can leverage AI to enhance risk detection and operational efficiency. At the same time, the chapter emphasizes the growing need for explainability, fairness, and responsible AI governance to meet regulatory expectations and maintain stakeholder trust. AI has evolved from being a lever for efficiency to being a strategic component of modern risk management – and this chapter provides institutions with a forward-looking blueprint for deploying AI safely, effectively, and at scale.

In recognition of the growing threat landscape and increasing regulatory scrutiny, this second edition introduces a new chapter 13 dedicated to cyber resilience. It highlights the need for financial institutions to strengthen their ability to prevent, withstand, and recover from cyber and ICT(information and communication technology)-related disruptions. Drawing on leading regulatory frameworks such as DORA and the NIST Cybersecurity Framework, the chapter outlines practical approaches to building cyber resilience, managing third-party risks, and embedding structured governance and response capabilities. Particular attention is given to the operational and reputational impacts of cyber incidents, the role of AI and cloud technologies in expanding attack surfaces, as well as the importance of continuous oversight, training, and strategic investment in cybersecurity. As institutions increasingly rely on a digital infrastructure, enhancing cyber resilience becomes a cornerstone of effective non-financial risk management.

## 1.8 Putting conduct and ethics at the center of sustainable non-financial risk management

Recent scandals in the corporate world have demonstrated that a lack of ethical values is often at the root of corporate misconduct. Hence, the role of conduct and ethics cannot be emphasized enough.

*Chapter 14* describes the subtle interplay between ethics, conduct and integrity in the context of the financial industry, and it outlines the implications for managers who must navigate today's increasingly complex and international regulatory landscape. Most business ethicists agree that, in general, financial institutions' ethical taxonomies can be divided into two categories: conduct/compliance-based ethics and integrity-based ethics. While the former constitute principles and codes born from government regulations, the latter are based on the establishment of core principles to which all employees are asked to adhere to and govern themselves accordingly. Organizations that combine both conduct-/compliance-based with integrity-based ethics could significantly mitigate conduct risk (market, client and employee conduct risk). These three categories are now widely used in conduct risk taxonomies and are increasingly referenced in both regulatory and institutional frameworks. Three major areas emerge as key focal points for regulatory oversight: expansion of the circle of stakeholders, elimination of "rolling bad apples" and greater cross-border collaborations. Supervisory bodies expect companies to behave ethically and maintain a strong focus on good conduct, not just towards their customers but towards all stakeholders. Technology, culture and behavioral metrics are playing an increasingly bigger role in the support, monitoring and implementation of conduct frameworks, including in areas such as AI governance, product suitability and whistleblowing.

*Chapter 15* examines two key trends in the regulation of conduct risk: *Treating Customers Fairly* (TFC) and the *Senior Managers and Certification Regime* (SM&CR). The idea of TFC as the standard for good conduct has made its way into financial regulatory frameworks all across the globe and has recently evolved further with the introduction of the UK's Consumer Duty. Another overarching global trend has been the shift away from a case-by-case approach towards treating conduct risk as a systemic phenomenon. As such, recent regulations have focused on extending individual liabilities through elaborate SM&CRs, with similar regimes now adopted in jurisdictions such as Hong Kong, Singapore, Malaysia, and Australia. Conduct risk figures prominently on the sustainability agenda for two main reasons: it is a key feature of a firm's governance framework and directly impacted by sustainability risks, and its occurrence is estimated to be on the rise as sustainability investing brings forth novel opportunities and new decision-making challenges.

To manage conduct risk, the development and implementation of an effective conduct risk framework is required, reflecting and tailored to a firm's culture, business environment and regulatory landscape, while it is also implemented through appropriate systems. Three key principles, however, should stand at the core of every framework: standardized metrics, customer centricity and clear definitions. Unfortunately, there is no one-size-fits-all approach. Each financial institution must remain vigilant about new conduct risks and develop its own approach based on its own exposures, activities and overall strategies.

## 1.9 A holistic approach to Sustainability Risk Management in Financial Institutions

Sustainability has emerged as a critical consideration for financial institutions, not just from a strategic point of view but increasingly as a key driver of financial and non-financial risks. Sustainability-related risks – ranging from climate-related physical and transition risks to social and governance challenges – are now understood as cross-cutting drivers that influence traditional risk categories such as credit, market, operational, and reputational risks. This evolving landscape is reshaping expectations from regulators, investors, and society at large. In response to these developments, regulatory authorities across jurisdictions have introduced frameworks that set clear expectations for the integration of sustainability into risk management. From the European Banking Authority's binding guidelines to the principles-based approaches by the MAS in Singapore and the HKMA, a global pattern is emerging: Financial institutions are increasingly required to demonstrate board-level accountability, perform scenario analysis, and embed sustainability risks in core governance and control structures. While the scope and prescriptiveness of these frameworks vary, they collectively underscore the need for a structured, enterprise-wide approach to sustainability risk management.

Building on this regulatory foundation, chapter 16 proposes a comprehensive Target Operating Model (TOM) tailored to the integration of sustainability risks into financial institutions' risk architectures. The model encompasses strategic alignment through taxonomies and risk appetite frameworks, governance mechanisms adapted to sustainability oversight, steering tools such as risk assessments and controls, as well as enabling factors including data, culture, and technology. This pragmatic approach not only ensures compliance with emerging regulatory requirements but also equips institutions with the internal structures needed to manage sustainability risks proactively and coherently – transforming sustainability from a compliance obligation into a source of long-term risk resilience and strategic advantage.

# 2 Definition of Non-Financial Risk in Financial Institutions

*Dr. Julia Gebhardt, Dr. Katharina Hefter, Jennifer Rabener, Dr. Carsten Wiegand*

## 2.1 Introduction

Risk management has always been a core element of financial institutions, which play a significant role in the transformation function of the financial markets, thereby transforming lot sizes, maturity and risk.[1] However, in recent years, not all loss events can be attributed to traditional financial risks. These so-called non-financial risks are, in fact, linked to operations.

As a first step in the discussion of risk management and the different types of risk, it makes sense to consider the definition of risk itself. According to the *Oxford Learner's Dictionary*, risk is defined as "the possibility of something bad happening at some time in the future; a situation that could be dangerous or have a bad result."

To offer products and services, financial institutions need business operations. These include headquarters and branch operations, such as physical assets like buildings, rental space or even vaults. These physical assets are complemented by IT infrastructure with both hardware as well as software.

Overall, there are five sources of potential operational risks or operational risk events.[2] These are people, processes, systems, external events and legal risks. All these components of the business and operating models give rise to a wide range of potential risks. These need to be identified, measured and managed. In managing these risks, banks must balance the expected return from risk-related activities with the amount of loss from these activities if risks materialise, as well as the costs of their management or mitigation. According to the Basel Committee, an effective operational risk management system and a robust level of operational resilience work together to reduce the frequency and impact of operational risk events.[3]

Financial business inherently includes numerous risk types, so complete risk avoidance in the sense of a "zero risk tolerance" is impossible. Risk taking and the management of risks is an integral part of the business. When providing loans to customers, financial

---

[1] Meyer 2000.

[2] OeNB/FMA 2006, 9.

[3] BCBS 2021b, 2.

institutions take on a credit risk. As the value of assets, such as securities, depends on certain underlying market parameters, such as interest rates, commodity prices or share prices, they are also exposed to market risks. Another core element of banking is taking deposits to fund loans. The management of the resulting cash inflow and outflow from assets and liabilities results in liquidity risks.

There are generally five basic management approaches to treating risks[4]: acceptance, avoidance, mitigation, sharing and transfer. Risk avoidance aims at fully evading the risk. This can mean that certain business activities need to be stopped or not performed, or processes need to be designed in a way to ensure that the particular risk does not arise. For example, when a bank wants to avoid any risk from outsourcing part of its value chain, the entire process needs to be done inhouse. If currency risks are to be avoided for certain currencies, then these currencies cannot be used either for trading, lending or payment services.

Risk mitigation describes the process of taking actions to reduce the possible loss event frequency or the possible impact of loss events. It is central to the mitigation strategy that an effective control environment is established, with preventive as well as detective controls. An internal control environment is an essential part of all risk management processes, and almost all regulators require financial institutions to have one. The European Banking Authority (EBA) publishes detailed guidelines on internal control frameworks in *Title V* of its guidelines on internal governance.[5]

In case internal controls do not adequately address risks, while accepting the risk is not a reasonable option, management can also share or transfer the risk to another party, for example by way of insurance products.[6] However, the Basel Committee points out that risk transfer is an imperfect substitute for sound controls and risk management programmes, hence, banks should view it as a complementary strategy rather than a replacement for thorough internal operational risk controls.[7]

Risk acceptance means that the risk is accepted without taking any specific measures. This can be the case when a certain risk type is deemed non-material for the financial institution. An indicator for this could be that the expected loss would be less than the costs related to the management activities to mitigate the risk.[8] In addition, this strategy is also

4 U.S. Department of Commerce/National Institute of Standards and Technology 2012.

5 EBA 2017.

6 BCBS 2021b, 16.

7 Ibid.

8 OeNB/FMA 2006, 43.

applied to the assessment of residual risks, in which the latter is the risk exposure after controls have been considered.[9]

The choice of the approach for any particular risk type depends on the individual bank's business model, i.e. its products, services, processes, people, transaction channels as well as physical and IT infrastructure. It further depends on the bank management's risk strategy and risk appetite, as well as on the relevance of the risk type in this combination. The general approach to risk management stated in the risk strategy is detailed in the risk appetite statement, which elaborates on the types and amounts of risk a financial institution is willing to take. For more details on risk appetite, especially from a non-financial risk perspective, please refer to chapter 3.

The practices of risk management vary depending on the size and complexity of business models and operations. However, a general approach to risk management always contains four core steps for each identified risk type. The first step is the determination, description and measurement of the inherent risk of the particular risk type. Inherent risk is defined as the amount of that type of risk without any mitigating measures or control processes. In a second step, based on this inherent risk, an assessment of potential mitigating measures is performed. These mitigating measures can have different forms, one of which could be the use of internal controls for a certain type of risk. These types of mitigating measures are intended to reduce the impact of a risk event. The implementation of controls around the processes related to the specific risk type can help reduce the risk event's probability and the impact of a risk event should it occur. Examples for such controls are the four-eyes principle or user access management. In a third step, the residual risk needs to be managed, if any remains after application of all mitigating measures and controls. Lastly, all of these steps need to be documented and reported to management, at least on an aggregated level.

## 2.2 History of non-financial risk and specifications by key regulators

Definitions of different types and clusters of risk are in use in financial institutions across the globe. Some of the risk types are standardised, with clear definitions by regulators; other risk types are not always clearly defined. The understanding and research of risks, root causes and effects gradually evolve. Laws, regulations and regulating authorities integrate, extend and adjust this knowledge, mostly driven by events and scandals. Therefore, we will take a look at the history of the development of non-financial risk here, and

9 BCBS 2021b, 10–11.

analyse commonalities and differences in regulatory definitions of risk types – with a focus on definitions around non-financial risks.

### 2.2.1 A short history of non-financial risk

Looking at the history of the development of non-financial risk, the starting point is perceived by many as the development of operational risk. In 1997, the Basel Committee on Banking Supervision (BCBS or Basel) issued a paper that set out 25 core principles for effective banking supervision.[10] One of the key risks faced by financial institutions was cited as operational risk, which was defined "as the risk of loss resulting from inadequate or failed internal processes, people and systems or from external events. The definition includes legal risk but excludes strategic and reputational risk."[11]

Two years later, BCBS issued a proposal for a new capital adequacy framework to replace Basel I, the capital measurement system launched in 1988.[12] Following the publication of the first round of proposals in 1999, the revised framework for capital measurement and capital standards, called Basel II, was endorsed in 2004. As part of the framework, operational risk, along with credit risk and market risk, was named as a risk type for capital requirements calculations. The scope of the definition of operational risk was contained in seven loss event types: (1) internal fraud, (2) external fraud, (3) employment practices and workspace safety, (4) clients, products and business services, (5) damages to physical assets, (6) business disruptions and system failures, and (7) execution, delivery and process management.[13]

The idea of Basel II was to measure the operational risk on a model basis by using loss data from operational risk loss events through one of the following three methods: the advanced measurement approach (AMA), the basis indicator approach (BIA) or the standardised approach (STA), which was mainly based on revenues over the past three years. However, the distributions used in the AMA were unable to appropriately consider extreme outliers because risk measurement and corresponding capital requirements were always based on some confidence level. In comparison with operational risk management, non-financial risk management is not only based on historical events but needs to include risk assessments that require organisations to familiarise themselves with their business models, risk appetites and the risks themselves. This means that financial risks are the original risks while non-financial risks are second-order effects of the original

[10] BCBS s.a., History.

[11] BCBS 2012.

[12] BCBS s.a., History.

[13] BCBS 2004.

risks. And while financial risks can be measured, it is still a challenge to measure non-financial risks.

Simultaneously to the BCBS developments, the history of the development of non-financial risk was supported by seven waves that triggered the development of the respective risks (Figure 1).

Figure 1: Development of non-financial risk

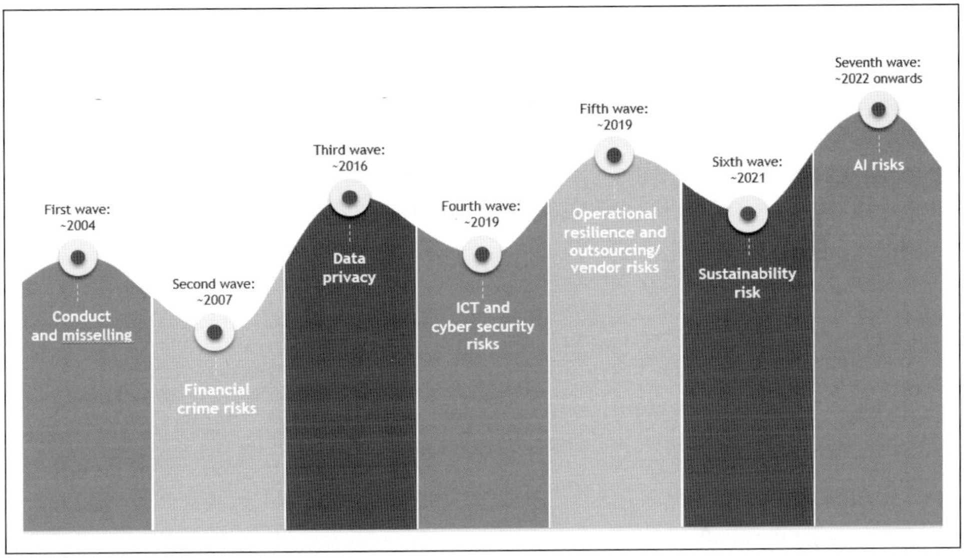


The first wave relates to the topic of conduct and mis-selling. As a result of the mis-selling scandals of the 1990s and early 2000s, including the dotcom bubble, and parallel to the development of Basel II, the European Markets in Financial Instruments Directive, also known as MiFID, was introduced in 2004 and has been applied since 2007. Its objective, amongst other things, was to set out the conduct of business and regulatory reporting to avoid market abuse.[14]

The second wave relates to financial crime risks. An understanding was gained that many compliance-related incidents included white collar-crimes. According to the U.S. Federal Bureau of Investigation, white-collar crime refers to the full range of frauds committed by business and government professionals and is independent of the application or threat

[14] ESMA s.a., MIFID II.

of physical force or violence.[15] In addition, it was noticed that retail customers were also involved in crimes, for example by committing tax evasion.

The third wave relates to the growing interest in data privacy that was triggered by the expanding use of data and online technology, including online banking. As early as 1992, the European Union published the European data protection directive, which came into force in 1995. It aimed to protect individuals with regard to the processing of personal data and the free movement of such data.[16] More than ten years later, in 2011, the European Union issued an opinion on a comprehensive approach on personal data protection.[17] This resulted in the European Union regulation on the protection of natural persons with regard to the processing of personal data and on the free movement of such data in 2016, commonly referred to as the General Data Protection Regulation (GDPR), which is in effect since 2018.[18] Other jurisdictions have adopted this regulation under other names and in other forms, such as the California Consumer Privacy Act (CCPA), introduced in 2018 to enhance privacy rights and consumer protection.[19]

The fourth wave relates to information, communication and technology (ICT) as well as cybersecurity risks. With the growing relevance of technology, these risks have gained in importance and a necessity for the position of a chief information security officer (CISO) arose. Therefore, the EBA reacted in 2019 by issuing the guidelines on ICT and security risk management that were enforced in 2020,[20] and, in 2021, by launching, with Europol's European Cybercrime Centre, a campaign called Cyber Scams 2.0 to spread public awareness of cybercrimes.[21]

The fifth wave relates to operational resilience and outsourcing/vendor risks. Along with increased technological risks, the need for the overall stability of financial institutions and the financial system triggered a regulatory push towards operational resilience. This was spearheaded by the UK regulatory authorities' policies both on operational resilience as well as on outsourcing and third-party risk management (published in 2019 and enforced since 2021).[22] The BCBS followed by publishing its principles for operational resilience

[15] Federal Bureau of Investigation s.a., White-Collar Crime.

[16] European Union s.a., Data Protection Directive.

[17] European Union s.a., Comprehensive approach on personal data protection in the European Union.

[18] European Union s.a., General Data Protection Regulation.

[19] State of California, DOJ s.a., California Consumer Privacy Act (CCPA).

[20] EBA 2019b.

[21] Europol 2021.

[22] FCA 2019a; Bank of England 2021.

in 2021.[23] The disintermediation of the value chain, driven by technological developments, lead to a higher importance of the understanding of both supply and process chains as well as knowing third parties such as vendors and contractors.

The sixth wave relates to sustainability risk as well as general strategic risks. The environmental element is found in supply chain management and the well-established know-your-supplier process. By contrast, the social element is generally associated with human resources and led to the introduction of anti-discrimination laws and quotas. With the increasing importance of the good citizenship model, an ethical change has taken place, and the public has developed higher expectations for moral behaviour in organisations. As such, sustainability risk is clearly embedded in strategy discussions and forms a part of the strategic risk faced by financial institutions and all other organisations.

The seventh wave relates to artificial intelligence (AI) risks, which are risks resulting from the use of AI models, including generative AI (GenAI). These risks are not perceived as a singular risk type in the risk taxonomy, since they influence, or materialize in, other risk types, and increase the importance of certain risk types, like model risk. With the launch of the ChatGPT AI large language model by OpenAI in 2022, AI models have been widely adopted by individual and corporate users. In 2023, the EU published the worldwide first AI regulation that will be fully applicable in 2026.[24] The US followed in 2023 by publishing an executive order for the safe, secure and trustworthy development and use of AI that was then revoked in January 2025.[25] Going forward, financial institutions need to manage the risks arising from AI systems, and also deploy AI to optimize their non-financial risk management (for more details see chapter 12).

### 2.2.2 Existing non-financial risk specifications by key global and regional regulators and associations

The term non-financial risk is not yet commonly used by regulators. While there are definitions for individual risk types, such as operational risk or AML risks, even with a somewhat widespread base, no catalogue of risk types has been summarised under non-financial risks by regulators. Thus, no clear regulatory definition of non-financial risk has been established.

On a global level, BCBS does not provide a definition of non-financial risk. The Basel Committee has, however, updated the principles for the sound management of opera-

23 BCBS 2021a.

24 European parliament 2025.

25 Executive office of the US president 2025.

tional risk and published a linked paper on operational resilience in March 2021. As with Basel, regulators more frequently advise on operational risk management and in part reference some of the non-financial risk types within those policies.

In Europe, Banco de España mentions certain examples of non-financial risks, such as misconduct, non-compliance, IT, reputational, cybersecurity or operational challenges. The basis for the delineation against financial risks is that the mentioned non-financial risks are not linked directly to financial decisions and have nothing but a downside. Also, according to Banco de España, a further defining element of non-financial risk is that it is hard to quantify precisely. Finally, there is a reference to operational risk as the specific part of the Basel Accord included a capital charge for these types of risk.[26] The ECB annually publishes a report on the outcome of the Supervisory Review Process (SREP) IT Risk questionnaire, which specifically deals with findings and weaknesses of IT-related risks.[27]

US regulators do not explicitly provide a definition of non-financial risk. However, in its November 2019 Supervision and Regulation report, the Federal Reserve Board (FED) gives examples of risk-management weaknesses for US banks with less-than-satisfactory supervisory ratings. These examples include compliance, internal controls, model risk management, operational risk management and/or data as well as information technology infrastructure. Further weaknesses mentioned concern the Bank Secrecy Act (BSA) and anti-money laundering (AML) programmes.[28]

Among Asian-Pacific regulators, the Australian Prudential Regulation Authority (APRA) refers to non-financial risks in its information paper on governance, culture, remuneration and accountability. However, it does not provide an explicit definition of non-financial risk.[29]

## 2.3 Differentiation of financial and non-financial risk

Given the lack of clarity concerning a standardised definition of non-financial risk, we here define the terms 'financial risk' and 'non-financial risk' the way we will use them throughout this book. The general approach considers regulatory definitions already in use and attempts to find a structure that encompasses all types of risk.

---

[26] Marita Delgado (Banco de España) at the SSM Round Table/Bankers Forum on 15 November 2019.

[27] ECB 2021.

[28] Board of Governors of the Federal Reserve System 2019.

[29] APRA 2019.

Financial risk can generally be defined as "the possibility of losing money on an investment or business venture."[30] Other categorisations of financial risk use the question of measurability, meaning whether methodologies are available to accurately model and measure risk.

However, as both approaches do not clearly define the risk types that would be considered under financial risk, our definition of financial risk is based on a positive-list approach, defining all risk types that belong in this risk category. Non-financial risk is then defined as the remaining risk types. Moreover, due to the importance of the term "operational risk," which is a supercategory for certain, yet not all non-financial risks, non-financial risk itself is subdivided into two key categories: operational risks and strategic risks. Taken together, this approach covers all types of risks possible in financial institutions.

### 2.3.1 Financial risk definition

Our definition of financial risk is based on the enumeration of all included individual financial risk types. For the purposes of this book, the three *financial risk types included in the definition of financial risk are credit risk, market risk and liquidity risk.*

The BCBS defines credit risk as "the potential that a bank borrower or counterparty will fail to meet its obligations in accordance with agreed terms."[31] For the purpose of risk quantification and the calculation of capital requirements, credit risk is separated into three main risk parameters. Those used to measure credit risk are probability of default (PD), loss given default (LGD) and the exposure at default (EAD). When all these parameters are estimated, their product equals the expected loss (EL), which can either be viewed on an individual loan, a customer or a portfolio level. However, the expected loss as such does not pose credit risk to a bank, as it is required to hold risk provisions for expected losses. The actual credit risk here is the risk of unexpected losses, or the deviation from the expected loss. This risk needs to be covered by banks by holding sufficient capital against potential unexpected losses, as specified by regulatory capital requirements.

Market risk, according to the BCBS, is defined as "the risk of losses in on and off-balance-sheet positions arising from movements in market prices."[32] In contrast to credit

[30] Investopedia 2021b.

[31] BCBS 2000.

[32] BCBS 2019.

risk, which is a pure downside risk, market price movements also include the possibility of gains instead of losses.

Liquidity risk as defined by the BCBS contains two components – funding liquidity risk and market liquidity risk:

> *"Funding liquidity risk is the risk that the firm will not be able to meet efficiently both expected and unexpected current and future cash flow and collateral needs without affecting either daily operations or the financial condition of the firm. Market liquidity risk is the risk that a firm cannot easily offset or eliminate a position at the market price because of inadequate market depth or market disruption."*[33]

### 2.3.2 Non-financial risk definition

The definition of non-financial risk is not as straightforward as for financial risk. In contrast to the positive definition of financial risk as being comprised of certain risk types, non-financial risks for the purposes of this book are defined *as comprising all risk types that are not included in the definition of financial risk*.

As pointed out previously, there is no clear catalogue or definition of non-financial risks. In addition, definitions of risk types overlap partially and cannot be as clearly established as financial risks.

The risk types under non-financial risk can, in turn, be structured into two key categories. The first category contains operational risks, which are those relating to banking operations. The other category contains those risks that we view as strategic risks, which makes them part of non-financial risks but sets them apart from risks related to operations. This approach combines the specification of operational risks according to the BCBS definition, including the fact that strategic risks are also non-financial risks.

## 2.4 Specific clusters of non-financial risk

This section takes a closer look at the different clusters of risk types that comprise all versions of non-financial risk according to the general definition in section 3.2.

[33] BCBS 2008.

Figure 2: Risk taxonomy in financial institutions

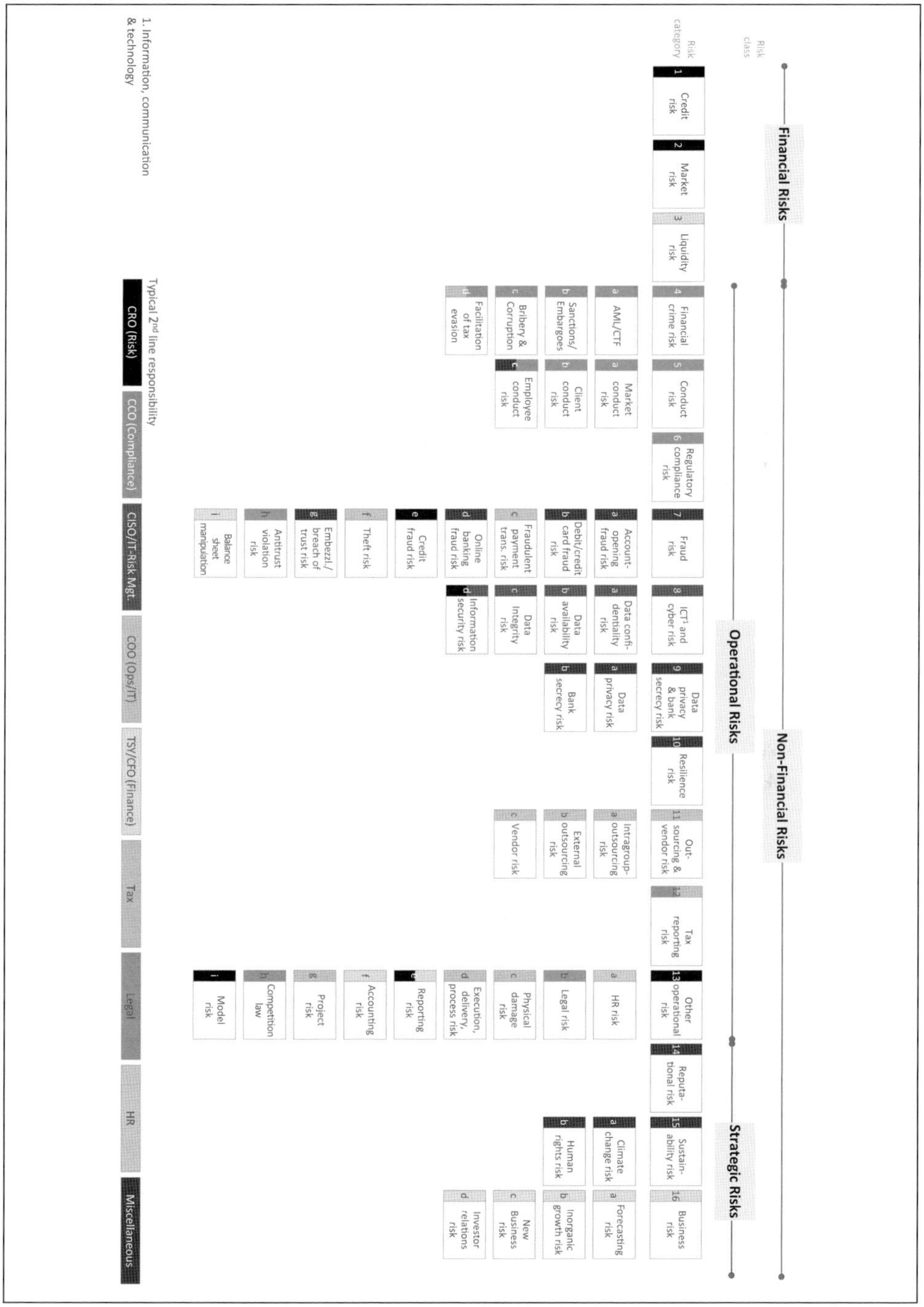

Non-financial risk contains the following risk types:

Operational risk:

- Financial crime risk
- Conduct risk
- Regulatory compliance risk
- Fraud risk
- Information, communication & technology (ICT) and cyber risk
- Data privacy and bank secrecy risk
- Resilience risk
- Outsourcing & vendor risk
- Tax reporting risk
- Other operational risk

Strategic risk:

- Reputational risk
- Sustainability risk
- Business risk

In the following section, we will provide definitions of the individual types of non-financial risks. If available, we provide an overview and comparison of definitions of the risk types as used by the different regulatory bodies or global associations.

We focus on the BCBS for global definitions. Concerning European regulators, we mainly cover the EBA, European Central Bank, the UK Prudential Regulation Authority (PRA) and the UK Financial Conduct Authority (FCA). Concerning North American regulators, we focus on the FED, the Office of the Comptroller of the Currency (OCC) and the Federal Deposit Insurance Corporation (FDIC). Concerning Asian-Pacific regulators, we mainly cover the Monetary Authority of Singapore (MAS), the Hong Kong Monetary Authority (HKMA) and the APRA.

### 2.4.1 Operational risk

Operational risk as a risk type has been in use by regulators since Basel II.[34] This risk type – along with the financial risk types of credit risk and market risk – is still the basis for the capital requirements calculation of the Basel framework's first pillar. According to the BCBS, operational risk is defined as "the risk of loss resulting from inadequate or failed internal processes, people and systems or from external events. This definition includes legal risk but excludes strategic and reputational risk."[35]

In Europe, the PRA makes use of the Basel definition. For the special case of funds, the FCA uses one further specification by stating that it includes "legal and documentation risk and the risk resulting from the trading, settlement and valuation procedures operated on behalf of the fund."[36] The EBA and the Central Bank of Ireland use definitions in line with the Basel definition.

Both in the US (Federal Reserve Bank of New York and FDIC) and in Canada (OSFI), the regulators use the Basel definition. In Asia-Pacific, the APRA also uses the Basel definition. Therefore, for the purpose of this book, we use the Basel definition of operational risk.

#### 2.4.1.1 Financial crime risk

Financial crime risk combines the risk of failing to prevent offenses related to financial crimes, such as money laundering, terrorist financing, fraud, bribery and corruption as well as insider trading. This risk type is high on the agenda of regulators and one of the core responsibilities of a bank's compliance function.

The International Compliance Association (ICA) defines financial crimes as two different types of conduct:

> *"First, there are those activities that dishonestly generate wealth for those engaged in the conduct in question. […] Second, there are also financial crimes that do not involve the dishonest taking of a benefit, but that protect a benefit that has already been obtained or to facilitate the taking of such benefit."*[37]

[34] Basel II refers to an international framework issued by the BCBS in 2006 in order to revise the standards governing the capital adequacy of internationally active banks; BCBS s.a., Basel II.

[35] BCBS 2017.

[36] FCA s.a.

[37] ICA s.a.

In the US, the OCC describes financial crime as ranging "from fairly simple operations carried out by individuals or small groups to highly sophisticated rings seeking funding for criminal enterprises or terrorism."[38]

There are several sub-categories of financial crime risks.

#### 2.4.1.1.1 Money-laundering/terrorist financing risk

The Financial Action Task Force (FATF) describes money laundering as the processing of criminal proceeds to disguise their illegal origin.[39] Terrorist financing refers to the financing of terrorist acts as well as of terrorists and their organisations[40] with funds coming from both legitimate and illegitimate sources.[41] A general global guideline regarding the management of money-laundering and terrorist financing risk is the BCBS's recently updated "Sound management of risks related to money laundering and financing of terrorism."[42] The EBA also published guidelines on money laundering and terrorism financing risk factors.[43] In Asia-Pacific, the APRA, refers to the money-laundering and terrorism financing risk as one "that a reporting entity may reasonably face that the provision by the reporting entity of designated services might (whether inadvertently or otherwise) involve or facilitate money laundering or the financing of terrorism."[44]

Based on these regulatory descriptions, we define *money-laundering/terrorist financing risk as the exposure to legal penalties and reputational loss faced by financial institutions failing to prevent money laundering or terrorist financing.*

#### 2.4.1.1.2 Sanctions and embargoes risk

In this context, sanctions refer to financial sanctions, which can be defined as restrictions on the free movement of capital and payments.[45] These restrictions are imposed on individuals or entities in an effort to curtail their activities and to exert pressure and influence on them. These restrictive measures include (but are not limited to) financial sanctions,

[38] OCC s.a.
[39] FATF s.a., Money Laundering.
[40] FATF s.a., Glossary.
[41] FATF 2019.
[42] BCBS 2020.
[43] EBA 2021b.
[44] APRA 2007.
[45] Deutsche Bundesbank 2021.

trade sanctions, restrictions on travel or civil aviation restrictions.[46] An embargo is defined as a prohibition on commerce.

The Wolfsberg Group published a guide on sanctions screening.[47] However, there is no explicit regulatory definition of the sanctions and embargoes risk. Therefore, we define the *sanctions and embargoes risk as the exposure to legal penalties and reputational loss faced by financial institutions failing to comply with existing sanctions or embargoes.*

##### 2.4.1.1.3 Bribery and corruption risk

Transparency International (TI) UK states that there is no universal definition of bribery, but all definitions have in common that it involves someone in an appointed position acting voluntarily in breach of trust in exchange for a benefit. The benefit does not have to involve cash or a payment, instead it can take on many forms, including gifts, hospitality and expenses, access to assets or a favour to a relative, friend or cause. Bribery is defined as "the offering, promising, giving, accepting, or soliciting of an advantage as an inducement for an action which is illegal, unethical or a breach of trust. Inducements can take the form of money, gifts, loans, fees, rewards or other advantages."[48]

Like TI, the Legal Information Institute of Cornell Law School in the US defines bribery as "the offering, giving, soliciting, or receiving of any item of value as a means of influencing the actions of an individual holding a public or legal duty."[49] On the other hand, corruption is defined as dishonest or fraudulent conduct by those in power, with bribery being one example of such conduct.

Based on these definitions, we define *bribery and corruption risk as the exposure to legal penalties faced if the company or its employees engage in bribery or corruption.*

##### 2.4.1.1.4 Facilitation of tax evasion

TI defines tax evasion as "the illegal non-payment or under-payment of taxes, usually by deliberately making a false declaration or no declaration to tax authorities – such as by declaring less income, profits or gains than the amounts actually earned, or by overstating deductions."[50] In the US, the IRS defines tax evasion as "the failure to pay or a deliberate

---

46 Central Bank of Ireland s.a.

47 The Wolfsberg Group 2019.

48 Transparency International s. a., Global Anti-Bribery Guidance.

49 Cornell Law School s. a., Legal Information Institute.

50 Transparency International s.a., Tax Evasion.

underpayment of taxes."[51] According to the European Commission, tax evasion "generally comprises illegal arrangements where tax liability is hidden or ignored, i.e. the taxpayer pays less tax than he/she is supposed to pay under the law by hiding income or information from the tax authorities."[52]

Based on these definitions of tax evasion, we define the risk for financial institutions from facilitation of tax evasion as *losses or penalties resulting from knowingly assisting or turning a blind eye to the evasion of taxes.*

#### 2.4.1.2 Conduct risk

As Copley asserts, there is no universal definition of either conduct risk, that is the risk stemming from a person's actions, or what good conduct means in practice.[53] While multiple, sometimes contradicting, definitions of conduct risk exist, we shall settle on the one by the Central Bank of Ireland that it published in its *Guide to Consumer Protection Management*: therein, conduct risk "is the risk a financial services firm poses to its customers from its direct interaction with them."[54] This definition is in contrast to the EBA's definition, which limits conduct risk to the risks relevant should something harmful happen to a banking institution. The three key types of conduct risk will be explored further in the following.

##### 2.4.1.2.1 Market conduct risk

First, market conduct risk can be defined as the risk of the market's integrity and transparency being harmed by unfair or abusive behaviour towards fellow market participants. The Fixed Income, Currencies and Commodities Markets Standards Board (FMSB) outlines six client misconduct patterns,[55] which can be observed in the market. While this analysis is not entirely original, a number of different authorities and reviews – most recently the Fair and Effective Markets Review (FEMR) by the Bank of England in 2015[56] – have recognised the importance of focusing on the behavioural patterns underlying market misconduct. In 2018, the FMSB became the first standard-setting body to collate, analyse and publish these behavioural patterns of market conduct risk as a single reference point for market participants.

---

[51] IRS s.a.

[52] European Commission s.a., Taxation.

[53] Copley 2016, 28–29.

[54] Central Bank of Ireland 2017, 7.

[55] FMSB 2018b.

[56] Bank of England/HM Treasury 2015.

#### 2.4.1.2.2 Client conduct risk

Client conduct risk can be defined as the risk of harm to clients by resolving conflicts of interest to their disadvantage, causing them financial loss or other detriment. There are seven key client misconduct patterns observable in the market, which form the basis of the conduct risk definition in the EBA guidelines on common procedure and methodology for the SREP.[57] Together with the FMSB's report, the EBA's guidelines serve as an exhaustive list of key conduct risk subcategories. While individual entities and institutions have adopted their own taxonomies, the above categories have served as the backbone for several conduct risk analyses.

#### 2.4.1.2.3 Employee conduct risk

Employee conduct risk can be defined as the risk of harm to the organisation by employees falling prey to conflicts of interests or violations of the code of conduct. The European Union defines conflict of interest as a situation

> *"where the 'impartial and objective exercise of the functions of a financial actor or other person' involved in budget implementation 'is compromised for reasons involving family, emotional life, political or national affinity, economic interest or any other direct or indirect personal interest.'"*[58]

According to the US Securities and Exchange Commission (SEC), organisations need to integrate conflict of interest risk into their three lines of defence structure and should consider conflicts of interest throughout their key business processes, including strategic planning, capital allocation, performance monitoring as well as evaluation of business units and individual business leaders.[59]

For further details on conduct risk, we refer to chapter 13.

### 2.4.1.3 Regulatory compliance risk

The FDIC defines compliance risk in its guidance for managing third-party risk as "the risk arising from violations of laws, rules, or regulations, or from non-compliance with internal policies or procedures or with the institution's business standards."[60]

[57] EBA 2014, 97–98.
[58] European Union 2021.
[59] SEC 2012.
[60] FDIC 2008.

In a slightly more general version, we define regulatory compliance risk as *the risk of failure of a financial institution to comply with all required laws, rules and regulations, across all jurisdictions and business operations in which the institution is active.*

A risk event of regulatory non-compliance can lead to significant penalties imposed by regulators. This implies that financial institutions need to be aware at all times of currently relevant regulations, and they need to permanently screen for changes, updates or new regulations both for existing business operations and for new products and service offerings.

#### 2.4.1.4 Fraud risk

Fraud, by definition, entails intentional misconduct, designed to evade detection. Fraud risk denotes the vulnerability that an organisation faces from internal or external individuals capable of committing fraud. The fact that fraud risk is considered a sub-risk of operational risk is also visible from the BCBS loss event categorisation within operational risk, as both internal and external fraud are loss event types for the collection of operational risk loss data.[61]

In 2016, the Committee of Sponsoring Organizations of the Treadway Commission (COSO) published a fraud risk management guide that contains both a definition of fraud as well as guidance for establishing an overall fraud risk management programme, based on principles and points of focus. The definition of fraud according to it is as follows: "Fraud is any intentional act or omission designed to deceive others, resulting in the victim suffering a loss and/or the perpetrator achieving a gain."[62] The guide, however, acknowledges that other definitions exist, including those developed by the Auditing Standards Board of the American Institute of Certified Public Accountants, the Public Company Accounting Oversight Board, and the Government Accountability Office.

In 2019, the OCC published fraud risk management principles under the heading of operational risks. The definition of fraud provided by the OCC is the following:

> *"Fraud may generally be characterized as an intentional act, misstatement, or omission designed to deceive others, resulting in the victim suffering a loss or the perpetrator achieving a gain. Fraud is typically categorized as internal or external:*
> *Internal fraud occurs when a director, an employee, a former employee, or a third party engaged by the bank commits fraud, colludes to commit fraud, or otherwise enables or contributes to fraud. [...]*

61 BCBS 2001.

62 COSO 2016.

*External fraud consists of first-party fraud and victim fraud. External fraud is committed by a person or entity that is not a bank employee, a former employee, or a third party engaged by the bank. [...]*
*Fraud risk is a form of operational risk, which is the risk to current or projected financial condition and resilience arising from inadequate or failed internal processes or systems, human errors or misconduct, or adverse external events."*[63]

The APRA defines fraud risk, similar to the OCC, as

*"the risk of loss from internal fraud or external fraud. These can be defined as: a) internal fraud – losses due to acts of a type intended to defraud, misappropriate property or circumvent regulations, the law or company policy (excluding diversity/discrimination events) which involves at least one internal party; and b) external fraud – losses due to acts of a third party that are of a type intended to defraud, misappropriate property or circumvent the law."*[64]

There are a number of sub-types for fraud risk, mainly based on the products or services for which fraud can happen.

##### 2.4.1.4.1 Account-opening fraud risk

According to the Association of Certified Fraud Examiners (ACFE), "new account fraud is generally defined as fraud that occurs on an account within the first 90 days that it is open. It occurs when it is found that the account was opened with the intent to commit fraud."[65] Based on this, we define account-opening fraud risk for a financial institution as *the risk of opening an account under a false identity and the subsequent misuse of such an account for fraudulent activities.*

##### 2.4.1.4.2 Debt/credit card fraud risk

According to Cornell Law School, "Credit card fraud is a form of identity theft that involves an unauthorized taking of another's credit card information for the purpose of charging purchases to the account or removing funds from it."[66] The resulting risk is *the risk of illegal use by a third party of a stolen or fake debit/credit card and the corresponding losses faced by the bank.*

63 OCC 2019a.
64 APRA 2015.
65 ACFE 2011.
66 Cornell Law School s.a.

### 2.4.1.4.3 Fraudulent paper-based payment transactions risk

We define this risk as *the risk of losses due to illegal use of means of payment by falsifying the payment media such as cheques or bank transfers.*

### 2.4.1.4.4 Online banking fraud risk

This risk refers to the illegal use of online banking based on obtained user account credentials. These credentials are usually obtained via cyberattacks such as phishing or whaling.

### 2.4.1.4.5 Credit fraud risk

Credit fraud can be described as the use of someone else's credentials and credit standing to borrow money without the intention of repayment. The corresponding risk from the perspective of a bank is then the risk of losses due to credit fraud.

### 2.4.1.4.6 Theft risk

This risk refers to the removal or illicit confiscation of property belonging to another person or entity with the intent to illegally assume ownership or to give it to a third party. In the context of financial institutions, this is the risk of information being stolen and handed to third parties outside the bank. As such, it may lead to data privacy violations as a result of theft risk events.

### 2.4.1.4.7 Embezzlement/breach of trust risk

Investopedia describes embezzlement as "a form of white-collar crime in which a person or entity misappropriates the assets entrusted to them. In this type of fraud, the embezzler attains the assets lawfully and has the right to possess them, but the assets are then used for unintended purposes."[67] The corresponding risk can then be defined as *the risk of losses resulting from the embezzlement or breach of trust.*

### 2.4.1.4.8 Antitrust violation risk

The European Union defines this risk as the violation of "agreements between market operators that would restrict competition, and the abuse of dominance."[68] According to

[67] Investopedia 2021a.

[68] European Union s.a., Antitrust Overview.

the International Chamber of Commerce (ICC), the intention of antitrust laws is to guarantee the delivery of goods and services to consumers at a fair price in an ethical manner. Non-compliance may lead to significant penalties as well as serious reputational damage.[69] The Procurement Collusion Strike Force of the US Department of Justice includes antitrust violations bid rigging, price fixing, and customer or market allocation.[70]

#### 2.4.1.4.9 Balance sheet manipulation

Balance sheet manipulation, also called financial statement fraud, refers to the manipulation of an organisation's financial statements. The ACFE defines it as a scheme in which an employee intentionally causes a misstatement or omission of material information in the organization's financial reports (e.g., recording fictitious revenues, understating reported expenses, or artificially inflating reported assets).[71]

### 2.4.1.5 Information, Communication & Technology (ICT) and cyber risk

ICT risk describes the general threats to IT and communication systems which can disrupt operations. The EBA defines this risk as

> *"risk of loss due to breach of confidentiality, failure of integrity of systems and data, inappropriateness or unavailability of systems and data or inability to change IT within a reasonable time and with reasonable costs when the environment or business requirements change (i.e., agility). This includes security risks resulting from inadequate or failed internal processes or external events including cyber-attacks or inadequate physical security."*[72]

The core of information security, IT security and cybersecurity lies in the protection of information and data. This is referred to as the protection of assets. Assets can be hardware as well as software, so they can encompass data and information or IT systems, products or processes. The U.S. National Institute of Standards and Technology (NIST) defines information security as the protection of information and information systems from unauthorised access, use, disclosure, disruption, modification or destruction in order to provide confidentiality, integrity and availability.

The term ICT risk is mainly used in Europe, with the European Parliament & Council using the following definition:

---

[69] International Chamber of Commerce s.a.

[70] U.S. Department of Justice/Procurement Collusion Strike Force 2021.

[71] ACFE 2004.

[72] EBA 2019b.

*"'ICT risk' means any reasonably identifiable circumstance in relation to the use of network and information systems which, if materialised, may compromise the security of the network and information systems, of any technology dependent tool or process, of operations and processes, or of the provision of services by producing adverse effects in the digital or physical environment."*[73]

The EBA provides a general definition of ICT risk:

*"'ICT risk' means the risk of loss due to breach of confidentiality, failure of integrity of systems and data, inappropriateness or unavailability of systems and data, or inability to change IT within a reasonable time and costs when the environment or business requirements change (i.e. agility)."*[74]

Accordingly, the aim of any policies "should ensure confidentiality, integrity and availability of a financial institution's critical logical and physical assets, resources and sensitive data whether at rest, in transit or in use."[75]

The EBA also provides a view on ICT and security risks from a payment perspective, stating that the

*"term 'ICT and security risks' addresses the operational and security risks mandate of Article 95 of the revised Payments Services Directive (PSD2). This term recognises that the operational risks for payment services refer predominantly to ICT and security risks because of the electronic nature of payment services (over ICT systems)."*[76]

The US National Institute of Standards and Technology (NIST) defines cyber risk as the "risk of depending on cyber resources, i.e. the risk of depending on a system or system elements which exist in or intermittently have a presence in cyberspace." A more detailed definition of cyber risk, also provided by NIST, is the following:

*"Risk of financial loss, operational disruption, or damage, from the failure of the digital technologies employed for informational and/or operational functions introduced to a manufacturing system via electronic means from the unauthorized access, use, disclosure, disruption, modification, or destruction of the manufacturing system."*[77]

[73] European Parliament 2020.

[74] EBA 2018.

[75] EBA 2019b, 18.

[76] Ibid.

[77] NIST s.a., cyber risk.

The Canadian OSFI states that

> *"'cyber risk' or 'cyber security risk' is the risk of financial loss, operational disruption or reputational damage from the unauthorized access, malicious and non-malicious use, failure, disclosure, disruption, modification or destruction of an institution's information technology systems and/or the data contained therein."*[78]

The APRA defines data risk as follows:

> *"Data risk encompasses the risk of loss resulting from inadequate or failed internal processes, people and systems or from external events impacting on data. Consideration of data risk is relevant regardless of whether the data is in hard copy or soft copy form. Examples include: (a) fraud due to theft of data; (b) business disruption due to data corruption or unavailability; (c) execution delivery failure due to inaccurate data; and (d) breach of legal or compliance obligations resulting from disclosure of sensitive data."*[79]

As compared to other risk categories, there are some possible sub-categories to ICT and cyber risks, as described in the following sections.

#### 2.4.1.5.1 Data confidentiality risk

According to NIST, "data confidentiality refers to protection of data from unauthorized access and disclosure, including means for protecting personal privacy and proprietary information."[80] Based on this definition, we define data confidentiality risk as *the risk of failure of protecting information from being accessed by unauthorised parties.*

This spans all types of confidential data in a bank, from personal customer data via employee data to all generated data used for internal operations and reporting.

#### 2.4.1.5.2 Data availability risk

The EBA defines data availability risk as "the risk that performance and availability of ICT systems and data are adversely impacted, including the inability to timely recover the institution's services, due to a failure of ICT hardware or software components, weaknesses in ICT system management, or any other event."[81]

---

78 OSFI 2021b.

79 APRA 2013.

80 NIST s.a., data confidentiality.

81 EBA 2017.

#### 2.4.1.5.3 Data integrity risk

The ECB defines data integrity risk as

> *"the risk that data stored and processed by IT systems are incomplete, inaccurate or inconsistent across different IT systems, for example as a result of weak or absent IT controls during the different phases of the IT data life cycle (i.e. designing the data architecture, building the data model and/or data dictionaries, verifying data inputs, controlling data extractions, transfers and processing, including rendered data outputs), impairing the ability of an institution to provide services and produce (risk) management and financial information in a correct and timely manner."*[82]

For the purpose of this book, we use this definition.

#### 2.4.1.5.4 Information security risk

Information security risk comprises the impacts on an organisation and its stakeholders that can occur due to the threats and vulnerabilities associated with the operation and use of information systems and the environments in which those systems operate. In this sense, information security risk is the risk type that is closest to what is usually called cybersecurity risk, even though the term cybersecurity risk might also include some of the elements of the other sub-types of ICT risk.

The APRA defines IT security risk as "the risk of loss due to inadequate or failed internal processes, people and systems or from external events, resulting in a compromise of an IT asset's confidentiality, integrity or availability," basically using the definition of operational risk, specifically applied to IT assets.[83]

The distinguishing factor for information security risk is that this risk does not materialise without an exploitation of vulnerabilities, i.e. it only happens in the case of a successful attack.

### 2.4.1.6 Data privacy and bank secrecy risk

Data privacy and bank secrecy risk describes the risk of a potential leakage of customer data and thus a breach in the bank secrecy. This risk is particularly sensitive as it pertains to highly personal individual data, its management is therefore a part of customer protec-

[82] ECB 2021.
[83] APRA 2013.

tion. Also, breaches of data privacy have a strong link to cybersecurity risk, as certain variants of cyberattacks aim at stealing protected customer data.

#### 2.4.1.6.1 Data privacy risk

Data privacy, sometimes also referred to as information privacy, is an area of data protection that concerns the proper handling of sensitive data including personal data but also other confidential data, such as certain financial data and intellectual property data, to meet regulatory requirements as well as protecting the confidentiality and immutability of the data.[84] Based on this definition of data privacy, we define data privacy risk as *the risk that unauthorised parties get access to confidential information which is protected by privacy laws.* This can either happen accidentally during internal processes or intentionally as part of a cyberattack aimed at stealing customer data.

Data privacy risk can be viewed as an extension of data confidentiality risk to a specific situation. It refers to the situation of violating the rights of the individual regarding the individual's data, for example using the data outside the scope of given consent, like the use in a marketing algorithm. This would not violate data confidentiality but data privacy. In the EU, the GDPR[85] provides the regulatory basis for this, an example in the US is the CCPA.[86]

#### 2.4.1.6.2 Bank secrecy risk

We define bank secrecy risk as *the risk that a bank violates the bank secrecy laws by leaking or giving access to bank customer data.* In contrast to data privacy risk, a risk event concerning a bank secrecy risk can only be triggered by the financial institution itself, i.e. by its processes or employees.

### 2.4.1.7 Resilience risk

Financial institutions always face the risk of operational disruption, due to, but not limited to, increased financial system interconnectedness, evolution of infrastructure complexity and potential impact from technology-related threats.

[84] SNIA s.a.

[85] EUR-Lex 2016.

[86] State of California, DOJ s.a.

Operational resilience is defined by the BCBS as

> *"the ability of a bank to deliver critical operations through disruption. This ability enables a bank to identify and protect itself from threats and potential failures, respond and adapt to, as well as recover and learn from disruptive events in order to minimise their impact on the delivery of critical operations through disruption."*[87]

We define resilience risk as *the risk of losses from unexpected events leading to disruptions of business operations*. It can be caused by poor identification of potential disruptive events and a failure to anticipate potential consequences from such events on the operations of a bank. In other words, the impact of this risk is strongly dependent on how well prepared the bank is, and how quickly and effectively its important business services are able to recover after a disruption, given the assumption that disruption cannot be prevented entirely.

Regulators are adopting a more structured approach towards operational resilience. Over the past approximately 15 years, there has been a visible expansion of the definition of operational resilience. In the years before 2008, it covered several rather heterogeneous risk elements, including operational risk, business continuity, information security, technological system integrity as well as physical security and safety.

After the global financial crisis, an evolution of the definition towards new and emerging risks could be observed. It was acknowledged that financial system and bank stability are a function of emergent risks. One example of such a risk is the topic of data privacy, as formalised and regulated by the GDPR in Europe and CCPA in the US. Other examples are cybersecurity and IT risks.

The next phase, which led to the current integrated view of operational resilience, started around 2017. At that time regulators across the globe, covering financial authorities in the UK, US, EU and Singapore, started to set structured expectations for a more comprehensive operational resilience framework. Now the focus is not only on the resilience of banks themselves but also on the effects of incidents on customers and other stakeholders. Regulators require a comprehensive understanding of business services, including the contributions and roles of third and fourth parties. The resilience of these business services now requires an analysis under low probability scenarios with a significant impact. Finally, regulators now expect an ongoing and holistic pressure testing and evolution of a bank's operational resilience framework.

[87] BCBS 2021a.

UK regulators have led the pack with their comprehensive regulatory frameworks on operational resilience. The FCA issued detailed guidance on how to build operational resilience in a series of consultative documents in 2019, culminating in the publication of final rules in 2021.[88] The FED, in collaboration with the OCC and the FDIC, published an interagency paper with recommendations on sound practices to strengthen operational resilience in 2020.[89] The BCBS issued a set of seven guiding principles for operational resilience in March 2021.[90] Also in March 2021, the MAS, together with the Association of Banks in Singapore, published a paper on risk management and operational resilience in a remote working environment.[91]

### 2.4.1.8 Outsourcing and vendor risk

European regulators have increased their focus on the management of outsourcing-related risks in recent years. In 2019, the EBA published guidelines on outsourcing arrangements. Therein, it defined the outsourcing risk as "the risk that engaging a third party to provide services may adversely impact an institution's performance and risk management."[92] Also, in 2019, the PRA published a consultation paper on outsourcing and third-party risk management.[93]

In the US, the FED, FDIC and OCC (collectively, the agencies) issued guidance on managing risks associated with third-party relationships which states that

> *"[T]he use of third parties can reduce a banking organization's direct control over activities and may introduce new risks or increase existing risks, such as operational, compliance, and strategic risks. [...] A banking organization can be exposed to adverse impacts, including substantial financial loss and operational disruption, if it fails to appropriately manage the risks associated with third-party relationships."*[94]

In Asia-Pacific, the APRA has published a prudential standard on outsourcing arrangements, however, without an explicit definition of outsourcing risk.[95] The MAS published guidelines on outsourcing in 2016.[96]

---

[88] FCA 2019a.

[89] Board of Governors of the Federal Reserve System 2020.

[90] BCBS 2021a.

[91] MAS/ABS 2021.

[92] EBA 2019a.

[93] Bank of England 2019a.

[94] Board of Governors of the Federal Reserve System 2013.

[95] APRA 2017.

[96] MAS 2018a.

### 2.4.1.8.1 Intragroup outsourcing risk

According to the Central Bank of Bahrain, intragroup outsourcing "is an arrangement in which one company within a group of companies provides services for another company within the same group that could also be or usually have been provided in-house."[97] Thus, we define intragroup outsourcing risk as *the risk that engaging another group entity to provide certain services adversely impacts the institution's operations and risk management.* In this situation, after a risk event or even after detection of weaknesses in the way services are provided, the group leadership can more directly influence adjustment measures to prevent further risk events or ensure mitigation of this risk before its occurrence.

### 2.4.1.8.2 External outsourcing risk

We define external outsourcing risk in line with the EBA definition of outsourcing risk as the risk that engaging another third party to provide certain services adversely impacts the institution's operations and risk management. Here, the strongest levers to mitigate such risks are clear and precise service-level agreements ("SLAs") with the third-party provider, and a clear definition of the interfaces, services and processes impacted by the third party.

### 2.4.1.8.3 Vendor risk

According to Gartner, "vendor risk management is the process of ensuring that the use of service providers and IT suppliers does not create an unacceptable potential for business disruption or a negative impact on business performance."[98] Based on this, we define vendor risk as *the risk of business disruption resulting from the use of service providers and IT suppliers.*

### 2.4.1.9 Tax reporting risk

Tax reporting risk describes the risk of incorrect/incomplete tax evaluation of the customers' transactions resulting in false reporting to the customers. This risk can lead to lawsuits against the financial institution with corresponding costs. It additionally carries the risk of reputational damage.

[97] Central Bank of Bahrain s.a.

[98] Gartner s.a.

### 2.4.1.10 Other operational risk

Operational risk in general, as described above, classifies any loss caused by inadequate or failed internal processes, people and systems, or external events. Other operational risks in this case comprise those that were not previously covered by the mentioned specific risk types.

#### 2.4.1.10.1 Human resources risk

We define human resources risk as *the risk of losses caused by inadequate human resources processes and decisions.* One example of human resources risk is employee shortage, i.e. not having the right persons for a specific job. Another example is the risk of key persons leaving and thereby causing friction in certain processes that ultimately lead to losses, for example due to foregone business opportunities.

#### 2.4.1.10.2 Legal risk

The BCBS states that "legal risk includes, but is not limited to, exposure to fines, penalties, or punitive damages resulting from supervisory actions, as well as private settlements."[99] The ECB's glossary defines legal risk as "the risk of a loss being incurred on account of the unexpected application of a law or regulation, or because a contract cannot be enforced." The FED states that "legal risk arises from the potential that unenforceable contracts, lawsuits, or adverse judgments can disrupt or otherwise negatively affect the operations or condition of a banking organization."[100]

From Asia-Pacific, a further description of legal risk is provided by the Reserve Bank of India:

> *"Legal risk may vary from institution to institution depending on the manner in which it conducts its business and the documentation it follows. The legal risks primarily arise either due to lack of clarity of the documentation of the product or the act of the counterparty. Change in legal environment due to legislative changes and Court interpretations/proceedings also result in legal risk. Legal risk includes risk of non-enforceability of contract or in-correct documentation resulting in the increased probability of loss. Broadly, legal risks may result in, (i) claims against institution, (ii)*

[99] BCBS 2017.

[100] Board of Governors of the Federal Reserve System 2021a.

*fines, penalties, punitive damages, (iii) unenforceable contracts resulting from defective documentation and (iv) loss of institutional reputation."*[101]

#### 2.4.1.10.3 Physical damage risk

Physical damage risk (also "damage to physical assets systems risk") is the risk of an unexpected financial or reputational loss from damage to physical assets owned or operated by the firm, ranging from natural disasters to other physical events such as vandalism, terrorism or sabotage.

#### 2.4.1.10.4 Execution, delivery and process risk

Business execution risk (in more detail: execution, delivery and process management risk) is the risk of unexpected financial or reputational loss as the result of poor execution of regular business tasks.[102]

#### 2.4.1.10.5 Reporting risk

This includes any risk resulting from incorrect/incomplete information about financial reporting standards and timelines, receipt of data from sources and subsequent analysis as well as the financial closing process at the end of each reporting period.

#### 2.4.1.10.6 Accounting risk

Accounting risk describes the risk of low accounting quality, with the worst case being that the financial statement does not show the true and fair view of a firm's financial position. This can result in restatements and corresponding regulatory scrutiny and penalties. In addition, low accounting quality is an information risk and can seriously distort the decision-making process.

#### 2.4.1.10.7 Project risk

The Project Management Institute (PMI) defines project risk as an uncertain event or condition that, if it occurs, has a positive or negative effect on a project objective. A risk

[101] Inaugural address by Ms Shyamala Gopinath, Deputy Governor of the Reserve Bank of India, at the Symposium on "Changing Dynamics of Legal Risks in the Financial Sector," Kochi on, 30 October 2009.

[102] Open Risk Manual s.a.

has a cause and, if it occurs, an impact.[103] A project risk can be internal to the business, it can involve external events, or it can stem from any other circumstances that can hamper the project's overall success and result in loss to the firm undertaking it.

##### 2.4.1.10.8 Competition law risk

According to the UK Institute of Risk Management (IRM), competition law is designed to protect businesses and consumers from anti-competitive behaviour in order to deliver open, dynamic markets and enhanced productivity, innovation and value. If competition law is breached, organisations can find themselves facing financial penalties, prison and fines, disqualification of directors and severe reputational damage.[104] Based on this, we define competition law risk as *the risk of losses to a company from violations to the respective competition law.*

##### 2.4.1.10.9 Model risk

The FDIC defines model risk as "the potential for adverse consequences from decisions based on incorrect or misused model outputs and reports" and provides guidelines on model risk management, however without a specific definition of model risk itself.[105] For the purposes of this book, we use the FDIC definition.

### 2.4.2 Strategic risk

Strategic risk is defined by the FDIC as "the risk arising from ill-advised business decisions or the failure to implement appropriate business decisions in a manner consistent with an institution's strategic planning objectives."[106] The OCC defines strategic risk as "the risk to current or projected financial condition and resilience arising from adverse business decisions, poor implementation of business decisions, or lack of responsiveness to changes in the banking industry and operating environment."[107]

#### 2.4.2.1 Reputational risk

Reputational risk refers to the potential for negative publicity, public perception or uncontrollable events to have an adverse impact on a company's reputation, thereby affect-

[103] Hillson 2000.
[104] IRM s.a.
[105] FDIC s.a.
[106] FDIC 2008.
[107] OCC 1996.

ing its revenue and market position. In Europe, the EBA defines reputational risk as "the current or prospective risk to the institution's earnings, own funds or liquidity arising from damage to the institution's reputation."[108]

The FED defines reputational risk as "the potential that negative publicity regarding an institution's business practices, whether true or not, will cause a decline in the customer base, costly litigation, or revenue reductions."[109] The FDIC defines reputational risk in an examination of third-party arrangements as

> *"the risk arising from negative public opinion. Dissatisfied customers, breaches of an institution's policies or standards, and violations of law can potentially harm the reputation of a financial institution in the community it serves. Negative publicity involving the third party, even if it is not related to the specific third-party arrangement, presents reputation risk to a financial institution."*[110]

### 2.4.2.2 Sustainability risk

Sustainability risk refers to the uncertainty in being able to sustain the growth of a given system (a corporation, household, community or economy) because certain practices may have negative externalities which result in the dilapidation of value chain of the system over a period of time or impact other related systems. Specifically, sustainability risk also includes the risk from relevant topics impacting on a company's strategy and direction.

The EU defines sustainability risk as "an environmental, social or governance event or condition that, if it occurs, could cause an actual or a potential negative impact on the value of the investment or on the value of the liability".[111] For more details, we refer to chapter 16.

#### 2.4.2.2.1 Climate change risk

Regulators have published guidelines and frameworks regarding the management of sustainability risk, with a strong focus on climate and environmental risk. The ECB published a comprehensive guide on climate-related and environmental risks in 2020. This

[108] EBA 2018.

[109] Board of Governors of the Federal Reserve System 2013.

[110] FDIC 2008.

[111] European Commission 2021b.

guide includes a definition of climate and environmental risks as being commonly understood to comprise two main risk drivers[112]:

- physical risk refers to the financial impact of a changing climate, including more frequent extreme weather events and gradual changes in climate, as well as of environmental degradation, such as air, water and land pollution, water stress, biodiversity loss and deforestation;
- transition risk refers to an institution's financial loss that can result, directly or indirectly, from the process of adjustment towards a lower-carbon and more environmentally sustainable economy.

In 2021, the EU published the transparency framework, the Sustainable Finance Disclosure Regulation (SFDR)[113], requiring financial market participants to disclose sustainability information for investors.[114] In the UK, the PRA has published a supervisory statement on the management of financial risks from climate change by banks and insurers.[115] The OSFI in Canada also uses a definition of climate change risk that is similar to the ECB definition.[116] In Asia-Pacific, the MAS has issued guidelines on environmental risk management for banks.[117] For this book, we use the ECB definition of climate change risk.

#### 2.4.2.2.2 Human rights risk

Human rights risks refer to the potential adverse impacts that a company can have on the enjoyment of human rights.[118] For financial institutions, we define human rights risk as *the risk of losses to the financial institution from violation of human rights, either by the financial institution itself or by its customers.*

The United Nations Environment Programme (UNEP) Finance Initiative has published a guidance tool to assist financial institutions identifying potential human rights risks arising from the activities of corporate customers/clients.[119] These risks depend on a company's business activities, products and services, its countries of operation, business relationships and the appropriateness of its existing prevention and mitigating measures.

---

112 ECB 2020a.

113 EUR-Lex 2019b.

114 European Commission 2024.

115 Bank of England 2019b.

116 OSFI 2021a.

117 MAS 2020a.

118 Deutsches Institut für Menschenrechte 2016.

119 UNEP 2014.

### 2.4.2.3 Business risk

Generally, business risk can be viewed as a threat to the company's ability to achieve its financial goals.[120] Based on this, we define business risk as *the risk that a failed or flawed business decision, or the lack thereof, poses to the financial situation of a company.* This risk is strongly related to the strategic direction and business strategy of the company. Risk events from business risk can imply the loss of market share or even the obsolescence of parts of the business due to changes in the competitive environment, for example from substitute products or technological advancement.

#### 2.4.2.3.1 Forecasting risk

Forecasting risk is the possibility that errors in projected data (e.g. cash flows) or forecasting models (e.g. on market growth, price and cost developments, attractivity of certain products and services to customers) will lead to incorrect business decisions and corresponding losses.

#### 2.4.2.3.2 Inorganic growth risk

Inorganic growth risk describes the risk involved in inorganic growth arising from mergers or takeovers rather than an increase in the company's own business activity. This includes the risks connected to the due diligence process and the post-merger integration.

#### 2.4.2.3.3 New business risk

This describes the risk of losses resulting from expanding the business activities into new products, markets, distribution channels or customer groups.

#### 2.4.2.3.4 Investor relations risk

This includes any risk resulting from insufficient or wrong communication between the company and its shareholders/investors, which can lead to financing struggles or a share price decline.

120 Corporate Finance Institute s.a.

## 2.5 Conclusion and outlook

Non-financial risk has been gaining significant importance over the recent years as incidents such as the financial crisis of 2008 and recent money laundering scandals have shown that organisations not only need to keep their financial risks but also their non-financial risks in mind. Given that there is no general definition of non-financial risk and that regulators of different jurisdictions have not yet developed a common view, financial institutions need to develop their own non-financial risk taxonomies based on their business models and risk appetites.

Generally, non-financial risk is divided into two main categories: operational and strategic risks. The former contains operational risks, i.e. risks related to banking operations, while the latter contains those risks that we view as strategic risks, which makes them part of non-financial risk but separate from operation-related risks. This approach combines the specification of operational risks according to the BCBS definition, considering that the risks falling under strategic risks are also non-financial risks. Historically, we have seen that the non-financial risk taxonomy constantly evolves parallel to emergent risk topics, e.g. cybercrime and resilience risk due to access to new technologies. It will be interesting to see which currently unknown risk topics will surface in the future. Therefore, all the better if organisations are already well-positioned concerning the known risk topics.

Whereas the management of certain non-financial risks such as fraud risk or outsourcing risk is already established quite well and follows a standardised process, emerging risks such as conduct risk and sustainability risk require more attention. Besides, well-established risks like ICT risk need to be monitored closely as new sub-risks occur from increasing digitisation and automation. Therefore, it is important to review risk types periodically in a holistic manner and to assess their inherent and residual risk in order to see if they still match the organisation's business model and risk appetite. Given the nature of non-financial risk, its measurement remains a challenge. Therefore, financial institutions need to develop robust methodologies for a more quantitative risk assessment of non-financial risks.

# 3 Risk Boundaries – Setting an Analytical Risk Appetite Framework for Non-Financial Risks

*Federico Truffelli, Dr. Ulrich Göres, Lorenzo Fantini, Michele Rigoni, Luca Rancan*

## 3.1 Introduction

### 3.1.1 Regulatory requirements

A risk appetite framework (RAF) sets the maximum level of risk an institution is willing to accept for the pursuit of its business plan and long-term strategic objectives, considering stakeholders interests and risk-specific regulatory requirements. The concept of risk appetite has evolved over the past ten years, reaching maturity not only through new regulatory standards but also the continuous hands-on efforts and tuning of financial institutions.

In 2009, the Senior Supervisors Group (SSG) under the Financial Stability Board (FSB) carried out an in-depth analysis of major failures and structural weaknesses in financial services' governance, risk management and internal controls systems, which were then identified as partial causes of the financial and banking crisis of 2008.[1] The analysis highlighted a significant disparity between the FSB's perception of risk management and appetite, and the actual performance of financial institutions. The FSB underlined the need for comprehensive and clear risk information, along with competences that allow for a proper risk oversight among board members and senior management, a message reinforced in recent years.[2]

Supervisory authorities called for a more structured, quantifiable and factual approach to the definition of risk appetite and management. In 2010, the SSG followed up on its findings and observed a general improvement in the identification of measurable indicators and in communication efforts towards (and from) senior management. However, such approaches were not yet fully consolidated within financial institutions.[3]

---

[1] SSG 2009.

[2] Ibid.; Bank for International Settlements 2010; Single Supervisory Mechanism 2016.

[3] SSG 2010.

In 2013, the FSB helped push the risk appetite framework further by collecting and rationalising lessons learnt and best practice observed among market players.[4] The FSB also contributed to the consolidation of key terminology and concepts, setting the minimum requirements in terms of:

- clear expression and identification of risk appetite and related limits, providing relevant vocabulary as well as guidelines to ensure significance and soundness;
- governance of risk appetite frameworks, clarifying expectations concerning roles and responsibilities of different actors within an institution.

In the ensuing years, market players have embedded such concepts and guidelines, and they have further evolved metrics and indicators in RAFs. Such refinement firstly focused on financial risks, the real culprits of the 2008 crisis. In the past five years, however, increased attention has been devoted to non-financial risks (NFR). The European Central Bank (ECB) gave a boost to the RAF evolution for NFR, paving the way for inclusion of non-financial risks as a measure of sound risk management in its *2016 Supervisory Review and Evaluation Process guidance*.[5] It stated that "Material non-financial risks (in particular compliance risk, reputational risk, IT risk, legal risk and conduct risk) are expected to be included more explicitly in the RAF, if not with quantitative proxies, at least with qualitative statements."[6]

From 2016 onwards, several financial institutions introduced a 'formal' RAF for non-financial risks. Still, most companies started approaching non-financial risks with broad qualitative statements, while only the most advanced institutions adopted a 'business steering' approach, with quantitative metrics cascaded into business operational limits, making explicit the trade-offs between business decisions and risk exposures. This business-oriented approach has marked an important step forward from the traditional slogan of 'zero tolerance' to a practical risk-based decision-making tool, which in the most advanced institutions is closely interlinked with other key business processes (e.g. strategic planning).

Nonetheless, the sophistication of quantitative indicators and level of granularity are not homogeneous across non-financial risk types. For some, it has proven convenient and feasible to transform a qualitative, high-level statement into quantitative metrics, to then further break them down into detailed indicators. In other cases, however, quantitative metrics are absent or still limited, and the RAF has remained mainly a qualitative exercise.

4 FSB 2013a.

5 ECB 2018a.

6 Single Supervisory Mechanism 2016.

This chapter will illustrate different ways adopted by market players to embed non-financial risks in RAFs.

### 3.1.2 RAF in practice

The core concepts underlying a RAF, unanimously recognised by regulators and transversely applied for financial as well as non-financial risks, are "appetite," "capacity" and "limit."[7] These express how risk is measured and the relevant thresholds are monitored:

- **Risk appetite** is intended as the express, formal statement concerning the aggregate type and levels of risks which an entity is willing to accept in its effort to pursue its strategic objectives. It can be expressed either as a quantitative measure or as a qualitative sentence. When detailed at a metric/indicator level, it is often identified as "**target**" and provides the reference threshold for the business' development and steering, indicating the risk level considered optimal for the organisation.
- **Risk capacity** (sometimes also referred to as "limit") is intended as the maximum level of risk that can be tolerated by the entity, before breaching relevant constraints (either regulatory or internal). Values beyond it are considered unacceptable, and both management and the board must take this into consideration when taking risk decisions in normal as well as in stressed conditions.
- **Risk targets/caution/limit levels** are the quantitative thresholds which cascade the aggregate risk appetite at the operational level (business line, entity). They represent the maximum acceptable deviation from the target level, and they are set leaving sufficient room to operate, also in stress conditions.

Considering the definitions above, market players typically define **three different levels** within their RAFs:

**Level 1: Overall risk appetite statement (RAS)**

A high-level formal declaration that sets out the types and level of risks that can be assumed in the pursuit of strategic business objectives, for each risk type. For the RAS to be actionable, it usually contains express indication of:

- key principles guiding response to non-financial risks, to be cascaded in risk appetite metrics;
- prohibited activities for the organisation for which "zero tolerance" applies.

[7] FSB 2013a.

### Level 2: Risk appetite metrics and tolerance levels

Primary metrics in which the overall RAS can be disaggregated and the related tolerance thresholds set. Usually linked to residual risk measures captured by a risk assessment, this is the primary step to allow measurement and monitoring of the entity's performance against applicable risk appetite objectives and limits.

### Level 3: Detailed risk indicators and thresholds

Key Risk Indicators (KRIs) that allow the institution to measure and monitor the performance of the defined risk appetite metrics, and allow for a definition of detailed tolerance thresholds (target, caution, limit) for each. The further disaggregation of risk appetite metrics into KRIs can simplify continuous monitoring and the implementation of remediating actions to decrease levels of risk if necessary.

An RAF's design and parametrisation involves all three lines of defence.[8] Given the strategic purpose of RAF, embedding business evaluation is critical to make RAF a steering tool for the organisation. The most mature market players involve key business functions across all the three levels of the framework (Figure 1).

Figure 1: Three levels in risk appetite frameworks

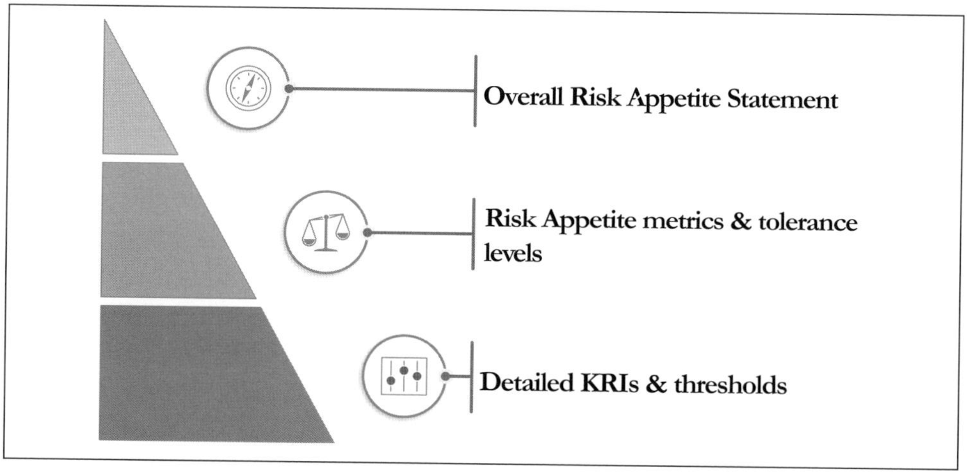


[8] ACAMS 2015.

## 3.2 RAF level 1: overall risk appetite statement

The first level is aimed at setting high-level principles driving risk appetite, and it is organised across two building blocks: overall statement and prohibited activities.

### 3.2.1 Overall statement

The overall statement outlines all levels and types of risk that the bank is willing to take on for each risk type within its risk capacity to achieve its strategic objectives and business plan. The statement, especially for non-financial risks, plays a pivotal role, thus, it should be sufficiently structured and specific to provide guidance and actionable implications for risk management decisions.

As general good practice, the following four RAF elements should be addressed in each statement:

- definition of the entity's ambition towards regulatory compliance (e.g. compliance to minimum applicable requirements versus full compliance also to non-mandatory requirements);
- translation of the ambition into objectives, expressed for example in terms of internal operations and customer interactions;
- expression of tracking mechanisms by which it is possible to acknowledge progress towards the objective;
- identification of the standards by which the bank measures its performance.

The table below shows exemplary non-financial risk RAF statements from large international banks.

Table 3: Example of Level 1 overall statement and related guidance for Level 2 metrics

| Level 1 Risk Appetite Statement | Guidance for Level 2 metrics definition |
|---|---|
| **Example 1**<br>*"We are committed to maintaining operational losses within a limited range, consistent with our business profile and operations [...]."* | This statement addresses non-financial risks globally, "capturing" them via operational losses. |
| **Example 2**<br>*"We are committed to ensuring formal and substantive compliance to all applicable regulations, to avoid sanctions and legal fines [...]."* | This statement addresses a specific non-financial risk (compliance), allowing further drill downs both at the second and third levels. |

The second approach is more commonly found in leading banks, using residual risk generated from risk assessment as the primary metric. This approach is in line with feedback collected by the ECB and has the following key advantages[9]:

- *Comprehensiveness*, given its ability to capture jointly intrinsic characteristics (inherent risk) and effectiveness of controls in place (controls' adequacy).
- *Maturity*, thanks to evolution over recent years of risk assessment methodologies, which cover a wide range of non-financial risk areas, as well as the use of advanced measurement methods.
- *Data Availability*, because of the consolidation over-time of reliable and high-quality input sources as well as the possibility of accessing data with sufficient historical depth.
- *Modularity*, thanks to the possibility of breaking down the aggregated metric and focusing on single non-financial risk areas (see also Section 3.4 below).

### 3.3.2 Metrics: setting the thresholds

In the paragraphs below, we describe the approaches adopted by primary industry players for the setting of thresholds respectively for a Level 2 metric based on operational losses and for another Level 2 metric based on risk assessment.

[9] Feedbacks collected during FIRM Compliance roundtable organised by the ECB (Frankfurt, 16 September 2020).

### 3.3.2.1 Thresholds based on benchmark and historical internal loss data for a metric based on operational losses

In the case of a Level 2 metric based on operational losses, the identification of relevant thresholds can take into consideration:

- Internal data capturing losses registered in past years and connected to a specific non-financial risk type.
- Benchmark data relating to comparable peers.
- Top management input reflecting preferences and expectations.

Top players often rely on a combination of the above-mentioned input sources, as exemplified below (aggregated example).

Figure 2: Definition of thresholds for a Level 2 metric based on operational losses

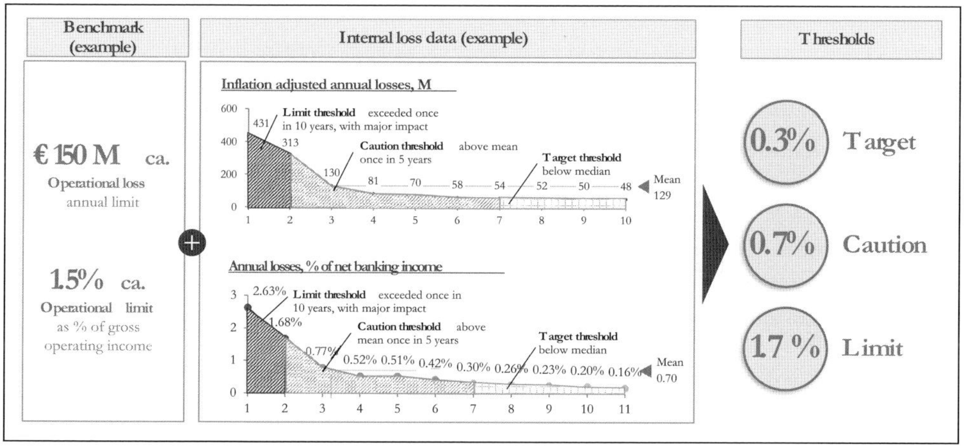


Starting from peers' tolerance levels for operational losses connected to compliance risks (both as absolute values and as a percentage of gross operating income), the bank in this example then carried out a detailed historical analysis of its own internal losses. As result, thresholds were defined as follows:

- *Target*: set to be below median of distribution.
- *Caution*: set to be above mean and exceeded only once in the past five years.
- *Limit*: set to be above mean and exceeded only once in the past ten years.

The bank in this example allowed for thresholds to be changed by +/- 10% based on managerial judgement.

### 3.3.2.2 Thresholds based on residual risk levels for a metric based on risk assessment

Among the main advantages of using risk assessment as second level metric, it is possible to provide a holistic overview of a broad set of non-financial risks and to prioritise the riskiest.

Figure 3: Definition of thresholds for a Level 2 metric based on risk assessment

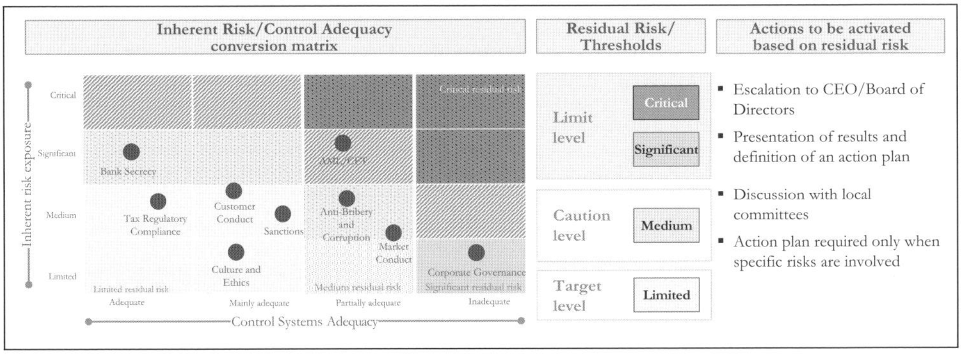


A top-down risk assessment of all non-financial risks will allow the institution to prioritise risk types for which the caution or limit thresholds are exceeded (e.g. in the example above AML/CFT, anti-bribery and corruption have a critical or significant residual risk, above the limit threshold). A bottom-up risk assessment analysis can follow, to identify i) underlying factors that led to a breach of the threshold (e.g. products vs. client geography vs. distribution channel) and ii) the entities or divisions most accountable.

To complement the Level 2 metrics, some players have introduced a synthetic indicator across all non-financial risks. The synthetic metric is calculated by aggregating the different residual risks with a quadratic weighting formula to over-weight elevated risk levels. The same escalation actions described before can be activated on this aggregated metric.

Figure 4: Aggregate Level 2 metric based on risk assessment results

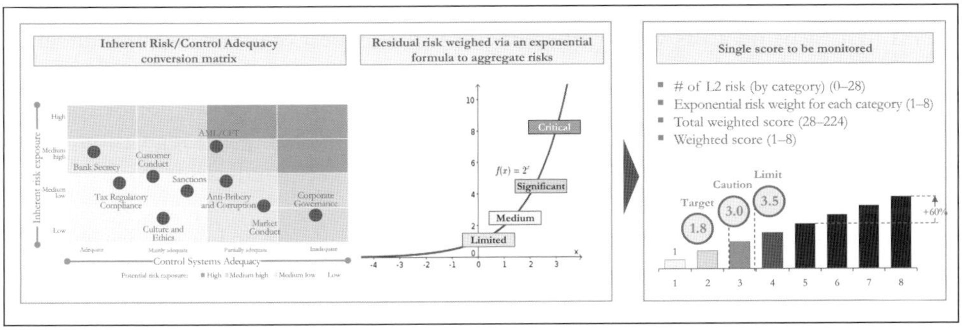


## 3.4 RAF level 3: Key Risk Indicators

Level 3 cascades the RAF down to the business lines and entity level via specific Key Risk Indicators (KRIs), which allow for the early detection of potential deviation from risk appetite objectives, facilitating timely intervention.

Currently, the majority of primary banks have only developed indicators at level 3 for prioritised risk types (based on, for example, internal audit or regulatory findings).

### 3.4.1 Selecting KRIs

Financial institutions typically use a sequence of three drivers to select the KRIs that are jointly the most meaningful and actionable.

Figure 5: Drivers for key risk indicators selection

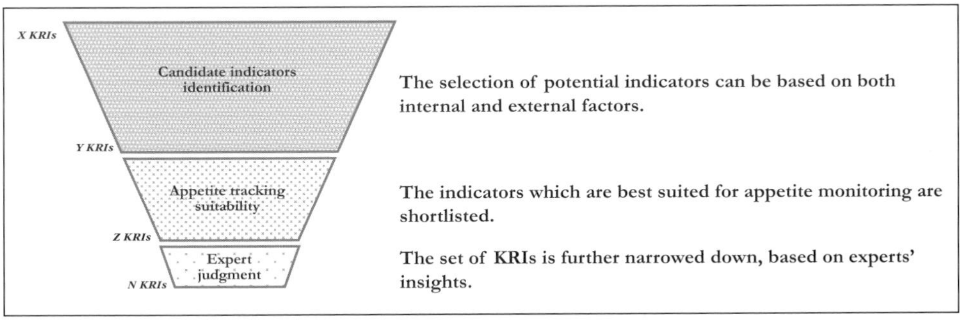

#### 3.4.1.1 Candidate indicators identification

Banks first focus on areas where inherent risk is the highest (e.g. for money laundering risk, indicators investigating non-active corporate customers or customers operating in risky sectors such as gambling). In addition, findings resulting from authorities' inspections, internal findings or critical areas affected by recent changes in regulation, might also represent relevant sources for the identification of Level 3 indicators.

Often, banks adopt internal rules to ensure that risks explored at Level 3 are correctly balanced, with the aim of achieving proper focus on the monitoring of more critical risks: as an example, it might be decided that medium-high risk categories cannot have a higher number of operational KRIs than a high-risk category.

#### 3.4.1.2 Appetite tracking suitability

The initial selection of potential key risk indicators undergoes further scrutiny with the aim of singling out those indicators whose characteristics are more likely to ensure reliable measurement of meaningful dimensions. The evaluation is performed in regards to three dimensions:

- *Feasibility of measurement*
  Given the objective to select indicators that are reliable and can be addressed with actionable measures, it is pivotal to evaluate the ease with which each indicator can be measured from existing information and the need to implement new processes/tools to do that.
- *Availability of data during ordinary business/control processes*
  Indicators based on data which are significant and ordinarily used in other processes can be more easily explained and assessed for consistency.
- *Relevance for regulators*
  Preferred indicators shall capture dimensions that are specifically targeted by applicable regulatory requirements and that, for this reason, can be typical areas of investigation for authorities and control functions.

#### 3.4.1.3 Expert judgement

Subject matter experts usually refine the final choice based on:

- emerging risks in the market (e.g. frequency/size of fines),
- identification of idiosyncrasies of certain indicators (e.g. indicators likely to have excessive/non-monitorable variability in different customers groups),
- identification of complementarity between indicators, which might be exploited to provide a more thorough representation of phenomena/performance.

Table 4: Example of KRI selection process in three steps

**1 – Large European bank (Customer Conduct)**

The bank identified six candidate KRIs for customer conduct risk. They were ranked based on their appetite tracking suitability, evaluating regulatory importance, data availability and feasibility of measurements, resulting in a shortlist of four candidates selected for expert judgment. Following the expert judgment, KRI four was excluded due to low materiality (i.e. values always close to zero), while KRI five was excluded as deemed less relevant for the purpose of compliance risk reporting. Only KRIs two and six where then selected to be included in the RAF.

Figure 6: Example of KRIs selection (Customer Conduct)

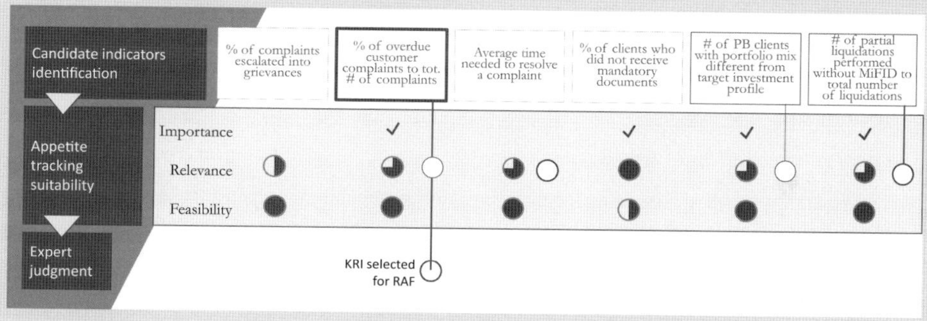


**2 – Large European bank (Data Protection)**

The bank identified six candidate key risk indicators for Data Protection risk. The evaluation of appetite tracking suitability led to the selection of four potential candidates for the last step; this, based on expert judgment, excluded KRIs 2 (for its similarity to KRI 3) and 4 (due to being partially captured by KRI 6). KRIs 3 and 6 were thus selected to be included in the RAF.

Figure 7: Example of KRIs selection (Data Protection)

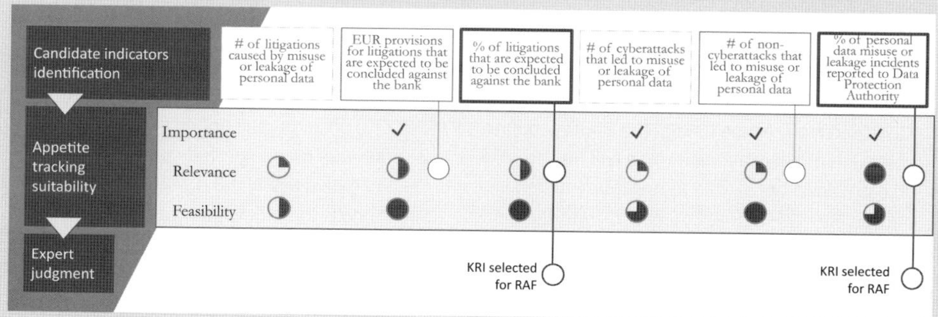

Table 5: Examples of KRIs monitored in the RAF

**1 – Large EU banking group – KRI shortlist**

Identified four KRIs for financial crime risk type.

- **Anti-Financial Crime (AFC) KRI 1** (Inherent Risk)

  $$\frac{\text{\# transactions connected to sanctioned countries (guarantees, letters of credit, loans)}}{\text{Total \# customers}}$$

  This indicator captures the weight of transactions which, although linked to sanctioned countries, were processed by the bank because they were either concluded before sanctions were imposed (currently blocked but present in bank's books) or permissible but exposed to high sanctions risk should regimes become more stringent (e.g. Russia).

- **AFC KRI 2** (Control adequacy)

  *# payments blocked by 3rd parties*

  This indicator is aimed at measuring the bank's controls system efficacy against those of another bank's for sanctions violation, i.e. payment having a nexus to a sanctioned regime. The indicator provides information on transactions that appear to be outside of other market players' risk appetite.

- **AFC KRI 3** (Control adequacy)

  $$\frac{\text{\# alerts in backlog}}{\text{Total \# alerts generated}}$$

  This indicator is aimed to increase focus on the transaction monitoring process and understand possible issues in timely finalising the analysis of alerts.

- **AFC KRI 4** (Control adequacy)

  $$\frac{\text{\# customers with overdue KYC}}{\text{Total \# customers}}$$

  This indicator provides information on relationships with customers whose risk has not been adequately assessed (yet). At the time of the expiration date, all those KYC positions still not recovered, need to be blocked in order to mitigate the risk. In case of KYC expiration due to unexpected risk events (e.g. increased level of risk due to previously unknown factors like negative news), 60 days' will be given to review the KYC before proceeding with the block (customer needs to be duly informed about this situation). No new products can be offered until the KYC has been reviewed.

**2 – Large EU commercial bank – KRI shortlist**

Identified eight key risk indicators in four risk areas having high or medium-high residual risks.

- **AML KRI 1** (AML Alerts backlog)

$$\frac{\text{\# outstanding (> 10 days) AML alerts}}{\text{Total \# AML alerts}}$$

- **AML KRI 2** (KYC Periodic Reviews backlog)

$$\frac{\text{\# outstanding (> 90 days) KYC periodic reviews}}{\text{Total \# AML alerts}}$$

- **AML KRI 3** (Incomplete KYC)

  # clients with missing KYC information

- **Market Conduct KRI** (Breaches by employees in permanent list)

  # of breaches regarding trading bank stock during restricted period for employees in the permanent insider list

- **Customer Conduct KRI 1** (Deal slips with outstanding signature)

$$\frac{\text{\# deal slips with outstanding signature on attached transaction documents for more than one month}}{\text{Total \# deals}}$$

- **Customer Conduct KRI 2** (Overdue[a] complaints)

$$\frac{\text{\# overdue customer complaints}}{\text{Total \# customer complaints}}$$

[a] A complaint shall be considered "overdue" when it takes longer than the target time the company establishes as maximum time to address a complaint.

### 3.4.2 KRIs: setting and calibrating the thresholds

For each risk indicator, different tolerance levels are defined, with the aim of providing straightforward, actionable guidance on how to evaluate the current situation – i.e. whether observed performance is ordinary or whether it is a symptom of emerging anomalies. The definition of thresholds at KRI level addresses the mandate expressed by the regulator, as risk limits are expected to be specific, measurable and reportable.[10]

As a matter of fact, RAFs bridge risk prioritisation coming from risk assessments (i.e. specific areas of focus) with operational KRI-based reporting and specific thresholds to activate remedial actions.

The process is usually articulated in the following three steps:

- Historical data analysis

  The core of threshold setting, in line with regulator's recommendations to "avoid defining limits only based on market references or existing regulatory limits."[11]

- Fine-tuning through peers' benchmarking and back-testing

  Mostly used to identify potential adjustments to the thresholds defined through the historical data analysis.

- Expert judgement

  Thresholds identified are typically refined based on expert insights, which embed, for example, market practice, regulatory guidance, relevant changes in the business model.

Given possible deficiencies in the internal data sources available (e.g. limited sample with few data points, high variability in distribution with large difference between minimum and maximum values for a given risk), financial institutions may decide to run simulations, to compare and identify the most suitable and robust methodology to apply.

Pragmatic examples of these three steps are provided below.

#### 3.4.2.1 Threshold calibration based on historical data analysis and percentiles

A possible approach for calibration relies on the analysis of the historical data of a selected KRI; the thresholds are then defined on selected percentiles of the value distributions.

[10] FSB 2013a.

[11] Ibid.

The percentile distribution approach is often considered a suitable option since it offers a dynamic risk factor assessment. The distribution is constantly updated as new data enters the dataset, thus allowing for a better representation of the evolution of the underlying risk factor.

Under an operational point of view, the percentile approach consists of three main steps:

1. *Building of the dataset through the calculation of the KRI values* (e.g. number of non-domestic customers resident in high-risk countries/total number of clients of all the legal entities within scope). It is important to leverage a sufficiently long set of reliable data series (for example, one large EU bank started with three years of data), to avoid having flat distributions potentially characterised by higher volatility; the resulting distributions may, in fact, lead to set thresholds that are triggered all too often.

2. *Computation of the KRI distribution*

   The KRI dataset must then be sorted from the lowest to the highest value, typically having higher percentiles corresponding to riskier values.

   In order to avoid having too many outlier values, it is important to consider homogenous data for the sample; in case of too heterogeneous data, it could be worth dividing the distribution into sub-distributions based on the characteristics of data (e.g. dividing customers into financial institutions and corporates, or small and large customers). The thresholds shall then be calculated for each of the sub-distributions.

3. *Choice of percentiles for limit, caution and target thresholds*

   The *limit threshold* should be set to contain the extreme values observed in the distribution. Most often simulations and backtestings are run in order to estimate the frequency of breaches of the selected limit threshold: this, in fact, in business-as-usual conditions should be triggered only on rare and high-risk occasions. Nonetheless, percentiles are also typically set in accordance with the institution internal broader RAF methodology, in order to have a consistent approach for the various risks managed within the RAF.

   The *caution threshold* should be set considering two main aspects:

   i. How frequently, in history, the breach of the caution threshold then actually led to the breach of a limit threshold, in order to have a significative caution threshold breach.

   ii. How long would it take to implement timely risk mitigating actions: the threshold should thus be set in order to allow the respective function to undertake the remedial action in a timely manner.

Finally, the *target threshold* should be set based on the risk appetite for the specific KRI that the control function, jointly with the first line, is willing to accept under business-as-usual conditions, and accordingly with overall risk appetite.

Figure 8: Example of thresholds calibration applying a percentile-based approach

| KRI example | Target 90th pct. | Caution 99.9th pct. | Illustrative distribution |
|---|---|---|---|
| 1 High risk customers/ tot # customers | 8.92% | 20.36% | |
| 2 Non-domestic clients resident in high-risk countries/ total number of customers | 0.17% | 0.74% | |

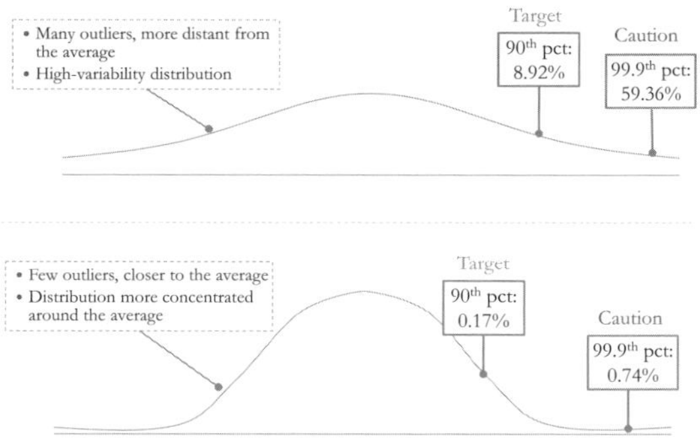


### 3.4.2.2 Threshold fine-tuning based on benchmarking and backtesting

Historical analysis run to determine the percentile to use for the Level 3 KRI thresholds should be complemented by peers' benchmark analysis and backtesting. These activities may lead to the fine-tuning of the defined thresholds, with the aim of better capturing both market practices and the financial institution's specificities.

A benchmark analysis among market peers on the selected KRI will determine the tolerances thresholds most widely in use. If the benchmark pool and the bank are comparable in size and business, the threshold for the selected KRI should be within this value range.

Backtesting should be performed to assess the relevance of selected thresholds in terms of frequency of incurrence. As an example, the analysis could highlight that, having set a specific threshold, over the past ten years too many breaches would have occurred. This could encourage the adjustment of the threshold so that the thresholds correctly identify the values which they are aimed at (e.g. extreme values).

Table 6: Example of KRI threshold calibration and fine-tuning

**1 – Large EU Banking Group**

The bank needed to set the limit, caution and target thresholds for the following KRI:

$$\frac{\text{\# non-domestic company customers resident in high risk countries}}{\text{Total \# comany customers}}$$

The bank firstly determined its data series collecting data points from all legal entities in the group and adding them to the data series of the previous two years. Then two different distributions were carved out of the original one: the first one referred to large company customers, the second one to small-size company customers.

In accordance with the overall RAF methodology, the bank set the following thresholds:

- Target: values in 80th–90th percentile.
- Caution: values above the 95th but below the 99th percentile.
- Limit: value above the 99th percentile.

This setting was backed up by simulations and backtesting, which showed that a breach would have occurred only three times in the past three years, thus being consistent with the definition of extreme values. Furthermore, a benchmark analysis was run, and it confirmed that the main market peers, comparable for volume of transactions and geographical fragmentation of business, used the same thresholds on average.

## 3.5 RAF governance

To enable support for business decisions, a firm's RAF should be underpinned by a strong governance framework, with clear roles for all stakeholders involved at every level of the institution (board, senior management, business lines, risk and control functions, legal entities etc.).[12] As was also highlighted by the Single Supervisory Mechanism, the responsibilities of all stakeholders should be clearly stated and described in the RAF documentation.[13]

As part of the overall corporate governance framework, risk appetite statements are expected to be used to promote robust discussions on risk and strategic issues not only on the board but also together with risk management and compliance functions.

[12] FSB 2013a, 2013b; ECB 2018a.

[13] Single Supervisory Mechanism 2016.

The RAF should also be cascaded within the institution. This means that risk appetite statements should be established for business lines and entities in order to ensure that their strategy and risk limits, as relevant, align with the institution-wide risk appetite statement. The EBA has made clear that internal policies and the risk culture should convey the straightforward message that the management board expects activities not to go beyond the defined risk appetite thresholds.[14] The RAF is a group-driven exercise, usually performed annually.

Figure 9: Annual RAF cycle

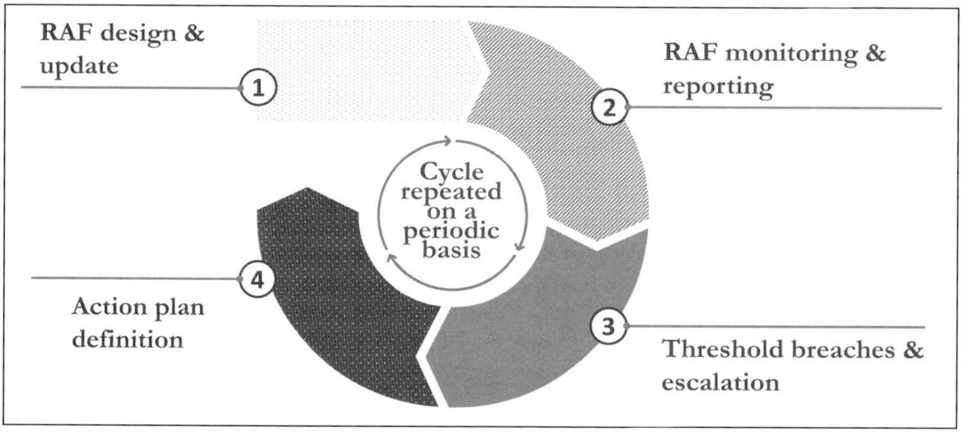


## 3.5.1 RAF design and update

A RAF's components must be periodically reviewed, to guarantee that they are meaningful, thorough and up-to-date; periodicity of review, however, varies depending on the framework's level. In addition, also the regulator mandates periodic independent reviews of the RAF by the internal audit function.[15]

*Level 1:* The overall Risk Appetite Statements (RAS) are reviewed ad hoc in case of senior management input or fundamental changes in business risk appetite or in the risk management framework. In general, variations at RAS level are less frequent than the tuning of other metrics because financial institutions should ensure stability and consistency to avoid strategic drift.

[14] EBA 2017, 2020a.

[15] Single Supervisory Mechanism 2016.

*Level 2:* Risk appetite metrics and corresponding thresholds are subject to periodic reviews – in general, annually – to account for major deviations in risk assessment results, new emerging risks or new business activities.

*Level 3:* KRIs and corresponding thresholds are reviewed more frequently – typically, on an annual basis – to ensure that changes in the risk categories are monitored, the regulatory framework and/or monitoring capabilities are embedded in a timely manner. For Level 3 indicators, any time new risk assessment results are published, it is verified whether there are changes in the residual risk level of the categories being monitored that require adjustments in the KRIs (e.g. new risk category with significant residual risk, requiring the identification of new operational indicators). Based on this preliminary assessment, control functions are expected to review the selection of indicators, based on predefined criteria (e.g. expert judgment):

- For confirmed risk categories, indicators and related thresholds are updated, revised or changed based on new priorities, capabilities or control processes.
- A risk committee with a representative from the board should usually approve any change to the RAF.
- For 'new' risk categories, ad hoc indicators are selected, and related thresholds are preliminarily defined, based on relevant regulation, organisational ambition and available information.
- For risk categories moving to 'non-monitored' levels, corresponding indicators are removed from the RAF.

### 3.5.2 RAF monitoring and reporting

RAF indicators are continuously monitored. However, the periodicity with which underlying data are provided can vary. While for some indicators the underlying data allow for continuous monitoring (e.g. rejected payments), in other cases calculations are periodic (e.g. quarterly, annually), based on the availability of the updated data.

Communications can be issued to inform key stakeholders and risk owners of the RAF indicators outcome, especially in cases in which values are deviating from expected trends and/or are approaching caution or limit thresholds. If thresholds are exceeded, however, specific escalation paths are provided.

Table 7: Example of RAF monitoring and reporting

**1 – Large European Bank**

The compliance unit of a large European bank collects data related to CIB business. Information is provided:

- annually, for related KRIs that are calculated only for the risk assessment.
- quarterly, for related KRIs that are used and calculated on a continuous basis.

Data is provided by the CIB business units, which also perform quality checks to ensure appropriate data quality. The compliance unit then shares the results with the key stakeholders and, if needed, triggers the escalation process.

Figure 10: RAF monitoring and reporting process

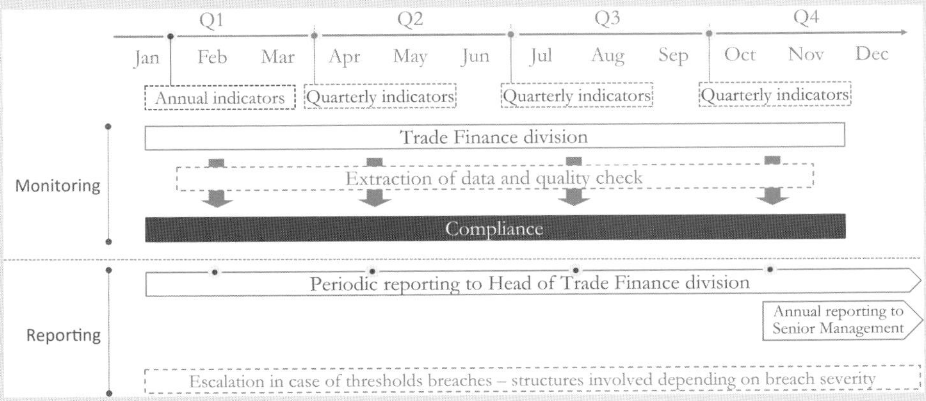


### 3.5.3 RAF threshold breaches and escalation

In case a metric or an indicator breaches caution or limit thresholds, escalation processes are activated in order to manage related risks, and communications are sent to inform the impacted structures/divisions/entities, to notify them about the violation and to investigate its causes.

Different escalation processes are designed in order to reflect the specific urgency, timeliness and severity of the breach, thus differentiating between those activated by the breach of the caution threshold (usually involving risk committees) and those activated by the breach of the limit threshold (typically involving the management board or supervisory board, depending on the legal entity).

Escalation processes should be designed considering:

- principles and criteria for escalation (e.g. confirmed materiality of risk, consistency with other alerts);
- scope of escalation (e.g. at local, regional and group level);
- involvement of appropriate risk type owners;
- identification of potential risk strategies to adopt (e.g. no action/mitigation/avoidance/transfer).

Tabelle 8: Example of RAF monitoring & reporting

**1 – Large European Commercial Bank**

A large commercial bank working across the EU has set up the Level 3 metrics tolerance thresholds, and the related escalation paths, as follows:

- The breach of the target level activates an early warning signal, entailing:
  - notification and request for a deep dive to investigate the reasons for the threshold breach;
  - close monitoring of the indicator;
  - evaluation of potential mitigating actions, involving the business functions in case of need.
- The breach of the caution level requires:
  - notification and request for a deep dive to investigate the reasons underlying the threshold breach;
  - increment of the monitoring frequency from the business-as-usual context, on at least quarterly basis;
  - definition of potential mitigating actions (review of existing or new ones), with involvement of central compliance along with all the relevant stakeholders;
  - reporting of the trigger breach to the local top management.
- A limit level breach requires:
  - notification and request for a deep dive to investigate the reasons underlying the threshold breach;
  - monthly monitoring frequency, increased vs. the base case and in case of trigger breach;
  - mandatory definition of immediate mitigating actions to bring the specific indicator below the limit threshold, jointly defined by the compliance function, involving all key stakeholders;
  - reporting of the limit breach to the local top management.

When a specific indicator breaches the limit threshold:

- the relevant business functions are involved and informed in a timely manner, in order to focus attention on the critical situation and induce a more prudential approach, even before the design and adoption of remedial actions;
- potential remedial actions are proposed and jointly defined with the impacted structures/divisions/entities;
- agreed remedial actions are promptly activated and monitored;
- further points of attention are escalated to relevant senior management;
- the indicator is subject to periodic updates and monitoring by internal control functions;
- after completion, the remedial action is reviewed by internal audits before the actions are closed.

The institution's management bodies are responsible for validating the methodology and are constantly informed about threshold breaches. Many advanced institutions have developed aggregated and consolidated risk appetite dashboards, in which they monitor the risk exposure and limits with respect to the firm's appetite for non-financial risks. These dashboards are regularly presented to the group-wide risk committee (e.g. monthly, quarterly) as well as to the management board and the supervisory board (at least quarterly for larger institutions) to support monitoring and to provide an overview of the institution's risk profile.

### 3.5.4 Action plan definition

Upon identification of "caution" or "limit" threshold breaches, four types of actions are typically undertaken:

1. the root cause is investigated;
2. findings are issued;
3. remedial actions are designed and launched;
4. the risk source (e.g. the division or legal entity) is put under enhanced monitoring, including a periodic reporting.

Based on the adopted metrics and indicators, entities shall define criteria to determine the severity of breaches and the priority of related remedial actions.

Table 9: Example of RAF thresholds breaches prioritisation (Findings Severity Matrix)

**1 – Large Italian Banking Group**

The compliance unit of a large European banking group defined the following criteria to assess the severity level of the remedial actions to be implemented after a threshold breach:

| Thresholds in breach | Inherent Risk from Risk Assessment of the Legal Entity/Foreign Branch | | | |
|---|---|---|---|---|
| | **Low** | **Medium-low** | **Medium-high** | **High** |
| **Target** | **Moderate** | **Moderate** | **Important** | **Important** |
| **Caution** | **Important** | **Important** | **Important** | **Major** |
| **Limit** | **Important** | **Important** | **Major** | **Critical** |

Prior to issuing findings in case of breaches, it should be taken into consideration whether analogous prescriptions have been identified by other sources (e.g. internal audit, risk assessments) and whether there are mitigating actions already ongoing to prevent duplication and promote synergic approaches. Potential remedial measures could be, for example, the review and potential reinforcement of second-level controls, the provision of additional training, the activation of a temporary task force to remedy a backlog of alerts or establishment of steering committees to monitor the remedial progress.

The risk owner for the respective area in which the breach occurred should be identified through the risk matrix within the organisational structure – and is thus the subject responsible for compliance with the external regulations/internal rules. The risk owner, in turn, must define the owners of the implementation of each remedial action to be undertaken.

Clear deadlines should be defined, and their related progress be monitored periodically. Furthermore, there should be clear rules for the definition and management of the due dates (e.g. maximum remedial action time span based on the severity of the related findings; rules and process for re-planning, also consistent with gap severity).

Furthermore, the issues that led to the breaches should be investigated and adequate actions should be taken, which can include cutbacks or the freezing of variable remuneration, up to the termination of employment.

# 4 The Three Lines of Defence Model: Key Success Factors for Effective Risk Management

*Dr. Georg Lienke, Dr. Oliver Engels, Marc Peter Klein, Peter Gürtlschmidt, Rei Tanaka*

## 4.1 Introduction

The origins of the three lines of defence (3LoD) model go back to the late 1990s. It became a prominent element of financial institutions' operational risk management in the aftermath of the 2008 global financial crisis, when a variety of post-crisis risk management regulations were introduced.

The Institute of Internal Auditors formally adopted the 3LoD model in 2013, mainly in response to gaps and duplication in risk management activities caused by diverse teams of risk management specialists, compliance officers, fraud investigators, internal control specialists and internal auditors dispersed across business segments and geographies. While it was a positive development that an increasing number of specialised risk and control professionals were managing risk exposure, it became obvious that an effective framework was necessary to align, delineate and coordinate various risk management activities.[1]

Regulators have since integrated requirements to define the roles and responsibilities of the 1st, 2nd and 3rd LoD in their regulatory standards and, the 3LoD model has been widely accepted as an effective risk management framework across the financial industry.[2] However, even though regulatory standards for 3LoD are similar across jurisdictions, a degree of variation exists regarding the regulatory split of activities between the 1st and 2nd LoD for specific risk types. This chapter will provide examples for such country-specific variations.

The 3LoD model caters for coordination of control responsibilities among various stakeholders in an effective and efficient manner. This is achieved by allocating and delineating distinct roles and mandates to business and operational functions in the 1st LoD, internal control and standard setting functions in the 2nd LoD as well as internal audit in the 3rd LoD. The benefits of the 3LoD model are widely accepted. Yet, several banking scandals have revealed limitations, which need to be addressed to maintain maximum effectiveness.

---

[1] IIA 2013.

[2] EBA 2021c; OCC 2014.

There is no one-size-fits-all approach to 3LoD. Financial institutions need to consider their individual exposures to non-financial risks when implementing 3LoD. That is, risk types with material exposure may require more oversight compared to risk types less relevant to their business models. In addition, institution-specific process questions play a role: exactly which controls are performed by 1st or 2nd LoD units varies between institutions, depending on risk profile, historic development, strategic focus and available resources and skills. These individual particularities must be addressed to achieve maximum effectiveness while maintaining the efficiency of 3LoD models.

This chapter starts with an overview of regulatory requirements for 3LoD in key jurisdictions, followed by a description of the key roles and responsibilities of the 1st, 2nd and 3rd LoD in financial institutions. For the 1st LoD, this includes looking at the benefits of a risk coordinating function (often called 1.5th LoD), which is a risk management coordinator between the 1st and the 2nd LoD. The chapter also describes the required level of 2nd LoD independence from the 1st LoD, as well as key success factors for effective 2nd LoD risk oversight, including methodological consistency across different 2nd LoD functions, adequate 2nd LoD participation in committees and information sharing as well as centralised governance of the institution's risk taxonomy. Finally, the chapter illustrates common pitfalls of the 3LoD model and makes suggestions on how to avoid them.

## 4.2 Regulatory framework in selected key jurisdictions

Global regulators have set regulatory standards with respect to roles and responsibilities of the 3LoD. The following is a summary of key regulations in the European Union, the United States, Hong Kong and Singapore.

### 4.2.1 European Union

In its guidelines on internal governance, the European Banking Authority (EBA) defines specific 3LoD requirements[3]:

- The business lines should be responsible for managing the risks they incur in conducting their activities, and they should have controls in place that aim to ensure compliance with both internal and external requirements.
- Institutions should install independent internal control functions including a risk management function and a compliance function.

[3] EBA 2021c.

- Institutions should set up an independent and effective internal audit function to independently review and provide objective assurance of the compliance of all activities and units.

At the time of editorial close, the European Central Bank was finalizing its *Draft Guide on Governance and Risk Culture* (July 2024). While not legally binding, this guide outlines supervisory expectations regarding the structure, authority, independence, and reporting lines of internal control functions – risk management, compliance, and internal audit – as part of a sound three lines of defence model. It also emphasises the role of the management body in empowering and overseeing these functions. The guide's final version was unavailable at the time of this book's editorial close.

### 4.2.2 United States of America

The US Office of the Comptroller of the Currency (OCC) has issued guidelines on the roles and responsibilities of the 3LoD.[4] In essence, the guidelines establish roles and responsibilities for the business, or 1st LoD (responsible for assessing and managing risks associated with their activities), independent risk management (2nd LoD; overseeing the institution's risk-taking activities and assessing risks independent of the 1st LoD) and internal audit (3rd LoD; assessing the design and effectiveness of the 3LoD model).

### 4.2.3 Hong Kong

In its supervisory policy manual, the Hong Kong Monetary Authority (HKMA) states that "it is generally expected that responsibilities among different functions of the institution are defined in such a way that there are three lines of defence which are independent from each other."[5] More precisely:

- The 1st LoD is responsible for the identification, assessment, management and reporting of risk exposures on an ongoing basis.
- The 2nd LoD oversees the institution's risk-taking activities, undertakes risk assessments and reports independently from the business lines.
- The 3rd LoD provides assurance on the effectiveness of the institution's risk management framework including the risk governance arrangements.

4 OCC 2014; the OCC is the primary regulator of banks chartered under the National Bank Act and federally licensed subsidiaries and branches of foreign banks.

5 HKMA 2017a.

### 4.2.4 Singapore

Equally, the Monetary Authority of Singapore has defined requirements for the segregation of duties between the 3LoD as well as defined key roles and responsibilities.[6]

### 4.2.5 Risk-type-specific qualifications of the 3LoD model: financial crime prevention

Regulatory requirements regarding the 3LoD model are similar across jurisdictions. However, regulators in some jurisdictions have defined individual roles and responsibilities of the 1st and/or 2nd LoD for specific risk types, to cater for local legal requirements or specific regulatory practice. These local specifics need to be factored in to be fully compliant with local regulatory frameworks. For illustration purposes, three examples are described below for the prevention of financial crime risk, an area under intense regulatory scrutiny.

#### 4.2.5.1 EU: remaining country-specific variation in 1st and 2nd LoD mandate

For the time being, EU member states individually define mandates of the 1st and 2nd LoD in financial crime prevention.[7] Even though, member states currently need to implement the EU money laundering directive,[8] there is room for a degree of country-specific variation. For example, the Swedish financial regulator, Finansinspektionen, requires financial institutions to appoint a Specially Appointed Executive (SAE) in the 1st LoD and an AML Compliance Officer in the 2nd LoD.[9] The mandate of the SAE primarily covers a money laundering risk assessment, the implementation of 1st LoD policies and procedures and monitoring measures. It must also ensure that procedures or other actions decided on by the undertaking are actually implemented in its operational activities, and that there is reporting on these items to the board of directors. The AML Compliance Officer is primarily responsible for monitoring compliance with external requirements and internal standards, providing training and advice to the 1st LoD, assessing the effectiveness of the overall Anti-Money Laundering (AML) framework of the institution and reporting suspicious activity to the Swedish authorities.

---

6 MAS 2021.

7 The Single EU AML Rulebook (Regulation (EU) 2024/1624; applicable from July 2027) will put an end to directive-based regulations in financial crime prevention, and will instead be directly applicable in all EU member states.

8 EUR-Lex 2015.

9 FFFS 2017, 11; FFFS 2024.

#### 4.2.5.2 United States of America: BSA Compliance Officer

Under US requirements, financial institutions must designate a 2nd LoD BSA Compliance officer.[10] The BSA compliance officer is responsible for coordinating and monitoring day-to-day BSA/AML compliance, including carrying out the board's direction and implementation of the bank's BSA/AML policies, procedures and processes. The BSA Compliance officer is also mandated to file suspicious activity reports to the relevant supervisory authorities.[11]

#### 4.2.5.3 Hong Kong: Money Laundering Reporting Officer and Compliance Officer

For the prevention of money laundering and terrorist financing, the HKMA requires financial institutions to appoint a Compliance Officer (CO) and a Money Laundering Reporting Officer (MLRO) in the 2nd LoD. The key mandate of the CO is to develop and review (group-wide) AML/Combating the Financing of Terrorism (CFT) systems, oversee all aspects of the institution's AML/CFT systems which includes monitoring effectiveness and enhancing of controls and procedures, provide training and advice to the 1st LoD as well as report to senior management. The MLRO is primarily responsible for evaluating potential cases of financial crime and deciding whether to report these to the Hong Kong Financial Intelligence Unit.[12]

## 4.3 Key roles and responsibilities of 1st, 2nd and 3rd LoD

Apart from the regulatory minimum standard, the scope of 3LoD mandates may vary between institutions, depending on factors such as size, business model and risk aversion. However, the following elements are common across large parts of the industry (Figure 1).

[10] Bank Secrecy Act (OCC 2021a); US law requires financial institutions in the United States to assist US government agencies in detecting and preventing money laundering.

[11] FFIEC 2014.

[12] HKMA 2023.

Figure 1: Overview key mandates 1st, 2nd and 3rd line of defence

| 1st LoD | 2nd LoD | 3rd LoD |
|---|---|---|
| • Risk ownership:<br>  • Identification of risk in business activities and operations<br>  • Risk management<br>• Execution of controls | • Setting of regulatory standards<br>• Testing of 1st LoD controls<br>• Risk-type specific risk assessments<br>• Training & advisory of 1st LoD | • Independent assurance:<br>  • Adequacy of risk management framework<br>  • Compliance with regulation<br>• Advisor to board of directors |

### 4.3.1 The first line of defence: risk owner

The 1st LoD spans across profit generating business lines (often referred to as front office) and support functions (middle and/or back office).

#### 4.3.1.1 Scope of 1st LoD mandate

Apart from business generating activities, the 1st LoD's responsibility covers two major elements: risk ownership and controls.

##### 4.3.1.1.1 Risk ownership

Risk ownership has two core elements. First, risks inherent in 1st LoD business and supporting activities must be identified by way of a structured top-down (i.e. risk agnostic) risk and control assessment[13]; second, identified risks must be managed to stay within risk appetite (potentially) defined by the institution and to avoid financial losses or violations of legal and regulatory requirements.[14]

[13] Please refer to chapter 7 for additional details on 1st LoD top-down risk and control assessments.

[14] Please refer to chapter 3 for details on non-financial risk appetite frameworks (RAF).

#### 4.3.1.1.2 Implementation and execution of 1st LoD controls

The 1st LoD must implement and execute controls to ensure proper business processes and compliance with laws and regulations. The latter includes scanning for any upcoming changes to the regulatory landscape and making adjustments to the control framework to cater for new or enhanced laws and regulations.

### 4.3.1.2 Allocation of 1st LoD responsibility

In principle, business lines and support functions are risk owners for the risks generated through their operating activities. Within these, there are risk types with a focus on customer-related misconduct, such as financial crime risk and client tax evasion risk. Other risk types focus more on middle and back office as well as staff-related errors (e.g. outsourcing and vendor risk, workplace safety risk). There are also risk types with relevance for both groups, including reputational risk, IT security and data privacy risk. In any case, risk ownership needs to be defined based on the individual operating model and risk exposure of the 1st LoD.

### 4.3.1.3 1st LoD risk-coordinating function (1.5th LoD)

In some of the larger financial institutions, non-financial risk management has grown into a complex, multi-facetted discipline, involving a variety of 1st and 2nd LoD stakeholders. Managing this complexity is often facilitated by a risk agnostic team (sometimes called the 1.5th LoD) with a mandate to coordinate 1st LoD risk management activities and act as interface to teams providing 2nd LoD oversight. Naturally, the scope and focus of these mandates vary depending on the institution-specific needs and particularities. The following three elements, however, are included in most mandates.

#### 4.3.1.3.1 Coordination of risk management activities

The risk coordinating team connects risk management professionals often scattered across 1st LoD segments, divisions and geographies, and can be approached for any questions regarding regulatory requirements. It also facilitates a consistent and sustainable implementation of the 1st LoD mandate across the organisation. The risk coordinating team supports the design, implementation and execution of 1st LoD controls by providing expertise and facilitating cross-functional exchange between 1st LoD risk managers. Finally, it enables non-financial risk reporting to senior management by defining harmonised reporting criteria, tools, formats and frequencies.

#### 4.3.1.3.2 Interface to 2nd LoD

Financial institutions need to manage a variety of non-financial risk types, often involving risk oversight provided by different 2nd LoD teams. In the 1st LoD, particularly in institutions with diverse product offerings and broad geographic footprints, risk managers are often found across segments, geographies and teams. Hence, an interaction between the involved parties can become complex and potentially duplicative or overlapping. A centrally implemented risk coordinating team acts as the main channel between the involved parties and improves overall communication, making it more effective and efficient.

#### 4.3.1.3.3 Regulatory advisor

When a 1st LoD risk-coordinating function is established, it often acts as a regulatory advisor to 1st LoD staff, backed by a good understanding of the institution's product offering and the relevant regulatory frameworks (Figure 2).

Figure 2: Key mandate 1st LoD risk-coordinating function

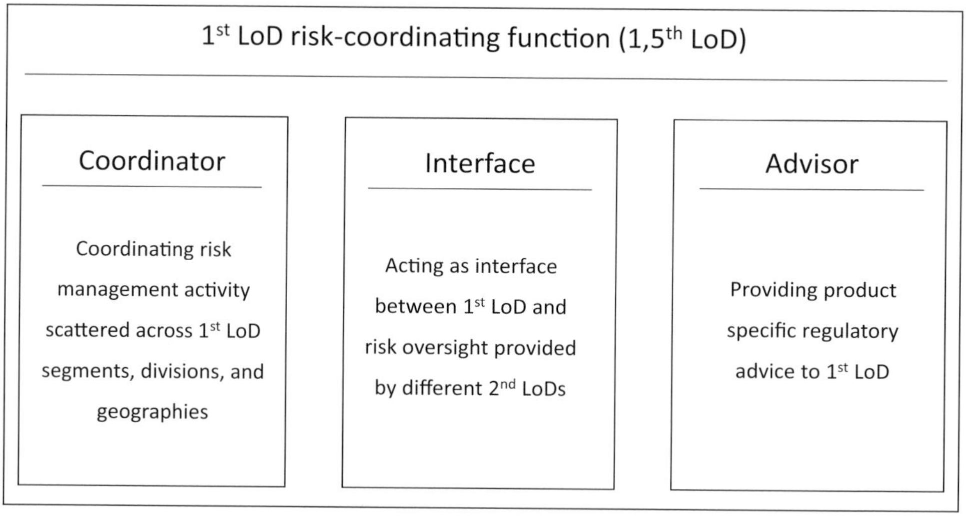


### 4.3.2 The second line of defence: internal control functions

Particularly material non-financial risk types such as financial crime, data protection and outsourcing risks have been under regulatory scrutiny for years. In most financial institutions such risk types are embedded in mature risk management structures and monitored by dedicated control functions, explicitly required to be established under legal or regulatory requirements in all key markets. Other risk types, such as human resources risk, accounting risk, reporting risk, project risk as well as processing and execution risk do not enjoy such a mature regulatory status. The question of which function performs 2nd LoD activities for these risk types may not be easy to answer in many institutions. Therefore, establishing comprehensive 2nd LoD coverage for all non-financial risk types often remains a challenge.

#### 4.3.2.1 Scope of 2nd LoD mandate

Although some variation may exist, the general scope of the 2nd LoD mandate is widely accepted across large parts of the financial industry.

##### 4.3.2.1.1 Standard setting

The 2nd LoD sets standards in policies, guidelines and/or procedures translating legal and regulatory requirements into an internal regulatory framework. This framework is intended to guide staff in their day-to-day operational activities and ensure compliance with both internal and external requirements.

##### 4.3.2.1.2 Testing of 1st LoD controls

A key responsibility of the 2nd LoD is to test the adequacy of 1st LoD controls in three dimensions: implementation, design and effectiveness. Tests of implementation determine whether controls exist, are integrated in operational activities and are executed. Tests of design determine whether controls address the root causes of risk and can prevent the relevant risks from materialising. Tests of effectiveness determine whether controls are executed as designed and consistently, and whether results are properly documented.

##### 4.3.2.1.3 Risk assessment

Internal control functions perform risk assessments for the non-financial risk types they cover as responsible 2nd LoD. These risk specific assessments complement the risk agnostic risk assessments performed by the 1st LoD and focus on risk-specific risk drivers and a corresponding control adequacy for individual risk types. For some material non-financial risk types, these risk assessments are explicitly required by regulators. These include financial crime risk, outsourcing risk and information security.[15]

[15] EBA 2021b, 2019a, 2019b.

#### 4.3.2.1.4 Training and advisory

The $2^{nd}$ LoD needs to create awareness among $1^{st}$ LoD staff, particularly for inherent non-financial risks, and regulatory implications for $1^{st}$ LoD activities. Trainings should be performed on a regular and/or ad hoc basis to transfer basic and advanced expertise. $2^{nd}$ LoD advisory for $1^{st}$ LoD staff is primarily performed on a transactional basis – for example, in the direct context of individual customer onboardings, client transactions or similar $1^{st}$ LoD questions or requests.

### 4.3.2.2 Risk materiality and corresponding intensity of $2^{nd}$ LoD risk oversight

For financial institutions, some risk types are more material than others because of the potential financial or reputational damage at stake or due to business or operating models with increased relevance for specific risk types. In practice, this translates into different degrees of oversight intensity by internal control functions, in line with the risk-based approach advocated by most regulators. Accordingly, when overseeing material, as opposed to non-material, risk types, $2^{nd}$ LoD functions are required to take a more vigorous approach. This may be in relation to standard settings (more detailed and stricter standards), control testing (higher testing frequency, larger sample population for control effectiveness testing), risk assessments as well as training and advisory (broader and deeper subject matter coverage).

### 4.3.2.3 Independence of $2^{nd}$ LoD risk oversight

Staff performing $2^{nd}$ LoD risk oversight require independence from the $1^{st}$ LoD. That is, they must be free of any (potential) conflicts of interest when executing their oversight activities. Otherwise, the honesty and quality of risk oversight will suffer. Independence requires an adequate segregation of roles and responsibilities between staff performing $2^{nd}$ LoD activities and $1^{st}$ LoD employees. This segregation can be achieved by taking an organisational or functional approach.

#### 4.3.2.3.1 Organisational independence

Organisational independence from the $1^{st}$ LoD requires a dedicated $2^{nd}$ LoD function or role outside the $1^{st}$ LoD, including a separate reporting line to a senior executive. Major regulators globally have made organisational independence mandatory for the compliance function and the officer responsible for the prevention of money laundering ("AML officer") due to the materiality of the underlying risks.[16] Some jurisdictions and regulators go further and require the appointment of 2nd LoD data protection officers to oversee compliance with data protection requirements.[17]

#### 4.3.2.3.2 Functional independence

Where organisational independence is not a regulatory requirement, independent risk oversight can be achieved by taking a functional, activity-based approach. With this approach, 2nd LoD activities can be performed by staff sitting in the 1st LoD, if they are not exposed to (potential) conflicts of interest. Three conflict constellations are especially critical and must be avoided using precautionary measures:

- Staff performing 2nd LoD activities cannot be integral to revenue-generating teams. The combination of revenue generation and risk oversight represents per se a conflict of interest
- Compensation of staff performing 2nd LoD activities must not be linked to the performance of teams under their oversight.
- Staff performing 2nd LoD activities may not be substantially involved in the processes, tasks or projects under risk oversight to prevent any type of self-monitoring. Accordingly, 1st LoD activities and 2nd LoD risk oversight must be clearly defined, segregated and allocated between the actors.

Financial institutions should document precautionary measures to be able to demonstrate 2nd LoD independence to internal and external auditors, senior management and supervisory authorities.

#### 4.3.2.3.3 Internal control functions performing 1st LoD activities

Internal control functions such as compliance take the role of 1st LoD in the following constellations.

[16] For the Compliance function: EBA 2021c, 49; HKMA 2017a; MAS 2021. For the officer/function responsible for the prevention of money laundering: EBA 2022; OCC 2019b, 50; HKMA 2023; MAS 2024c, 31.

[17] For instance, under the EU General Data Protection regulation and the Singaporean Personal Data Protection Act.

#### Role as genuine 1st LoD for generalist risk types

Just like any other bank department, the compliance function qualifies as 1st LoD when it comes to risk types such as project risk, workplace safety, outsourcing risk or IT security risk. When running projects, the compliance function must comply with relevant policies and guidelines and own the risk, for example of projects running over budget. Similar, outsourcings of compliance operations must be in line with the institution's outsourcing policies, and any failures or omissions in the outsourcing process must be borne by the function. Accordingly, the compliance function is subject to risk oversight by the responsible 2nd LoD for these risk types.

#### Financial crime prevention: possible outsourcing of specific 1st LoD controls to AML team

In financial crime prevention, some institutions outsource the execution of complex controls in AML transaction monitoring and financial sanctions name screening and payment filtering from the 1st LoD to the 2nd LoD AML Officer and their team. This is mainly due to the expertise and experience required to evaluate monitoring and screening alerts, and to decide whether to discount alerts or report to external authorities. Where such delegation occurs, the AML team must take action to ensure independent 2nd LoD risk oversight of the delegated controls by separate 2nd LoD staff members.

### 4.3.2.4 Key success factors for effective 2nd LoD risk oversight

In many financial institutions, risk oversight across risk types is provided by different 2nd LoDs. This is particularly challenging in two ways. First, different methodologies are likely applied in 1st LoD control testing and risk assessments, making it difficult to compare and consolidate outputs. Also, adequate 2nd LoD participation in risk committees and the sharing of information from bodies and committees can be difficult to establish.

### 4.3.2.4.1 Methodology consistency across 2nd LoD functions

Being able to compare and consolidate outputs of different risk oversight functions is essential for effective risk management. Banks must be able to compare key insights on control quality or risk exposure between different risk types to put these into proportion and derive implications for bank-wide risk management and steering. This requires a level of consistency across non-financial risk types in three key methodologies (see below). While aiming to create consistency in methodologies, risk oversight functions must continue to have the flexibility required to cater for risk-type specific challenges.

First, a consistent approach to core testing activities is required across non-financial risk types, regarding the following underlying aspects[18]:

- **Testing scope and frequency**: a risk-based approach should be taken when determining the scope (i.e. which controls to test) and frequency of controls (i.e. how often to test them). Controls in high-risk activities should be tested more frequently than in medium- or low-risk areas. The scope and frequency of testing should be informed by the results of 2nd LoD risk assessments and/or (where available) by internal or external audit insights.
- **Sampling**: the effectiveness of controls is tested by selecting a sample population of control occurrences and testing each sample by using different techniques. These include interviews with control owners and/or control performers and process walk-throughs. A consistent approach to selecting and sizing the sample population should be defined, which will avoid controls in some areas being over-tested while others remain undertested.[19]
- **Qualitative control assessments**: a set of bank-wide, actionable criteria must be applied when determining the quality of controls (i.e. inadequate, weak, to be improved, established).

Second, consistency is essential when it comes to risk assessments performed by the 2nd LoD across different risk types, and should be achieved along the following key parameters:

- **Evaluation of inherent risk:**
  - selection of financial (e.g., operational losses) and non-financial impact factors (including supervisory repercussions, negative impact on customers)
  - determination of impact severity and rating scores of likelihood
  - determination of inherent risk rating scores and approach to their calculation
- **Assessment of control adequacy:**
  - selection of types of controls assessed (e.g., governance, policies, training)
  - determination of control adequacy scores (also need to be aligned with qualitative criteria applied in control testing described above)
  - where applicable, approach to weighting different control pillars

[18] The key components of 1st LoD control testing have been described above: test of implementation, test of design and test of effectiveness.

[19] Common approaches to sample sizing include: sample sizing based on the frequency at which controls occur or based on the total population of control occurrences.

- **Evaluation of residual risk:**
  - determination of residual risk rating scores
  - approach to calculate residual risk

Third, 2nd LoD policies, guidelines and/or procedures should be drafted according to a minimum set of harmonised standards defined in a group-wide policy framework.[20]

#### 4.3.2.4.2 Bodies and committees: adequate 2nd LoD participation and information sharing

Legal requirements and effective corporate governance require financial institutions to establish governing bodies and committees on entity and (where applicable) group levels. In most jurisdictions with a two-tier board structure, the work of the management board is supported – at a minimum – by a (financial and non-financial) risk committee, a credit committee and a treasury committee. The supervisory board must establish (financial and non-financial) risk, audit, nomination and compensation control committees. On group level, committees are established to ensure alignment with group entities on key topics including (financial and non-financial) risk, finance, information technology, human resources and audit. Depending on their size, strategy, business model and geographic footprint, institutions set up additional (group) committees e.g., on compliance, digitisation, sustainability and individual client segments.[21]

Financial institutions must establish transparent rules regarding the sharing of information from bodies and committees with 2nd LoD functions and 2nd LoD participation in specific committees. This will ensure the 2nd LoD has access to the required information. For each 2nd LoD function the degree of shared information and any committee participation(s) should be determined in accordance with the non-financial risk type(s) covered as well as the individual mandate. The following graded options are generally available:

- active participation, including voting rights, prior access to meeting documents and access to meeting minutes;
- passive (guest) participation, including prior access to meeting documents and access to meeting minutes;
- prior access to meeting documents and access to meeting minutes;
- access to meeting minutes.

[20] Please refer to chapter 6 for detailed guidance on harmonised policy frameworks.

[21] Under a one-tier board structure, similar committees are established under the board of directors and the group executive committee.

#### 4.3.2.4.3 Appointment of primus inter pares non-financial risk governance function

Financial institutions should consider appointing a primus inter pares (first among equals) risk governance function from the existing non-financial risk control functions to facilitate and institutionalise a consistent methodology across the 2nd LoD. The mandate should cover the following key elements:

- identify material consistency gaps between control functions, particularly in control testing and risk assessment, design harmonised methodology and align with key stakeholders from 2nd LoD;
- closely liaise with internal audit to monitor the application/implementation of a harmonised approach (in control testing and risk assessment) by control functions;
- consolidate individual 2nd LoD risk reports to holistic non-financial risk report;
- create and align consistent criteria for the participation of control functions in committees and the information sharing by bodies and committees.

The effort of this exercise obviously depends on various factors, including the number of involved stakeholders, the degree of complexity and variance between existing methodologies, the potential level of fragmentation in 2nd LoD processes and underlying IT applications as well as, finally, the institution's geographic footprint, potentially triggering a variety of local regulatory specifics.

### 4.3.3 The third line of defence: internal audit as provider of independent assurance

Internal audit plays a key role in the 3LoD model, with two major responsibilities: independent assurance and advisement of the board.

#### 4.3.3.1 Independent assurance

The 3rd LoD audits the financial institution's entire risk management framework, including the internal control system.

##### 4.3.3.1.1 Adequacy of risk management framework

Internal audit examines whether the risk management framework corresponds to the specifics of the business and operating model and the financial institution's risk exposure. Internal audit must identify missing, insufficient or poorly designed elements of the framework, such as risk types subject to inadequate risk oversight by the 2nd LoD, incomplete internal standards or guidelines and poor 1st LoD controls. The risk management framework must reflect the product and process specifics of the institution and follow a risk-based-approach. That is, areas with a higher operational risk require more diligent risk management efforts.

#### 4.3.3.1.2 Design and operating effectiveness

Internal audit must identify whether the institution's risk management – both 1$^{st}$ LoD risk identification and control activity and 2$^{nd}$ LoD risk oversight (including standard setting, risk assessment, monitoring of 1$^{st}$ LoD controls and training and advisory) – is operating in the designed and intended manner, or whether any of the underlying risk management processes are poorly (or not) executed, or are insufficiently documented. Internal audit needs to test both the design effectiveness of controls (do controls satisfy the institution's control objectives and can they effectively prevent or detect error?) and their operating effectiveness (are controls operated as designed?).

In that context, internal audit can deliver value by helping the 1$^{st}$ and 2$^{nd}$ LoD better understand:

- how consistent risk management is across segments, subsidiaries and jurisdictions, and which inconsistencies need particular attention;
- how overall risk management effectiveness evolves over time and how this supports or stands in the way of the institution's overall goals and strategy;
- how an evolving business and risk environment impacts the role of the 1$^{st}$ and 2$^{nd}$ LoD.

#### 4.3.3.1.3 Compliance with regulatory requirements and internal standards

Independent assurance provided by internal audit also covers regulatory conformity of risk management by the 1$^{st}$ and the 2$^{nd}$ LoD. Hence, the 3$^{rd}$ LoD needs to identify whether the 1$^{st}$ or 2$^{nd}$ LoD complies with legal or regulatory standards as well as any internal policies, guidelines or directives of senior management.

### 4.3.3.2 Advising the board of directors

Where relevant, internal audit plays a key role as independent senior advisor to the board of directors in any matters regarding overall bank management.

## 4.4 Common pitfalls of the 3LoD model and precautionary measures

Although 3LoD is the financial industry's clear market standard, it is necessary to anticipate the following potential pitfalls and take appropriate precautionary measures.

### 4.4.1 Insufficient risk ownership by 1st LoD

A fundamental cornerstone of 3LoD is 1st LoD risk ownership. Yet, often stakeholders from business departments or support functions falsely consider risk management as an exclusive task of the 2nd LoD and perceive their own mandate only as a business generating or business supporting role, without a significant mandate in risk management. When not addressed adequately and sustainably, insufficient risk ownership in the 1st LoD will stand in the way of effective risk management and expose the institution to increased levels of operational, regulatory and reputational risk. Most likely, the root cause can be found around a lack of 1st LoD senior management commitment or, more generally, an insufficient compliance culture. Measures must be taken early on to prevent the 1st LoD from alienating itself from its risk management responsibilities: there is a need for awareness for the roles and responsibilities of the 1st LoD as well as for the importance of 1st LoD risk management for the overall success of the financial institution. And, where necessary, 1st LoD stakeholders must be reminded of their specific roles and responsibilities in the risk management context. To that end institutions need to establish:

- a tone from the top regarding the values of 1st LoD risk management and its role in reaching the institution's goals;
- mandatory training programs covering the roles and responsibilities of 1st LoD staff in risk management;
- regular internal communication on risk management topics to refresh 1st LoD staff risk management awareness.

### 4.4.2 Lack of 2nd LoD expertise

Exercising the mandate of the 2nd LoD requires a wide range of skills, which in combination lay the foundation for effective risk oversight. Three elements stand out: first, regulatory expertise is mandatory, meaning a thorough understanding of the legal framework and regulatory requirements for banking operations in general and for non-financial risk management specifically; second, a detailed understanding of a bank's operating model is required, with a focus on the process and IT landscape and controls; and, finally, effective risk oversight requires an understanding of products, transactions and services. The challenge for 2nd LoD functions is to find (and keep) adequate staff for all three areas. While regulatory skills can be developed over time by following the relevant standard setters and regulators, the other two areas (operating model and product landscape) ideally require a professional banking career outside the 2nd LoD. Hence, winning well-deserved 1st LoD process or product experts for the 2nd LoD is a great asset and, together with strong regulatory expertise, is an unbeatable combination.

To attract and keep highly-qualified experts, the 2nd LoD needs to develop dedicated career models in the risk management field, offering sustainable career steps and a pathway to leadership positions. In addition, 2nd LoD risk management experts need to stay on top of market developments and industry trends to anticipate potential impacts on their own institution: adequate training programs, participation in industry forums and bilateral exchanges with market peers are three common options to refresh skills and expertise.

### 4.4.3 Inadequate assurance by 3rd LoD

Recent corporate scandals have highlighted the urgent need for independent, comprehensive and truthful assurance. For senior management, internal audit is the last (internal) resort to disclose corporate malpractices. Still, internal auditors could often be more relentless in exposing deficient controls and less yielding in negotiating the severity of shortcomings. This requires a strong audit culture, in which the role and importance of internal audit is frequently accentuated by senior management and potential roadblocks to effective assurance (such as insufficient cooperation and fragmented information transfer) are immediately escalated and adequately addressed.

## 4.5 Conclusion

The 3LoD framework lays the foundation for effective risk management, particularly in financial institutions. Yet, 3LoD is not a self-fulfilling prophecy. It requires institutions to answer fundamental questions and take corresponding action: is the 1st LoD fully committed to risk management or "just playing along"? Are there 2nd LoDs for all non-financial risk types? How effective is risk oversight across the risk universe covering the broad range of risk types in the risk taxonomy? How much can senior management rely on 3LoD assurance and what measures can be taken to strengthen internal audit? Still, if appropriate measures are taken, the 3LoD model can be the solution to key questions in non-financial risk management: who is responsible for what? What needs to be done? How do you draw the line between the parties involved? Hence, senior management of financial institutions should put the 3LoD model high on their agendas and commit to creating the necessary conditions for excellent excellence.

# 5 Global Functional Lead in Non-Financial Risk Management: Ensuring Consistency and Integration in Complex Organisations

*Ulrike Brouzi, Dr. Michael Lange, P. Robert Mieszkowski, Jannik Leiendecker, Dr. Georg Lienke, Florian Seiferlein, Norbert Gittfried, Rei Tanaka*

## 5.1 Introduction

Most global financial organisations with a broad product portfolio active across multiple geographical regions are managed with a matrix organisation covering product divisions, infrastructure functions (including risk management) and geographical regions.

While they are the market standard for most, if not all, major financial organisations, matrix organisations bring about complexity challenges. In non-financial risk management, key risk management activities such as regulatory screening, training and advisory, controls and risk assessments are executed regionally, increasing the risk of divergence, inconsistent results across the group as well as ambiguous implications for group risk steering.

Insufficient consistency in group non-financial risk management not only exposes banking operations to an intolerable level of risk of financial loss and reputational damage, but it also breaches the fundamental requirements of all major financial industry regulators. Standards defined by the European Banking Authority, the U.S. Federal Reserve and major Asian regulators explicitly require risk management programmes to reflect the organisation's geographic reach, to produce an aggregate view of the organisation's non-financial risk exposure across business lines, support units, legal entities and jurisdictions of operation, as well as to operate based on an integrated approach to managing those risks.

Efforts to achieve sustainable integration across global financial organisations in non-financial risk management are often labelled under the rubric "global functional lead" (GFL).[1] GFL stands for a combination of strategic, governance and risk management elements aimed at:

[1] This chapter focuses on non-financial risk management, but other departments or initiatives in a financial organisation also apply a GFL concept to their work.

- central setting of global risk management standards by horizontal risk management functions with a comprehensive understanding of the organisation's business model and geographic footprint. Standards typically cover risk-specific requirements and key supporting activities embedded in the organisation's risk management life cycle;
- full (or predominant) execution by vertical product or region focused functions with direct or indirect reporting lines into horizontal risk management functions. Unless restricted by regulatory or organisation-specific constraints, institutions should aim to achieve the highest possible level of execution consistency across regional organisations to facilitate consistent risk steering at group level. Vertical functions represent respective legal entities and branches in local jurisdictions. Depending on regulatory requirements, historical developments and strategic ambitions, vertical risk management staff can operate in regional hub, local or hybrid setups.

Effective GFL cannot operate standalone. Instead, it must be enabled by a global framework defining the organisation's minimum standard for non-financial risk management, specifically including:

- a group-wide non-financial risk taxonomy, defining a common understanding and definition of risk types across the financial organisation to achieve a consistent understanding of non-financial risk;
- a risk appetite framework to define, monitor and steer the maximum level of (non-financial) risk an institution is willing to accept to pursue its business plan and long-term strategic objectives. Horizontal and vertical functions must commit to staying within the boundaries of the defined risk appetite;
- a consistent understanding of the mandates, roles, and responsibilities of the 1$^{st}$, 2$^{nd}$ and 3$^{rd}$ lines of defence (LoD) to ensure harmonised activity levels cross all layers of the organisation;
- a policy and procedure governance framework, defining group-wide criteria for document ownership, including creation and update (on different levels of a policy pyramid), approval and roll-out.

This chapter starts with a summary of key regulatory requirements in the context of GFL, and it examines key corporate parameters that are essential to define an institution-specific solution. The chapter analyses three major components essential for the implementation of a GFL in non-financial risk management: an operating model defining the balance between global standards and regional execution, adequate reporting lines of risk management staff into global risk management functions and a meeting governance to ensure effective management of the global risk function. The chapter concludes with a summary of key takeaways and an outlook on major considerations.

## 5.2 Regulatory framework in select key markets

Global financial regulators require financial institutions to apply an integrated, consistent approach to non-financial risk management across their group organisation. The following sections describe key regulatory expectations in the European Union, the United States of America and Asia (Hong Kong and Singapore). However, additional regulatory frameworks may need to be considered, depending on the institution's operating model and geographic footprint.

### 5.2.1 European Union

Integrated, consistent group-wide non-financial risk management is a cornerstone of the EU legislative and regulatory framework for financial institutions exemplified by the following references:

- under the Anti-money laundering Directive financial institutions "that are part of a group need to implement group-wide policies and procedures [...] and those policies and procedures shall be implemented effectively at the level of branches and majority-owned subsidiaries in member states and third countries"[2];
- in its guidelines on internal governance, the European Banking Authority (EBA) requires "parent undertakings [...] to ensure that governance arrangements, processes and mechanisms are consistent and sufficiently integrated on a consolidated and sub-consolidated basis; the management body of a subsidiary [...] should adopt and implement on the individual level the group-wide governance policies established at the consolidated or sub-consolidated level"[3];
- according to the EBA's outsourcing guidelines, financial institutions are required "to ensure that their outsourcing policy is implemented, as applicable, on an individual, sub-consolidated and consolidated basis."[4]

### 5.2.2 United States of America

The Federal Reserve requires large banking organisations[5] to establish organisation-wide compliance risk management programmes, spanning across business lines, legal entities

[2] EUR-Lex 2015.

[3] EBA 2017.

[4] EBA 2019a.

[5] Defined as having 50 billion US-Dollars or more in consolidated total assets.

and jurisdictions. Organisations are also required to oversee the local implementation of the programme.[6]

### 5.2.3 Hong Kong

The Hong Kong Monetary Authority (HKMA) requires financial institutions to develop

> *"risk management policies and procedures [...] on a comprehensive review of all business activities of an institution, [...] covering all material risks [...] associated with the institution's activities. Policies and procedures should be prepared on a firm-wide basis and, where applicable, on a group-wide basis."*[7]

In addition, the HKMA requires the board of a financial institution to "ensure that there are [...] policies and procedures in place appropriate to the structure, business and risks of the group as a whole and its component entities."[8]

### 5.2.4 Singapore

Under the Singaporean regulatory regime, the senior management of financial institutions must establish a (non-financial) risk management system to identify, measure, evaluate, monitor, report and mitigate risks regularly, where applicable across and within the group of which the institution is a member.[9]

## 5.3 Global functional lead: individual corporate parameters to consider

There is no one-size-fits-all solution for a successful global GFL. Instead, several parameters must be considered when defining a proper, "tailor-made" approach for a financial institution, including the following.

### 5.3.1 Corporate culture

An institution's corporate culture refers to the values, beliefs and behavioural patterns of senior management and staff, determining how an operation is managed and run short-,

[6] Board of Governors of the Federal Reserve System 2021b.

[7] HKMA 2017a.

[8] HKMA 2017b.

[9] MAS 2021a.

mid- and long-term. Corporate culture also affects how regional and local organisations are managed, how much trust is placed in local execution and how much leeway local stakeholders are granted.

### 5.3.2 Organisation's complexity

The degree of an organisation's complexity – driven primarily by the breadth of the product portfolio, the number of domestic and foreign entities and branches – and the density of inter-company related governance arrangements determine the environment in which GFL is embedded.

### 5.3.3 IT landscape

Key activities in non-financial risk management rely heavily on functioning IT systems and applications as well as the availability of high-quality (internal and external) data. Relevant examples include the scanning and identifying of new financial sector regulations, surveillance of security transactions to detect market manipulations or the collection of data to monitor key performance indicators across a portfolio of outsourcing contracts. The level of IT fragmentation, the (in)consistency of data formats, the degree of process automation across divisions and the potential use of artificial intelligence need to be factored in when aiming for a realistic level of consistent execution across regional organisations.

### 5.3.4 Geographical footprint

Finally, regional execution must comply with local regulatory regimes, potentially requiring a deviation from or an add-on to global standards. Organisations active in a variety of jurisdictions may face a considerable regulatory complexity.

## 5.4 Major components of global functional lead in non-financial risk management

A GFL in non-financial risk management is built on three major components. First, an operating model defining and delineating the mandates of global risk management functions and vertical execution teams. Second, adequate reporting lines of vertical functions into global risk management functions. Third, a meeting governance framework supporting effective management of a global, branched risk function.

Figure 1: Major GFL components

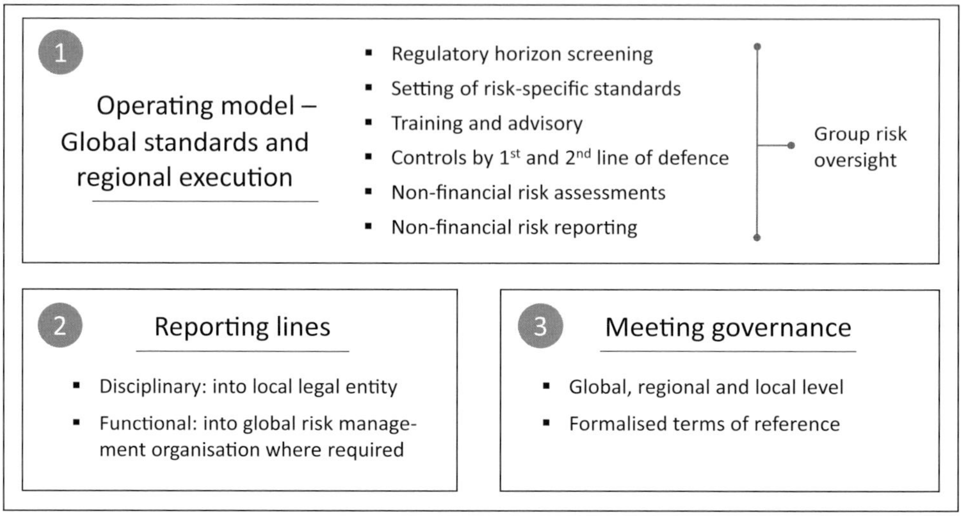


When defining and implementing a GFL, institutions should proactively align key elements with regulatory authorities to ensure that regulatory concerns can be appropriately addressed – i.e. the home state's regulator and potentially, depending on the geographic footprint, additional regulators.

### 5.4.1 Operating model: striking a balance between global standards and regional execution

Global standards set out by central $2^{nd}$ LoD risk management functions (also referred to as "global head") need to include risk-type-specific guidance and instructions for supporting activities. Ideally, global standards are embedded in an operating model following major steps in the organisation's risk management cycle. Risk-agnostic-supporting activities should be aligned and consistent across non-financial risk types. The operating model determines the boundaries between the mandates of the global risk management function and the $1^{st}$ and $2^{nd}$ LoD teams responsible for vertical execution (in regional hub, local or hybrid setups).

When establishing an operating model for a group of entities, an organisation needs to consider the following criteria:

- *level of entity participation:* typically, controlled entities are consolidated i.e. entities subject to capital quota or voting rights of more than 50% or controlled based on individual dependency or similar agreements; entities subject to a reduced level of participation (less than or equal to 50%) may still expose an organisation to non-financial risk, thus, measures to manage that risk should be considered separately;

- *entity type:* when defining global standards, entity types such as banking (including retail, corporate and investment banking), payment services, asset management and insurance need to be reflected. Complexity and a potential for error in the local execution typically vary depending on the entity type;
- *business purpose:* specific entities may have a limited business purpose and hence reduced exposure to global standards and group risk oversight (e.g. special purpose vehicles (SPV), real estate management, shelf companies, holding companies).

The following section describes an operating model along six common steps in non-financial risk management. The criteria described above and potentially additional individual circumstances of a financial organisation need to be factored in when designing an operating model to achieve the optimal level of effectiveness.[10]

#### 5.4.1.1 Regulatory horizon screening

Financial organisations are required to screen the regulatory horizon and identify potential changes in the legal or regulatory environment that are likely to impact their business and operating models. A global standard for regulatory horizon screening should determine the following key items:

- key process steps for regulatory screening, implementation of identified regulatory requirements, assignment of ownership including corresponding escalation mechanisms, and effectiveness testing;
- tracking of screening and implementation status and reporting mechanism;
- group-wide legal and regulatory topics/areas subject to regulatory screening;
- domestic, foreign and supranational legislators, regulators and standard setters included as potential sources of regulatory changes;
- criteria to ensure consistent use of data feeds/tools/external providers to support regulatory screening.

The execution of regulatory screening is often characterised by a split between global and vertical responsibilities. The responsible central 2nd LoD risk management functions, e.g. the global head of anti-money laundering or global head of IT security, screen globally relevant developments and track vertical screening and implementation efforts in the legal and regulatory areas under their responsibility to ensure consistent interpretation and implementation of regulatory changes across group organisations.

[10] The balancing of global vs. local execution described is intended as a guidance – individual constellations may require a deviating model.

Vertical 1st and/or 2nd LoD teams focus on the following regulatory screening and implementation efforts including:

- implementation and monitoring of local data feeds to support regulatory screening;
- evaluation of business-specific and regional/local regulatory changes and their impact on the business and operating model;
- implementation of changes to cater for new/changed regulatory requirements;
- reporting on implementation progress to global heads.

### 5.4.1.2 Setting of risk-specific standards

Standards need to be defined for non-financial risk types, representing the regulatory guard rails for 1st LoD operational activity. Responsible global heads need to define risk-specific regulatory standards applicable to the entire organisation (e.g. on IT security, data protection, anti-money laundering and outsourcing). When setting global regulatory standards, organisations need to find the right level of global harmonisation, with two general approaches available:

- determination of a global minimum standard, being further enriched by local entities based on their individual industry and local requirements;
- determination of a global maximum standard, being determined by industry and local requirements of all group entities.

Most financial organisations adopt the "minimum" approach, aiming to reduce the regulatory burden on the organisation. Typically, global 2nd LoD standards cover:

- key drivers of risk;
- components of group-wide risk management programmes, including controls and monitoring efforts;
- roles and responsibilities of 1st, 2nd and 3rd LoD;
- oversight of major policies and procedures.

Building on global minimum risk standards, vertical organisations need to complement those requirements from two perspectives. First, vertical 2nd LoD teams need to draft local additions to global standards to cater for jurisdiction-specific legislation or regulation. Local additions should be subject to formal global head approval. Second, vertical 1st LoD teams need to apply global risk standards to their business and operating model and draft business-specific policies where required (e.g. know-your-customer policies for corporate and retail customer segments), with necessary regulatory advice coming from regional 2nd LoD teams. Where global standards cannot be fully applied by vertical functions or require deviations due to local regulatory requirements, global heads need to be informed and give their approval (sometimes referred to as "comply or explain").

#### 5.4.1.3 Training and advisory

1st LoD staff in vertical organisations must be empowered to execute their operational duties consistent with global and local standards provided by the 2nd LoD. This requires training and advising staff on a variety of risk-specific and related matters. Global heads need to define a training and advisory framework, applicable to business and regional organisations globally. The framework should define:

- minimum risk-specific training coverage (functional scope and content);
- trigger occasions and frequency;
- formats (online vs. physical training);
- participation tracking, penalties for non-participation.

Vertical organisations provide physical or virtual training and give advice to 1st LoD staff. Training needs to be provided at the required frequency (potentially required by local regulation) and in adequate formats by the 1st and/or 2nd LoD, depending on the focus of the training sessions. Where relevant, the scope and content of local training needs to be supplemented according to local regulatory requirements. Transaction-specific, ad hoc advice is likely to come from regional 2nd LoD teams with sufficient expertise in global and local regulatory standards.

#### 5.4.1.4 Controls by the 1st and 2nd line of defence

Controls, performed by the 1st and the 2nd LoD, are essential tools to mitigate risk by identifying deficits, weaknesses and regulatory shortcomings in operations. 2nd LoD controls focus on the effectiveness of 1st LoD controls and overall compliance with 2nd LoD standards. For 2nd LoD control output and insights to be consistent across business and regional organisations, global heads need to define globally applicable minimum standards for 2nd LoD controls. First, global heads need to determine a consistent methodology for 2nd LoD controls, e.g. by making the following parameters mandatory for 1st LoD control testing:

- test of design;
- test of implementation;
- test of operating effectiveness based on selection of samples.

Second, global heads need to require regional 2nd LoD teams to establish risk-based control plans. These determine the degree of control scrutiny based on the level of risk of the underlying process/activity, informed by the latest 2nd LoD risk assessment. 2nd LoD controls are performed by central or regional teams focusing on compliance with global and business-/region-specific risk management standards.

#### 5.4.1.5 Non-financial risk assessment

Risk assessments are at the very core of non-financial risk management as their outcomes define risk management agendas. In complex organisations, risk assessments need to be performed across different vertical organisations, with results consolidated on a global level to derive implications for group risk steering. Effective group risk assessments require regions to follow consistent approaches as increased regional divergence prevents prioritisation of risks and mitigating measures at a group level and hence limits the overall value of the risk assessment exercise.

For non-financial risk types or categories of risk types subject to their responsibility, global heads need to establish consistent 2nd LoD risk assessment standards. These should include:

- overall assessment methodologies, i.e. evaluation of inherent risk, control adequacy and residual risk. Global heads need to factor in potential jurisdictional regulatory specifics for certain risk assessments[11];
- consistent rationales to quantify inherent and residual risk (e.g. high, medium-to-high, medium-to-low and low risk categories);
- consistent rationales to rate control adequacy (e.g. satisfactory, needs improvement or deficient).

Assessing non-financial risk in a global organisation is a joint effort by global 2nd LoD risk management functions and regional/local 2nd LoD teams. Vertical organisations perform the risk assessment in their respective areas of responsibility by retrieving the required data from the 1st LoD, potentially performing interviews, and evaluating risks and controls. In many cases, 3rd LoD audit reports are also a viable source to consider. 2nd LoD risk management functions provide regional results to the responsible global heads, who consolidate inputs to create a group-wide risk view, which, in turn, forms the basis of recurring (annual, bi-annual) reporting to senior management.

[11] For example, the German BaFin has defined detailed requirements for the money laundering risk assessment.

#### 5.4.1.6 Non-financial risk reporting

To perform their mandate, global heads depend on data provided by vertical organisations on a regular basis. Reporting needs to follow a consistent standard across individual segments for global heads to derive sustainable conclusions for group risk management.

A global risk-specific reporting standard should cater for consistent reporting in a harmonised format at recurring intervals across vertical organisations. Key items covered by global reporting standards should, with potentially diverging delivery frequencies, include:

- regulatory horizon screening (status of local regulatory changes);
- non-financial risk standards (implementation status of global and local standards);
- training and advisory (status on staff participation in regional/local training);
- controls (summary results of controls performed in vertical organisations);
- risk assessment (results of regional risk assessments);
- key risk indicators (pre-defined key risk indicators that monitor business or operational activities).

Based on the defined global standard, regional and local 2nd LoD teams provide their global heads with the required data. Global heads then consolidate the reports and build the global risk-type-specific risk report, including the results of the risk assessment exercise.

#### 5.4.1.7 Group risk oversight

Applying a risk-based approach, global heads (as the responsible central 2nd LoD risk management functions) need to establish a review process and verify to what degree local entities comply with global regulatory standards. The following elements should be considered in the review process:

- provision of formal feedback (in writing) with regards to adherence to global standards: this can be a simple "comply" statement but might require additional information ("explain") in case of non-adherence or deviation from global standards due to local regulatory standards;
- definition of key risk indicators (KRIs) to assess the current and evolving risk situation in local entities. KRIs help to create risk transparency on local entities and subsequently on group-level. KRIs might be further enriched by Key Performance Indicators (KPIs) to determine the effectiveness of 2nd LoD staff in local entities (for example,

measurement of adherence to initially planned NFR review plans or closing of internal and external audit findings);

- on-site visits in local entities by global head representatives: Assessment of regular day-to-day operations (based on group-wide standards) following a standardised assessment scheme. In addition, these on-site visits can be used to draw a sample for the verification of former "compliance statements" (especially when any non-compliance is expected) and adherence to global standards.

### 5.4.2 Reporting lines: establishing implementation accountability in vertical functions

To ensure global standards are consistently executed across the group, adequate reporting lines of vertical risk management staff into global risk management functions must be defined. As shown above, risk management staff in vertical functions operate in regional hub, local or hybrid setups. They are typically formally employed by legal entities or branches in local jurisdictions. Where required, reporting lines of vertical risk management staff should be split into solid (disciplinary) and dotted (functional) reporting lines.

Figure 2: Reporting lines under GFL

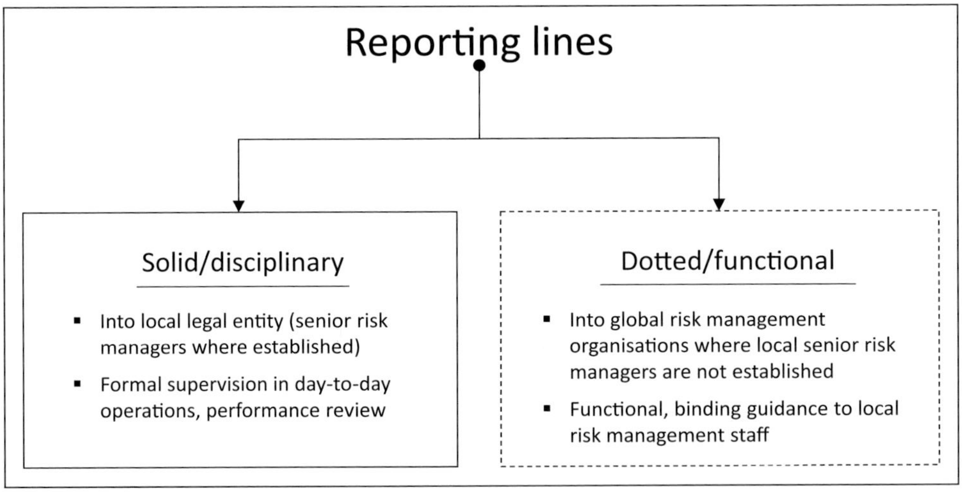


#### 5.4.2.1 Solid reporting lines into local legal entity and branch

Vertical risk management staff should have solid reporting lines into senior risk managers or, where these are not locally available, general managers of the legal entity or branch by which they are employed. Solid reporting lines comprise formal supervision in day-to-day operations, performance reviews, performing potential powers in accordance to local employment laws and ownership of financial budget, where applicable. A solid reporting line into senior risk managers also covers functional, risk-specific guidance.

#### 5.4.2.2 Dotted reporting lines into global risk management organisation

Where a setup does not provide for solid reporting lines into local senior risk managers, local risk management staff should have dotted reporting lines into the global risk management organisation (for the relevant non-financial risk types), either directly to the global head or indirectly to the global head via a regional head. Dotted reporting lines establish a functional relationship between risk management staff in legal entities or branches and higher-level positions in the risk management hierarchy, providing functional, binding guidance to lower-level risk management staff.

Where dotted reporting lines are established, the scope and reach of solid and dotted reporting lines need to be aligned to avoid overlap or redundancy. Also, adequate measures need to be agreed upon by relevant local parties to ensure that local risk management staff can perform their risk management duties independently from local 1st LoD (senior) staff (e.g. documented risk management mandate or job description).

### 5.4.3 Meeting governance: supporting effective management of a global risk function

Managing risk in a global financial institution requires effective leadership on various levels and layers of the organisation. A clear top-down management approach, facilitated by an effective, cascaded meeting governance, is essential to ensure senior risk management decisions are properly communicated and implemented throughout the group.[12] Delays, inconsistencies and any implementation white spots must be prevented to achieve sustainable and high-quality operational outcomes. Depending on the individual setup, senior risk executives should consider the following layers when defining group meeting governance:

- *global level:* monthly or weekly meetings of global head with direct central and regional reports. Key focus topics should include global risk steering, overall alignment with business and risk strategy, risk-specific global regulatory trends as well as short-, medium- and long-term planning of the risk management agenda;

[12] Risk management may also require active or passive participation of 2nd LoD risk management functions in an institution's (group) bodies and committees (e.g. risk committee) and need-to-know access to information from these bodies and committees. Please refer to chapter 4 for more information.

- *regional level:* monthly or weekly meetings of regional heads with direct local reports. Key focus should be on regional implementation of the global agenda, alignment with regional initiatives, regional and local regulatory environment as well as short- and medium-term planning of the risk management agenda;
- *local level:* weekly meetings of local heads with local risk management staff. Key focus should be on local operations as well as current and upcoming implications of regional risk steering.

The meeting governance should be formalised in dedicated terms of reference covering pre-communication of meeting agendas, mandatory attendance, decision-making and circulation of meeting minutes.

Figure 3: GFL meeting governance

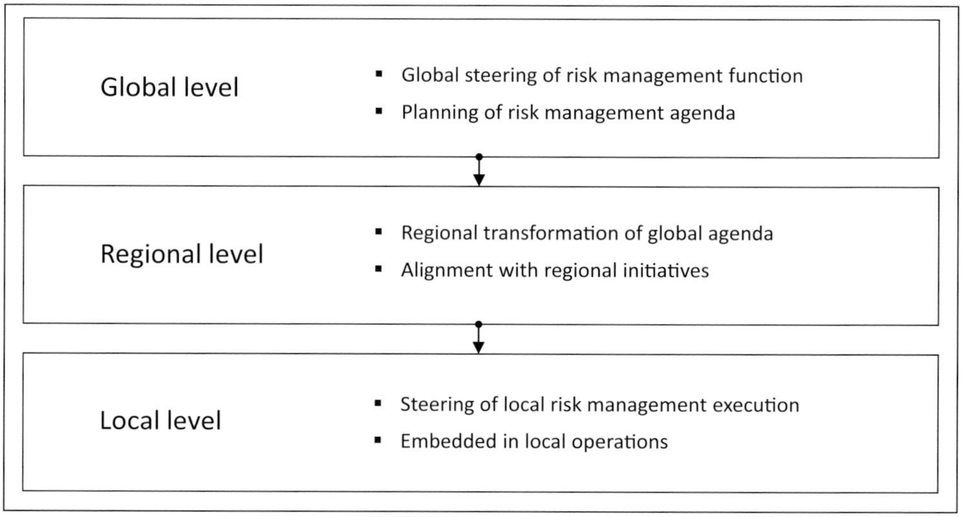


## 5.5 Conclusion

Financial institutions need to manage the complexity in non-financial risk management. Any negligence exposes institutions to operational risks, potential financial losses and regulatory repercussions. Financial institutions have their own mix of product divisions, infrastructure functions and geographical regions. Hence, setups to tackle GFL need to consider these individualities. Still, overall principles apply across organisations and these need to be in the focus of risk management functions. They include defining the right balance between global standards and regional execution, establishing functional reporting lines into horizontal risk management organisations and setting up adequate top-down, cascaded meeting governance.

When designing GFL or rethinking an existing framework, three considerations are likely to make a difference. Institutions should consider their medium- and long-term strategic agendas to prevent unnecessary disruptions down the road and help make the solutions storm-proof. They should involve regional and local stakeholders early on in the process and ensure their buy-in to enhance the solution acceptance on the ground. Finally, they should keep their "regulatory eye" open and stay aware of dynamics in global regulation to anticipate hurdles early on.

# 6 Policies and Procedures: Framework and Governance Requirements in the Financial Sector

*Dr. Erasmus Faber, Björn Stauber, Dr. Georg Lienke*

## 6.1 Introduction

Document governance is a key pillar of financial institutions' risk management frameworks. A stringent policy and procedure framework enables the firm to ensure that external and internal legal and regulatory requirements are linked to the firm's values and overarching risk appetite, and are ultimately translated into actionable behavioural expectations. Policies and procedures are essential tools in conveying the management boards' values and the risk profile to every employee. Keeping documents up to date and available to the relevant employees is essential in this process. Hence, the real value of a policy governance framework lies in effective implementation of standards and sustainable employee buy-in. The primary intention of a policy framework is to build a structural policy hierarchy, allocating the financial institution's documents – specifically including board directives, policies and procedures – to different hierarchy levels and structuring them along risk types, business segments and geographies.

Comprehensive policy governance defines a process for document creation and updates, and it determines criteria for alignment, ownership, approval and publication as well as communication and roll-out. It also needs to include a structured workflow governing the whole policy life cycle. The mapping of regulatory changes to policies is as much a key requirement as the mapping of policies to internal processes, so that the responsible process owners are informed automatically about policy changes to review and determine policy adjustments when necessary. The outcome needs to be a user-friendly, efficient way of organising the firm's policies and documents to ensure effective implementation. Board directives, policies and procedures must be stored in a repository that can be structured along business segments. The repository defines the key base data for each document, such as document type, scope, document's owner and document version.

## 6.2 Regulatory framework in selected key jurisdictions

Regulators around the globe have issued guidelines on how firms should structure their document governance frameworks and what target state institutions should aim to achieve.

### 6.2.1 European Banking Authority (EBA)

In its *Guidelines on internal governance*,[1] the EBA aims to harmonise institutions' internal governance arrangements, processes and mechanisms in the EU. While targeting a sound risk culture overall, the guidelines also provide guidance on the implementation of standards and policies.

The EBA clarifies that

> *"the management body should develop, adopt and promote high ethical and professional standards, considering the specific needs and characteristics of the institution, and should ensure the implementation of such standards (through a code of conduct or similar instrument)."*

The EBA states that firms "should have clear and documented policies for how these standards should be met."[2] It prescribes that institutions should "establish, maintain and regularly update adequate written internal control policies, mechanisms and procedures, which should be approved by the management body" and should "communicate those policies, mechanisms and procedures to all staff and every time material changes have been made."[3] According to the EBA, policies should contain principles and examples of both acceptable and unacceptable behaviour, especially in the fields of misconduct, financial misreporting as well as economic and financial crime.

In 2024, the European Banking Authority (EBA) issued guidelines to ensure the effective implementation of the European Union's and national restrictive measures (sanctions) by financial institutions. Among others, these guidelines establish specific requirements for internal policies, procedures, and controls that institutions must adopt to comply with restrictive measures, with a particular focus on due diligence, transaction monitoring, and reporting obligations. A key aspect of the guidelines mandates that institutions develop and maintain comprehensive policies and procedures to identify, assess, and manage risks associated with (the circumvention of) restrictive measures.[4]

1 EBA 2017.
2 No. 103 in ibid., 28.
3 No. 146 in ibid., 36.
4 EBA 2024 (applicable from 30 December 2025).

### 6.2.2 US regulators

#### 6.2.2.1 The Federal Reserve

In 1995, the Federal Reserve addressed the question of adequate policies, procedures, and limits in its policy letter on *Rating the Adequacy of Risk Management Processes and Internal Controls at State Member Banks and Bank Holding Companies*. Whilst the focus at that time was heavily on financial risk and its management, some of the general principles are still valid for managing non-financial risks. According to that letter, directors and senior management should tailor their "policies and procedures to the types of risks that arise from the activities the institution conducts."[5]

In its 2008 policy letter *Compliance Risk Management Programs and Oversight at Large Banking Organizations with Complex Compliance Profiles*, the Federal Reserve stated that the "boards of directors are responsible for setting an appropriate culture of compliance within their organisations, for establishing clear policies regarding the management of key risks, and for ensuring that these policies are adhered to in practice."[6]

In its supervisory letter *Consolidated Supervision Framework for Large Financial Institutions*, the Federal Reserve states that firms should "implement and maintain effective policies, procedures, and systems to ensure compliance with applicable laws and regulations."[7]

#### 6.2.2.2 Office of the Comptroller of the Currency

The Office of the Comptroller of the Currency (OCC) states in its *Corporate and Risk Governance Handbook* that the board is responsible for approving and reviewing key risk policies.[8] The OCC provides a non-exhaustive list of policies that require board approval, which include policies on banking secrecy, compensation, safe and sound banking practices as well as information security standards.[9]

[5] Board of Governors of the Federal Reserve System 1995.

[6] Ibid. 2008.

[7] Ibid. 2012, Sec. B2d.

[8] OCC 2019b, 30.

[9] Ibid., Annex B, Table 2.

### 6.2.3 Hong Kong Monetary Authority

The Hong Kong Monetary Authority (HKMA) provides guidance on both the principles to be applied to a policy and procedure framework as well as the content and risk areas to be covered. The rules are distributed across various sections of the HKMA's supervisory policy manuals.[10]

The HKMA states that institutions "should have clearly defined and documented policies and procedures that enable firm-wide risks to be managed in a proactive manner," while achieving, (i) objective and consistent risk identification and measurement approaches; (ii) comprehensive and rigorous risk assessment and reporting systems; (iii) sound valuation and stress-testing practices; and (iv) effective risk monitoring measures and controls.[11]

The Hong Kong regulator also emphasises overall board responsibility and the need for "risk management policies and key risk management procedures to be approved by the Board (or its designated committee(s) with the necessary delegated authority)." Firms are encouraged to implement an (at least) annual review cycle, which should be conducted by the board or its designated committee.[12] This is in line with the wider expectations the HKMA issued in its *Supervisory Policy Manual – CG 1 – Corporate Governance of Locally Incorporated Authorized Institutions*[13] in which is stated that the board should annually approve risk management strategies, key risk policies and the firm's risk appetite.

According to the HKMA, various factors should be considered when developing policies and procedures. Among these are (i) the overall business strategy and activities; (ii) the appropriateness of the framework to the size, nature and complexity of the institution's business activities; (iii) risk appetite; (iv) the results of sensitivity analysis and stress tests; as well as (vii) any legal and regulatory requirements.[14] The HKMA also refers to key risk areas that need to be covered in policies including compliance, remuneration, whistleblowing, conflicts of interests and insider trading.[15]

---

[10] HKMA 2017a.

[11] Ibid., Sec. 4.1.1.

[12] Ibid., Sec. 4.1.5: if the annual review is not conducted by the board but by the board's committee(s) or senior management, any material amendment to the policies and procedures should be approved by the board.

[13] HKMA 2017b.

[14] For a full view on the factors: HKMA 2017a, Sec. 4.1.3.

[15] Explaining the main processes by which compliance risks are to be identified and managed through all levels of the organisation: HKMA 2017b, Sec. 2.5.2, 2.5.5, 2.6.7, 2.6.8, 2.6.10, 2.6.13, 2.7.1.

### 6.2.4 Monetary Authority of Singapore

The Monetary Authority of Singapore (MAS) takes a similar approach to that of the HKMA. The regulatory requirements cover both formal principles and risk topics to be addressed in the policy framework.

In its *Guidelines on Risk Management Practices – Internal Controls*, the MAS primarily refers to the principles of a policy and procedure framework and states that "an institution should have comprehensive and sound policies approved by the Board for prudent management of significant risks arising from its business activities and operations."[16] The MAS puts an emphasis on effective implementation of the policies by requiring institutions to establish appropriate implementing procedures and processes, which need to be documented in procedural manuals.[17] Both the policies and procedures, as well as the procedural manuals, should be subject to periodical review by senior management to ensure their adequacy and appropriateness.[18]

## 6.3 Policy framework: key implications for a target concept

Institutions can rely on regulatory guidance only to a certain extent when it comes to the design of their policies and procedures frameworks. This has led to heterogenous approaches across the industry.

### 6.3.1 Status quo: need for structured approach

Many institutions struggle with challenges when it comes to the design and implementation of their policy and procedure frameworks. Hastily created documents to address urgent regulatory findings and historically evolved inconsistencies are just two reasons. In trying to address the shortcomings, the following pain points should be prioritised.

#### 6.3.1.1 Lack of a harmonised approach

A common shortcoming is the lack of a harmonised approach and a clear structured institution-wide framework – business segments may have their own, deviating frameworks with the same risk topic being covered in different documents across the institution.

---

16 MAS 2024a, Sec. 2.1.2.

17 Ibid., Sec. 2.1.3.

18 Senior management is only explicitly responsible for the review of the policies and procedures, not of the procedural manuals; MAS 2013, Sec. 2.5.3, 2014, Sec. 2.1.3.

Some institutions also lack sufficient transparency, availability and awareness regarding their policies and procedures. Sometimes even the whole governance process is undefined, with unclear ownership for updating and communication of documents, leading to employees not knowing about or not being able to find the relevant documents.

#### 6.3.1.2 Policy gaps and redundancies

Another common pain point relates to vague and unprecise wording of documents, resulting in non-actionable content and readers not knowing about the expected behaviour. When firms have varying levels of detail and granularity in policies between risk types, business segments and/or geographies, the result is usually that some areas are covered well, while others are insufficiently covered or not covered at all. Resulting gaps again create the risk of activities outside the institution's risk appetite. Whilst having such policy gaps is obviously critical, the opposite can be a major shortcoming as well. If redundant policies exist, risk topics are covered in a duplicative way and outdated policies remain in place, the overarching objective of a policy framework – to transform both external and internal legal and regulatory requirements and the firm's values into actionable behavioural expectations – can be put at risk.

### 6.3.2 Policy framework: design concept and hierarchies

#### 6.3.2.1 Design concept: key hypotheses for an effective policy framework

With the discussed shortcomings in mind, the following seven design principles form the basis for an effective policy framework: (i) harmonised design approach, (ii) completeness, (iii) uniform naming conventions, (iv) precise wording, (v) assignment of responsibilities, (vi) governance rules as well as (vii) linkage to internal processes and controls.

##### 6.3.2.1.1 Harmonised design approach

Of foremost importance is a harmonised policy framework design approach across the institution. Only one framework should exist, applicable across all business segments, risk types, geographies as well as subsidiaries and branches. This will avoid fragmentation, gaps and duplication. The hierarchical framework also needs to be built consistently, meaning that every lower hierarchical level document must be in line with (and potentially specify) the content and requirements set at a higher level ("parent-policy principle"). Lower-level documents should be linked to one or more higher-level policies.

#### 6.3.2.1.2 Completeness

The holistic approach needs to ensure that no major risk areas remain uncovered.[19] The framework also needs to ensure that only relevant risks are covered. Focusing on key risks and not trying to overwhelm an institution with excessive numbers of documents is necessary to allow for an effective implementation.

#### 6.3.2.1.3 Uniform naming convention

Whilst there is no universal recommendation on how documents on different levels should be named, it is important that an institution follows a consistent approach, both for the naming of the document levels and the documents themselves.

#### 6.3.2.1.4 Precise wording

Besides naming, the actual content of policies should be written in clear, precise and easy-to-understand language. Ambiguous and vague wording must be avoided. Using uncommon technical terms or acronyms can cause misinterpretations or misbehaviour.

#### 6.3.2.1.5 Assignment of responsibilities

Policies need to contain a clear assignment of responsibilities, meaning that the target group is clearly defined and every process or control has an identified owner or responsible unit (e.g. risk owners, oversight teams, person responsible for implementation).

#### 6.3.2.1.6 Governance rules

The policy framework should contain clear governance rules on the document life cycle, covering policies' ownership, approvals, reviews and updates, awareness (availability and publication of documents) as well as training and assurance.[20]

#### 6.3.2.1.7 Linkage to internal processes and controls

Finally, documents need to create linkages to internal processes and controls to allow for a smooth implementation of the documented requirements.

---

[19] Please refer to chapter 2 for more details on a non-financial risk taxonomy.

[20] See below in section 6.3 for more details on governance requirements.

### 6.3.2.2 Suggested hierarchy levels: key criteria and examples

There is no single truth when it comes to defining an institutional policy hierarchy. It rather depends on the individual firm's business model and organisational structure.

In the following sections, a four-tiered policy hierarchy is analysed, assuming a corporate and retail business bank registered and based in Europe with major business operations in the US, Hong Kong and Singapore.

Figure 1: Example for four-tiered policy hierarchy

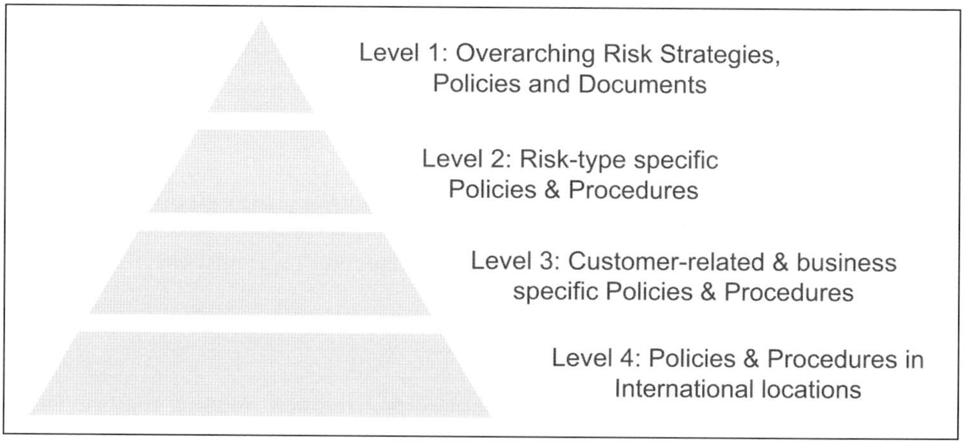


### 6.3.2.3 Level one: overarching risk strategies, policies and documents – risk and business segment agnostic

#### 6.3.2.3.1 Key criteria

The top hierarchical level of a policy and procedure framework is reserved for addressing overarching topics and the elementary values governing the institution and its risk management. It should clarify "why" something needs to be done. Documents on this level typically have a cross-functional application and a global validity irrespective of risk type, business segment and jurisdiction. They usually do not contain procedural elements and generally require an implementation on subsequent hierarchy levels.

#### 6.3.2.3.2 Key risk type and business segment agnostic topics

The following topics should be covered on level one of a policy hierarchy:

- **code of conduct:** compendium comprising an institution's values, ethical foundations and professional standards for all employees;
- **board directives**: board guidance on behavioural expectations or unacceptable behaviour for comprehensive topics like non-bribery or environmental impact;
- **risk appetite statement**: general principles of an institution's risk policy and acceptance with qualitative statements on risk tolerance;
- **strategy documents**: risk-agnostic strategy documents with cross-functional application, not linked to a single risk type;
- **group corporate governance**: overarching document dealing with organisational structure, group oversight and senior management responsibility.

### 6.3.2.4 Level two: risk-type-specific policies and procedures

#### 6.3.2.4.1 Key criteria

The next hierarchical level addresses the questions of "what" needs to be done and "how" it can be achieved. This comprises the risk-type-specific core policies and procedures for relevant non-financial risks. Within each risk type, both policies and procedures on this level generally have global validity and serve as a foundation for level-three and level-four documents. Level-two policies translate an institution's overall risk understanding and senior management's overarching risk topics set on level one into both implementable and tangible instructions and behavioural expectations. They form the link between an institution's documented high-level values and risk profile and an actionable control environment.

Procedures are significantly more practical and serve as specification of policies. They address the "how" and specify in detail the necessary actions designed to implement the content of both the policies and level-one documents.

### 6.3.2.4.2 Risk-type-specific documents

Based on the exemplary institution's risk taxonomy, the following non-financial risk topics are generally subject to policies on level two of a policy hierarchy[21]:

- individual risk strategies, including on operational risk, reputational risk and compliance (including financial crime)[22];
- compliance;
- anti-money laundering including know-your-customer (KYC);
- sanctions and embargoes;
- anti-fraud (internal and external);
- anti-bribery and corruption;
- sustainability;
- securities trading, including market and customer conduct;
- gifts and entertainment;
- private account dealing;
- client tax reporting;
- regulatory change management;
- data privacy and bank secrecy;
- third-party management, outsourcing and vendors;
- information and communication technology, including cyber security;
- operational resilience, including business continuity management;
- recovery and resolution;
- project management;
- legal contract management;

[21] Exemplary corporate and retail business bank, registered and based in Europe with major business operations in the US, Hong Kong and Singapore.

[22] As the focus of this chapter is on non-financial risk types, financial risk types are not covered (e.g. credit or market risk).

- human resources, including diversity, equity and inclusion as well as
- workplace safety.

Depending on the business and operating model, additional level-two topics may be relevant.

### 6.3.2.5 Level three: customer-related and business-specific policies and procedures

#### 6.3.2.5.1 Key criteria

Where applicable, the third policy level defines "how" different business segments should implement the requirements created on the higher hierarchy levels. Level-three policies and procedures should be formulated in accordance with level-one and level-two policies and contain business line-specific, actionable, process-oriented and sufficiently detailed guidance. Documents on this level are segment, business type and/or customer-specific policies and procedures.

#### 6.3.2.5.2 Customer-related and business-specific topics

On the third level, institutions should translate level-two policy requirements into customer-type and business segment specific standards, where necessary. In the case of our example institution, this would require defining the necessary level-three policies for its corporate and retail business.[23] Typically, some non-financial risk types require a higher degree of level-three specifications. Customer conduct standards, for example, vary between retail customers and institutional investors, and institutions have separate policies for the two client segments. In financial crime prevention, the onboarding and ongoing monitoring of corporate customers requires a different approach than for retail customers, and again, different AML/KYC policies should specify the relevant standards. Level-two requirements for risk types such as outsourcing or project management typically require less or no specifications to business segments because they are generally client or business type agnostic. In essence, the scope of level-three policies and procedures strongly depends on the individual business model, risk exposure and client segmentation of an institution.

[23] Exemplary corporate and retail business bank, registered and based in Europe with major business operations in the US, Hong Kong and Singapore.

### 6.3.2.6 Level four: policies and procedures in international locations

Institutions with an international footprint must deal with various regulators in different jurisdictions, and they need to address the question of how diverging laws or regulatory views and expectations across these jurisdictions need to be met. Depending on the involved jurisdictions, topics with a considerable degree of international variation include anti-money laundering, anti-bribery and corruption, data privacy and bank secrecy.

#### 6.3.2.6.1 Scope of applicability: subsidiary companies and branch offices

Subsidiary companies that are fully owned or controlled by a parent company and branch offices fall under the parent's policy framework and should comply with the criteria and governance requirements thereof.[24]

#### 6.3.2.6.2 Key criteria

In terms of the example institution's international setup, there are three potential outcomes with regards to diverging expectations between the European home regulator and regulators elsewhere.[25] Regulatory expectations can be (i) stricter than in Europe, (ii) weaker or (iii) just different but not contradictory. When designing level-four policies and procedures, these constellations and the interplay between home state and host state regulation for the various risk topics should be carefully considered. For all local deviations, it is crucial that a feedback and approval process exists to enable central group functions to obtain and keep both oversight and control over the institution-wide policy framework.

[24] A branch office does not constitute a separate legal entity.

[25] Mid-sized business bank with small investment banking and retail business, registered and based in Europe with major business operations in the US, Hong Kong and Singapore.

Figure 2: Financial crime policy hierarchy (example for a corporate and retail bank)

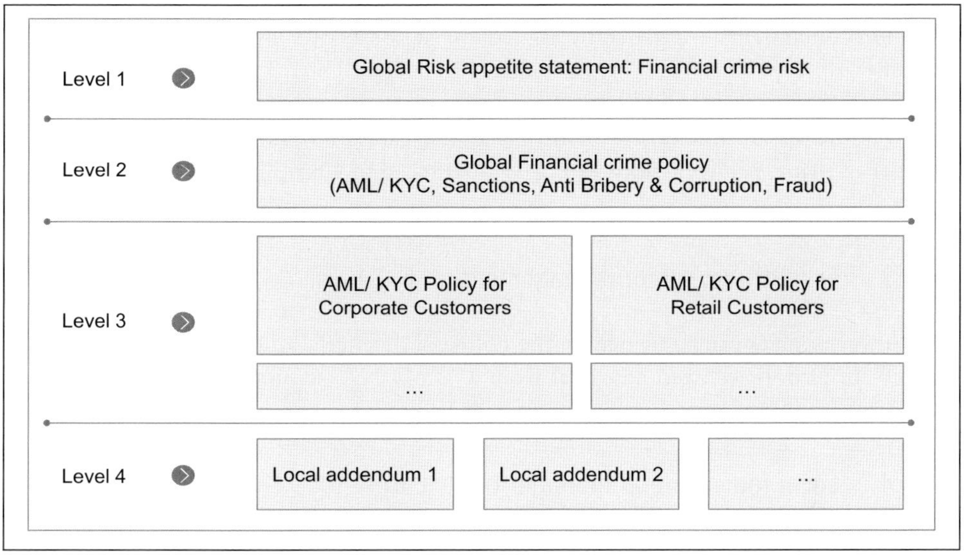


## 6.4 Policy governance, repository and workflow tool

A policy framework requires clear governance rules. Without a structured process for document creation and updates, as well as well-defined criteria for ownership, approval and publication, it will fall short of expectations. A governance framework should cover an approval process for policies and procedures, an update and ownership process as well as a policy repository tool.

### 6.4.1 Approval of policies and procedures

An adequate approval process is a core governance element. The approval hierarchy must be linked to the policy hierarchy and ensure that responsibility for signing off on key documents is placed on staff with necessary seniority.

#### 6.4.1.1 Level one: board of directors

Generally, level-one documents need to be signed off and approved at the board level. This is in line with requirements by regulators in the EU, the US and APAC.

#### 6.4.1.2 Level two: responsible board member

Level-two documents are generally signed off at the board level. Still, since they are generally risk-type-specific, it is not standard to have full board approval. Instead, these policies can be approved by the responsible board member. For relevant procedures on this level, the responsible board member may delegate the signing off to the N-1 senior manager of the respective risk type (e.g. Global Head of Compliance or Global Head of AML).[26]

#### 6.4.1.3 Level three: senior management on N-1 level

Level-three policies can be owned by the 1$^{st}$ line of defence (LoD) or the 2$^{nd}$ LoD. Generally, 1$^{st}$ LoD policies need approval from 1$^{st}$ LoD N-1 senior management. 2$^{nd}$ LoD policies are approved by risk-type-specific 2$^{nd}$ LoD N-1 senior managers.

#### 6.4.1.4 Level four: general manager or 2$^{nd}$ LoD N-1

As with level three, level-four documents can come from the 1$^{st}$ or the 2$^{nd}$ LoD. 1$^{st}$ LoD documents need approval from the general manager of the subsidiary or branch office. 2$^{nd}$ LoD documents need risk-type-specific 2$^{nd}$ LoD approval. Depending on the size and organisational setup of the subsidiary or branch office, the approval would usually come from local or regional 2$^{nd}$ LoD senior management.

### 6.4.2 Authorship, ownership, creation as well as update of policies and procedures

Ensuring the appropriate approval of documents is one part of document governance. Other pivotal parts are the document's authorship and ownership, the process to create any such documents and having a clearly structured and stringent update process.

#### 6.4.2.1 Document authorship

The author(s) create a document's content and corresponding intellectual property.

[26] N-1 = Management level, one level below the highest hierarchy level.

### 6.4.2.2 Document ownership

A document's owner is ultimately responsible for managing the document's life cycle, accuracy and timely updates. The document's owner can be, yet is not necessarily, identical to the document's author.

### 6.4.2.3 Document creation process

New documents can become necessary, due to regulatory changes or interventions, audit findings or compliance testing results. The document creation process should follow a clearly structured approach. First, the target solution needs to be determined, meaning the content needs clarification. In the next steps, the target audience must be defined before the first draft of the document. This draft needs to be coordinated frequently with all relevant $1^{st}$ and $2^{nd}$ LoD stakeholders. It is also advisable to consult with $3^{rd}$ LoD stakeholders where relevant. While finalising the wording and obtaining the necessary approvals on the adequate level, a plan for communication and implementation (e.g. trainings, new tools etc.) must be drafted. Once the document has been approved, it needs to be communicated to the relevant target group(s).

### 6.4.2.4 Stringent management of update process

One of the basic principles of a policy framework is that no policies or procedures that are out of date exist. Institutions therefore need to have a system in place that guarantees regular and ad hoc reviews of documents to consider a changing regulatory environment or other trigger events. Once an update is initiated, it must follow the same general steps as for the document's creation. It needs emphasis here that an updated document requires a new approval unless only minor editorial changes were conducted. Again, it is crucial for a successful implementation to ensure a clear communication of an updated document to the relevant target group(s).

#### 6.4.2.4.1 Regular validation based on time intervals

All documents need to be regularly reviewed and checked for continuing accuracy and fitness for purpose. This means that every document should be validated after a pre-defined time interval. While it is mandatory only in some jurisdictions to have key risk policies validated at least once a year, an annual review of key risk documents is recommended. For less critical documents, some institutions tend to apply a two-year review cycle. Some institutions also apply a split approach and require just an annual prolongation (respectively a signing off) by the document's owner to confirm that no major changes require a full makeover, while demanding a detailed review and validation of content only biannually. The review cycle needs to be in line with the respective regulator's expectations.

When conducting a detailed review, institutions should consider lessons learned from assurance testing to enhance a policy's implementation. Minor findings from internal or external audits or compliance testing that did not require immediate and a document's ad hoc revision should also be considered.

##### 6.4.2.4.2 Ad hoc updates

A review might be triggered outside the usual review cycle. This usually happens when significant external or internal events occur. Examples are major changes in the regulatory environment, regulatory interventions and/or sanctions, major identified internal deficiencies such as money-laundering incidents, or major findings from audits, quality assurance or internal testing.

Ad hoc updates can also become necessary on changes to an institution's business model, business activity or operating model. Typical examples are the launch of new products, new client segments and entering new or withdrawing from geographical regions. In any such cases, the relevant policies need to be reviewed to ensure their future accuracy and to avoid critical gaps.

### 6.4.3 Policy repository, including workflow tool: centralised management of policies and procedures

It is essential for institutions to have a centralised policy repository to manage the complexity that comes with a large body of policies and procedures on a broad range of topics across business segments, entities and geographies.

A policy repository primarily serves the following three key purposes:

- facilitation of access to current policies and procedures;
- management of policy life cycles and workflow support for document's owners;
- audit-proof tracking of any changes and updates to policies and procedures.

The following core features are required for a repository to achieve these purposes.

#### 6.4.3.1 Facilitation of access

Policies and procedures should be clustered and accessible along the hierarchy levels of the policy framework.

Within the repository, documents should be mapped to business segments and processes, to help staff identify relevant policies quickly. This is particularly helpful when faced with large volumes of documents, which in many institutions are most likely to exist on levels two, three and four of the policy hierarchy.

#### 6.4.3.2 Document lifecycle management

To enable a fully digital life cycle management, the repository should allow for the mapping of policies and procedures to the respective document's owners and approvers. In that context, two types of validations are relevant.

##### 6.4.3.2.1 Regular validation of documents

An integrated workflow solution should automatically trigger regular, time-based document update cycles and allow for digital approvals.

##### 6.4.3.2.2 Ad hoc updates

Apart from regular reviews, documents may need to be updated ad hoc.

###### 6.4.3.2.2.1 Changes in business and operating model

First, ad hoc updates may be triggered by changes to an institution's business model, business activity or operational model, which can impact specific policies. With a workflow tool, documents can be selected based on thematic relevance, requests can be sent to respective owners to check whether any policy updates are necessary and change execution can be logged accordingly.

###### 6.4.3.2.2.2 Changes in regulatory framework

Updates can become necessary due to newly published or changed external requirements. Policies and procedures first need to be linked to regulatory clusters that can, for example, be defined along the risk categories established in an institution's risk taxonomy. Once the relevance of potential changes has been validated centrally (e.g. by the compliance function), the document's owners for policies and procedures linked to these clusters can be informed via a workflow tool to confirm whether any policy updates are necessary.

#### 6.4.3.3 Audit-proof change log

Details of any updates, modifications or changes made to any policy or procedure and key steps in the life cycle management process need to be securely logged to enable internal or external auditors to fully comprehend the complete history.

## 6.5 Conclusion

A policy and procedure framework and adequate policy governance are key elements of effective non-financial risk management. They define internal operating standards binding for all staff members and thereby lay the foundation for compliance with regulatory requirements. Staff misconduct (both intentional and negligent) can only be fully pursued and sanctioned when the expected (and proper) behaviour is adequately documented and communicated. When policies and procedures are insufficient, incomplete or outdated, the prevention and mitigation of misconduct is less likely to be successful, thus resulting in increasing operational, regulatory and reputational risk for the organisation. Hence, key stakeholders in financial institutions need to be aware of the significant role of policy and procedure frameworks in the context of risk prevention and mitigation, and they need to ensure these are adequately implemented, updated and communicated.

# 7 Top-Down Risk and Control Assessment: A Forward-Looking Approach to Evaluate Company-Wide Non-Financial Risk Exposure

*Hurdogan Irmak, Burcu Nasuhoglu, Dr. Erasmus Faber, Lorenzo Fantini, Benedetta Testino, Jannik Leiendecker, Barbara Fojcik, Dr. Georg Lienke*

## 7.1 Introduction

Assessing non-financial risks has become a crucial task for financial institutions worldwide. With new regulations, large supervisory fines and growing internal costs in administering compliance, it has become ever more important to understand, measure and manage risk exposures. The traditional slogan of "zero risk tolerance" must be translated into a contemporary, risk-based decision-making process based on full risk transparency. Institutions need to be enabled to take risk decisions and make appropriate investments on what is important for their business models, client bases and strategic priorities.

Currently, the financial services industry takes a fragmented approach to evaluation of non-financial risks, with advanced institutions having implemented two major types of non-financial risk assessments, with different objectives, scopes and methodologies. One is a bottom-up approach, with assessments owned by 2nd line of defence (LoD) control functions. These define mitigating actions by process or non-financial risk type, analysing specific drivers and related controls for each risk (such as money laundering or cyber risk) or process (such as client onboarding). Bottom-up risk assessments are specific to individual non-financial risk types, applying indicators that vary according to the risk and relevant regulations.

Sophisticated institutions additionally apply a top-down approach to their risk assessment, using risk-type-agnostic criteria to evaluate their overall exposure to non-financial risk, enabling them to put risk exposures between different risk types into proportion, prioritise risk areas (e.g. where to run a bottom-up exercise) and derive the proper implications for bank-wide non-financial risk management and steering. Top-down risk and control assessments are owned by the 1st LoD with a substantial involvement from senior management.

Top-down and bottom-up risk assessments can effectively co-exist, each approach delivering valuable, complementary outcomes. However, while risk-specific, bottom-up risk assessments are standard across the industry, top-down risk assessments are often limited to the more sophisticated organisations, even though they offer unique benefits including:

- *synergies in deployed resources:* this is due to coordinated time plans and removal of duplicated activities, especially for interaction with business units;
- *consistent messages delivered:* these harmonise the level of granularity and use of consistent rating scales for likelihood and severity across non-financial risks.

This chapter focuses on the benefits of top-down risk and control assessments, providing a detailed demonstration of the underlying approach. The chapter starts with a summary of the key differentiators and benefits of the top-down versus the bottom-up approaches, followed by illustrations of key regulatory requirements and standard setter guidelines that comprise the "foundation" of risk assessments. The chapter outlines the methodology of each risk assessment framework component (inherent risk, internal controls and residual risk), adding practical examples. The chapter makes suggestions on the handling of residual risk and gives examples of potential measures for its different severity categories. The chapter closes with a summary of key considerations for the annual risk assessment process, suggesting a formalised approach following pre-defined phases.

## 7.2 Top-down vs. bottom-up: different approaches based on desired outcomes

Although they apply different approaches, both top-down and bottom-up assessments of non-financial risk adopt the framework suggested by both major regulators and standard setters. Under this approach, residual risk is evaluated primarily based on its inherent risk profile and the effectiveness of its control framework. According to this framework, inherent risk (gross risk) represents the amount of risk that exists in the absence of controls. It is the natural level of risk in a process or activity without doing anything to reduce likelihood or to mitigate the severity of an accident. On the other hand, internal controls represent the system of procedures and controls implemented to reduce inherent risk under a tolerable threshold. As a result, residual risk (net risk) refers to the amount of risk that remains after internal controls are accounted for.

### 7.2.1 Approaches: risk-specific focus vs. overarching non-financial risk coverage

Risk assessments using the bottom-up approach focus on single risk types, while top-down assessments are aimed at the full set of non-financial risks a financial institution is exposed to. Correspondingly, both approaches have distinct characteristics, described below.

#### 7.2.1.1 Bottom-up approach: risk-specific, granular focus

Organisations typically assess non-financial risks through methodologies tailored to the type of risk being evaluated or the process being considered. These assessments are performed using a bottom-up approach, often by means of checklists and detailed questionnaires addressed to risk management or compliance staff, with limited backup from quantitative data.

Bottom-up risk assessments help companies formulate detailed actions to counter individual risks, but they cannot really help control overall non-financial risk, since they are:

- performed by control functions, with limited involvement from the business;
- based mainly on qualitative information and hence on subjective judgments;
- focused on controls, with limited evaluation of the inherent risk and relevant business profile;
- based on current and past information, with a limited focus on possible future internal or external factors of significance, such as corporate strategy or new regulations.

Bottom-up risk assessments are focused on a single process or risk, are directed to compliance or operational risk management (driven by control functions) and are backward-looking (based on past records). The main objective of bottom-up risk assessments is to identify potential corrective measures for types of business or, more frequently, to recommend enhancements in controls.

#### 7.2.1.2 Top-down approach: overarching, holistic non-financial risk coverage

Top-down risk assessments enable financial institutions to manage company-wide, overall non-financial risk. Among their key attributes are the following:

- they can be used to gauge the full range of non-financial risks at group or legal-entity level, thereby evaluating an institution's entire risk exposure with a view to implementing actions and investments (at the legal-entity or group level) after prioritising areas for intervention;
- they are based on key risk indicators common across risk types, allowing a risk-agnostic view of an institution's full risk exposure;
- they are owned by the business (and facilitated by control functions) and are forward-looking, taking into account expected risk exposure evolutions, as depicted by the institution's business management;

- they rely on engagement by the $1^{st}$ and $2^{nd}$ LoDs, making agreed outcomes more sustainable, including agreeing on relevant actions, depending on the stated level of inherent risk and control adequacy – for example where to run bottom-up risk assessments.

### 7.2.2 Potential outcomes: different scope of risk-coverage and level of granularity

Bottom-up and top-down approaches in risk and control assessments bring different benefits. The outcome of a bottom-up risk and control assessment is focused on the level of exposure to a specific risk type and enables optimisation of the exposure to that risk type by reducing inherent risk (e.g. in clients, products, transactions) or improving the effectiveness of the risk-specific control framework. Bottom-up risk assessments are an essential working tool for the $2^{nd}$ LoD to plan efforts and initiatives on a risk-based approach and sustainably optimise standards, controls, training and $1^{st}$ LoD advisory.

Top-down risk and control assessments enable the financial institution to take a broader perspective, put exposure into proportion and prioritise risk areas (e.g. due to higher inherent risk or weaker controls). Using the top-down approach, senior management can take a consolidated approach to managing and steering all non-financial risk by categorising additional actions, depending on the risk exposure:

- new projects and investments for further mitigating high and medium-high risks;
- further tuning of controls to enhance effectiveness for medium-low risks;
- simplification of controls or no action in low-risk areas.

Top-down risk assessments are key to managing and steering an institution's overall exposure to non-financial risk, delivering valuable insights across risk types and allowing risk prioritisation at senior management level.

## 7.3 Key success factors: maximising the effectiveness of top-down risk and control assessments

Successful top-down risk assessments depend on several factors, of which the following are particularly relevant:

- *fact-based:* top-down risk assessments should use clear and objective key risk indicators and rigorous criteria for assessment, thereby reducing the influence of subjective judgment;
- *clearly framed:* financial institutions are expected to follow the guidelines for an inherent risk – control – residual risk framework, evaluating the inherent risk and business

profile separately from an appraisal of controls, since these two considerations can lead to different actions (i.e. reduction of inherent risk profile and strengthening of control framework). In addition, a numerical scoring system should be adopted to rank risks, supported by a standardisation of the scales used to determine the likelihood and impact of risks. A standardised approach provides a comparable view across different non-financial risk types. Equally, inconsistent risk assessments can lead to bad risk management decisions, potential violations of regulatory mandates and an overall poor risk management culture;

- *forward-looking:* a top-down risk analysis should incorporate emerging risks (e.g. evolving regulatory environment, emerging business trends, changes in customers' behaviours), embedding future internal and external developments;
- *action-oriented:* top-down results and related discussions should be translated into concrete actions for the business, to either lower the risk or enhance the controls;
- *business-oriented:* top-down results must be discussed at a sufficient level of seniority, with business senior managers actively involved in the assessment through the review and challenge process. 1st LoD business engagement ensures that this is not a 'check-the-box' exercise, reported to senior management once and then forgotten until the next year. Instead, institutions should use the results to drive decisions around control mitigation, investment and business strategy.

## 7.4 Regulatory framework, best practice and standard setter guidelines

A top-down risk assessment is a business managerial exercise, which is gaining traction among sophisticated institutions and is derived from supervisory expectations. In contrast to bottom-up risk assessments, which are regulation-driven and apply indicators derived from relevant regulations, there is no one single 'golden source' for a top-down methodology. Yet, a top-down approach can be gleaned from a holistic analysis of international banking regulations and standard setters' guidelines. In this context, to get a view of the top-down risk assessment scope, objectives and methodology, it is essential to also look at other market players (leading EU banks, large insurers etc.). With this approach, the industry is likely to develop a common analysis framework for non-financial risks.

### 7.4.1 COSO ERM framework

Internationally, the COSO ERM framework explains how risk assessments should examine the risk sizes, both individually and collectively, and focus management's attention on the most important threats and opportunities, as well as to lay the groundwork for a risk response.[1] According to COSO, a private-sector group aimed at reducing fraudulent financial reporting, risk assessment is the tool implemented so that risk levels are managed within defined tolerance thresholds without being overcontrolled or forgoing desirable opportunities. They should also be used to finding the 'sweet spot' or optimal risk-taking zone to effectively pursue strategic goals. COSO has published a series of papers that highlight the importance of risk assessments in managing risk exposures across organisations so that, at any given time, they incur just enough of the right kinds of risk to effectively pursue strategic goals. To accomplish this, enterprises require a risk assessment process that is practical, sustainable and easy to understand, supported by a structured and disciplined process. In its overview of risk assessment approaches and techniques that have emerged as the most useful and sustainable for decision-making, COSO strongly recommends the adoption of (i) an inherent risk framework, (ii) internal controls and (iii) a residual risk framework in risk analysis.

### 7.4.2 Bank for International Settlements

On the same trajectory, the Bank for International Settlements' "Management of non-financial risks, Issues in the Governance of Central Banks" recognises how central banks have become more systematic in their risk management by adopting more structured approaches and enhancing oversight of their risk management activities.[2] The Bank highlights how a substantial number of central banks, particularly those with major supervisory responsibilities, tend to apply the Basel II framework for operational risk or the Enterprise Risk Management Framework devised by COSO.

### 7.4.3 EBA and ECB

The European Banking Authority (EBA) and the European Central Bank (ECB) evaluate inherent risk and control adequacy of banking risks separately in their Supervisory Review and Evaluation Process (SREP), with specific key performance indicators allotted to both these dimensions.[3] In addition, the EBA guidelines on internal governance suggest leveraging a mix of quantitative and qualitative indicators (including expert judgement and critical analysis) to build a sound risk analysis framework.[4]

According to the EBA, when assessing risks, an institution should deploy methodologies allowing for the aggregation of risk exposures across business lines, supporting the iden-

[1] COSO 2004.
[2] BIS 2009.
[3] EBA 2014.
[4] EBA 2017.

tification of risk concentrations and including both forward-looking and backward-looking risk elements.

## 7.5 Methodology of top-down risk and control assessment: evaluation of inherent risk, control adequacy and residual risk

This section outlines the methodology for each risk assessment framework component (inherent risk, control adequacy and residual risk).

### 7.5.1 Non-financial risk taxonomy as a starting point

Top-down risk and control assessments are intended to create transparency on risk exposure across different non-financial risk categories. Hence, the starting point needs to be a comprehensive risk taxonomy for non-financial risks, as illustrated in chapter 2. With a taxonomy in place, large organisations need to establish a set of inherent risk indicators and control adequacy indicators for all risk categories, thereby facilitating comparisons and prioritisation of mitigating actions.

### 7.5.2 Measurement of inherent risk

The COSO ERM framework defines inherent risk as the risk to an entity in the absence of any action management to alter either the risk's likelihood or impact. As such, inherent risk is the 'gross risk,' representing the natural level of risk in a process or activity without doing anything to reduce the likelihood or mitigate the severity of an incident. Some entities interpret inherent risk to be the level of risk assuming existing responses fail, and residual risk to be the level of risk assuming existing responses operate according to design. Other entities interpret inherent risk to be the current level of risk assuming existing responses operate according to design and residual risk to be the estimated risk after the responses under consideration are put into place. The first approach is focused more on control effectiveness and the second approach on evaluating risk-response options. There is no *one* right answer, and either approach may be useful depending on the purpose of the assessment and the nature of the considered risks.

Inherent risk is typically measured as the combination of severity and likelihood of risk realisation per risk category without controls, adjusted for organisation-specific and industry context:

- *severity:* result, effect or consequences that a given event could cause (e.g. monetary loss, reputational damage);
- *likelihood:* probability of incurring a loss when controls are not in place.

In the next sections, quantitative and qualitative risk indicators that should contribute to inherent risk are discussed, highlighting key features, scoring criteria and weighting, complemented with real case examples.

### 7.5.2.1 Calculation of severity

Severity is calculated across two dimensions (organisation-specific risk indicators and industry adjustments) and assigned a value out of four possibilities: low, medium-low, medium-high and high (tagged 1–4). Based on market practice, severity is the result of three organisation-specific risk indicators and two industry adjustments, each evaluated per risk category:

- *organisation-specific risk indicators:* potential loss, reputational damage and risk relevance/process diffusion;
- *industry adjustments:* operational risk loss data and expert scenarios.

While risk indicators are organisation-specific and forward-looking, industry adjustments account for precedent and context, providing a point-in-time representation of the industry background.

#### 7.5.2.1.1 Organisation-specific risk indicators

Organisation-specific risk indicators are evaluated through the following quantitative and qualitative risk metrics.

The risk indicator "potential loss" is evaluated per risk category along the following two dimensions:

- *economic impact:* measuring the monetary impact of internal losses, supervisory sanctions and costs of adjustment, assessed together to create a holistic vision;
- *additional impact:* accounting for non-quantifiable economic impacts (e.g. profit disgorgement) and other administrative (e.g. license withdrawal) or criminal sentencing.

The risk indicator "reputational damage" is evaluated along the following two dimensions:

- *visibility:* measuring the frequency and intensity of potential publicity around compliance breaches;
- *sensitivity:* embedding the degree of public perception on the severity of potential compliance breaches.

The purpose of the "reputational damage" indicator is to measure the impact of a change in public perception, based on the spread of a risk that the organisation is exposed to negative news in the media.

The risk indicator "risk relevance/process diffusion" is evaluated per risk category along potential process diffusion, accounting for the degree of relevance of a given risk across an organisation's processes.

To drive the risk assessment execution, the dimensions described above are further cascaded into measurable risk elements. The dimension "economic impact" is measured based on the combination of three quantitative risk elements:

- financial sum of *impending firm-specific internal loss* per annum due to operational failures associated with each risk category;
- *maximum fine amount* permissible by law for compliance violations (e.g. data breaches, financial sanction circumventions) associated with each risk category;
- *expected cost of remediation* (e.g. new IT implementation, consulting fees) in case of regulatory breaches.

Applying these risk elements can be challenging. By way of practical example, the application of the second element may seem overly punitive for large organisations with well-established control frameworks, suggesting the use of a managerial discounting factor or a differentiation to account for the maximum fine amount, specifically for those risk categories that relate to a deliberate misconduct (e.g. misselling) by the organisation itself.

"Additional impact" is derived from a combined applicability of three qualitative risk elements:

- non-quantifiable economic sanctions (e.g. interdiction, profit disgorgement, private enforcement actions),
- criminal sentencing (e.g. detention),
- administrative sentencing (e.g. compulsory administration, license withdrawal).

"Reputational visibility" comes from the combination of:

- number of organisation-specific negative press/internet articles, TV reports and blog/social media posts related to each risk category;
- volume of circulation/audience of media for organisation-specific news (e.g. number of copies, clicks per day).

"Reputational sensitivity" is a synthetic qualitative score measuring public perception for each risk category (e.g. on a five-grade scale from 1. Unimportant to 5. Critical).

Finally, "risk relevance/process diffusion" is the sum of process relevance score (0–4) across processes for each risk category, where a 0 score stands for "irrelevant" (risk does not affect process) while 4 stands for "crucial" (risk affects business model). For each risk, a quantitative score is assigned by summing the scores across all processes.

#### 7.5.2.1.2 Industry adjustments

Industry adjustments correct risk indicators to account for precedent and context, providing a representation of industry trend and background, with a different applicability across risk indicators:

- *operational risk loss data:* collecting historic financial loss data across the industry as a result of operational failures associated with each risk category;
- *expert scenarios:* representing the relevant financial and reputational impact for the industry, based on rankings of risk scenarios by operational risk experts.

Industry-specific internal loss data due to operational failures is typically borrowed from industry data sources, such as the Operational Riskdata Exchange Association (ORX), and may require a mapping of standard risk categories to the financial institution's risk taxonomy.

Expert scenarios are qualitative evaluations by internal experts to adjust for potential downsides of quantitative models such as:

- historic data, focused on past performance rather than future potential;
- organisation-specific data, missing the wider banking industry perspective;
- comparability, at the expense of reflecting risk particularities.

In this context, expert scenarios capture insights into regulatory trends and emerging priorities. They account for specificities of certain risk types and offer a wider perspective on how other institutions are performing. In a typical scenario-based conversation with experts (e.g. an AML [anti-money laundering] specialist conducting customer due diligence, a cyber risk team conducting penetration tests/attack simulations), "what-if" questions should be asked, covering a set of adverse scenarios (e.g. if such an event occurs, how significant can the potential financial and non-financial sanctions be?). The scenarios (two or three for each risk category) can be based on events at peer institutions, drawn from parallels in other industries, or be purely hypothetical. For example, how would risk levels change if:

- regulators start to focus on new topics that weren't relevant in the past, such as chat boxes for customer interactions;
- money laundering scandals (e.g. laundromat scandals) affecting peer banks bring renewed regulatory attention to AML;
- new business trends (e.g. cryptocurrencies) gain traction among banks' customers, posing new challenges.

Expert scenario scores are used to adjust the quantitative model scoring. The goal of this exercise is not to produce an exact estimate of severity risk exposure but to develop a thinking about possible consequences of risk events and their impacts cascaded throughout the organisation, and to assess to what extent the institution is prepared for them.

#### 7.5.2.1.3 Weighting of risk indicators based on data source reliability

To calculate the severity of risk realisation for each risk type, each risk indicator is assigned a score (1–4) based on values attributed to quantitative and qualitative risk elements. To foster objectivity, weights for each risk indicator should be defined based on data source reliability, attributing higher weights to risk indicators demonstrating:

- *coverage:* dataset covering all or most of the risk categories in scope (does the data source apply to almost all or most of the risks, not just one or two?);
- *quality of matching:* dataset fitting the purpose of the exercise (how confident about the data source "fitting the purpose" can the organisation be?);
- *forward-looking view* (i.e. not historic).

Each applicable risk indicator score is multiplied with its respective adjusted weight, and all the scored weighted indicators are summed up to generate a final severity score per risk type. For adjusted indicators (such as potential loss), adjustments are scored independently on both risk and weight, and the risk indicator is re-estimated as adjusted, with a new weight average.

### 7.5.2.2 Calculation of likelihood

The second dimension for measurement of inherent risk analysis is likelihood, representing the frequency of confirmed incidents (occurred or intercepted, prevented before taking place) the financial institution experienced over a one-year time frame. Likelihood is assessed based on:

- internal and external operational risk loss data, coming from an organisation's internal loss database and/or external data consortiums (e.g. ORX), typically collected over a ten-year time frame;
- expert scenarios, serving as aggravating adjusters.

Likelihood thresholds are defined based on the maximum score across risk types, divided in quartiles: low, medium-low, medium-high and high (1–4). Metric risk scores are weighted and combined to produce the overall likelihood score.

#### 7.5.2.3 Inherent risk matrix

The combination of the assessments of severity and likelihood enables institutions to plot each non-financial risk type on an inherent risk matrix in which the value for inherent risk exposure is assessed on four level scales: low, medium-low, medium-high and high (1–4).

The overall inherent risk for each legal entity is reached by aggregating the sum of all such risks by factor, weighted according to their attributes.

The design of the inherent risk matrix represents a cornerstone in the methodology of top-down risk assessment. While there is no standard approach, the following design principles are typically followed in best practice:

- *four-tier risk rating*, in order to prevent the concentration effect on the central value (medium);
- *symmetry pursued in risk tier plotting*, to avoid miscalibration of risk exposure;
- *severity, forward-looking and industry-adjusted*, "valued" more than likelihood (e.g. "high" severity resulting in "high" inherent risk three times vs. twice for likelihood), institution-specific and backward-looking.

### 7.5.3 Measurement of internal control adequacy

Controls are programmes, policies or activities put in place by financial institutions to protect against materialisation of risks or to ensure that potential inherent risks are promptly identified. In the context of top-down risk assessments, internal control adequacy measures the ability of deployed internal controls to mitigate inherent risk and is instrumental to the residual risk evaluation. Control adequacy assessments are performed using proxies (e.g. internal audit findings, litigations or customer complaints), aimed at allowing a "synthetic" view of the effectiveness of the existing control framework.

#### 7.5.3.1 Control indicators

Control indicators are applied to each non-financial risk category, enabling comparability across risk categories. Based on market practice, controls are typically assessed via the following internally enforced or externally triggered control indicators:

- internally enforced control indicators:
  - policy enforcement
  - internal audit findings
  - internal control findings
  - training
  - IT system failures and branch outages
- externally triggered control indicators:
  - external inspections
  - litigations
  - complaints

Control indicators should be linked to measurable metrics to allow for allocation of different adequacy scores, e.g. as set out below.

Internal audit findings:

- *findings incidence:* number of findings per risk category and average severity;
- *remedial action:* number of recommended remedies and implementation progress.

Trainings capture:

- *execution:* number of trainings conducted per year per selected risk categories;
- *coverage:* target population and percentage of attendance.

IT system failure and branch outages:

- number of interruption events;
- severity of events, based on the disruption time of the event or interruption.

Customer complaints:

- *complaints incidence:* number and repetitiveness of customer complaints, per year and per risk type;
- *resolution time:* average duration of complaints resolution (in working days).

For each internal control metric, qualitative or quantitative scales are defined, which signify different levels of risk contributions: low, medium-low, medium-high and high.

#### 7.5.3.2 Weighting of control indicators

As with inherent risk factors, the response to each area under examination is assigned a score, which, when aggregated, reflects the relative strength of that control. The final score by risk type depends on the assigned weight: each area can be assigned a weighting based on the importance that the institution places on a given control. Similar to inherent risk factors, weights for internal control indicators should be anchored to data source reliability, attributing higher weight to risk indicators demonstrating:

- *coverage:* dataset covering all or most of the risk categories in scope;
- *quality of matching:* dataset fitting the purpose of the exercise;
- *link to controls.*

Practical examples:

- internal audit findings may receive higher weights, thanks to relatively good risk coverage, straightforward mapping vs. risks and intuitive links to controls;
- internal control findings may have a "medium" weight, given relatively limited coverage compared to other indicators, still straightforward mapping vs. risks and intuitive links to controls;
- complaints obtained a lower weight, due to very limited coverage of risks, poorer matching quality and no direct links to controls.

Additionally, weights can be adjusted to account for indicator applicability to risk categories. Any time an indicator is not applicable to a given risk (e.g. no complaints for money laundering risk), the respective weight is distributed to other indicators.

#### 7.5.3.3 Control rating

A risk-type-specific control framework is rated according to a pre-defined rating scale or based on qualitative factors, e.g. 'satisfactory', 'needs improvement' or 'deficient' for each control metric.

As an alternative method, based on the uniformly distributed value of complaints among all non-financial risks, it determines how much higher or lower the number of complaints matched to a risk are, compared to the uniformly distributed value.

### 7.5.4 Determination of residual risk

Once both the inherent risk and the adequacy of the internal controls have been assessed, the residual risk can be determined. Residual risk is the risk that remains after controls are applied to inherent risk. It is determined by balancing the level of inherent risk with the overall strength of the risk management activities/controls. The residual risk rating is used to indicate whether risks are being adequately managed.

In a residual risk matrix, risks are represented in homogeneous buckets, allowing risk prioritisation to drive identification of mitigating actions and required investments.[5] While there is no industry standard, best practice suggests that the following design principles should apply when establishing the residual risk matrix:

- strong controls can lower residual risk in comparison to inherent risk by one rate (one shift);
- in the presence of low or medium-low internal control adequacy, residual risk confirms the inherent risk rating (i.e. inherent risk not reduced);
- to reduce residual risk, either the inherent risk can be reduced or the controls strengthened.

Once the residual risk is computed, it is necessary to determine whether the residual risk is equal to or exceeds risk appetite.[6] With the latter, measures must be agreed upon to either reduce the inherent risk or strengthen the control environment to ensure residual risk comes back into line with risk appetite. Alternatively, it may lead to discussions as to whether the risk appetite is correctly positioned (or not). The importance of senior management's involvement is especially critical here, as a financial institution's risk appetite is a key influence on its strategic goals and drivers.

---

[5] To emphasise highest risk categories and boost risk-based prioritisation, some financial institutions adopted exponential weighting, normalising the resulting exponential score via binary logarithm: first, all risk categories scores (1–4) are converted to exponential, with a base of 2 (2–16); second, the exponential scores are averaged and the resulting score normalised to the 0–4 range through a binary logarithm; as a result, logarithmic equation provides the overall weighted risk score across risk categories.

[6] See chapter 3 for details on risk appetite frameworks.

It is a critical part of the process that roles and responsibilities are clearly defined to ensure that if risks are beyond both the appetite and the remit of the control framework, that a management procedure is then put in place.

## 7.6 Breakout: building an institution-wide internal control system

Control frameworks are a pivotal element of risk management systems in general and non-financial risk management systems in particular.

### 7.6.1 Introduction

Financial institutions face non-financial risks in almost every area of activity, from financial crime, conduct, data privacy and operations to fraud, resilience and tax. To counter increased regulatory scrutiny over the past years, institutions have invested heavily in their 2nd LoD functions and created various internal functions to mitigate risks. To a large extent, the evolving risk types have therefore been dealt with by different functions. As part of their risk management arrangements, these different and mostly independent operating functions have created their own, independently operating control systems. Based on this historical development, institutions nowadays often face the challenge of lacking a harmonised, institution-wide control framework that connects the underlying individual control systems. This leads, in consequence, to a lack of comparability between the different control systems and makes effective and efficient institution-wide risk steering difficult. To remedy the inconsistency across internal control systems, some organisations have taken the next step – creating a single institution-wide control system that spans all risk categories but retains existing risk-specific underlying structures.

### 7.6.2 Alternative path to building an internal control framework: top-down, risk-based approach

When institutions try to tackle the challenge of building an institution-wide control framework, many firms start by looking at their existing processes and controls first. This means extensively collecting existing process and control data from all LoDs and aggregating them in one control oversight document, which can then be used to build an overarching control system. While this approach has the advantage of gaining necessary buy-in and involvement from 2nd LoD functions, and leveraging their expertise and knowledge through close alignment during the data collection process, there are severe disadvantages. Data collection is a time-consuming process and can lead to an informational overflow when it is not executed in a focused and concise way, while completeness of controls cannot be guaranteed. In addition, divergent views on controls between the different functions and inconsistencies during aggregation make it difficult for senior decision makers to gain a user-friendly, comprehensive overview on the control environment. Using this control-based process to design an overarching control framework is therefore associated with high operational risk.

An alternative method for building an institution-wide control framework is to apply a top-down methodology that leverages an understanding of market standards and a detailed view of an institution's underlying business and operating model. Assuming 2nd LoD validation and buy-in, the approach is a much faster way to obtain a holistic view of the risk as well as ensure comparability across risk types and corresponding control requirements, leading to a more efficient risk management framework. This alternative approach is described in the following section.

### 7.6.3 Five-step approach: building an internal control framework

The key activities in building an internal control framework using a top-down methodology can be grouped along the following five key steps.

#### 7.6.3.1 Step 1: determination of NFR criticality

The starting point needs to be a holistic risk taxonomy, creating a comprehensive view on relevant risks categories, risk types and corresponding risk definitions.[7] "Relevant risks" are those that are inherent to the institution's business and operating model. However, institutions should take a risk-based approach when building a top-down internal control system and focus on those risks responsible for most of the underlying risk exposure, allowing them to distinguish between 'critical' and 'less critical' (but still relevant) risks. For example, critical risks could be those with medium-high and high inherent risk classifications (considering the severity and likelihood of risk materialisation). Focusing on critical risks does not mean putting non-critical risks aside, but it enables institutions to prioritise the mitigation of risk types that have the highest potential for regulatory breach, financial loss and reputational damage.

#### 7.6.3.2 Step 2: mapping of key risks to process landscape

Risks should not be assessed in an isolated manner but in the context of the process in which they potentially materialise. Hence, a mapping of critical risks (and corresponding controls) to an institution's key processes is material, both to fully understand the risk exposure and to design effective mitigating measures. The challenge many institutions face is that existing process landscapes are often heterogenous because processes have

[7] See chapter 2 for more information on non-financial risk definition and risk taxonomy.

been designed from a department-specific perspective, without a comprehensive end-to-end (E2E) view. However, an E2E perspective in the process landscape covering an institution's key processes (e.g. including bank steering, sales, key products, including credit, capital markets, payment transactions, structured finance, customer service as well as supporting activities like IT, procurement, HR) is essential to the understanding of where risk can materialise and how controls should be designed to deliver an impacting mitigation.

#### 7.6.3.3 Step 3: definition of control objectives, key controls and control repository

Once critical risks have been determined and mapped to processes, key controls need to be defined. As a starting point for the definition of control activities, control objectives should be determined. Control objectives define the required characteristics or circumstances of a process (e.g. accuracy, completeness, diligence, segregation of duties, documentation) subject to review by the control activities. Once control objectives are determined, two potential approaches are available for the definition of controls.

The common *bottom-up approach* would comprise the collection of controls, involving time-consuming interviews with 1st and 2nd LoD functions. These may lead to the creation of an initial control catalogue, but there is often variability in respect of scope and granularity or controls across risk types.

Instead, institutions can apply a *top-down approach*, defining controls based on an analysis of their business and operating models, alongside regulatory requirements and market standards. As an output of step 3, the key control repository should include a short description of the control, alongside references to the responsible 1st/2nd LoD units, the relevant processes (in the logic of the previously established E2E process map) and underlying IT applications or control documentation.

#### 7.6.3.4 Step 4: assessment of controls

In step 4, controls need to be tested against the following criteria:

- *test of implementation:* control is executed in the relevant processes in which risks can materialise;
- *test of design:* when operated properly, control is adequately designed to address the control objectives and prevent the relevant risks;
- *test of operating effectiveness:* based on testing an adequate control sample, the control is consistently operated in the designed manner and is properly documented.

The assessment exercise should be performed by or in close conjunction with the responsible 2nd LoD functions. Based on the outcome of the assessment, controls should be rated based on a pre-defined rating scale or qualitative control factors with a summary of the underlying rationale. For example:

- Control is satisfactory.
- Control needs improvement.
- Control is deficient.

Control shortcomings need to be addressed, and adequate remedial actions including action timelines should be agreed upon with the relevant 2nd LoD functions.

### 7.6.3.5 Step 5: design NFR control report

As a final step, an NFR control report should be produced. This will summarise the key results of the previous steps and enable senior stakeholders to take informed risk management decisions. The report should cover at least:

- a summary of the current risk situation (leveraging information used to determine individual risk criticality), closely linked to the results of the (top-down) risk assessment;
- descriptions of key risk indicators, including their historic evolution and potential limitations (e.g. number of high-risk customers or KYC backlogs);
- the results of the control adequacy and effectiveness assessments, based on regular 2nd LoD reviews;
- required remedial measures, including assignment of individual responsibilities, agreed timelines and status updates.

## 7.7 Approach to handling residual risk

As described at the beginning of this chapter, the main objective of a top-down risk assessment is for business and control functions to agree upon priorities for intervention, depending on the stated level of inherent risk and control adequacy.

While bottom-up risk analyses recommend deploying actions to reduce business risk exposure and mitigating gaps or deficiencies in the control environment, a top-down risk assessment may instead suggest running a bottom-up risk analysis. Following the completion of a top-down risk and control assessment exercise, and supported by an NFR control report based on a comprehensive control assessment, gaps or deficiencies in the control environment may be identified, prompting different types of actions. Based on market experience, a residual risk matrix can trigger different follow-up actions for different levels of residual risk.

### 7.7.1 High residual risk: project and investment imperative to mitigating residual risk

In this scenario, risk management, compliance or other control functions are expected to plan and perform a bottom-up risk analysis to deeply assess gaps or deficiencies in the control environment. As a result of the bottom-up risk analysis, risk owners are requested to develop rigorous action plans and trigger investments with the support of control functions. In addition, internal audit is expected to intervene with tailored audits.

### 7.7.2 Medium-high residual risk: action plan to reduce inherent risk exposure

Risk management, compliance or other control functions are expected to plan and perform a bottom-up risk analysis to assess gaps or deficiencies in the control environment. As a result of the bottom-up risk analysis, risk owners are requested to develop a rigorous action plan, with a special focus on inherent risk reduction (e.g. product limitations, high risk customers termination).

### 7.7.3 Medium-low residual risk: continuous control testing and selected action requested

Control functions are expected to keep monitoring these risks, running periodic independent testing exercises. In addition, risk management, compliance or other control functions are recommended to selectively conduct a bottom-up risk analysis, to assess gaps or deficiencies in the control environment.

### 7.7.4 Low residual risk: periodic, risk-based controls

With a risk-based approach, in a scenario in which limited risks occur, it is recommended to establish regular control adequacy checks to ensure controls are not deteriorating. Risk management, compliance or other control functions should perform a bottom-up risk analysis with tactical timing (e.g. only when new relevant regulations come into force, internal reorganisation is under way or new products are being launched). Where residual risk is low, it is recommended to simplify and streamline controls, thereby reorienting resources towards more significant risks.

The mitigating actions mentioned above need to be tracked centrally, retaining full oversight of completion. Business acceptance of residual risk is crucial as the business is best positioned to effect change to the inherent risk profile and the effectiveness of the internal control environment.

The issues identified during a top-down risk and control assessment should inform annual planning, monitoring and testing as well as management information. As such, there should be a sufficiently robust quality assurance process to check whether proposed actions appropriately address the raised issues.

Triggered actions may have a significant impact on the residual risk rating once they are completed and therefore must receive the utmost attention and support from senior management and other relevant stakeholders. It is recommended that, wherever possible, the triggered actions are remediated before the next top-down risk assessment is carried out, to assess whether the residual risk position has improved.

## 7.8 Integrated process to perform annual top-down risk and control assessment

A top-down risk and control assessment is an integrated exercise, jointly conducted by business risk owners in the 1st LoD and 2nd LoD control functions, while capturing issues identified by both parties. Unlike bottom-up risk analyses, which are performed by control functions with limited engagement of the business at most financial institutions, ownership of the top-down risk and control assessment lies with the 1st LoD, with process execution potentially delegated to control functions. This may include tasks such as methodology development, maintenance, periodic refresh process/activity initiation and record keeping of completed assessments. Given the number of stakeholders involved, top-down risk and control assessments require a structured and formalised process for annual execution in the three phases explained below.

### 7.8.1 Phase 1: pre-assessment by control functions

In the first phase, control functions prepare the stage for business engagement and execute a pre-assessment of both inherent risk and internal control adequacy to get a preliminary view of residual risk for each applicable risk category. In the pre-assessment phase, control functions gather and process relevant data (e.g. internal audit findings, customer complaints, bank-specific negative news flow) by risk category, tune the assessment scale and consolidate preliminary results. Parallel, control functions map key business stakeholders to engage in the following phases. The preparatory phase typically happens in the third quarter of the year, setting the stage for formal engagement by the business in the fourth quarter.

### 7.8.2 Phase 2: assessment by business senior management

During the assessment phase, business senior managers are involved to preview preliminary results built by control functions and suggest adjustments, based on a forward-looking business evolution. Business senior management inputs are typically collected in a plenary workshop facilitated by control functions, who are then responsible for processing proposed changes offline and providing new results.

### 7.8.3 Phase 3: validation and reporting

As the final step of an annual top-down risk and control assessment, consolidated residual risk figures are validated in the institution's risk committee. The results of the assessment, supported by an NFR control report produced based on a comprehensive control assessment, must be communicated to relevant stakeholders and business divisions, including but not limited to the group's senior management and internal audit. Regulatory and supervisory authorities should be advised as seems appropriate.

Reporting should include clear, action-oriented implications for the business, to lower inherent risk by enhancing controls, limiting certain business activities, or to adopt a risk transfer mechanism, such as insurance, where applicable. The exact action should be based on the institution's risk appetite and both should be discussed at senior levels.

The reporting should be designed so that the results can be presented in several ways, highlighting risks by any factor recorded, for example by business division or geography. In addition to providing for inherent risk scores or control environment scores, trend indicators for risk can also be used, such as a scale of increasing, stable and decreasing risks to assess the stability of risk exposure over time.

Overall, these process steps should prevent the top-down risk and control assessment from turning into a "check-the-box" exercise and keep business leaders engaged.

# 8 A Top-Down Approach to Non-Financial Risk Reporting: Collaboration Across Risk Types for Sustainable Risk Steering

*Valérie Villafranca, Dr. Georg Lienke, Florian Seiferlein, Kai Gammelin, Dr. Katharina Hefter, Norbert Gittfried*

## 8.1 Introduction: the imperative of top-down non-financial risk reporting

Financial institutions are confronted with increasing non-financial risks, both in number and severity. Moreover, they face a range of non-financial risk types, including financial crime, compliance, conduct, information & communication technology (ICT) security, data privacy, resilience, fraud, tax, and sustainability. Due to a heightened regulatory pressure, institutions have long established 2nd line of defence (LoD) functions to perform the independent risk oversight, which has led to the creation of multiple distinct responsibilities and roles. The 3rd LoD executes internal audits that encompass the activities of the 1st and 2nd LoD on a risk-based approach.

At many institutions, the proliferation of roles and responsibilities has led to heterogenous risk frameworks, including reporting mechanisms for different non-financial risks. There is a variety of bottom-up, risk-type-specific reports from different functions and often diverging criteria to measure risk. The situation makes it difficult for executive management to put risk categories into accurate proportion and derive key implications for overall risk oversight and steering.

Financial institution's risk exposures are increasingly subject to volatile environments, impacting operating models and corresponding parts of risk taxonomies. Due to the ongoing digital transformation of business and operating models, substantial parts of banks' value chains are being converted from physical to virtual performance. This conversion significantly amplifies exposure to risk types such as ICT security (including cyber) and availability risk, while it relativises non-data related areas such as physical damage risk and workplace safety.

Executive management of financial institutions is in ever stronger need of an overall non-financial risk reporting framework, spanning across risk types and consolidating the measurement of risk and the adequacy assessment of risk-mitigating measures and controls. Such a top-down report can give the executive management the fact base and the institutions further to have reporting frameworks in place covering operational risk under local capital adequacy requirements.[9]

### 8.2.4 Singapore

The Monetary Authority of Singapore (MAS) requires financial institutions to "ensure that senior management establishes a risk management system for identifying, measuring, evaluating, monitoring, reporting and controlling or mitigating risks regularly."[10] MAS expressly requires reports for specific risk types, including technology risk.[11] Under the local risk-based capital adequacy requirements, MAS requires financial institutions to

> *"ensure that there is regular and comprehensive reporting of its operational risk profile, risk exposures and loss experience to the board, senior management and business unit management, to enable them to understand, assess, monitor and control operational risk."*[12]

## 8.3 Current state of non-financial risk reporting: formats with inconsistent scopes and methodologies

Traditionally, financial institutions report non-financial risk-related information across three major channels.

### 8.3.1 Operational risk reports

The unit mandated with the quantification and steering of operational risk for the purposes of determining operational risk regulatory capital provides regular reporting (OpRisk report) to executive management, other internal stakeholders and regulators on three major items. First, the OpRisk report summarises the key outcomes of the operational risk identification and assessment process, based on the following tools used by the majority of institutions:

- *Risk and control self-assessments*, in which 1st LoD units evaluate the financial impact and likelihood of pre-defined operational risk scenarios (e.g. cyberattacks resulting in reduced availability of IT systems, flawed settlement of transactions, change in legislation adversely impacting the offering of products and services);

9 HKMA 2022b (6.2.2).
10 MAS 2024a.
11 Ibid.
12 MAS 2024b.

- *key risk indicators*, capturing risk-relevant data on pre-defined reference points, potentially limited by tolerance thresholds (e.g. business relationships with high-risk customers, number of customer complaints, overdue KYC reviews);
- *operational risk loss data* derived internally and from external loss data providers, supporting quantification of risk events based on previous internal events and industry benchmark intelligence
- *key performance indicators capturing data of outsourcing risks (provider and service).*

Second, the OpRisk report shows the current overall risk exposure for operational risk, often displayed per risk scenario and organisational unit, identifying the scenarios and units with a higher-than-average and potentially critical risk exposure.

Third, the OpRisk report highlights calculated regulatory capital for operational risk and the corresponding allocation to business divisions. The calculation technique depends on the approach selected by the financial institution (either advanced measurement approach subject to regulatory approval, basic indicator approach or standardised approach).

### 8.3.2 Additional 2$^{nd}$ LoD reports on specific non-financial risk types

Control functions with a mandate to perform 2$^{nd}$ LoD risk oversight for a specific risk type typically produce risk reports, annually, semi-annually, quarterly or, depending on the risk situation, at higher frequencies. Risk reports focus on the following:

- *results of the most recent risk assessment:* inherent and residual risk exposure and corresponding adequacy of risk-specific 1$^{st}$ and 2$^{nd}$ LoD controls, quantification of risk exposure (e.g., high, medium-high, medium-low, low);
- description of risk incidents in reporting period and corresponding mitigating measures;
- key 2$^{nd}$ LoD activities in reporting period, particularly around standard setting, risk monitoring, training and advisory;
- investigations into potential misconduct and major interactions with regulatory agencies (where applicable).

2$^{nd}$ LoD risk reports are typically addressed to, in the case of two-tier board structures, a dedicated member of the board of directors as well as to the chairman of the supervisory board and to, in case of one-tier board structures, a dedicated executive member of the board of directors as well as the chair of the risk committee.[13]

[13] Diverging reporting channels exist depending on legal entity type and jurisdictional regulatory specifics.

Although there is a trend toward consolidating $2^{nd}$ LoD risk oversight and reporting for non-financial risk, the landscape of reporting $2^{nd}$ LoD functions will continue to be heterogenous. On that note, the ECB and other regulators have clarified that compliance-related risk types (e.g. data protection) may be allocated to the compliance function but not other risk types (such as outsourcing, ICT security, business continuity). This is designed to prevent conflicts of interest and dilution of the original compliance mandate.[14] Hence, involved $2^{nd}$ LoD non-financial risk control functions will continue to be fragmented, which makes it even more important to ensure the harmonisation of underlying reporting principles across relevant risk types.

### 8.3.3 Reports on internal control system

Depending on the scope and corresponding governance of internal control systems (bank-wide and centralised versus topic- or risk-focused and decentralised) senior management receive regular reports on the adequacy of controls, potentially broken down into design adequacy and operating effectiveness. Typically, these reports are based on a pre-defined rating scale or qualitative control factors (design and operating effectiveness), e.g. 'control is satisfactory,' 'control needs improvement' or 'control is deficient' with a summary of the underlying rationale.

## 8.4 Key parameters of top-down non-financial risk reporting: methodology, required input and results

To establish top-down non-financial risk reporting as a sustainable tool for executive management, the reporting should take into account the full list of risk types that are relevant to the operating model, apply a consistent methodology to evaluate risk and controls and generate actionable output.

The top-down approach to non-financial risk reporting described in this chapter follows a three-step approach:

- identification and evaluation of key risk indicators;
- assessment of controls as risk-mitigating measures;
- determination of residual risk and required risk-mitigating actions.

[14] ECB 2020b.

The operational risk department, the 2nd LoD non-financial risk control functions and the unit(s) mandated with operating internal control systems should be closely integrated in all three steps.

### 8.4.1 Identification and evaluation of key risk indicators

Key risk indicators (KRI) are at the heart of top-down non-financial risk reporting. KRIs indicate how risky an activity is and provide early signals of increasing risk exposures in various areas of a financial institution.

#### 8.4.1.1 Determination of key risk indicators, thresholds and potential input sources

For each non-financial risk type, KRIs should be defined in a three-step approach described below. In most cases, the necessary information and data to perform these steps can be found in the risk reports referred to in section 8.3 above or retrieved directly from the relevant 2nd LoD control functions.

##### 8.4.1.1.1 Step 1: understand risk factors

In step 1, financial institutions need to understand how non-financial risks materialise, i.e. which factors and root-causes need to occur in their market and back-office operations.

##### 8.4.1.1.2 Step 2: identify key risk indicators

Once it is clear how risks materialise, institutions need to identify the drivers, i.e. KRI's behind the risk factors.[15] To the degree possible, the NFR report should integrate KRI's already established, e.g. in the context of the identification and evaluation of operational risk.

##### 8.4.1.1.3 Step 3: derive institution-specific thresholds

Once key risk indicators have been identified, it is essential to define indicator-specific thresholds. This definition should include the senior management's risk appetite and budgeting of risks. Thresholds represent the volume of a given risk-generating activity, either pending on a specific date or performed in a specific period. Thresholds can be

[15] For more technical details on the determination of KRIs see chapter 3 on risk appetite frameworks.

expressed in absolute numbers or as percentages of underlying business volumes. Where adequate, three levels of thresholds should be defined, with respective degrees of consequences and action plans in case of breaches, unless regulatory requirements explicitly call for zero tolerance.

The 'target' threshold determines the optimal (green) level of risk and should be set based on the risk that the institution is willing to accept under business-as-usual conditions and in line with overall risk appetite (e.g. target threshold for financial crime high-risk customers is set at less than or equal to 6% of the total customer population). No dedicated, additional remedial action is required if business volumes stay within target thresholds.[16]

'Caution' thresholds describe heightened (yellow) but generally still acceptable risk levels, triggering the implementation of predefined mitigating measures and dedicated management reporting (e.g. caution thresholds for high-risk customers are set at more than 6% and at less than or equal to 10% of the total customer population).

'Limit' thresholds describe the level of risk the institution is no longer willing to accept (red) and represent the highest escalation level, requiring more stringent and concrete consequential action (e.g. management reporting, more frequent tracking, intensification of controls) within a specified timeline (e.g. limit threshold for high-risk customers is set at more than 10%).[17]

#### 8.4.1.2 Example KRI's: financial crime risk, outsourcing risk and human resources risk

The following sections provide examples of KRI's for financial crime risk, outsourcing risk and human resources risk.[18] These examples would need to be adjusted to an institution's risk profile to fully address the specifics of an individual business and operating model.

[16] Enhanced monitoring of high-risk customers is required in the normal course of business.

[17] For more details on the calibration of KRI thresholds see chapter 3.

[18] Including money laundering, financial sanctions violations, fraud as well as bribery and corruption.

#### 8.4.1.2.1 Key risk indicators for financial crime risk

The following key risk indicators for financial crime risk are structured along five risk factors.

Table 1: Financial crime risk key risk indicators

| Financial crime risk factors | Key risk indicators |
|---|---|
| 1. Customers associated with illicit funds or subject to financial sanctions | • high money laundering risk business relationships (PEP, high-risk industry and jurisdiction, adverse media, other)<br>• (potential) customers subject to financial sanctions:<br>  • onboarding aborted due to identified/suspected sanction hit<br>  • customer relationship terminated due to identified/suspected sanction hit<br>• overdue KYC checks<br>  • onboarding of new customers<br>  • risk-based review of existing customers |
| 2. Correspondent banks with inadequate safeguards against financial crime | • business relationships with correspondent banks<br>  • volume overall<br>  • with high-risk profile e.g. registered in high-risk jurisdictions<br>• overdue due diligence on correspondent bank relationships |
| 3. Transactions associated with illicit funds or subject to financial sanctions | • indications of potential money laundering (ex-powst transaction monitoring):<br>  • cases incl. overdue cases requiring deeper analysis<br>  • suspicious transaction reports filed<br>• transactions involving sanctioned individuals/entities (real-time sanction payment filtering):<br>  • cases incl. overdue cases requiring deeper analysis<br>  • transactions aborted |
| 4. Fraud, bribery and corruption | • allegations raised via whistleblowing channel, 2nd/3rd LoD, external auditor<br>• formal inquiries by regulators, prosecutors, other agencies<br>• detections according to the internal control system |
| 5. Staff with inadequate risk awareness | • insufficient participation in trainings<br>• individual violations of rules and guidelines |

### 8.4.1.2.2 Key risk indicators for outsourcing risk

The following key risk indicators for outsourcing risk are structured along four risk factors.

Table 2: Outsourcing risk key risk indicators

| Outsourcing risk factors | Key risk indicators |
|---|---|
| 1. Inadequate outsourcing dependency | • volume of outsourcings in relation to overall business activity<br>  • number of intra-group outsourcings<br>  • number of outsourcings to external service providers<br>• volume of outsourcings of critical business activities<br>• concentration risks (provider, service)<br>• incomplete contractual obligations (e.g., service level, regulation, control rights, key performance indicators, exit strategies) |
| 2. Service providers with critical risk profiles | • service providers with high-risk status<br>  • service providers with multiple outsourcings<br>  • service providers with sub-outsourcings<br>• service providers with medium/medium-high risk status (e.g., adverse media results, information & communication technology, financial stability)<br>• overdue risk assessments incl. reviews of service providers<br>• problematic location of the service provider and service provided (e.g., data protection, sustainability, geopolitics) |
| 3. Inadequate service provision | • service providers with insufficient performance balance<br>  • non-performance<br>  • delay in service provision<br>  • poor performance and incidents<br>• service providers with insufficient licensing/registration status |
| 4. Ineffective outsourcing governance | • lack of selection process (provider, service)<br>• incomplete documentation in institution's outsourcing register<br>• inadequate operational and organizational structure, fluctuation rate in service providers |

#### 8.4.1.2.3 Key risk indicators for human resources risk

The following key risk indicators for human resources risk are structured along five risk factors.

Table 3: Human resources risk key risk indicators

| Human resources risk factors | Key risk indicators |
|---|---|
| 1. Shortage of skilled workforce | • extended vacancy in critical positions despite substantial hiring efforts |
| 2. Inadequate staff fluctuation | • volume of employee terminations in critical areas and key roles<br>• frequency of staff entries and subsequent exits |
| 3. Critical temporary staff dropouts | • staff absence due to medical indications<br>• staff absence due to pandemic |
| 4. Dependence on critical employees | • significant overdependence on individuals in steering or day-to-day operations<br>• volume of undocumented expertise, intellectual property critical for operations |
| 5. Underperforming workforce | • negative performance evaluations |

### 8.4.1.3 Evaluation of key risk indicators

The evaluation of KRI's identifies potential breaches of target, caution or limit thresholds in the reporting period (Figure 1).[19] While the frequency of the NFR report dictates how often key risk indicators need to be evaluated, the necessary data can be found in the risk reports referred to in section 8.3 above or needs to be retrieved directly from the relevant 2nd LoD control functions. The evaluation should be performed in a cascaded approach. First, individual KRI's are evaluated by capturing relevant volumes of (business) activity, e.g. from the 1st LoD to determine whether any corresponding thresholds have been breached (target, caution or limit).

Second, individual KRI evaluations should be aggregated for a consolidated risk evaluation of the overarching risk factor, often bundling a selection of key risk indicators. Two options are available for the determination of the aggregated risk factor evaluation. In the first option, the most severe KRI evaluation dictates the overall risk factor evaluation ('highest of' approach) as individual KRI's within risk factors are closely interlinked and impact each other. In the second, more differentiated option the aggregated risk factor

[19] Please refer to chapter 3 for guidance on immediate (during the year) escalation procedures in case of breaches of KRI thresholds.

evaluation is determined based on the arithmetic mean of the underlying risk indicator evaluations (target: 1; caution: 2; limit: 3), with the following spreads for the risk factor evaluation:

- target: 1–1.6
- caution: 1.7–2.3
- limit: 2.4–3

Finally, risk evaluations for all risk factors are cumulated to derive a consolidated risk evaluation for the overarching risk type. Again, the two options described above are available to determine the risk type evaluation. Yet, to cater for a differentiated risk assessment, it is recommended to deploy the second option (arithmetic mean), as risk factors are not as closely interlinked as risk indicators but represent different focus areas under a risk type.

Where adequate, the second option (arithmetic mean) to derive a risk evaluation for key risk indicators or risk factors can be adjusted by applying a risk-based weighting approach. Under that approach, specific key risk indicators or risk factors are given more weight (e.g. by factor 1.5 or 2) compared to their peers, resulting in an overall risk evaluation tending more towards the weighted components. Such an approach helps highlight areas of specific concern in need of more scrutiny and attention to mitigate risk going forward.

Figure 1: Evaluation of key risk indicators

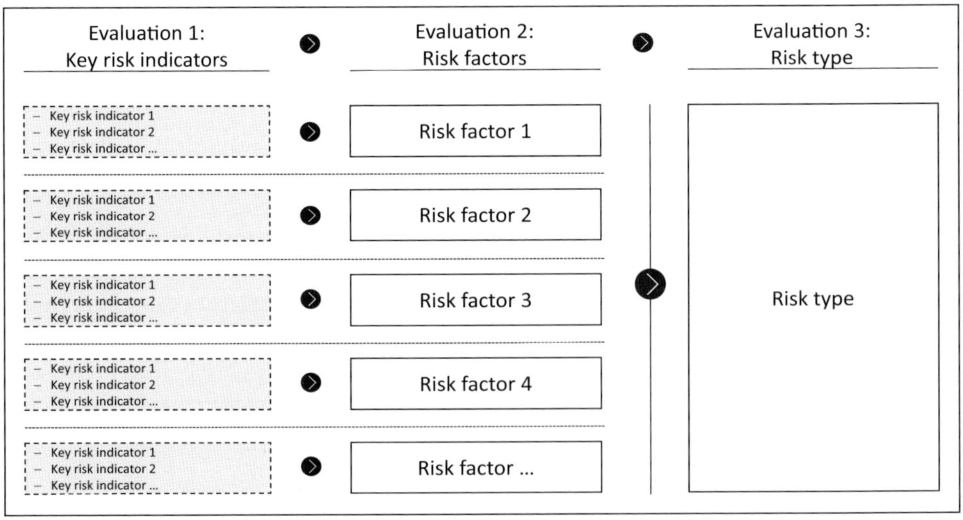

### 8.4.2 Assessment of key controls as risk-mitigating measures

The assessment of key controls is performed along the two following steps.

#### 8.4.2.1 Step 1: capturing and allocation of controls

In a first step, existing key controls in non-financial risk types need to be captured and allocated to KRI's and risk factors respectively. A structured approach is essential to derive further risk-mitigating actions along risk factors and KRI's further down the process. Relevant data and information required for this step should come from the responsible 2nd LoD functions, including from risk reports prepared by them.

Table 4: Examples of key controls to mitigate financial crime risk

| Financial crime risk factors | Key controls |
|---|---|
| 1. Overall risk exposure | • financial crime risk assessment<br>• 2nd LoD AML officer with mandate to perform financial crime risk oversight<br>• internal audits on effectiveness of financial crime risk prevention framework |
| 2. Customers associated with illicit funds or subject to financial sanctions | • risk-based customer due diligence (CDD), incl. explicit sign-offs/approvals for high-risk customers:<br>  • CDD onboarding process: new customers<br>  • CDD review process: existing customer base<br>• sanctions name screening procedure:<br>  • onboarding of new customers<br>  • daily screening of existing customer base |
| 3. Correspondent banking | • risk-based due diligence on correspondent banks focusing on financial crime controls:<br>  • onboarding of new correspondent banks<br>  • regular review of existing correspondent banks |

| Financial crime risk factors | Key controls |
|---|---|
| 4. Transactions associated with illicit funds or subject to financial sanctions | • money laundering transaction monitoring to identify financial crime indicators/ cases:<br>• screening of alerts automatically generated<br>• assessm<br>• ent of cases by analysts requiring deeper analysis<br>• filing of suspicious transaction reports where required and exiting of corresponding customers<br>• sanctions payment filtering to identify transactions involving sanctioned individuals/entities:<br>• screening of alerts automatically generated<br>• assessment of cases by analysts requiring deeper analysis<br>• aborting transactions where required and exiting of corresponding customers |
| 5. Fraud, bribery and corruption | • four-eye principle, segregation of duties, validations etc. in procurement, payment, trading and settlement processes<br>• business partner due diligence<br>• whistleblowing channel |
| 6. Staff with inadequate risk awareness | • policies, procedures on financial crime risk<br>• training on financial crime risk incl. tracking and sanctioning of non-participation |

### 8.4.2.2 Step 2: assessment of controls

As a second step, controls need to be assessed against three key criteria:

- *existence:* control is implemented;
- *design:* when operated properly, control is adequately designed to address and prevent the relevant risks;
- *operating effectiveness:* based on testing of a control sample, control is operating in the intended manner, consistently and is properly documented.

The assessment exercise should be performed by, or in close conjunction with, the responsible 2$^{nd}$ LoD functions, and supported by the OpRisk department. Based on the assessment outcome, controls need to be rated according to a pre-defined rating scale or qualitative control factors with a summary of the underlying rationale. These may be:

- Control is satisfactory.
- Control needs improvement.
- Control is deficient.

After individual controls have been assessed, the ratings should be aggregated on a risk factor level. Two options are available for the determination of the aggregated control adequacy assessment on a risk factor level. The first option applies the 'highest of' approach, whereby the aggregated assessment is dictated by the most severe individual control assessment. In the second option, the aggregated control adequacy assessment is determined based on the arithmetic mean of the underlying control evaluations (satisfactory: 1; needs improvement: 2; deficient: 3), with the following spreads for the aggregated control assessment on risk factor level:

- Satisfactory: 1–1.6
- Needs improvement: 1.7–2.3
- Deficient: 2.4–3.0

Finally, control adequacy assessments of risk factors should be aggregated on risk type level, applying one of the two options described above (Figure 2). It is recommended to deploy the second option (arithmetic mean) to allow for a differentiated representation of control qualities across a number of risk factors. Control adequacy assessments applying the second option (arithmetic mean) can be adjusted by applying a risk-based weighting approach, i.e., giving controls for specific risk factors more weight compared to their peers.[20]

Figure 2: Control assessment on aggregated levels

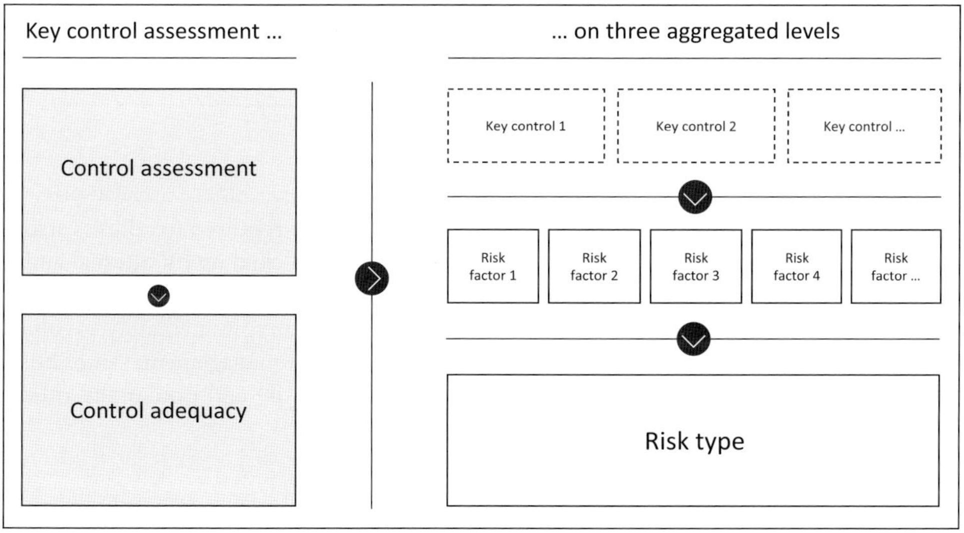


[20] Risk-based weighting approach to key risk indicators and controls should be aligned.

### 8.4.3 Determination of residual risk and required risk-mitigating actions

In a final step, further action needs to be determined based on the level of residual risk, derived from a combination of the risk level and control adequacy (Figure 3). Depending on the intended use and audience, residual risk can be demonstrated on the level of individual key risk indicators, risk factors or risk types.

Figure 3: Representation of residual risk levels

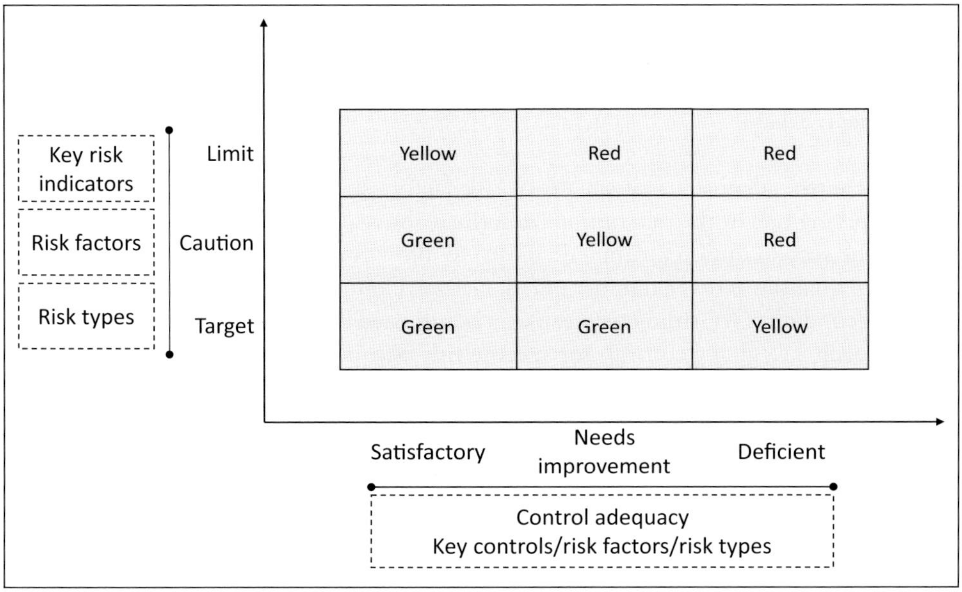


#### 8.4.3.1 High level of residual risk

In case of red (i.e. high) residual risk, substantial measures are required to address structural deficits. If not already the case, deficits are likely to be picked up by internal audit, the external auditor or even regulators – resulting in remediation pressure. Due to the remediation's impact and the potential risk of regulatory scrutiny, immediately involved stakeholders should include a responsible member of executive management, senior business and/or back office representatives of the 1st LoD, 2nd LoD and potentially others (e.g. internal audit).

#### 8.4.3.2 Medium level of residual risk

Residual risk on yellow (i.e. medium) level is somewhat less urgent but still requires full attention. Depending on the individual situation, remedial measures should focus on a further reduction of the underlying risk-generating (business) activity (e.g. suspending the onboarding of high-risk customers or the outsourcing to external service providers), vacant positions in risk critical areas or the strengthening of existing controls.

#### 8.4.3.3 Low level of residual risk

A low level of residual risk should not trigger mitigating measures. Instead, the responsible $2^{nd}$ LoD control function should monitor the situation. It must be noted that only medium and low inherent risks can result in low residual risk. High inherent risks, regardless of control adequacy, should not qualify for low residual risk.

## 8.5 Reporting process and governance

To cater for effective and efficient NFR reporting, sound governance and reporting arrangements need to be in place.

### 8.5.1 Governance arrangements

The following roles and corresponding responsibilities should be defined to cover key activities in the context of NFR reporting.

#### 8.5.1.1 Board of directors

The NFR report is primarily addressed to the board of directors,[21] which should take note of the results and, where appropriate, decide on risk steering measures required to mitigate non-financial risk exposures.

#### 8.5.1.2 Chairman of the supervisory board

The NFR report is also addressed to the chairman of the supervisory board, who needs to monitor whether the measures initiated by the board of directors based on the NFR report are adequate, effective and sufficient, or if any additional steps are required.[22]

---

[21] All members of board of directors in two-tier board structures, executive members of board of directors in one-tier board structures.

[22] In one-tier board structures, the NFR report is typically addressed to the chair of the risk committee.

### 8.5.1.3 Central reporting unit

An existing or newly-created unit should take over the role of central reporting unit and be responsible for the following key reporting tasks:

- consolidation of NFR data provided by 2nd LoD and other functions;
- quality assurance of NFR data;
- drafting of NFR report;
- communication with senior stakeholders regarding NFR reporting;
- overall coordination of reporting process.

### 8.5.1.4 2nd LoD control functions

2nd LoD control functions should assume the following responsibilities in the context of NFR reporting:

- gathering, consolidation and quality assurance of required information from 1st LoD units;
- provision of NFR data to central reporting unit;
- monitoring and documentation of risk-mitigating actions.

### 8.5.1.5 Operational risk department

The operational risk department (mandated with the quantification and steering of operational risk for purposes of determining operational risk regulatory capital) should have the following responsibilities in the context of NFR reporting:

- plausibility and consistency check across NFR and operational risk reports;
- where applicable, consideration of information from NFR report in operational risk steering.

## 8.5.2 Reporting process

Ideally, the NFR reporting process should be structured along the following key steps:

- based on the full scope of data provided by the 2nd LoD, the central reporting unit performs quality assurance, drafts the NFR report and forwards the report to the operational risk department and 2nd LoD functions;

- the operational risk department performs a plausibility and consistency check across the draft NFR report and the operational risk report to ensure key measures and messages are aligned and potential contradictions are eliminated. Upon feedback from the operational risk department and 2nd LoD functions, the central reporting unit makes any necessary modifications and produces a final draft version;
- once the NFR report is finalised, the central reporting unit provides it to the board of directors and the chairman of the supervisory board. Based on the report's outcomes, the board of directors decides on any required risk steering or mitigating measures.

## 8.6 Conclusion

Without a top-down approach to non-financial risk reporting, executive management faces an ever larger challenge across a variety of non-financial risks. Risk reports from different functions with diverging methodologies delivering outputs in different formats make sustainable risk steering difficult. Still, much of what is needed to set up a consistent approach to top-down non-financial risk reporting is already there in most institutions: a deep understanding of risk drivers and controls along non-financial risk types in 2nd LoD control functions, expertise on the quantification and steering of operational risk, including 1st LoD risk and control self-assessments focusing on a variety of risk scenarios and, finally, know-how around (bank-wide or topic-focused) internal control systems. Still, currently many of these efforts are operated in parallel and potential insights and synergies are lost across silos.

A top-down approach eliminates the downsides of the silo-approach by harmonising underlying methodologies and joining efforts across involved stakeholders from the 1st and 2nd LoD, including the operational risk department. The created value gives the executive management the tools for sustainable steering of non-financial risk. These include transparency across risk types, consistent results on risk exposure and control adequacy as well as a harmonised view of further required measures to mitigate residual risk in different risk categories. To improve their resilience to non-financial risk, financial institutions need to establish top-down non-financial risk reporting on top of existing, risk-specific reporting formats.

# 9 Internal Investigations into Corporate Misconduct: Applying an Investigative Approach to Enable Proactive Risk Oversight

*Lora von Ploetz, Florian Seiferlein*

## 9.1 Introduction

To effectively combat corporate crimes, the EU has moved towards harmonisation of European corporate law with that of the US and UK over recent years. Still, harmonisation of factors such as legal scope, criminal offences and liabilities, following minimum compliance requirements, is only half the story. Companies also need to take concrete steps to prevent violations and crimes. This includes establishing comprehensive compliance and risk management programmes, investigating incidents and proactively reporting to authorities and regulators.

While quite a few European countries like France have a well-established corporate criminal liability, others like Germany still have not yet enacted a dedicated corporate criminal liability law, such as the proposed Corporate Sanctions Act ("VerSanG"). While the draft legislation aimed to introduce significant changes– including full corporate liability, fines of up to 10% of annual revenues for intentional misconduct, and incentives for internal compliance programs[1] – these provisions have not been adopted into law, while the EU is continuously pushing toward a greater consistency.

With these factors in mind, investigative assessments become a crucial element of effective risk management across different non-financial risks. This chapter focuses on proactive investigations to detect and evaluate relevant incidents for insights on risk exposure and adequate risk oversight. It will also touch on investigations of employee misconduct, which may be required as a result of investigative assessments.

Proactive investigations cover more than just the detection and interception of financial crime. They are relevant for all cases in which inadequate conduct by external and internal parties puts the company at risk of prosecution and regulatory scrutiny, including potential data protection violations, cyber security incidents or outsourcing irregularities.[2] External expectations for the proactive identification of relevant incidents and

[1] BMJ 2020; Bundesregierung 2021.

[2] Europol 2017.

assessment sophistication are rising, and hence intelligence-led approaches are becoming a standard across the industry. An intelligence-led or contextual assessment requires companies to use enhanced knowledge of the threat and context to direct operational resources into the highest priority areas.[3]

The following sections will cover selective insights on legal and regulatory requirements, a concept for proactive risk oversight using an intelligence-led investigative approach as well as key lessons learned, success factors and common pitfalls.

## 9.2 Selected laws, regulations and standards

As part of proactive risk oversight, more regulators, authorities and standard setters expect institutions to put effective measures in place to proactively identify high-risk incidents, to perform structured investigations and to respond adequately to violations and deficiencies, including disclosure and reporting to law enforcement, regulators and other stakeholders.

The new ISO standard 37301, outlining requirements for compliance management systems, says that an "organization shall develop, establish, implement and maintain processes to assess, evaluate, investigate and close reports on suspected or actual instances of non-compliance."[4] A similar requirement was defined in the recently updated US Department of Justice guidance on the evaluation of corporate compliance programs. According to the guidance, compliance program reviews should "[...] evaluate the quality of a company's internal investigation [by looking whether the organization] has established corporate governance mechanisms that can effectively detect and prevent misconduct."[5]

Legislation increasingly expects institutions to put proactive mechanisms in place to assess potential wrongdoings. For instance, the draft German Corporate Sanctions Act will provide courts with the right to reduce fines and mitigate the imposed sanction, only if the enterprise carried out a "substantial contribution to the clarification" in the context of its internal investigation.[6]

[3] Ibid.

[4] ISO 2020, 15.

[5] DOJ 2020, 6.

[6] Bundesregierung 2020, 14.

Related laws, regulations and standards very often have in common that they require companies to disclose relevant incidents and expect close cooperation and structured as well as sometimes independent assessments. On the cooperation prerequisite, investigations need to be performed to detect, defer, prevent and dissolve such incidents, and to be in a position to report relevant misconduct. For instance, the US Foreign Corrupt Practices Act (FCPA) supports the detection of misconduct and requires companies to report specific instances of misconduct.[7] Obviously, to make an accurate report of misconduct, management will need to conduct an investigation into alleged wrongdoings. Agencies such as the Securities and Exchange Commission require accurate financial reporting by the companies they oversee, and have the power to impose penalties for reports that are inaccurate or omit facts that could affect the accuracy of the reported information.[8] An investigation can ensure that all relevant facts are known and reported.[9]

This connects the two very important steps: investigation and cooperation. Still, not every investigation requires voluntary self-disclosure and reporting. Obviously, cooperation and openness are a natural ambition and undisputable, where legally required. However, not all incidents are necessarily required to be reported. Companies need to evaluate the pros and cons of conducting an investigation and disclosing the results.

Companies may be faced with criminal or civil liability, administrative fines and reputational damage if misconduct becomes public knowledge. History shows that noncompliant business conduct may also have a significant negative impact on a company's financial capabilities and business prospects. Internal investigations provide external investigators with additional evidence. An internal investigation may also result in discovery of misconduct beyond the scope of the initial allegations or evidence of wrongdoing, while the credibility of an investigation may suffer if relevant leads are not pursued. To the extent that apparently unrelated misconduct is identified, a thorough assessment should be undertaken to determine whether it should be included in the scope of the investigation.[10] Furthermore, ensuring adequate investigations may result in costs, expenses and potential business disruptions.[11]

7 ACFE 2017, 5.

8 Harvard Law School Forum 2016.

9 ACFE 2017, 2.

10 Bicker et al. 2021.

11 ACFE 2017, 7.

Still, investigations provide companies with the opportunity to understand their risk exposures, recover losses when misconduct occurs, and close control gaps to prevent systemic recurrence. Furthermore, legal duties and requirements may outweigh a company's desire to ignore offences.[12]

### 9.2.1 Supervisory sanction relief based on voluntary investigation and cooperation

Very often, companies are rewarded for effective cooperation, with reduced sanctions or even complete avoidance of enforcement actions. In addition, self-driven investigations may ringfence liability, financial and reputational risks.[13] Both the US SEC and DOJ consider a corporation's willingness to undertake and voluntarily disclose the results of a properly conducted internal investigation when imposing civil or criminal penalties. The government welcomes internal investigations and self-disclosure, and it sees it as part of effective cooperation because it preserves enforcement resources.[14] By contrast, failure to investigate reported wrongdoing or to respond effectively to red flags can bolster the case for imposing a penalty.[15]

In general, one can distinguish between three scenarios: (1) a legal framework provides option to reduce sanctions and enforcement actions due to effective investigation and cooperation by companies, (2) a legal framework does not explicitly provide a bonus for self-disclosure and cooperation, but it is common practice, and (3) a company's investigation and cooperation does not change the assessment of law enforcement agencies and regulators.

The following paragraphs provide a non-exhaustive view into corporate criminal laws of selected countries, outlining the incentives for investing in compliance programmes and risk management as well as investigation capabilities and proactive cooperation.

---

[12] Ibid.

[13] Bicker et al. 2021.

[14] Missal et al. 2010, 7; see also U.S. Securities Exchange Commission 2001: factors in the decision to forego an enforcement action include hiring outside counsel to conduct a thorough inquiry, dismissing employees for proven wrongdoing. producing the details of its internal investigation to the SEC (including notes and transcripts) and choosing not to invoke the attorney-client privilege, work product protection or other privileges.

[15] Missal et al. 2010, 7.

#### 9.2.1.1 Jurisdictions potentially reducing sanctions and enforcement actions due to effective investigation and cooperation

The following jurisdictions provide options to reduce sanctions and enforcement actions due to effective investigation and cooperation by companies:

- **USA:** investigations and cooperation are taken into account in fine calculation and other sanctions so that, for instance, the Department of Justice can end the investigation based on sufficient insights or enter into a non-prosecution agreement (NPA) or a deferred prosecution agreement (DPA), in which criminal charges are filed along with an agreement that the charges will be dismissed within a specified period if the company fulfils the DPA's requirements. If the company refuses to enter any such agreements, it can plead guilty or take the matter to trial. A guilty plea, an NPA and a DPA typically require the company to admit wrongdoing or to accept the government's statement of facts.[16]
- **UK:** a similar situation exists in the UK, where there are four options, which are also influenced by the company's willingness to cooperate: (1) no further actions, (2) DPA, which requires cooperation and proving compliance improvements, (3) prosecution and guilty plea or (4) prosecution and conviction or acquittal by jury.[17]
- **Germany:** national legislation draft in Germany can provide companies with a reduction in fines of up to 50% for effective investigation and cooperation according to the well-defined criteria. Considering that penalties can be as much as 10% of the average annual turnover, investigation and proactive cooperation may seem appealing.[18] It is, however, noteworthy that this draft has been discussed for a couple of years and was not explicitly part of the newly elected government's roadmap.
- **France:** Sapin-II (anti-corruption law) allows corporate entities to obtain termination of the criminal prosecution in exchange for a fine, which could amount to up to 30% of the company's annual turnover, the implementation of a compliance programme under the supervision of the Agence Française Anticorruption for a period of three years and the compensation of the loss incurred by the potential victim of the offence within one year.[19]
- **Austria:** the Verbandsverantwortlichkeitsgesetz (VbVG) entered into force on 1 January 2006. The law governs the prerequisites under which entities may be held liable for criminal offences, as well as proceedings and possible sanctions. There is no legal

[16] Cravath, Swaine & Moore LLP 2020.

[17] Ibid.

[18] Bundesregierung 2021.

[19] Lasry et al. s.a.

provision establishing the type of compliance model to be adopted in Austrian law. However, effective compliance models may provide two mitigating factors in case of prosecution: (1) compliance models that have been introduced by a company before the criminal offence can reduce the sanctions, if preventive measures were established; (2) introduction and maintenance of a proper compliance model after the commission of a criminal offence will also constitute a mitigating factor.[20]

- **Netherlands:** a new policy on self-disclosure and cooperation was introduced, wherein self-disclosure can result in a fine reduction of up to 25% and cooperation may qualify for an additional fine reduction of up to 25%.[21] Although there is no prosecution or liability exemption due to the existence – and implementation – of a compliance programme under Dutch criminal law, such a programme may reduce the risk of exposure to criminal behaviour and/or mitigate the severity of a possible sanction.[22]

### 9.2.1.2 Jurisdictions not explicitly providing a bonus for self-disclosure and cooperation

The following jurisdictions do not explicitly provide a bonus for self-disclosure and cooperation, but it can be seen as common practice:

- **Switzerland:** since the Swiss Criminal Code (SCC) creates a direct link between corporate criminal liability and the company's lack of organisation, companies may potentially mitigate their criminal liability, if they adopt an effective compliance programme, despite the fact that SCC does not officially admit such programme as mitigating circumstances of criminal liability. In practice, leniency is achieved by an unreserved and truthful cooperation during the entire investigation and prosecution of the offence, including producing all requested documents, assisting in the analysis of the incriminated acts, providing for the possibility of interviewing all relevant employees, repairing – to the extent possible – any harm caused and voluntarily disclosing or confessing to any committed offences.[23]
- **Italy:** under Italian law, there is no formal mechanism for corporations to cooperate with the investigation or to disclose violations in exchange for reduced penalties. However, a certain degree of cooperation with prosecuting authorities in terms of removal of the concerned officers or members, responsible implementation of compli-

[20] RIS 2005; Petsche/Krakow s.a.

[21] Mondaq 2024.

[22] Dutch Criminal Code and the Economic Offenses Act (EOA); van den Berg s.a.

[23] Swiss Criminal Code (SCC), Criminal Administrative Code (CAC), Financial Market Supervision Act (FMSA); Gautier s.a.

ance programmes aimed at preventing the same types of offences and compensation for damage, can have a significant impact on pre-trial and final sanctions.[24]

#### 9.2.1.3 Jurisdictions where investigations and cooperation do not change assessment of law enforcement

Finally, in the following jurisdictions investigations and cooperation does not change the assessment of law enforcement agencies and regulators:

- **Luxembourg:** Luxembourg introduced the concept of corporate criminal liability in 2010. However, it does not allow a legal entity to benefit from an exemption from liability for implementing an effective compliance function and provides specific provisions for settling proceedings with a plea bargain.[25]
- **Sweden:** Swedish criminal law is built on the idea of personal criminal liability and only private individuals are considered capable thereof. A corporation cannot commit a criminal act and therefore it cannot be liable to criminal sanctions. This is in line with concepts that are currently established in Germany.[26]
- **Belgium:** Belgian criminal law does not provide for measures or models of prevention of corporate liability. In addition, Belgium does not have a leniency programme for corporates or any other formalised incentive to report violations and cooperate with prosecutors. The corporation can establish mitigating circumstances (e.g. proper internal control systems) that the judge can take into account when determining the sentence. However, the judge is not under any obligation to take these circumstances into account.[27]

### 9.2.2 Statutory disclosure requirements

On top of investigations as a form of cooperation to reduce potential fines, companies are required to fulfil certain statutory disclosure requirements (e.g. civil law duties to a company and its stakeholders) as well as monitoring and public reporting statutes, which require minimum transparency. Non-compliance may result in penalties. For instance, the American Sarbanes-Oxley Act requires companies to establish audit committees with the mandate to investigate complaints of financial fraud involving auditing, accounting or

---

[24] Legislative Decree No. 231, 8 June 2001 ("Law 231"); Studio Legale Pisano s.a.

[25] Law of 3 March 2010 ("2010 Law"); Findling/Schmitt s.a.

[26] Swedish Criminal Code and Swedish Companies Act; Hedwall s.a.

[27] The Act of 4 May 1999, Belgian Criminal Code, Belgian Code on Company and Associations (2019); Gutermann/De Winter s.a.

internal control issues.[28] Other statutes require companies to monitor themselves, file accurate reports and statements as well as keep accurate records (e.g. Anti-Money Laundering regulations). Investigations are sometimes the only way to create the necessary transparency to fulfil these disclosure and reporting requirements. A lack of transparency and ignoring well-known weaknesses to fulfil these requirements may lead to liability risk, as cases have shown previously.[29]

Without a proactive risk oversight in the form of investigation of relevant incidents, companies are left with white spots on their risk exposures and are not necessarily in a position to make informed decisions enabling them to meet law enforcement and regulators' expectations on cooperation as well as on disclosure and reporting requirements.

### 9.2.3 Investigation standards and requirements

The regulatory and criminal investigations become increasingly global and the cross-border data sharing prohibition and privacy issues are more critical than ever, especially given the data privacy laws worldwide. Depending on local legislation and scenarios, certain investigation standards and requirements need to be evaluated and followed during assessments:

- **Data privacy**: data privacy and data protection laws restrict investigations relating to personal data. Inclusion of personal data is only possible when the law allows it and the company's interest prevails.[30] Internal investigations must be conducted in compliance with the applicable laws (e.g. General Data Protection Regulation requirements in Europe) and documented appropriately.[31]
- **Information sharing:** another key aspect is the sharing of information in the company and, in particular, cross-border to achieve a true and fair view of the exposure. If the respective statutory law allows for it, companies may even share information outside the company.[32]
- **Attorney–client privilege:** when investigations are started by law enforcement, it can be of particular interest whether investigation documentation can be seized based on the provisions of the national criminal procedure code and case law.[33]

---

[28] Sarbanes-Oxley Act of 2002; Donaldson 2003.

[29] ACFE 2017, 5.

[30] Alford et al. 2020.

[31] Bicker et al. 2021.

[32] Your Europe 2021.

[33] Schürrle et al. 2020.

- **Employee misconduct suspicion**: depending on local laws, employees may have the right not to incriminate themselves. However, this may contradict the company's ambition for effective cooperation with authorities. There are several measures intended to encourage employees to cooperate during an investigation, in particular amnesty or leniency programmes. These include the waiver of employment law measures, the waiver of assertion of claims for damages and the assumption of the costs for the employee's legal counsel and a guarantee of confidentiality. On the other hand, it is impossible to protect employees against potential investigations by public authorities.[34]

## 9.3 Concept for proactive risk oversight using an investigative approach

To proactively identify various risks, companies can implement a risk oversight framework based on assessments that highlight cases requiring thorough or independent investigations. In particular, a legitimate interest exists in conducting internal investigations when there is a risk or suspicion of violations of laws that carry criminal or financial penalties. Internal investigations are intended primarily to detect, stop and prepare for the sanction of misconduct and are aimed at enabling the company's officers to make informed decisions for the benefit of the company, its employees and its customers. They are also necessary to avoid liability on the part of senior management.[35]

While misconduct or a cyber incident may occur in one jurisdiction, the relevant data may be held, collected or reviewed in several other locations. With so many countries potentially involved, multi-jurisdictional legal requirements, as well as country-specific company policies and procedures for the processing, review and collection of data, need to be considered carefully at the beginning of any investigation.[36] The GDPR requires financial institutions, when processing personal data, to inform data subjects about the ways in which their data will be processed by way of a privacy notice. Article 6 of the GDPR states that banks must rely on a lawful basis to process personal data.

In order to detect different risks proactively, such as financial crime events, information security threats or other non-financial risks on a global level, companies should appoint

[34] Bicker et al. 2021.

[35] The Bundestag is expected to adopt the Corporate Sanctioning Act (Verbandssanktionengesetz "VerSanG"), which would authorise the criminal prosecution and conviction of a corporate entity and would introduce the principle of corporate criminal responsibility.

[36] Roos et al. 2022.

dedicated personnel or even team(s). These will perform most likely global assessments identifying cases requiring thorough or independent investigations.

Setting up a dedicated team to receive, track, analyse and report critical data is crucial for successfully identifying and managing key events. The team's size and structure will vary depending on the organisation's size, complexity, business model and the types of risks involved. Made up of risk experts, these teams will work on categorising common intelligence insights and help improve the understanding of threats and risks – especially by defining clear risk indicators. They will also, where legally allowed, support the sharing of operational or tactical intelligence connected to ongoing investigations.

These teams should be equipped to carry out intelligence-led, or so-called contextual, investigations into large-scale events or trends with similar impacts, using information gathered from around the world. The sharing and exchanging of information allows companies the building of a comprehensive view of the risk landscape. This, in turn, improves risk assessment methods, strengthens monitoring and surveillance strategies through better resource alignment, and ensures that the organisation can respond swiftly to identified vulnerabilities – such as by updating internal controls and procedures. It also helps identify irregularities that may require independent investigations by external parties, as well as potential disclosure and cooperation with authorities when necessary.

Furthermore, teams or units should adopt an agile way of working, across departments and across jurisdictions, by which the workload can be centrally coordinated. In addition, they should be responsible for a more effective global and proactive risk management, central intelligence and the operation of a communications hub from which relevant information is disseminated.

To ensure global coverage, interaction principles for foreign entities and branches need to be established. Communication channels and reporting structures should be clearly defined, in line with banking secrecy and data privacy laws. The central team can then assess and decide who may be impacted by new trends and patterns in order for it to establish appropriate and timely preventative measures.

### 9.3.1 Investigation process

The financial industry has made significant progress over the past few years in widening the use of intelligence-led investigations and implementing automated solutions for the detection of suspicious activities. It has also made progress on timely reporting to law enforcement agencies and other authorities, in particular in terms of financial crime events. In November 2021, the US DOJ introduced significant policy changes that mark a shift in tone, strengthening the department's response to corporate crime. In particular, the policy changes signal greater scrutiny of past corporate misconduct, broader expectations for corporate disclosures regarding individuals and an increasing reliance on corporate monitorships.[37] EU policymakers shall ensure an adequate approach to investigating compliance wrongdoing by encouraging leverages data and modern methods of intelligence, evidence gathering, including the use of proactive approaches like data mining.

COVID-19 has urged on a number of already visible trends in digitalisation and has opened up new opportunities for the use of digital and contactless payments as well as changed the global trade in advanced and emerging economies. All of those were triggered by the unprecedent lockdowns, long-term lasting e-commerce and teleworking, the emergence of new fintech companies, neo banks which has also changed the preferences and expected approach for investigations. The increasing digitisation of financial services results in growing volumes of transactions and extremely large data sets, which require advanced computational analysis to reveal patterns, trends and associations. The use of analytics is therefore becoming essential for both reporting entities and authorities to cope with information and fully exploit its potential.[38]

Many companies are proactively working to improve internal analytical and forensic capabilities. Using advanced analytics – such as machine learning, artificial intelligence and natural language processing – has become increasingly important in this effort. These technologies enable organisations to efficiently screen and analyse massive volumes of structured and unstructured data, uncover hidden patterns, and detect subtle anomalies that might otherwise go unnoticed. By applying predefined rules, visualising complex relationships, and using network analyses to reveal indirect connections, investigators can gain deeper insights more quickly and accurately. This data-driven approach is now a standard part of investigators' daily work, helping companies respond faster and more effectively to potential threats.

Big data technologies including clouds, data lakes and data processing engines provide a central infrastructure, allowing companies to gather data, make more searches as well as store and promptly access vast amounts of information across jurisdictions. This is a clear prerequisite for companies to run intelligence-led investigations.

#### 9.3.1.1 Proactive risk management

There is a legitimate interest in conducting an internal investigation where there is a suspicion of regulatory or legal violations that are subject to criminal or monetary penalties. Internal investigations are intended primarily to detect, stop and prepare for the sanction

[37] Bruce et al. 2022.

[38] Europol 2017.

of misconduct and are aimed at enabling a company's decision-makers to make informed decisions for the benefit of the company, its employees and customers. They are also necessary to avoid liability on the part of senior management.[39]

Where events require an investigation, it is critical to define the background, scope, methodology and minimum requirements for the assessment, create a communication protocol, track progress, implement reporting mechanisms and perform stakeholder management. In many cases, investigative teams need to perform cross-border investigations. With that in mind, they need to assess and follow required information sharing protocols and define solutions for effective cross-border investigation efforts.

An investigation itself is a temporary activity, where analysts will assess a pre-defined internal data set retrospectively (e.g. SWIFT and/or SEPA transactions) and other external available data, in order to examine potential violations, illegal activities or breaches of internal policies, regulations or business restrictions. An investigation may include one or even a series of interrelated activities. An intelligence-led investigation goes beyond the usual forensic activities and looks at further connected issues.

There is no one-size-fits-all approach to complex investigations. However, it is critical to identify relevant events, decide on and perform contextual assessments when necessary and share information when required. The aggregated oversight and screening for risk-related trigger events should be conducted centrally and build the basis for initiating an investigation. Hence, the decision to initiate, either at the group or local level, should also be coordinated centrally.

To this end, companies need a well-defined operating process for the initiation of investigations. They should also describe the type of events that are legitimate for investigation, or so-called trigger events. Those usually fit into one of three categories:

1. regulatory inquiries,
2. internal control activities and other findings,
3. adverse media and market trends.

For each risk type, relevant trigger events and corresponding actions need to be defined (e.g. a recent cyber attack on competitors, new money laundering schemes). The purpose of an initial assessment is to evidence the basic facts, assess if those can be substantiated, check the supporting documentation or other available information, preserve and secure basic evidence and assess whether the opening of an investigation is justified. In case a

[39] See footnote 35 on "VerSanG".

preliminary assessment shows facts indicating risk relevance, the company should conduct an investigation. At this stage, senior management may need to be involved if certain limits are met or a decision needs to be made whether it requires an independent investigation by a third party. This will be a reflection of the issue at hand and reputational, regulatory or financial risks, amongst other things. The degree of impact also determines whether the event affects more than one geographic location or is of a systematic nature.

In several recent money laundering cases, non-resident accounts – that is, bank accounts opened in a country or territory where the account holders do not reside - were heavily exploited. In such instances, rather than limiting the investigation to specific customers, it is advisable to validate the identified transactional patterns across broader customer groups. Additionally, recent money laundering scandals and academic research have highlighted the central role that third-party actors – such as lawyers, accountants, company service providers, and notaries – play in organising and processing illicit funds. Therefore, when designing an investigation, companies should take root causes and structural patterns into account to appropriately define its scope.

For the identification of such trigger events, the respective team(s) should:

- review external databases, websites, research tools and newsletters of regulatory authorities, law enforcement agencies, industry associations and media outlets to identify events, information and patterns that have potential relevance;
- attend meetings of industry associations working groups or other risk-specific related events and conferences to learn about current trends, patterns, risk indicators, linkages and illicit activities;
- meet with personnel from law enforcement agencies, authorities and related associations to learn about developments.

### 9.3.1.2 Strategic and tactical investigations

In general, there are two types of investigations:

- **strategic investigation** refers to proactive assessments with unclear exposure for the company. Trigger points may be regulatory trends, external media reports or new patterns, and the analysis may be based on different information sources. Investigation results may include mitigating measures of a strategic nature, where the company proactively decides, for example, to restrict certain business activities.
- **tactical investigation** is reactive in nature and focuses on events that already occurred (e.g. internal findings on customer groups, complex cases with multijurisdictional scope). The investigation usually includes data analysis and reviews, following a risk-based approach, and leverages root cause analysis for adequate risk mitigation. Due to

Financial institutions face particular sanctions risks as a result of their clients' exposure to sanctions targets. Transactions that do not appear to violate sanctions regulations may in fact involve, or be for the benefit of, sanctions targets or sanctioned jurisdictions. It is essential, therefore, for financial institutions and regulated entities to identify and manage these risks.[44]

Additionally, OFAC notes that further risks may be posed by "products, services, supply chain, intermediaries, counterparties, transactions, and geographic locations, depending on the nature of the organization."[45] Investigating payment flows that go through foreign affiliates can be challenging for financial institutions. Criminal syndicates create layered corporate entities or use shell companies, front companies, subsidiaries and multiple intermediaries to gain access to the international financial system. Some of these business structures are very complex. Also, many banks systematically apply intelligence led investigations in order to manage the risks associated with correspondent banking transactions.

Sanctions-related investigations review retrospective data sets. Such analyses range from a basic pivot-table analysis to more advanced software applications or automated analytical tools and platforms to stratify, synthesise and flag data from a variety of ecosystems. The key to effectively using data analysis is the ability to link transactional evidence from disparate sources buried in a multitude of data fields to identify hidden relationships or correlations. With the assistance of analytical tools, robust forensic analysis can be performed to help thwart sanctions violations.[46] If an internal investigation uncovers sanctions violations or attempts to circumvent sanctions, a voluntary self-disclosure (VSD) should be submitted promptly to the Office of Foreign Assets Control (OFAC). Voluntary self-disclosures can demonstrate an institution's commitment to compliance and may result in reduced penalties. However, it is important to note that financial institutions risk losing the benefit of voluntary self-disclosure credit if the same infringement has already been reported by another party or identified through other means.

In addition to OFAC, the Bureau of Industry and Security (BIS) actively encourages entities to submit VSDs when they believe they may have breached the Export Administration Regulations (EAR). Early disclosure to BIS can facilitate a more cooperative resolution and may mitigate enforcement actions.

44 Ibid.

45 OFAC 2019.

46 For more information on voluntary self-disclosure, refer to the website of the Bureau of Industry and Security (www.bis.doc.gov).

Furthermore, financial institutions should have clear protocols in place for reporting and escalating potential sanctions breaches, ensuring a timely communication with relevant regulatory bodies. This proactive approach helps manage regulatory risk, supports ongoing compliance efforts and reinforces the organisation's reputation for transparency and integrity.

### 9.3.2 Information sharing and global risk management

Information sharing is critical to combat global risks. Barriers to it may therefore negatively impact the effectiveness of controls and investigative efforts and facilitate cross-border operations of criminal networks. This underscores the importance of rapid, meaningful and comprehensive sharing of information from a wide variety of sources, on national and/or global scales.

In the last years many international initiatives devoted serious attention to the regulatory impediments for information sharing. The FATF itself has encouraged its members to take action on the national and global level to address barriers to information sharing, including the review of data protection and privacy laws.[47]

#### 9.3.2.1 How to connect needles in the same haystack (in a financial institution)

For effective risk oversight, financial institutions need to make every effort to ensure a constructive and timely exchange of information on trend analysis, patterns of behaviour, targeted investigations and geographical vulnerabilities. This will enable them to better manage their risk exposures and monitor transaction flows group-wide.

Where investigations are conducted without ensuring adequate information sharing with other units, entities or jurisdictions, risks may be overlooked. Additionally, sharing information is key to promoting financial transparency and protecting the integrity of the financial system.

For effective risk management, financial institutions must possess a thorough understanding of the risks to which they are exposed. Such risks may stem from customers, products, geographical exposures, transaction patterns or factors associated with affiliates within the group. A comprehensive identification and analysis of these risks enables institutions to more accurately structure their risk profiles, implement commensurate controls, and establish robust risk management frameworks.

[47] FATF 2016.

Accordingly, information from affiliates and other business units should be incorporated into a consolidated risk assessment. This facilitates the identification and evaluation of the nature and magnitude of risks associated with each affiliate, as well as the aggregate risk at a global level – particularly where shared information pertains to cross-border relationships and interdependencies. It is therefore imperative that relevant teams are granted appropriate access to such information to inform their assessments.

Nonetheless, group-wide information sharing is often constrained by divergent legal frameworks governing data protection, the handling of Suspicious Activity Report (SAR) information, privacy and banking secrecy – including confidentiality – across jurisdictions. Restrictions on branches and subsidiaries sharing information with head office compliance and oversight functions vary significantly depending on the jurisdiction involved.

In principle, the sharing of information and transfer of personal data and customer-related information shall only be performed where legally permissible and on a need-to-know basis. Transfers of personal data to any other country require companies to provide appropriate safeguards, generally by adopting binding corporate rules (for transfers within multinational groups) or by introducing standard data protection clauses, adopted or approved by the EU Commission, in contracts with third-party service providers.[48]

### 9.3.2.2 How to connect needles in different haystacks (between different financial institutions)

Well-timed and adequate identification and mitigation of risks can be facilitated by sharing relevant information between financial institutions or with governments, regulators, and other relevant authorities, both domestically and internationally. However, inconsistent legal frameworks, data privacy restrictions and confidentiality obligations present barriers inhibit intelligence sharing. It is important to adopt the highest standards for data protection, data security and customer privacy. However, the result is often that financial institutions, law enforcement and regulators are constrained in seeing the complete picture of underlying activity.

Notable developments continue to take place in this area. For example, FinCEN issued an updated guidance on Section 314(b) of the USA Patriot Act, which allows financial institutions to share information with one another under a safe harbour that provides protection from liability. This facilitates better identification and reporting of activities potentially linked to money laundering or terrorist financing. The new guidance also

[48] For more information on potential data transfer restrictions: www.ec.europa.eu.

clarifies that there is no restriction under Section 314(b) on sharing personally identifiable information, nor are there limitations on how the information may be shared. This clarification is significant, as it explicitly includes, for instance, attempted transactions or attempts to induce others to engage in transactions.[49] This provision plays a critical role in enhancing the collective ability of financial institutions to detect and report suspicious activities.

Also, the Financial Action Task Force (FATF) has made progress in addressing information barriers.[50] For instance, banks shall share financial crime information where the principle of "legitimate interest" under the data protection and privacy requirements applies. The priorities of the two-year German FATF Presidency also includes the update of respective FATF recommendations and guidance (e.g. Digital Transformation of AML/CFT is an objective of the FATF Presidency[51]).

Furthermore, there are several initiatives by banks and start-ups that aim to apply privacy-enhanced technology for data sharing. Such technologies include homomorphic encryption, secure multiparty computation and zero-knowledge proofs.[52]

In addition to direct exchange between financial institutions, there is a trend to set up public private partnerships (PPP), providing an opportunity for analysing and sharing strategic information on recent risk and crime trends, methods, techniques, common typologies and modus operandi. Such information, provided in a sanitised manner (with no reference to personally identifiable information or operational intelligence), would not compromise relevant data protection and privacy laws. Sufficient safeguards concerning the information and data shared should be established to ensure the non-disclosure of the information and data, including against tipping off.

- **Example 1:** Europol launched the Europol Financial Intelligence Public Private Partnership (EFIPPP) in 2017. This was the first transnational financial information sharing mechanism. The members, comprising experts from financial institutions and competent authorities, aim to share strategic financial intelligence in a trusted environment. Ultimately, the objective is to facilitate, in accordance with applicable domestic legal frameworks, the exchange of operational or tactical intelligence associated with ongoing investigations. The EFIPPP also aims to identify ways in which the regulations for information sharing could be improved.

---

[49] FinCEN 2020.

[50] Some jurisdictions in particular, including the United Kingdom and Singapore, have produced effective guidance in this context: HM Treasury/Home Office 2020; or Singapore's FATF Guidance on Private Sector Information Sharing: MAS 2018b.

[51] FATF 2020.

[52] Wass 2020.

- **Example 2:** The Anti Financial Crime Alliance (AFCA) is a public-private partnership established in Germany to enhance the fight against money laundering and terrorist financing through collaborative efforts between public authorities and private sector entities. Initiated on 24 September 2019 by the Financial Intelligence Unit (FIU), the Federal Financial Supervisory Authority (BaFin) and the Federal Criminal Police Office (BKA), AFCA aims to foster strategic cooperation and information exchange among its member. AFCA's primary goal is to improve the identification and mitigation of financial crime risks by leveraging the combined expertise and resources of both public authorities and private institutions. The alliance facilitates the development of analytical papers on current issues, provides guidance on compliance matters, and promotes best practices. As of February 2025, AFCA comprises 58 members from both the financial and non-financial sectors. Membership is open to all obligated entities under Germany's Money Laundering Act (GwG), including banks, insurance companies, real estate firms and other relevant institutions.

## 9.4 Success factors and common pitfalls

Given rising legal and regulatory scrutiny, proactive risk oversight is critical. Investigative assessments are an elementary component of effective and proactive risk management across different non-financial risks. As discussed here, proactive investigations provide a method to detect and evaluate relevant risk incidents. This can lead to insights on new or changing risk exposures and enable mitigating measures before these are required by external factors.

Recent cases have shown that key reasons for failure of investigative assessments include a lack of management attention, imbalance in power and authority between business and control functions, insufficient resourcing of control functions and a lack of adequate risk culture. The common misperception that 'bad things only happen to others' often leads to underinvestment in risk management. Even if this is not the case, critical pitfalls remain. For instance, inadequate data quality and disconnected datasets, which may only exist in paper form, undermine any initiative to evaluate risk exposure and detect relevant risk incidents. Furthermore, technologies and data analytics need to be leveraged to enable the required intelligence.

To avoid these common pitfalls, the following seven success factors have proven relevant when advancing risk assessments with a proactive investigative component:

- **adequate authority for investigative assessments:** investigative teams need to be granted authority and be independent when performing their assessments. There is no benefit to a financial institution in a biased assessment, when it comes to variables such as decision-making on mitigating measures or even discussions with authorities;

- **sufficient resourcing for screening of trigger events and for conducting critical assessments:** the investigative teams need to be equipped with sufficient resources so that relevant trigger events are adequately identified, and critical risk incidents can be appropriately investigated. Prioritisation of assessments and potential temporary support by external parties may help overcome peaks of needed resources;
- **assurance of a structure and integrated risk management approach:** the investigative team needs to be seen as an integral part of the risk management approach, which is responsible for independent assessments of arising or changing risks. The results of such investigations should be considered, amongst other things, for improvement of the internal control system (e.g. new or adjusted controls) or adjustment of annual risk assessments (e.g. consideration of new risk factors);
- **data quality and information access is key:** financial institutions need to ensure that relevant data is recorded, stored and available for investigative teams. This may include connecting data points for different risks, but also ensuring access to relevant personnel or third parties;
- **enhanced data analytics are the basis for well-informed decision-making and efficient resource usage:** the implementation of new technologies allows financial institutions to perform more accurate data analyses and apply adequate and proportionate risk management strategies, enabling informed decisions. Furthermore, advanced technologies will also decrease operational risk related to human errors as well as anticipated costs;
- **information sharing improves decisive actions:** the ability of financial institutions to share data across multiple jurisdictions associated with the group, with authorities and other financial institutions around the globe will allow a prompt, actionable and adequate response to disruptions by risk incidents;
- **a setup enabling cooperation reduces liability risk:** conducting investigations, where necessary in cooperation with authorities, will significantly mitigate corporate liability risks in multiple jurisdictions. Early identification and assessment of warning signs is a prerequisite to demonstrate awareness, good culture and willingness to cooperate.

In essence, intelligence-led investigations and the systematic sharing of information constitute fundamental components in the contemporary fight against increasingly sophisticated financial crimes. The complexity and transnational nature of modern financial criminal activities necessitate approaches that are both proactive and intelligence-driven. By leveraging comprehensive data analyses, pattern recognition and network mapping, intelligence-led investigations facilitate the early identification of emerging threats and vulnerabilities within the financial ecosystem. Moreover, information sharing among financial institutions, regulatory bodies, and law enforcement agencies – both domestically and internationally – enhances situational awareness and fosters a collaborative environment crucial for disrupting illicit financial flows. Such collaboration mitigates the challenges posed by jurisdictional fragmentation, enabling a coordinated and timely response to criminal conduct that often transcends national borders.

# 10 Technical Application and Data Architecture for Non-Financial Risk Management

*Kai Gammelin, Björn Stauber, Dr. Christian N. Schmid, Dr. Jan-Oliver Fröhlich, Annika Melchert, Daniel Wagner*

## 10.1 Introduction

From data to tax, legal and operational, the list of non-financial risks (NFR) facing financial institutions continues to grow. In the regulatory space alone, institutions are often confronted with hundreds of regulatory changes a week, many of which require both, software-based and manual implementation.[1] Managing this barrage comes at a significant cost. The average bank spends 40% to 60% of its change budget on compliance.[2] As the number and scope of non-financial risks expand, banks need to think afresh about how they can reduce workloads and build more efficient risk management frameworks.

The challenges associated with NFRs are a function of their number and diversity. Indeed, they can be manifested in institutions or from the environment, stakeholders, the supply chain or clients. Further, there is no single measure of NFR that can be applied across the business and its interests. This lack of standardisation inevitably creates a burden on compliance functions, amid frequent communication breaks, fragmented documentation and a lack of clarity on data ownership.

Here, we describe the challenges many banks face in designing information and communication technology (ICT[3]) architectures for NFR management and discuss potential ways to help them standardise (within organisational limits) and manage their resources. These include optimising data models and streamlining interfaces between systems. Through these efforts, combined with agile management approaches, banks can respond more quickly, stay in sync with regulatory expectations and be more confident in taking a holistic approach to risk management.

---

1 Masters 2011.

2 Gittfried et al. 2017.

3 EU regulations such as the Digital Operational Resilience Act (DORA) and the revised NIS 2 Directive deliberately adopt the broader term Information and Communication Technology (ICT), replacing the older IT terminology; further information on these regulations can be found in chapter 13 on cyber resilience.

### 10.1.1 A fragmented ICT landscape

At a large number of banks, specific challenges are associated with ICT resources. Simply, the technology required to manage NFR consists of a huge variety of applications (custom-built, spreadsheets, packaged solutions, SaaS etc.), many of which are run on outdated systems. Many banks do not yet have the core ICT architecture and project management capabilities that would enable faster software production cycles. This deficit inevitably slows time to market and means the business lacks access to tools that would make a difference to risk management efficiency and effectiveness. In addition, many banks are stuck with semi-manual reporting, particularly in aggregating reports for management dashboards.

Figure 1: Illustrative decentralised NFR ICT landscape

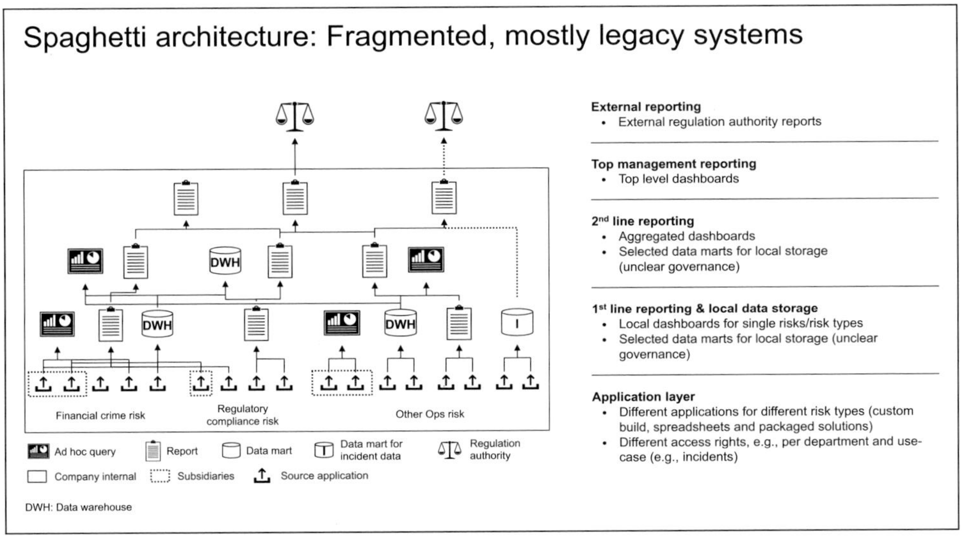


### 10.1.2 ICT's impact on data availability

Amid a fragmented ICT landscape, central access to consistent NFR data is often limited (see Figure 1 for a typical architecture). There are exceptions – for example, there are usually decent data resources for anti-money laundering (AML) or counter-terrorism financing (CTF). However, apart from these specific topics, data is often fragmented and unstructured. It may be contained in paper documents and/or isolated Excel spreadsheets rather than in databases that can be accessed automatically via APIs. See Figure 2 for an indication of data availability by risk type.

Often the root cause of the challenge is the lack of an accessible and centralised data source. As a result, data and reports need to be requested from, and deployed by, the data-producer – for example via SQL queries. If quantitative incident data (by risk type) is available, it is usually not protected by consistent access management. Rather, it is only available on a 'need-to-know' basis for exactly those requesting the data.

Figure 2: Typical data availability by NFR risk type

| NFR cluster | NFR type | Data availability |
|---|---|---|
| Financial crime risk | AML/CTF | High |
| Financial crime risk | Sanctions/Embargoes | High |
| Financial crime risk | Bribery & corruption | High |
| Financial crime risk | Facilitation of tax evasion | High |
| Conduct risk | Market conduct risk | Low |
| Conduct risk | Client conduct risk | Low |
| Conduct risk | Employee conduct risk | Low |
| Regulatory compliance risk | Regulatory compliance risk | Low |
| ICT risk[a] | Data confidentiality risk | High |
| ICT risk | Data integrity risk | High |
| ICT risk | Data availability risk | High |
| ICT risk | Cybersecurity risk | High |
| ICT risk | AI usage risk | High |
| Data privacy & bank secrecy risk | Data privacy risk | High |
| Data privacy & bank secrecy risk | Bank secrecy risk | High |
| Resilience risk | Resilience risk | Low |
| Outsourcing & vendor risk | Intragroup-outsourcing risk | High |
| Outsourcing & vendor risk | External outsourcing risk | High |
| Outsourcing & vendor risk | Vendor risk | High |
| Fraud risk | Account-opening fraud risk | High |
| Fraud risk | Debit/credit card fraud risk | High |
| Fraud risk | Fraudulent payment trans. risk | High |
| Fraud risk | Online banking fraud risk | High |
| Fraud risk | Credit fraud risk | High |
| Fraud risk | Theft risk | High |
| Fraud risk | Embezzlement risk | High |
| Fraud risk | Antitrust violation risk | High |
| Fraud risk | Balance sheet manipulation | High |

| NFR cluster | NFR type | Data availability |
|---|---|---|
| Tax Reporting Risk | Tax reporting risk | High |
| Other operational risks | HR risk | Low |
| Other operational risks | Legal risk | Low |
| Other operational risks | Physical damage risk | Low |
| Other operational risks | Execution/process risk | Low |
| Other operational risks | Reporting risk | Low |
| Other operational risks | Accounting risk | Low |
| Other operational risks | Project risk | High |
| Other operational risks | Competition law | Low |
| Other operational risks | Model risk | Low |

a.See chapters 12 and 13 on the deployment of artificial intelligence and cyber resilience.

## 10.1.3 Data availability across borders

Where companies operate across borders, NFR and incident data is often siloed in local divisions, making it difficult for institutions to comply with regulations in other jurisdictions. Further, regulations specific to locations and types of data transfer sometimes restrict movement of data across borders. For companies operating in multiple jurisdictions, international data transfers are often only permitted if conditions are met by the company carrying out the transfer and/or by the country in which the recipient is based.

Typical requirements include security safeguards, specific contractual clauses with offshoring partners (affiliates or third-party vendors; for example, the right to on-site inspections) or the need to obtain informed customer consent. Conditions pertaining to the recipient generally relate to local data protection laws. These conditional frameworks can prevent the transfer of data or undermine the economic case for offshore processing.

## 10.1.4 Additional challenges associated with group companies

To effectively comply with multiple regulatory requirements, the parents of group companies need to ensure aggregated and adequate NFR reporting across all subsidiaries. However, many group companies face challenges when identifying NFR or managing reporting requirements across the group.

The challenges outlined in the previous paragraphs – fragmented ICT landscapes, no centralised data access, differentiated availability of base data – are also often relevant for subsidiaries. As a result, consolidated reporting requires a significant manual effort to aggregate and assemble heterogeneous data sources and formats. The complexity of requirements rises even further when subsidiaries are themselves subject to a range of regulatory regimes – for example across borders or industries.

## 10.2 Regulatory requirements

Given the fast pace of regulatory change, any list of regulations is bound to be incomplete within a few months. Hence, the following paragraphs should be understood only as a starting point for screening the regulatory landscape. In any case, a diligent regulatory screening and internal alignment with the lines of defence is required.

Data handling and retention are typically subject to the respective local requirements, e.g. GDPR in the EU or the Sarbanes-Oxley Act (SOX) in the US, but regulations might differ in key aspects of their scope. For example, while GDPR offers protection to all natural persons' data, for clients and staff alike, this is different in Switzerland where only client data enjoys the special protection of the DSG (data protection law) so far, however, a further harmonisation with GDPR is already in the making. In general, differences in regulatory requirements can be handled by inserting specific clauses in the contracts with subsidiaries and partners. In this way, they can all be held to the same standard as the parent entity. However, there might be little support by the respective local regulators and auditors in auditing and enforcing such contract clauses with subsidiaries and partners.

Other areas of ICT and data architecture that are typically subject to specific regulations include (cloud) outsourcing[4], general technology[5] or emerging technologies like AI.[6] Furthermore, internal controls often should or have to adhere to certain standards, e.g. to the COSO framework in the US, to the "Management, Supervision and Internal Control Guidelines" by Hong Kong's SFC[7] or BCBS 40.[8]

## 10.3 Seven challenges in NFR management and reporting

Even if adequate data resources are put in place, the road to excellence in NFR management and reporting is often bumpy. Institutions often lack a dedicated strategy, run un-

4 For instance, in the EU: EBA 2019a.

5 BaFin 2021a (for Germany); HKMA 2021a (for Hong Kong).

6 HKMA 2019; please refer to chapter 12 on the deployment and risk of AI in NFR management.

7 SFC 2003.

8 BIS 1998.

certain governance frameworks and routinely must make trade-offs in software roll outs. In addition, data and ICT architectures are often insufficient for the task at hand.

### 10.3.1 Challenge 1: the lack of a defined NFR-ICT strategy

Banks are confronted with strategic challenges in terms of both functional and non-functional requirements. These requirements have been further extended by DORA which requires the definition and implementation of a DOR strategy for ICT risk management, including third-party risk management.[9]

- Challenging functional requirements:
  - *identity/access* management and authorisation levels on highly confidential incident data – for example, while non-personal details of an incident can be accessible to all compliance staff, the names of involved employees should only be accessible to compliance management and relevant line managers;
  - the *creation of external interfaces* to ingest and export data in the right formats;
  - enabling the *searchability* of NFR data and reports;
  - *data integrity, versioning and archiving/retention:* solution must support proper audit trails (spreadsheets make it nearly impossible to track edits) as well as have the capacity to archive, search, and leverage NFR data for analytics/tracking;
  - *implementation of ICT risk management frameworks,* e.g., support protection needs assessment along four central criteria: confidentiality, integrity, availability, and authenticity.
- Challenging non-functional requirements:
  - *adaptability of systems* to include new or updated regulations;
  - *auditability for the three lines of defence* and regulatory authorities;
  - *standardisation:* defining a common and standardised list of definitions/glossary and documentation;
  - *integrability/extensibility:* difficulty to integrate with existing and external systems. No solution currently provides either an exhaustive list of features to track NFR or the potential to do so;
  - *operability:* heavy reliance on manual inputs;
  - *sufficient ICT risk knowledge and skills in management body*;

[9] Further details on DORA can be found in chapter 13 on cyber resilience.

- *reporting of major ICT-related incidents* to competent authorities within certain timeframes;
- *regular digital operational resilience testing,* including stress tests;
- *stringent oversight of third-party service providers* through register of dependencies and integration of security as well as risk management provisions into contracts.

### 10.3.2 Challenge 2: responsibility for and execution of NFR reporting-related activities (operational unit vs. NFR management)

The three lines of defence (LoD) framework has become established among financial service providers as a best-practice approach to managing risk at strategic and operational levels, and is required by DORA (other risk management and control models are possible).

Each LoD has a specific role to play. The 1st LoD, the business itself, should own its risks. The business provisions, designs, implements and integrates the solutions that carry out controls – for example regular checks of adherence to a clean desk policy. The business is also responsible for proactively seeking out new solutions.

The 2nd LoD is responsible for monitoring and reporting on NFR management. It sets standards and details guidelines, which may comprise NFR definitions and a taxonomy. The 2nd LoD should also manage process documentation to enable operational units and technical teams to translate business/regulatory language to code and swiftly act on incidences and emerging risks. It must ensure the company has the proper data assets, technologies, tools, procedures and methodologies. It must also ensure there are minimum standards for NFR management across the business – including auditable standards/protocols and training protocols and manuals. In addition, the 2nd LoD should approve controls designed, monitor adherence and run tests of control effectiveness. It must prepare reports for the board, operate regular risk assessments and provide proofs of completion. In recent years, regulatory reporting has seen a further increase in significance. For instance, the 2nd LoD needs to ensure adherence to regulatory reporting standards, such as described in DORA Art. 17 for the ICT-related incident management process. This could involve notifying the relevant financial authority of incidents which then relays the information to other relevant bodies.

Finally, the 3rd LoD, or audit function, provides independent assurance on the efficacy of risk management through internal/external audits. The 3rd LoD should also independently validate that ICT systems comply with the latest regulations – for example through web scrapes or a subscription to relevant publications as well as contacts with regulators.

A significant challenge in adhering to the three LoD framework in the context of NFR is a blurred line between the 1st and 2nd LoD, i.e. determining risk ownership in a heterogenous/siloed risk landscape and establishing a corresponding risk data governance.[10]

### 10.3.3 Challenge 3: consistency and transparency of ICT architecture

Many banks struggle to build the ICT capability for continuous automated oversight of NFR applications, instead relying on ad hoc oversight and spreadsheets. The same applies to oversight of risk clusters and monitoring of personnel. In addition, banks lack consistency in application design across regions and sub-functions, heightening the risk of gaps in compliance coverage.

Often banks do not have standardised tools, procedures and methodologies across all business units, leading to mistakes in naming, archiving and version control. There is a further perennial challenge in ensuring that applications meet prescribed regulatory and legal standards, especially where the bank employs custom-built or heavily customised solutions.

From an internal perspective, there is a need to ensure that solutions are reliable and represent the most cost-efficient way of working with regards to the regulatory possibilities. In the case of automation, banks are often challenged to achieve quick wins, which in turn can create barriers to wider adoption and scaling.

**Application owners.** Application owners, the business and ICT departments often do not take joint ownership of applications and share management of NFR reporting requirements and resources. They lack the range of skills and expertise that would enable them to define services and ownership, capture and agree business requirements, plan resources and infrastructure, monitor and report performance, review and iterate as necessary. The process is neither circular nor continuous. Additionally, IT departments often do not have access to dedicated workflows (such as automated processing) to effectively manage NFR reporting requirements.

**The role of the business.** The business often does not provide sufficient input. To capture business requirements for application operations, departments should appoint owners for each business service, which are supposed to work closely with the ICT. These should be responsible for helping design and manage services provided by the IT department. This would include identifying business requirements and agreeing on them via service level agreements with IT; for example, in relation to availability or performance of sys-

[10] For more information, see chapter 11 on NFR data governance.

tems. The owners should document adherence to business requirements through regular reports, escalating issues where necessary. Individual owners should spot necessary changes and act as a single point of contact for solution designers/ICT operations for each application.

**The role of IT.** Deficits in ICT are often the result of structural shortfalls. In an ideal world, departments should assign ICT service owners for each service, capturing and implementing business requirements in daily application runs. Service owners should be mandated to manage services provided by applications. They should also agree on business requirements with the business and formalise them in service level agreements. They should monitor applications and forward the results to business service owners. In addition, they should be informed when tweaks are required and work with both business service owners and solution designers to identify possible solutions.

IT departments should appoint service managers to 'run the business' and manage the service catalogue centrally. To ensure coverage where employees are absent, there should be owners for important applications and rules of representation in the event of absence. Key responsibilities would include:

- facilitating the service management process and acting as the contact for service owners on process-related issues;
- taking ownership of service definitions and corresponding SLAs and supporting service owners with initial setup of documentation;
- conducting regular evaluations of services in terms of accuracy, soundness and completeness;
- evaluating the effectiveness of service management processes;
- taking ownership of ICT service management tools as necessary.

Since many ICT architecture decisions – such as access controls, system integration, and incident detection – directly influence cybersecurity posture, readers may refer to chapter 13 on cyber resilience for a deeper exploration of these interrelated challenges.

### 10.3.4 Challenge 4: alignment of data architecture for transparency on data lineage

Data architecture should be aligned to provide as much transparency as possible on data lineage. Preconditions for data architecture alignment include agreed upon data formats, usually per risk type, and the appointment of individuals to take end-to-end responsibility for data (e.g. data owners for each risk domain, data stewards for sub-risk domains, data custodians for risk domains from an ICT perspective). In addition, it is important to ensure that decision-makers have a holistic view of ownership and interfaces.

Banks should interrogate their ability to prevent faulty data changes in reporting pathways, for example during aggregation or data merging. A typical source of error is differences in accounting standards across subsidiaries, where data cannot be merged directly (e.g. IFRS vs. HGB in Germany). However, the problem may, more prosaically, be the result of input errors, oversights, arithmetic mistakes, misdirected queries or queries on the wrong data assets. Tools such as a meta-data catalogue can help reduce these kinds of errors.

### 10.3.5 Challenge 5: implementing a solid ICT target architecture

When looking to implement an ICT architecture with the ability to accurately measure and report NFR on a group-wide basis, banks face both short- and longer-term challenges. In the short-term, they need to aim to target a basic reporting capability within about six months but are often unable to do so. Over the longer-term (one to three years), the aim should be a comprehensive reporting capability backed by analytics. Again, few achieve this benchmark.

Modern ICT strategies increasingly rely on cloud-native architectures that support elasticity, scalability and resilience – key capabilities for dynamic non-financial risk environments. Microservices-based systems further enhance agility by enabling modular development, deployment and maintenance of risk-related applications, which is especially valuable in environments that face frequent regulatory updates and evolving risk typologies.

Often, transformation of regulatory and data architecture is viewed as risky, time-consuming and expensive. This militates against concerted action. Further, the task's complexity can lead to uncertainty of where to start. Institutions need to consider both the upfront cost of overhauling existing ICT infrastructure, and the timeframe involved.

That said, the benefits of engagement are potentially significant and include a more accurate fulfilment of regulatory requirements, lower 1st LoD data collection costs and reduced costs for data aggregation and management reporting.

### 10.3.6 Challenge 6: cost-benefit considerations

It is common to satisfy a regulatory requirement by implementing a temporary solution. However, this generates a short-term (sunk) cost. Leaders, therefore, should undertake an early cost/benefit analysis, weighing the higher sunk cost but better long-term solution against an immediate but less efficient solution that avoids the sunk cost. Put another way, the short-term goal should always be to become regulatory compliant fast, while the long-term goal should be to maintain regulatory compliance with lower costs, faster processes and less risk of mistakes in manual workarounds. Planning should be aligned with ICT and data architecture strategy, supported by Enterprise Architecture Boards and in alignment with Compliance.

### 10.3.7 Challenge 7: "make-or-buy" decision

The seventh challenge is the make-or-buy decision for ICT services and components. Banks must weigh the customisation potential and direct control of in-house solutions against the potential economic benefits or availability of specialist know-how when buying external services or components. These options have different risk profiles and implications on risk management which are challenging to compare in a structured manner. Thinking of procurement in two flavours helps structure the considerations around risk trade-offs:

- *ICT service providers*: fully managed component offerings (software/infrastructure/platform-as-a-service), pure services (e.g., cyber-security operations, penetration testing), and classic external support along the software lifecycle (development, testing, operations). Service providers involve concentration and lock-in risks, as well as heightened compliance risks, e.g., around data protection or incident management.
- *ICT components*: standalone products (hardware, firmware, software); in the financial industry, typically, make-or-buy decisions are only relevant for software, such as the core banking system. Purchased components carry the risk of integration and specification errors, hidden vulnerabilities, external patch and maintenance cycles as well as an end-of-life exposure.

Risk ownership stays with the financial service provider, whether a solution is built or bought. This means the financial service provider must still exercise full governance and accountability: embed compliance and security obligations in contracts, maintain oversight and audit rights, have exit planning in place for critical or important functions (mandated under DORA), align vendor choices with the overall ICT strategy (such as wider decisions on architecture, ICT vendor strategy, potential volume discounts etc.), and track every outsourced function in the risk register so the residual risk remains transparent and controllable.

## 10.4 A target ICT architecture for NFR

A key step in constructing a high-performance NFR management architecture is to design and implement a target architecture (see Figure 3). An ideal longer-term aim would be to design architecture for a cloud-based data platform, which would incorporate risk and incident data as well as offer flexibility and scalability.

The architecture model should be characterised by the following capabilities:

- data should be stored in a (physically or virtually) centralised data hub platform, typically via an ELT ("extract, load, transform") model, meaning data is not transformed before storage. The data hub contains a data lake which should have sufficiently powerful big data capacity available (possibly on-demand to save costs);
- data should be located in the data lake via structured metadata. A 'need-to-know' principle should be applied, along with data protection requirements like GPDR;
- beyond risk quantification, banks should store incident data and quantification of damage or impact, mapped to the corresponding risk type and the affected teams/departments. This information is critical because it will enable management teams to identify trends and track remedial progress;
- mitigating measures should not be more expensive than (the average cost of) the risk they are addressing. The "business case" should be documented;
- queries should be made directly to a data lake (of unstructured data). The data can then be structured via a virtual data warehouse. Incident data should be available on a strict 'need-to-know' basis;
- the platform should include a process for incorporating new regulatory requirements.

Figure 3: An illustrative target architecture

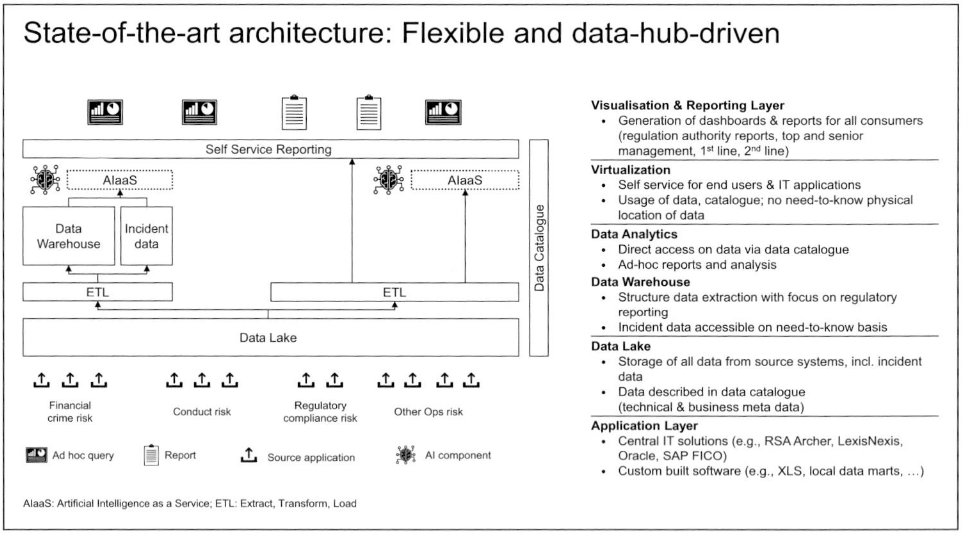

A short-term plan for NFR ICT architecture design would comprise three key steps:

1. achieve transparency on the status quo: applications, data stores, data responsibilities, data objects, data lineage;
2. identify gaps: spots where regulatory compliant reporting is not possible within the current ICT infrastructure;
3. align with responsible operational units on how to bridge the gaps.

### 10.4.1 The NFR architecture ecosystem

The NFR architecture should provide interfaces to other systems via APIs, enabling connectivity with sub-contractors and subsidiaries. This will enable an evolution from manual processes – in some cases comprising a PDF-file downloaded every six months – to an interface with granular data ready for analysis, providing a wide range of use cases.

One benefit of this approach is that it allows an institution to digitise its vendor risk, incorporating data from ongoing Request for Proposals (RfPs) and vendor management to enable automatic flagging of items such as insurances near expiry or missing documents (contracts, insurances, staff information like CVs). These impacts will cut risk and reduce processing costs.

Ideally, a data hub would allow for incorporation of external data sources, such as relating to asset management funds, private label funds or alternative investment funds. Additionally, the data hub should provide for remote audits, so that the regulator does not have to be on premise.

Regulatory audits ideally would be metaphorically similar to the servicing of modern cars. Put simply, all of the information is encoded in the car's computer. It is tracked automatically and available for reading and analysis. In the long run, banks should aim for the same: audits should be automated, and regulators should be able to automatically check that processes have been put in place to comply with regulations (the computer reports data that is aligned with regulatory requirements). Also, that responsible managers are making sure those processes are being carried out correctly.

### 10.4.2 Dashboards and reporting

If all data is readily available on the data hub, ad hoc reporting and analysis can be elicited directly from the hub. Users can define dashboards, combining queries into custom key risk indicators (KRIs) and there may be a link back to the institution's risk limits. These might take the form of "traffic lights": "no action required" (green), "action required" (amber) or "exceeding risk appetite" (red). The system would also allow users to define custom alerts based on KRIs, triggering pre-defined responses. It is best practice to agree on specific countermeasures ahead of time.

Dashboards would also enable comparability of external inputs, such as relating to outsourcing or tenders. For example, if a bank gets three offers for service provision, these, alongside supplementary documents such as insurance policies, can be stored in a centralised database. This would allow the user to compare documents and perform an automated plausibility check, thereby meeting reporting obligations in relation to third-party services.

Customised reports should also be accessible on a 'need-to-know' basis. 2$^{nd}$ LoD reports must be invisible to the 1$^{st}$ LoD, as this will avoid any incentive to "play the system."

### 10.4.3 Other key enabling technologies

A range of additional technologies can create more flexibility, enabling adjustment as regulation evolves, facilitating rules-based oversight and supporting analysis of complex dependencies.

*Cloud technologies* are still regarded by some regulators with suspicion.[11] Therefore, cloud users are likely to be more under the spotlight than firms relying on classic outsourcing.

There are jurisdictional variations in relation to the storage of data on the cloud. In some tax jurisdictions, for example, beneficial owner data cannot be transferred to another territory. For example, Swiss rules relating to employee data and payroll outsourcing data are different to those in Germany.

Some countries do not adhere to the global Automatic Exchange of Information (AEoI) standard or Foreign Account Tax Compliance Act (FATCA), which can create barriers to commercial relationships in those countries. It makes sense to bear in mind the restrictions and obligations in the GDPR. There are also uneven requirements across jurisdictions. For example, the US Safe Harbor Principles are more focused on commercial aspects of data use than Europe's GDPR, which is weighted toward consumer protection.

[11] Ahlawat et al. 2021.

*Rule engines* offer significant advantages in risk management, especially when used for NFR-compliant data ingestion and business actions/approvals. These include:

- the ability to pinpoint fraudulent behaviours, rather than honest mistakes, through application of high numbers of detailed criteria. Checks can usually be conducted in real time, which is particularly valuable in a securities trading context;
- more time for compliance FTEs to focus on the highest-risk incidents;
- the option to monitor changes to rules across geographies.

Rule engines can also be used for general compliance monitoring. For example, they can evaluate gifts given to employees or clients, flagging potentially fraudulent behaviour or conflicts of interest. This can be achieved based on variables including frequency, contract dates, public functions and the number of functions beyond the job (political, charity etc.).

*Graph databases* can be leveraged to analyse complex dependencies, can visualise and develop risk/compliance checks relating to transaction data.

*Artificial intelligence*, particularly machine learning, plays a growing role in enhancing NFR detection and response. For instance, natural language processing (NLP) can be used to monitor unstructured data from internal emails or chat systems to flag potential conduct risks or early signs of employee misconduct. Similarly, anomaly detection algorithms can analyse historical incident logs and flag atypical event patterns – such as a spike in operational errors before system outages – which allows for an early intervention and risk mitigation.

AI technology can be applied to common use cases for NFR including as a classifier for AML and CTF behaviours, to flag potential debit/credit cards and fraudulent payments frauds or to reveal online bank account hacking. Still, AI should not be seen as a panacea. Certainly, some employee knowledge of models is critical for regulatory and auditability purposes. Chapter 12 elaborates further on the usage of AI in NFR management and how to manage risks emerging from its use including an overview of existing regulations.

# 11 Data Governance in Non-Financial Risk Management

*Björn Stauber, Dr. Christian N. Schmid, Dr. Jan-Oliver Fröhlich, Annika Melchert, Daniel Wagner*

## 11.1 Introduction

In a highly digitised business environment, excellent non-financial risk management is predicated on effective data governance. Organisations that are able to marshal, store and interrogate data effectively are more likely to accurately model their risk positions. However, a common misstep in rolling out data-driven applications is to overlook the governance frameworks required to institutionalise data tasks and processes. The absence of effective governance increases data risks and exposes the institution to potential regulatory sanctions. Conversely, a dedicated governance framework promotes effective decision-making, saves costs and boosts regulatory compliance.

Non-financial risk management takes in a huge range of potential liabilities that cut across strategy and operations. In managing risk data, organisations face common challenges that include unclear lines of responsibility for data across reporting hierarchies, a lack of clarity over data ownership and redundant storage of data assets – leading to overlapping records and the absence of a single source of truth. A perennial challenge is data quality, with data often too inaccurate to be useful or presented in a variety of fields and formats, inhibiting comparability. Data cleansing and reconciliation is often undertaken manually, creating delays and increasing the risk of mistakes in data entry. This lack of automation is partly due to the absence of useful metadata (source, date, time until obsolete, data lineage etc.), which would enable a more purposeful standardisation. In many cases, legacy IT infrastructure does not support the required level of granularity. Indeed, in a few cases, institutions still rely on spread sheets, leading to version conflicts and gaps in reporting.

Underlying many of the pain points in data management are issues of governance. Often responsibility for data assets is spread across the organisation, with no single role or unit taking end-to-end responsibility. Data producers and consumers often operate under different sets of rules and standards. The problem is exacerbated by the inherent fuzziness of non-financial risk, which is resistant to the type of quantification that can be applied to financial exposures. Often the risks in question, such as legal or HR risk, are abstract and their measurement is subjective – or at least partially so. Data quality, meanwhile, is often not governed by an overarching framework, and institutions often do not have the tools in place to make specific improvements. Many have failed to optimise their processes to analyse data from transactional systems and line of business applications. The data structures are therefore not defined in advance to optimise for fast queries. Data is not cleansed, enriched, and transformed; it therefore cannot be the users' 'single trustworthy source of truth'.

Another common deficit is the absence of master data management to ensure the uniformity and accuracy of master data. Master data is static data, usually concerned with business entities, that tends to remain the same over time or changes only occasionally, rather than something like the more fluid reference data. Furthermore, institutions do not have automated workflows to enforce data rules and policies, while interfaces for data exchange are missing or unstandardised.

The way to resolve many of these pain points and underlying drivers is effective data governance. Therefore, there is an imperative for institutions, many of which are mainly focused on financial risk governance, to adapt their governance frameworks to ensure their management of non-financial risks is as effective as possible.

## 11.2 Regulatory requirements

Given the fast pace of regulatory change, any list of regulations is bound to be incomplete after only a few months. Hence, the following paragraph should be understood only as a starting point for screening the regulatory landscape. In any case a diligent regulatory screening and internal alignment with the lines of defence is required.

While initially introduced for the Global Systemically Important Banks (G-SIBs) the BIS regulation BCBS 239 "Principles for effective risk data aggregation and risk reporting" came with a recommendation to local regulators to make this a requirement for Domestic Systemically Important Banks (D-SIBs) as well and is, by today, a global de facto standard.

The EU AI Act further reinforces the importance of robust data governance by mandating high data quality, transparency, and risk management processes for AI systems – particularly those used in high-risk applications, such as compliance monitoring or fraud detection in financial institutions (see also chapter 12 on deployment of AI).

Moreover, regulations such as the EU's Digital Operational Resilience Act (DORA) and increasing scrutiny from data protection authorities globally underscore the need for harmonised data governance frameworks that can adapt to rapid regulatory changes.

## 11.3 Data governance to support NFR management

Effective data governance can go a long way toward equipping organisations with the tools to construct a high-performing non-financial risk management framework. This will enable more automation which then improves efficiency as well as data quality, insight and accountability – as well as more accurate risk-decisioning. Furthermore, it will ensure that institutions are aligned with the growing regulatory focus on data governance.

Effective governance will also create tangential benefits away from NFR risk management, some of which will add value to the bottom line. It will, for example, save the costs of highly manual processes and improve data quality, i.e. decrease data errors that need manual reconciliatory steps to detect and correct. Indeed, some banks have shown that the efficiency gains from good data governance through, e.g. less legacy technologies, offset the resources required to fund the journey.

Having said all of that, NFR does not need its own governance framework. Instead, existing frameworks, such as those designed for the Basel requirements or Europe's General Data Protection Regulation should be leveraged whenever applicable to suit the needs of alternative risk landscapes.

Figure 1: Key building blocks of data governance

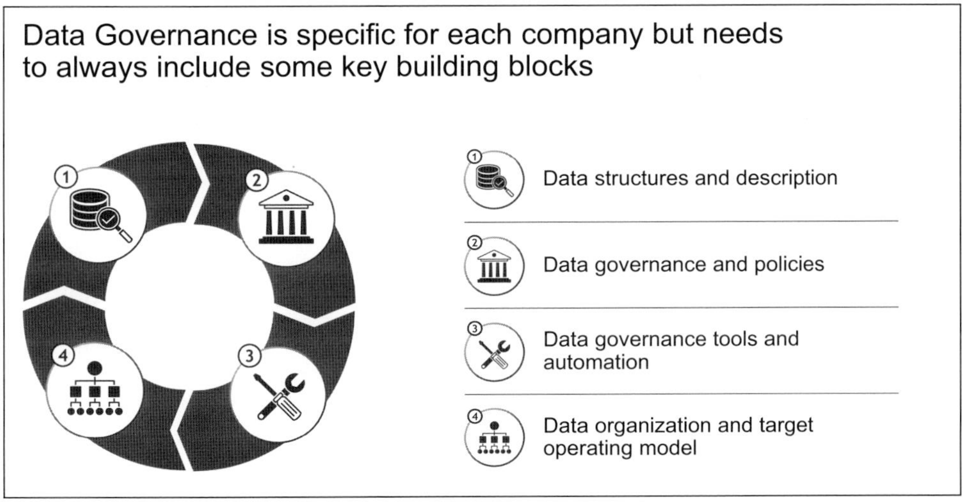


Four key buildings blocks will support optimisation of data governance frameworks (see Figure 1). Each has specific requirements for an effective adaption to NFR.

### 11.3.1 Data structures and description

The foundation of efficient non-financial risk management are data structures that accurately identify and describe the various risks the institution faces. Leading institutions have put in place risk taxonomies that define those risks under headings that include Information and Communication Technologies (ICT) risk, data risks and resilience risk. Other key risk categories include those relating to fraud, tax and operations, while strategic risks include those concerned with sustainability and reputation.

MECE (mutually exclusive, collectively exhaustive) is a principle that suggests that to understand and fix any large problem, you need to understand your options by sorting them into categories that are mutually exclusive (fitting into just one category) and collectively exhaustive, meaning all items fit into one of the categories. To create effective NFR structures, data leaders need to take a MECE approach, leveraging data domains (and their owners), families and business data objects. Typical NFR data domains will include types of events and associated parameters (incident probability, financial impact, relevant assets and risk appetite) as well as past incidents, including the impacted units, the damage and the area where the fault occurred. To increase comprehensiveness, most institutions will need to access external databases, as there are likely insufficient internal incidences available for a representative profile.

In addition, institutions require data glossaries, models, dictionaries and flow maps. 'Data glossary' means definitions that can be read and understood by the business, while data dictionaries describe datasets based on enterprise-wide specifications. This will allow for a standardised use of data. Data models are a more technical description of data in a visual format, stating data domains (e.g. 'client'), relevant data fields (e.g. 'client name') and their relation to each other (e.g. 'a client must have 1 to n addresses'). Finally, flow maps are useful visualisations of data usage along a chain of processes. They enable institutions to develop or describe data transformation logic in a non-code format.

Unlike financial risks, NFR metadata does not need to be fully consistent. The reason is that the range of non-financial risks is larger than that of financial risks so that full consistency is likely to be elusive in any event. However, financial institutions should still aim to establish clear standards and mappings as well as the APIs to connect to third-party databases. Additionally, data domain maps can support the organisation of data into clearly defined, coherent, globally shared and balanced datasets or data domains.

### 11.3.2 Data governance and policies

In setting data policies, the priority should be to ensure that the policies themselves are directed at concrete issues and root causes of potential breaks. Policies should exist only if they address identified problems, the solution to which will create value that is higher than the cost of implementation (as long as regulatory compliance is ensured). As a rule of thumb, organisations need no 'Ministry of Data' – every data governance policy needs to be backed by a business case or address an important regulatory requirement.

As a starting point, institutions must ensure they have drafted comprehensive rule books, covering matters including data quality, data documentation, data accessibility, data privacy and master data management. Most policies will be optional, the inclusion of which will be contingent on the specific organisation. However, to ensure a common mission across the organisation, a policy related to data quality is a definitive 'must have.' It should clearly define what 'quality' means for a specific company. Leading institutions often base that judgement on a list of eight parameters per domain: clarity, unicity, completeness, consistency, accuracy, integrity, accessibility and privacy.

### 11.3.3 Data governance tools and automation

Data tools are key enablers of excellent data quality management, providing a root to functionalities that include deduplication, data enrichment, data matching and merging as well as data quality validation. These can be enhanced though metadata management solutions that scan and index data, which will enable users to identify and understand data, define data and create a shared understanding, apply data governance rules to validation workflows as well as finally reveal data quality and compliance levels.

Governance project leads should establish a data catalogue or organised inventory of data assets. The catalogue uses metadata to help organisations manage their data. It also helps data professionals collect, organise, access and enrich it to support data discovery and governance.

To create a comprehensive catalogue, organisations must put the tools and applications in place to answer questions such as, "Do I have the most recent data?" and "Can I make sure that only authorised persons can access the data?" Should there be multiple truths on a dataset, for example in respect of versions or temporal viewpoint, then the question may be, "Do I have the 'truth' I require for my report?"

The basic tools for data hygiene include second- and third-generation data catalogues, automated quality checks and the creation of metadata during extract, transform, load (ETL)/live-crawling.

To support robust non-financial risk data governance, many institutions are moving toward hybrid data architectures that leverage both, data lakes and data warehouses. A data lake stores raw, unstructured or semi-structured data at scale, making it ideal for capturing diverse incident reports, emails and log files from across the organisation. In contrast, a data warehouse provides structured, cleaned and curated datasets that support reporting, analytics and compliance dashboards. While the former are flexible and cost-effective for storage, the latter offer high performance for analytics and business intelligence. When used together, the lake handles large-scale ingestion while the warehouse transforms that data into actionable insights for risk management and regulatory reporting (see Figure 2).

Figure 2: Comparison table

| Feature | Data Lake | Data Warehouse |
|---|---|---|
| Data type | Raw, unstructured or semi-structured | Cleaned, structured |
| Purpose | Storage, exploration, machine learning | Reporting, analytics |
| Speed | Slower query performance | Optimised for fast queries |
| Flexibility | High (schema-on-read) | Lower (schema-on-write) |
| Example | Ingesting incident response tool logs | Generating NFR dashboards |

Besides, cryptographic technologies like blockchain also offer potential in enhancing non-financial risk data governance, particularly for ensuring data immutability, auditability, and traceability – critical features for regulatory reporting and internal compliance audits.

### 11.3.4 Data organisation and target operating model

Organisations must establish roles and responsibilities for non-financial risks in line with the current overall data governance, e.g. in the context of BCBS 239. This will, in turn, facilitate high-quality data and date lineage. Responsible persons will ensure that reporting is consistently reliable, whether it be for single NFRs or for aggregated dashboards. They should be charged with setting guidelines and ensuring that business and IT are aligned.

Data ownership is often defined as a function of how it presents across the organisation. Where data is highly heterogenous, responsibility may be in the hands of individual business units, while these may be responsible for the data associated with that business's assets, for example in relation to data availability risk. Other times, data ownership may be assigned by risk type. This will work best with homogenous risks – for example in relation to compliance data, for which a single person may be deemed ultimately responsible.

Given the close interplay between data governance and cybersecurity – particularly in areas like data access, confidentiality, and incident response – these themes are further explored in detail in chapter 13 on digital resilience.

## 11.4 Scaling up state-of-the-art NFR data governance

Once the building blocks are in place, organisations should start to identify and prioritise use cases that will enable the scaling-up of data governance capabilities. The first step in doing so will be to bring the 1st and 2nd lines of defence (LoD) on board, disseminating a strong vision of how NFR data governance and responsibilities will operate across the organisation. Roadmaps will help the 1st and 2nd LoD see how the change will affect both them and their processes.

Once the groundwork is complete, the responsible data officers should all be about creating compelling NFR use cases. This will mean prioritising them, improving data governance and data lineage on live objects as well as unifying data domains and families based on the organisation's projects and pipeline. The 1st and 2nd LoD should be closely involved, so that they continue to build their awareness and commitment. Teams should work simultaneously to boost data quality in prioritised reports, for example those that may attract more regulatory scrutiny – which makes it possible for timelines of only a few months.

After the initial phases, teams should seek to gradually scale up NFR data capabilities and data quality in manageable waves of three to six months (see Figure 3). Success can be measured by quality of regulatory reporting, particularly in the first instance, where initial estimates are still often far off the mark.

Figure 3: Scaling up NFR data governance

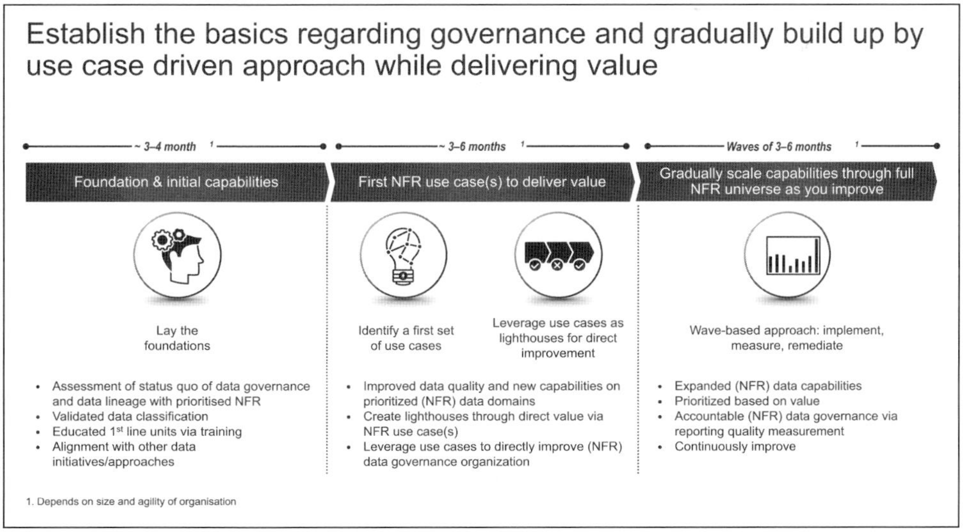

### 11.4.1 Specific roles and responsibilities

A key element of an effective operating model will be clear delineation of roles and responsibilities (see Figure 4). Many leading firms appoint a dedicated chief data officer (CDO), who should be responsible and accountable for the target data model set-up and overall data management. The CDO's remit should cut across business functions and IT.

In addition to the CDO, there should be an end-to-end NFR data owner for each risk domain and an NFR data steward for each sub-risk domain. These should oversee data generation/creation, content and quality – critical tasks that need to service the expectations of the business and NFR use cases.

Furthermore, organisations should appoint a responsible IT person for each source system relevant to NFR data domains – a so-called NFR data custodian. As organisations set up their data organisations, data custodians will be responsible for ensuring the IT architecture is aligned with functional needs.

Figure 4: High-level roles and responsibilities in data governance

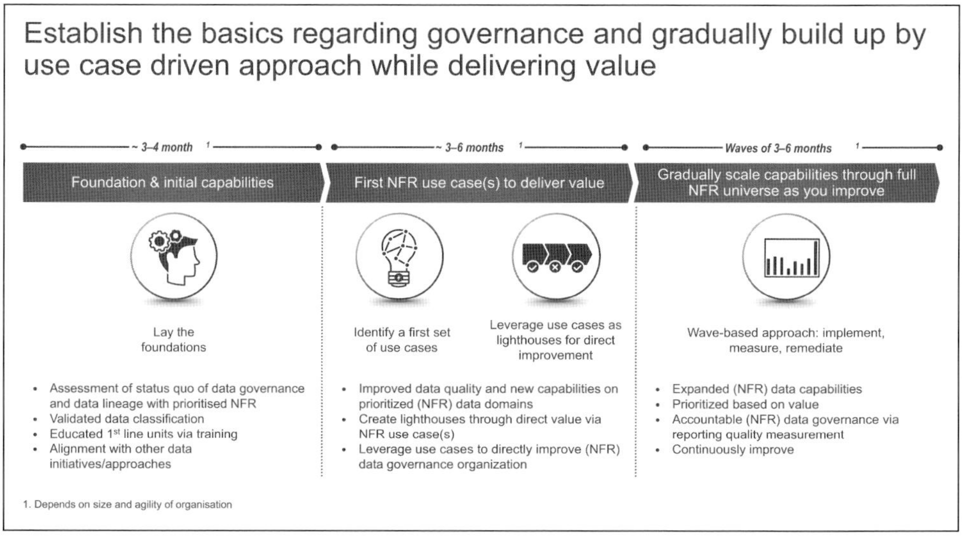


The wider NFR team will be responsible for data catalogues and metadata: The data custodian creates a data catalogue and defines non-functional metadata, whereas data owners (or data stewards) define functional metadata. This ensures that stakeholders can automatically retrieve relevant NFR data which facilitates reporting. Technology can support tasks including lineage definition, consistency checks, data leakage prevention and master data management. Large cloud providers offer these services as SaaS products.

### 11.4.2 Tool optimisation

In state-of-the-art solutions, organisations should acquire (and potentially customise) metadata management tools, which will enable them to effectively retrieve metadata for all their activities. This would, for example, allow users to more easily monitor details of data evolutions or retrieve data without knowing its physical storage location (e.g. database, application report). Metadata can also support management of granular data access rights. For example, where users are unauthorised for any subset of the requested data, they would receive an automatic notification and be directed to the relevant data owners.

Where organisations are structured as groups, all of these principles need to be applied across subsidiaries. Provision should also be made for the consolidation of reporting, which, in general, requires a large amount of manual aggregation.

Finally, organisations require the capabilities to effectively implement master data management. This would encompass a complimentary set of solutions that provide a physical/virtual single source of truth for specific types of master data. These offer benefits including removal of duplicates, standardisation, elimination of incorrect data (or overrides) and sending automatic error corrections to dependent systems.

## 11.5 Conclusion

In conclusion, good governance is a vital element of non-financial risk management that will both improve efficiency and sharpen decision-making as well as protect organisations from a range of potential liabilities. Moreover, as regulators increasingly focus on governance issues, a streamlined data operating model will foster confidence and support both timely and reliable reporting. The key to making that happen is to put a robust strategic agenda in place, which should be connected to strong basic structures and the appropriate tools to enable scaling.

# 12 Optimizing Effectiveness and Efficiency: Deployment of Artificial Intelligence in Non-Financial Risk Management

*Dr. Jochen Papenbrock, Dr. John Ashley, Dr. Georg Lienke, Florian Seiferlein, Norbert Gittfried, Dr. Stiene Riemer, Hanjo Seibert*

## 12.1 Introduction

Artificial intelligence (AI) is transforming how financial institutions manage risks. What once relied on manual oversight, rule-based detection, and retrospective analysis is now evolving into an AI-driven ecosystem, where risks are identified earlier, decisions are made faster, and compliance processes are increasingly automated. The ability to process vast amounts of structured and unstructured data in real time is redefining non-financial risk management, thus offering financial institutions new tools to reduce risk exposure, enhance compliance, and strengthen resilience against emerging threats. However, this shift presents the industry with both opportunities and challenges. On one hand, AI improves detection accuracy, reduces the number of false positives, and automates complex workflows, thus allowing financial institutions to manage risks more effectively and efficiently. On the other hand, AI-driven decisions must remain transparent, explainable, and aligned with regulatory expectations, requiring strong governance frameworks and ethical oversight. As regulators all over the world introduce new AI compliance requirements, financial institutions must ensure their AI deployments adhere to evolving standards while maintaining operational effectiveness.[1]

AI has evolved from a tool for operational efficiency into a critical enabler of proactive, data-driven risk management. Ever more institutions leverage AI to process vast datasets, detect complex patterns, and support real-time decision-making in ways that traditional methods could not and cannot achieve. AI's ability to enhance early risk detection across multiple areas of non-financial risk has become a game changer:

- Financial Crime Risk: AI enhances KYC/CDD[2] processes and strengthens transaction monitoring, by analyzing transaction patterns and anomalies.
- Conduct & Market Integrity Risk: AI monitors employee behaviors, detects trading anomalies, and flags misconduct in financial markets.

---

[1] For further details on the role of AI in risk management by financial institutions see: ECB/Financial Stability Review 2024; ESMA 2023.

[2] Know your customer/Customer due diligence.

- Regulatory & Compliance Risk: AI automates compliance reporting and scans regulatory updates.
- Cyber & Third-Party Risk: AI helps detect cybersecurity threats, assess vendor risks, and monitor external attack surfaces in real time.
- Sustainability Risk: AI supports climate risk assessments, compliance monitoring, and greenwashing detection.

However, while AI can significantly enhance the effectiveness and efficiency of selected risk-related processes, financial institutions must also strengthen foundational areas in which AI is not necessarily the key driver of improvement. These include organizational and governance frameworks, data quality management, and training as well as upskilling of employees – all of which are critical to setting up a resilient and future-ready risk function. In addition, organizations must invest in cross-functional collaboration and change management capabilities to ensure that innovation efforts are integrated and sustainable. In this context, AI should be viewed as a powerful enabler instead of a standalone solution. Sustainable performance improvement requires institutions to also "do their homework" on these non-AI fundamentals.

Given the increasing complexity and sophistication of financial crime, this chapter will take a deep dive into AI's role in preventing financial crime risk, focusing on key challenges such as detection accuracy, compliance automation, and data quality. Financial crime – including money laundering, sanctions violations, bribery, corruption, and fraud – remains a top concern for financial institutions and regulators alike. AI is being deployed to enhance, e.g., transaction monitoring, optimize alert handling, and strengthen negative news screening, all of which are essential for the improvement of financial crime risk management. Advances in natural language processing allow AI to interpret regulatory updates, assess adverse media, and refine risk modeling, while making sure that AI-driven decisions are auditable and transparent.

It is important to recognize that the degree of regulatory scrutiny – and the corresponding governance requirements for financial institutions – depends heavily on the type of application of AI. Broadly speaking, two categories can be distinguished: First, AI replaces key components of an existing process – e.g., when an institution shifts from human analysts reviewing transaction alerts to an AI model for triage or resolution decisions. In such cases, the potential impact of model failure is significant because alerts that would previously have been reviewed by trained analysts the model might now incorrectly dismiss or overlook, thus increasing the risk of undetected financial crimes. As a result, financial institutions must implement robust oversight mechanisms, such as continuous model performance monitoring, independent model validation, explainability tools, regular bias testing, and human-in-the-loop (HITL) safeguards for high-risk decisions. Regulators will expect clear evidence of governance, testing, and control processes to ensure that risks are appropriately mitigated. Second, AI is added to an existing rule-based setup to enhance detection – e.g., by identifying complex patterns that traditional systems might miss. Since the AI model is not replacing critical decision-making, the potential impact of model failure is less significant and, hence, the associated regulatory scrutiny tends to be more moderate (though measures to ensure transparency and documentation are still expected).

## 12.2 The transformative journey of AI: from rule-based systems to advanced analytics, machine learning and generative AI

Artificial intelligence has evolved significantly over the past decades, progressing from rule-based automation to complex, self-learning systems that continuously adapt to new data. This transformation has enabled AI to move beyond static decision trees and predefined logic into an era of predictive modeling, deep learning, and generative AI, reshaping how financial institutions manage risks and optimize processes. The evolution of AI can be divided into four key stages, each contributing to the increasing sophistication of risk management in financial services.

While the AI landscape continues to evolve rapidly, it is important to recognize that many financial institutions have not yet fully realized the benefits of classical AI, such as rule-based automation. These foundational tools still hold untapped potential, and many operational challenges can be effectively addressed using classical AI, advanced analytics, or traditional machine-learning techniques – without immediately turning to more complex solutions like generative AI. Institutions are well advised to focus on getting the basics right – establishing reliable data pipelines, strong governance, and robust traditional models – before attempting to implement highly advanced AI systems. In many cases, sustainable impact comes not from complexity but from the consistent and thoughtful application of proven approaches.

### 12.2.1 Classical AI: rule-based systems and early automation

Classical AI refers to the early stage of artificial intelligence, in which systems followed predefined rules and logic-based decision trees to automate repetitive tasks. These systems relied on if–then statements and expert-defined rules rather than learning from data, making them useful for structured and predictable processes but ineffective in handling dynamic or evolving risks.

In non-financial risk management, classical AI was primarily applied in automating regulatory reporting, rule-based transaction monitoring, and early fraud detection systems. Robotic Process Automation also emerged during this phase as a complementary tool for automating highly repetitive and rule-based processes, such as populating compliance reports, cross-checking system records, or triggering alerts based on simple thresholds. Robotic process automation (RPA) bots followed fixed workflows without learning or adaptation, making them a natural fit for operational tasks governed by stable business rules.

Another enabling technology during this period was Optical Character Recognition, which allowed institutions to extract structured data from scanned or handwritten documents. OCR facilitated early forms of digital compliance by converting paper-based KYC forms or ID documents into machine-readable texts. While OCR itself lacked decision-making intelligence, it laid the groundwork for downstream automation by enabling rule-based systems or RPA tools to electronically process documents.

While effective for basic risk screening and document-driven automation, these classical AI approaches struggled with adaptability, often leading to a large amount of false positives and a limited ability to recognize emerging threats. Nonetheless, they laid the foundation for risk process automation, paving the way for more sophisticated AI approaches that integrate real-time data and self-learning capabilities.

### 12.2.2 Advanced analytics: from description to prediction

The next phase in AI's evolution saw the emergence of advanced analytics, which introduced key capabilities to risk management:

- Descriptive statistics: summarize and present data in a meaningful way, using measures such as averages, percentages, and distributions, helping to identify patterns or trends in historical data.
- Statistical modeling: uses mathematical formulas to identify relationships between variables and estimate the likelihood of future outcomes based on historical data.
- Regression analysis: statistical method used to estimate the relationship between variables and predict outcomes, such as identifying how changes in one factor – like income or transaction frequency – might influence the likelihood of a risk event.
- Probabilistic forecasting: uses historical data and statistical models to estimate the likelihood of various future outcomes.
- Anomaly detection: identifies data points, events, or observations that deviate significantly from the norm, which may indicate critical incidents, such as fraud, system failures, or errors.

With these tools, institutions were able to summarize data, identify correlations, predict trends, and quantify risks based on historical patterns – providing a deeper insight than rule-based systems. In addition to traditional statistical techniques, graph analytics emerged as a powerful tool to map and analyze complex relationships in risk environments.[3] In financial crime prevention, for instance, knowledge graphs visualize hidden connections between entities – such as individuals, accounts, or transactions – revealing networks of suspicious activity that are difficult to detect using linear models alone. This capability allows institutions to go beyond trend recognition and gain structural insight into how risks propagate across systems. While these methods improved risk prediction, they remained heavily dependent on structured data and historical trends, limiting their effectiveness in dynamic or high-velocity risk environments. This gap led to the rise of machine learning and deep learning, which could analyze complex data patterns and continuously refine risk models.

### 12.2.3 Machine learning & deep learning: from pattern recognition to adaptive decision-making

Machine learning (ML) and deep learning (DL) represent a significant add-on in AI-driven risk management:

- With machine learning, systems can learn from data and make decisions with minimal human input. This happens by training algorithms on historical data, allowing them to identify patterns, and improve their performance over time as they are exposed to new information.[4]
- Deep learning is a subset of machine learning that uses multi-layered neural networks to process large and complex datasets.[5] It enables systems to automatically extract features from unstructured data such as texts, images, or audio, making it particularly powerful in applications like natural language processing, facial recognition, and fraud detection.

These technologies form the core of what is often referred to as predictive AI, enabling systems to learn from data, identify patterns, and forecast risk events with increasing pre-

[3] Graph analytics is a method of analyzing relationships between entities – such as people, transactions, or organizations – by mapping how they are connected through interactions or associations, often using a visual network graph to uncover hidden patterns, anomalies, or risk networks.

[4] An algorithm is a set of rules or instructions a computer follows to solve a problem or perform a task. In the context of AI and machine learning, an algorithm is the method used to analyze data, learn patterns, and make decisions based on said data.

[5] Multi-layered neural networks are AI models composed of multiple layers of interconnected nodes that process data in a sequence of steps. Each layer extracts increasingly complex features from the data, enabling the network to recognize patterns and make decisions in tasks such as image recognition, language understanding, or fraud detection.

cision. Unlike previous models, ML and DL systems continuously adapt to new inputs and improve over time, making them highly effective for specific use cases including fraud detection, transaction monitoring, and early warning systems. One of the most impactful applications of ML and DL in non-financial risk management is natural language processing (NLP). NLP enables AI systems to understand, interpret, and generate human language, making it possible to analyze the vast volumes of unstructured text data that financial institutions routinely encounter. This includes regulatory updates, adverse media reports, internal emails, policy documents, customer interactions, legal filings, and more. In practice, NLP can play a critical role across multiple non-financial risk domains:

- In compliance and conduct monitoring, NLP is used to screen internal communications for indicators of misconduct, identify sentiment shifts, or flag potential insider threats.
- For KYC and onboarding, NLP models extract key customer data from scanned documents, such as IDs or incorporation certificates, reducing manual processing time.
- In adverse media screening, NLP enhances name-matching by accounting for variations, spelling differences, or multilingual aliases, while also classifying articles by relevance and risk category.
- In regulatory intelligence, NLP enables automated parsing of new regulations or enforcement actions, helping compliance teams assess the impact of emerging rules more quickly.
- And in reporting, NLP supports the automatic drafting of suspicious activity narratives, regulatory filings, and audit logs, contributing to a more efficient and standardized documentation.

By turning raw text into structured, actionable insights, NLP expands the scope of what AI can analyze, and it enables financial institutions to better navigate the complexities of real-world language – especially in high-volume, multilingual, or high-context environments. Combined with machine learning and deep learning, NLP equips risk teams with tools that are not only intelligent but also context-aware, scalable, and responsive to the increasing demands of modern risk oversight.

### 12.2.4 Generative AI (GenAI): transforming risk intelligence and compliance

Generative AI (GenAI) introduces capabilities that go beyond analysis and prediction – it can generate new content, synthesize complex information, and automate compliance tasks with human-like precision. GenAI's ability to process unstructured data, interpret contextual risk factors, and simulate risk scenarios is revolutionizing how institutions approach risk mitigation, regulatory compliance, and financial crime prevention. However, its adoption also raises concerns around AI model transparency, hallucinations, and ethical considerations, requiring strong governance frameworks to ensure responsible deployment. As AI continues to evolve, financial institutions must adapt their risk management frameworks to incorporate these advancements, leveraging AI's strengths while ensuring compliance, fairness, and accountability.

As institutions scale the use of generative AI, it is increasingly important to consider the sustainability implications of accelerated computing. Training and deploying large-scale AI models requires substantial computational resources, leading to significant energy consumption and environmental impact. A 2025 report by the International Monetary Fund projects that global electricity demand from AI could more than triple by 2030, reaching levels comparable to India's current national usage of 1,500 terawatt-hours (TWh). Under existing energy policies, this increase could contribute to a rise of 1.2% in global greenhouse gas emissions.[6] For financial institutions, this trend is more than abstract: Under the Corporate Sustainability Reporting Directive (CSRD) and the European Sustainability Reporting Standards (ESRS), companies are expected to disclose the environmental impact of their digital infrastructure – including outsourced AI compute capacity – when it constitutes a material driver of energy consumption or emissions. As a result, energy-conscious model design, vendor selection, and cloud sourcing – calibrated to balance performance requirements and sustainability aspects – will become core components of responsible AI governance, alongside risk and regulatory alignment.

## 12.3 Global approaches to AI regulation

The rapid adoption of AI in financial services has led to increased regulatory scrutiny, as policymakers seek to balance innovation with ethical responsibility, transparency, and risk management. Regulators around the globe are responding by implementing AI governance frameworks, sector-specific guidelines, and risk-based compliance models. AI regulation in financial services varies significantly across the EU, U.S., and China, reflecting different priorities in governance, transparency, and risk management. The EU AI Act imposes strict risk-based compliance requirements, the U.S. has shifted towards deregulation, and China enforces strong government oversight, prioritizing financial stability and cybersecurity.[7]

---

[6] IMF 2025.

[7] For further insights on AI regulation in the financial sector see: Financial Stability Institute/Bank of International Settlements 2024.

### 12.3.1 The need for AI regulation in financial services

As AI adoption increases, so do the risks associated with algorithmic decision-making, data biases, regulatory non-compliance, and an unintended model drift. Without proper oversight, AI models used in risk management could lead to unfair outcomes, reinforce systemic biases, or fail under extreme market conditions. Many regulators around the globe are seeking to ensure that AI governance frameworks prioritize fairness, transparency, and explainability.

### 12.3.2 European Union: the AI Act and its impact on financial institutions

The AI Act represents the world's first comprehensive regulatory framework for artificial intelligence.[8] It uses a risk-based classification, categorizing AI systems into prohibited, high-risk, limited-risk, and minimal-risk categories. Financial services are considered high-risk, meaning institutions must comply with strict requirements for governance, explainability, and model validation. Key provisions of the AI Act relevant to non-financial risk management include:

- Mandatory Risk Assessments: Institutions using AI, e.g., for fraud detection, compliance monitoring, or credit risk analysis, must conduct regular risk assessments.
- Explainability & Transparency: AI-driven decisions must be explainable and auditable.
- Regulatory Reporting Requirements: Institutions deploying AI for compliance or fraud prevention must document AI model performance, bias mitigation efforts, and governance frameworks.

### 12.3.3 United States: recent shift to AI innovation and deregulation

The U.S. approach to AI governance has recently undergone a significant shift following a change in executive policy direction in 2025. Initially, on October 30, 2023, President Joe Biden signed Executive Order 14110, introducing federal oversight for AI in financial services. The order tasked agencies such as the SEC, Federal Reserve, and OCC[9] with strengthening AI risk governance, including developing standards to address bias, fraud, and systemic risks. It also required institutions to ensure transparency and explainability

[8] Regulation (EU) 2024/1689 of the European Parliament and of the Council of 13 June 2024 laying down harmonised rules on artificial intellligence: EUR-Lex 2024b.

[9] U.S. Securities and Exchange Commission, Board of Governors of the Federal Reserve System, Office of the Comptroller of the Currency.

in AI-driven decisions and mandated regulatory evaluations of AI's use in areas such as fraud detection, compliance, and lending.[10]

In January 2025, President Donald Trump rescinded EO 14110, citing overregulation of AI. Three days later, he signed Executive Order 14179,[11] shifting focus to AI innovation instead. Here, key elements include:

- Economic Growth Priority: AI development is encouraged with fewer regulatory constraints.
- Relaxed AI Ethics & Bias Rules: Fairness assessments in AI-driven lending and fraud detection are no longer federally mandated.
- Reduced AI Oversight: The SEC, Federal Reserve, and OCC are instructed to minimize regulatory intervention.

### 12.3.4 China: AI regulation, cybersecurity, and data sovereignty

China has taken a state-driven approach to AI regulation, focusing on financial stability, cybersecurity, and data localization. The People's Bank of China and the Cyberspace Administration of China oversee AI applications in financial services and ensure these align with the country's national security and fintech governance policies. Key regulatory priorities in China include:

- AI Security & Risk Management: AI systems used in risk management must comply with cybersecurity standards and financial stability policies.
- Data Sovereignty & Localization: Financial institutions must store and process AI-related data within China to ensure regulatory oversight.
- Ethical AI & Fairness Standards: AI models must be designed to prevent systemic bias and financial instability.

China's AI regulatory framework reflects a strong focus on risk containment and regulatory control, requiring global financial institutions operating in China to align AI governance with national policies.[12]

---

[10] Executive Order 14110 – Safe, Secure, and Trustworthy Development and Use of Artificial Intelligence (Oct. 30, 2023).

[11] Executive Order 14179 – Removing Barriers to American Leadership in Artificial Intelligence (Jan. 23, 2025)

[12] Office of the Central Cyberspace Affairs Commission: Interim measures for the Management of Generative AI Services (July 13, 2023).

## 12.4 Deep dive: AI-driven prevention of financial crime

Financial crime remains one of the most significant threats to the stability and integrity of the financial system, encompassing a broad range of illicit activities such as money laundering, fraud, terrorist financing, sanctions violations, and corruption. Financial criminals' increasing sophistication has made traditional rule-based detection systems less effective, thus necessitating the integration of AI-driven solutions that enhance detection, streamline compliance processes, and improve data integrity. AI's ability to analyze vast volumes of structured and unstructured data, recognize complex risk patterns, and detect emerging threats in real time is starting to transform how financial institutions combat financial crime.

### 12.4.1 Overall challenges in financial crime prevention

Financial crime prevention is becoming increasingly difficult as criminals develop more advanced methods to evade detection and exploit weaknesses in financial systems. At the same time, financial institutions face growing regulatory pressure, operational inefficiencies, and data challenges, making it harder to identify risks, streamline compliance, and ensure accurate reporting.

#### 12.4.1.1 Enhancing detection accuracy in complex risk environments

Conventional detection models rely heavily on predefined rules (e.g., transaction thresholds, geographic risk factors), potentially leading to a large number of false positives, missed risks, and inefficiencies. A major challenge in detection accuracy is the constant evolution of criminal tactics. Fraudsters continuously adapt their methods, employing layered transactions, mule networks, and AI-assisted (fraud) techniques to bypass traditional detection mechanisms. As financial crime schemes become more sophisticated, rule-based models often fail to recognize new fraud patterns, leaving institutions exposed to emerging threats. Another key issue is the high rate of false positives and false negatives. Many rule-based detection systems tend to generate excessive alerts, overwhelming compliance teams with large volumes of flagged transactions, many of which turn out to be low-risk or even uncritical (false positive). At the same time, these systems often fail to detect subtle but high-risk activities, allowing illicit transactions to go unnoticed (false negative). The challenge is further compounded by the complexity of cross-border transactions in an increasingly globalized financial system. Criminals exploit differences in regulatory frameworks, transaction monitoring standards, and jurisdictional enforcement, making it difficult to track illicit financial flows. Effective financial crime detection requires AI models that can analyze diverse regulatory requirements and transactional data in real time, ensuring that institutions can respond proactively to evolving risks.

#### 12.4.1.2 Reducing manual burden in compliance operations

Many financial institutions invest heavily in compliance operations, yet many processes remain highly manual, resource-intensive, and often inefficient. One key challenge in financial crime compliance operations is the overload of transaction monitoring alerts, which frequently inundates compliance teams with high rates of false positives. The sheer number of flagged transactions makes it difficult to prioritize genuine risks, leading to inefficiencies in resource allocation and delays in identifying truly suspicious activities. A connected challenge lies in the manual nature of case investigations, data collection, pattern analysis, and preparation of suspicious activity reports (SARs). The reliance on manual processes not only slows down risk assessments but also increases the likelihood of inconsistencies in investigative outcomes. Also, financial crime compliance operations face significant hurdles in internal and external reporting requirements. Financial institutions must frequently generate detailed reports for both regulatory bodies and internal stakeholders, often compiling information from multiple, disconnected data sources. The lack of streamlined reporting processes introduces risks of errors, inefficiencies, and delays, making it harder for organizations to ensure a timely compliance while still maintaining operational oversight.

#### 12.4.1.3 Ensuring data availability, quality, and consistency

Effective financial crime prevention depends on data availability, quality, and consistency. Institutions often struggle to access complete and up-to-date risk data, as information is spread across multiple systems, business lines, and jurisdictions. Gaps in data availability create blind spots in financial crime detection, making it harder to track suspicious activities and emerging threats. Poor data quality due to inaccurate, incomplete, or unstructured data further weakens risk management owing to ineffective transaction monitoring, delayed fraud detection, and compliance failures. Strengthening data governance frameworks is essential to ensuring accessible, accurate, and consistently structured risk data, ultimately enhancing financial crime prevention and compliance effectiveness.

### 12.4.2 Case studies: deployment of AI in financial crime prevention

The following case studies showcase successful implementations of AI in financial crime prevention, demonstrating how institutions have leveraged AI to enhance detection accuracy, streamline compliance, and improve operational efficiency. These real-world examples highlight the tangible benefits of AI-driven solutions in tackling complex financial crime challenges and ensuring more effective risk management.

### 12.4.2.1 Case study 1: using digital fingerprinting and synthetic identity coherence to prevent application fraud

Application fraud in credit lending has become an escalating concern, with fraudsters employing increasingly sophisticated tactics to bypass traditional identity verification systems. Affected institutions face a growing number of fraudulent applications, including those submitted using stolen identities, synthetic identities, and AI-assisted automation. If not detected early, fraudulent credit applications can result in significant financial losses, reputational damage, and regulatory scrutiny.

#### 12.4.2.1.1 Starting position & specific challenges

One of the most pressing challenges is synthetic identity fraud, in which fraudsters create fictional identities by combining real and fabricated information. Unlike conventional identity theft, synthetic identities evolve over time, establishing a seemingly legitimate credit history before being used to commit large-scale fraud. Once approved for credit, these accounts are often maxed out and abandoned, leaving leading institutions to absorb the losses. Another major concern is the use of AI-powered fraud techniques that enable fraudsters to automate applications and manipulate digital footprints. Fraud networks leverage deepfake technology, AI-generated identity documents, and credential stuffing attacks to bypass verification processes undetected. Additionally, they use virtual machines, bot networks, and virtual private networks to disguise their digital presence, making it harder for traditional fraud detection systems to identify anomalies. Existing fraud prevention methods, such as rule-based transaction monitoring, credit bureau checks, and manual identity verifications, have become insufficient. These approaches generate high rates of false positives, leading to unnecessary friction for genuine applicants, while still allowing sophisticated fraudsters to slip through the cracks. To combat these challenges, institutions require advanced, AI-driven fraud detection mechanisms that go beyond static identity verification and incorporate real-time digital fingerprinting and synthetic identity coherence analysis.

#### 12.4.2.1.2 Solution: applying digital fingerprinting & synthetic identity coherence analysis

To effectively counter sophisticated application fraud, leading institutions are leveraging AI-powered digital fingerprinting and synthetic identity coherence analysis, which provide a multi-layered approach to fraud prevention. These solutions analyze device characteristics, user behavior, and identity data consistency to detect fraudulent applications before approval. Digital fingerprinting allows institutions to analyze unique digital and behavioral attributes of an applicant's device, internet connection, and user interactions to determine the fraud risk. Unlike the traditional identity verification, which relies on personal data that can be stolen or fabricated, digital fingerprinting examines how an application is submitted. AI models assess factors such as device characteristics, connection anomalies, and behavioral biometrics to distinguish between legitimate users and fraudsters.

Device intelligence plays a critical role in fraud detection by analyzing screen resolution, browser type, and operating system to assess whether an applicant is using a real personal device or attempting to manipulate identity verification controls. Fraudsters often rely on virtual machines, remote desktops, and automation tools to obscure their true identities and submit fraudulent applications. Screen resolution is a key factor in detecting virtual environments. Most legitimate users have standard resolutions based on personal devices, whereas fraudsters with virtual machines often use fixed, low-resolution settings that do not match typical consumer behavior. Anomalies in screen resolution can indicate the use of bot-driven fraud or automated application attempts, helping financial institutions flag high-risk cases. The browser type also provides insights into fraud attempts: While real users access financial services through common browsers like Chrome or Safari, fraudsters frequently use headless browsers or automation frameworks to bypass verification processes. Identifying browser inconsistencies helps detect scripted attacks, credential stuffing, and mass application fraud. The operating system further strengthens fraud detection by highlighting device inconsistencies. Most users operate from mainstream systems like Windows, macOS, iOS, or Android, whereas fraudsters may use virtualized or emulated environments that are uncommon for standard financial transactions. Frequent OS switching or mismatches between declared and detected systems often signal identity spoofing or fraudulent intent. By analyzing these factors, AI-driven fraud detection systems can identify anomalies, reduce the number of false positives, and enhance identity verification accuracy, allowing financial institutions to proactively mitigate fraud risks while maintaining a seamless user experience.

Connection anomalies such as VPN usage, proxy networks, and mismatched geolocation data can indicate fraud attempts, particularly when multiple applications originate from the same network but claim different applicant identities. Behavioral biometrics further enhance fraud detection by analyzing typing speed, mouse movements, and navigation patterns. Fraudsters using automated scripts or bot networks often display robotic or inconsistent behaviors, which AI can flag in real time. By correlating digital fingerprint data across multiple applications, leading institutions detect patterns of fraudulent activity, prevent duplicate submissions, and flag high-risk identities for further review.

While digital fingerprinting focuses on identifying fraudulent application methods, synthetic identity coherence ensures that the identity itself is legitimate and logically consistent. AI models analyze identity attributes to determine whether personal details align across different databases and behavioral patterns. Leading institutions cross-reference identity data across multiple sources, including credit bureaus, fraud watchlists, and external verification services, to validate applicant authenticity. AI-driven coherence analysis assesses whether an applicant's name, date of birth, phone number, and address align with historical records. Inconsistencies – such as a recently created email address linked to multiple high-risk applications – can indicate a synthetic identity attempt. By integrating machine learning-driven cross-validation, AI can detect suspicious identity mismatches, unusual application patterns, and conflicting background data that may suggest fraudulent intent. This analysis helps ensure that affected institutions are not approving credit for non-existent individuals or synthetic profiles designed to manipulate credit scoring models.

##### 12.4.2.1.3 Benefits for financial institutions

The implementation of digital fingerprinting and synthetic identity coherence analysis provides leading institutions with three key benefits:

- Enhanced Fraud Detection & Risk Mitigation: AI-driven identity verification detects and blocks fraudulent applications before credit is issued, minimizing financial losses from synthetic identity fraud and stolen credentials.
- Improved Compliance & Regulatory Alignment: AI-powered identity validation strengthens adherence to KYC and anti-money laundering (AML) regulations, reducing fraud-related compliance risks.
- Seamless & Secure Customer Onboarding: legitimate applicants experience faster approvals with minimal friction, as AI can efficiently differentiate between real customers and fraudulent applications.

By leveraging AI-powered fraud prevention strategies, leading institutions can stay ahead of emerging fraud tactics, improve operational efficiency, and ensure regulatory compliance in credit lending.

#### 12.4.2.2 Case study 2: automating KYC file creation and maintenance

KYC processes remain a critical pillar of financial crime prevention, yet they continue to be highly manual, time-consuming, and resource-intensive for many financial institutions. From collecting and verifying customer information to compiling structured KYC documentation, the effort required to maintain up-to-date and audit-ready KYC files can stretch onboarding timelines, drive up compliance costs, and expose firms to operational risks.[13] To address these challenges, leading institutions are deploying AI-powered solu-

[13] A KYC file is a structured record that consolidates all relevant customer identification, verification, and risk assessment information required to meet regulatory KYC obligations.

tions to automate the creation and maintenance of KYC files, improving speed, consistency, and governance across both onboarding and periodic review processes.

#### 12.4.2.2.1 Starting position & specific challenges

Traditionally, KYC files are assembled manually during onboarding or periodic reviews. This process requires gathering and validating data from a range of internal systems and external sources, such as company registries, identification documents, and media reports. Compliance analysts must then synthesize this information into a format that meets regulatory expectations. However, this manual approach often results in inefficiencies, bottlenecks, and inconsistencies. Assembling KYC files is particularly burdensome for complex customer types, such as corporates or high-risk individuals, where a variety of data points must be pieced together with the client across multiple touchpoints. Discrepancies, missing documentation, and a lack of standardization can lead to delays and increased operational risk – e.g., overlooking politically exposed persons, or failing to detect ownership links to sanctioned entities. Moreover, since updates are handled manually, maintaining a consistent and auditable history of changes over time becomes a significant challenge – especially as regulatory scrutiny continues to increase.

#### 12.4.2.2.2 Solution: modernizing KYC documentation with AI

Modernizing KYC documentation requires a structured approach that aligns with key compliance activities – from verifying the customer identity to assessing risk and maintaining audit-ready documentation. The following framework outlines as to how each stage of the KYC lifecycle can be streamlined and enhanced with a more integrated and intelligent operating model.

The process begins with customer identification and verification, with which institutions collect and validate basic identity information. AI technologies can play a key role in automating this step: Optical character recognition combined with natural language processing can extract data – such as names, addresses, and ID numbers – from scanned documents, while robotic process automation retrieves and reconciles the information across internal systems. Entity resolution techniques help match fragmented records and flag inconsistencies, accelerating the onboarding process while improving data quality and consistency.

Once the core customer profile is set up, the next step involves identifying connected persons and ultimate beneficial owners (UBOs). Machine learning models and graph analytics are used to map ownership structures and detect hidden relationships between legal entities, shareholders, and controllers. Fuzzy matching and a multilingual name resolution improve the ability to identify individuals across different data sources and jurisdictions, helping institutions build a more accurate and complete picture of control and influence within complex customer groups.

Establishing the source of a customer's wealth and funds is another critical element of due diligence. NLP models can extract and interpret source-of-wealth narratives from customer documentation, forms, or onboarding interviews, while machine learning is used to assess plausibility based on known income levels, professions, or regional benchmarks. Robotic process automation can collect and validate supporting documents – such as bank statements or asset records – ensuring that evidence aligns with declared information and risk expectations.

Screening for politically exposed persons (PEPs), sanctions exposure, and adverse media is one of the most resource-intensive parts of the KYC process. AI significantly alleviates this step by improving name matching, reducing the number of false positives, and enabling real-time monitoring. NLP is used to classify and filter news articles as well as regulatory notices based on relevance and risk category, while machine learning models prioritize alerts by assessing severity, recency, and source credibility. Combined with sanctions list screenings, this creates a more accurate and scalable approach to reputational and legal risk detection.

Based on all collected information, institutions determine the customer's overall risk rating – typically categorizing them as, e.g., low, medium, or high risk. Machine learning models, trained on historical onboarding and investigation data, support this classification by identifying risk patterns across customer types, industries, jurisdictions, and behaviors. These models ensure more consistent and explainable outcomes, while also adapting gradually to reflect new typologies, regulatory expectations, and internal policy updates.

Once all relevant checks have been completed, the final step in the KYC process is to consolidate the information into a complete, reviewable, and regulator-ready file. This stage often requires assembling identity data, ownership structures, screening results, and risk assessments into a standardized format that can be easily audited and updated over time. AI and automation technologies significantly streamline this process. RPA and intelligent document assembly tools are used to pre-fill templates with the latest data from various systems, ensuring consistency, while reducing manual work at the same time. NLP supports the generation of narrative elements – such as risk rationales, due diligence summaries, and compliance justifications – based on structured inputs and a case history. To meet regulatory expectations for traceability and governance, institutions also include full version control, metadata tagging, and audit trails on their compliance platforms. These features allow for a transparent oversight, easy retrieval of historical records, and seamless updates during periodic reviews or triggered events. As a result, KYC files become not just more efficient to produce but also more resilient under internal scrutiny and external regulatory audits.

### 12.4.2.2.3 Benefits for financial institutions

Modernizing KYC documentation with AI and automation provides financial institutions with clear advantages:

- Accelerated onboarding and reviews: Automation of data capture, document parsing, and risk assessments significantly reduces the manual workload, speeding up KYC processes while freeing up compliance teams to focus on high-risk cases.
- Improved consistency and auditability: AI ensures structured, explainable, and traceable decisions across the KYC lifecycle – supporting better internal oversight and meeting evolving regulatory expectations.
- Scalable and risk-based compliance: Institutions can handle greater volumes and complexity without increasing cost, while continuously adapting risk assessments in real time through dynamic, intelligence-driven workflows.

### 12.4.2.3 Case study 3: optimizing transaction monitoring E2E

Transaction monitoring (TM) is a cornerstone of financial crime prevention, enabling financial institutions to detect and investigate suspicious activities such as money laundering, fraud, and terrorist financing. However, traditional TM systems rely on rule-based models, which tend to generate high rates of false positives, slow down alert resolution times, and create inefficiencies in compliance operations. These limitations overburden compliance teams, increase operational costs, and potentially lead to regulatory scrutiny due to missed high-risk activities.

### 12.4.2.3.1 Starting position & specific challenges

The increasing sophistication of financial criminals, combined with the evolving regulatory landscape, has created a growing need for more intelligent, data-driven TM solutions. Money launderers exploit weaknesses in static monitoring systems, using layered transactions and AI-assisted money laundering techniques to bypass any detection. Meanwhile, regulators continue to push financial institutions to demonstrate stronger AML compliance controls and reporting accuracy. One of the major issues with traditional TM systems is the lack of an end-to-end (E2E) optimized process, where detection, alert triage, investigation, and suspicious activity report (SAR) filings are fully integrated. Without seamless workflow automation, TM operations experience long resolution times, redundant investigations, and a suboptimal case prioritization. Many institutions still rely on manual alert handling and fragmented case management systems, leading to delays in suspicious activity reporting, compliance backlogs, and an increased regulatory risk. To address these inefficiencies, to enhance detection accuracy, streamline investigations, and improve compliance reporting, leading financial institutions are adopting AI-driven E2E transaction monitoring optimization, leveraging advanced analytics, machine learning, and workflow automation.

### 12.4.2.3.2 Solution: AI-powered holistic optimization of TM

Optimizing TM requires a holistic approach, integrating AI across the stages of detection, investigation, and reporting. AI-driven TM solutions improve detection capabilities, prioritize high-risk alerts, and enhance investigative workflows, ensuring that compliance teams focus their efforts on high-risk transactions. By leveraging AI across the transaction monitoring process, institutions have achieved two to three times faster alert handling and realized up to 40% savings in the overall cost base, combining automation, risk-based prioritization, and workflow optimization.

One of the critical weaknesses in conventional transaction monitoring systems is the high rate of false positives, which leads to an inefficient use of compliance resources. Traditional rule-based models rely on fixed thresholds and deterministic logic that are often too broad to capture the nuances of evolving money laundering patterns. As a result, they tend to over-flag legitimate transactions while missing more sophisticated or subtle forms of illicit activity. Modern AI-powered alert processing addresses these limitations by enhancing both the accuracy and efficiency of detection. The process typically begins with the application of descriptive statistics, which help summarize and analyze historical transaction data, alert volumes, and typologies – establishing a baseline for understanding normal behavior. This statistical foundation is then used to inform more advanced machine learning models that identify anomalies, learn from past investigation outcomes, and refine risk scoring over time.

Unlike static systems, machine learning models can continuously adapt to new information. They assess transaction patterns, behavioral risk indicators, and the investigation history to assess the likelihood of a flagged alert representing true suspicious activity. These models substantially reduce the number of false positives while improving true positive rates, ensuring that investigative capacity is focused on what matters most. To further improve performance, institutions are increasingly deploying challenger models – alternative AI-driven risk models that operate alongside the primary monitoring setup. These models apply different analytical techniques or data perspectives to test and improve the effectiveness of existing controls. By learning from real-time transaction behaviors and identifying complex patterns missed by rule-based systems, challenger models support a more dynamic and responsive approach to risk detection.

By integrating these AI capabilities – including descriptive analytics, adaptive risk scoring, and model-based prioritization –financial institutions are better able to triage alerts based on true risk, reduce unnecessary manual reviews, and thus accelerate resolution times. The result is a more targeted, resilient, and scalable transaction monitoring framework that evolves with emerging financial crime threats.

Furthermore, financial institutions often struggle with fragmented compliance workflows, in which transaction alerts are reviewed across disconnected manual processes before finally reaching a resolution. This lack of integration results in case-handling delays, an inefficient alert escalation, and inconsistent risk decision-making. However, an AI-driven workflow orchestration provides a centralized, automated approach to TM case handling, ensuring alerts are processed, investigated, and escalated based on real-time risk assessments. Key optimizations include:

- Whenever possible, automation of Level 1 (L1) investigations, allowing AI to rapidly close low-risk alerts without human intervention.
- Standardization of Level-1 and Level-2 workflows, reducing investigative redundancies and ensuring that compliance teams operate more efficiently.
- Network analysis integration, enabling AI to detect hidden linkages between suspicious transactions, revealing complex financial crime networks that a traditional monitoring may overlook.

By automating case routing, AI ensures that high-risk alerts are escalated faster to senior analysts (L3), whereas low-risk cases are hibernated or auto-closed, improving efficiency while maintaining compliance integrity. Institutions leveraging AI-driven TM workflows report considerable reductions in case-handling times and a significant improvement in their SAR filing accuracy.

The final step in TM optimization is streamlining the SAR preparation and compliance reporting process. Filing SARs is traditionally a labor-intensive, documentation-heavy process that requires compliance teams to manually extract and summarize transaction details, investigation findings, and risk justifications. GenAI models automate SAR preparation by extracting key case information, summarizing transaction narratives, and generating structured SAR templates that align with regulatory expectations. These AI models contextualize transaction risk, ensuring compliance teams can generate comprehensive, high-quality SARs in significantly less time. By integrating automated SAR documentation and reporting tools, institutions can accelerate compliance workflows while maintaining reporting accuracy, reducing regulatory exposure and ensuring timely submission of SARs.

#### 12.4.2.3.3 Benefits for financial institutions

AI-driven E2E TM optimization can deliver three major benefits for financial institutions:

- Faster Alert Resolution & Cost Reduction – AI-driven automation significantly accelerates TM alert handling, reducing manual workload and operational costs while ensuring a more efficient resource allocation.
- Improved Detection Accuracy & Risk Prioritization – AI models enhance risk scoring, substantially reducing the number of false positives and improving the identification of truly suspicious activities, allowing compliance teams to focus on high-risk cases instead.
- Enhanced Compliance & SAR Reporting Efficiency – GenAI-driven automation streamlines SAR preparation and reporting workflows, improving regulatory compliance while minimizing documentation efforts and processing time.

### 12.4.2.4 Case study 4: enhancing sanctions screening with AI-powered intelligence

The geopolitical landscape is undergoing a fundamental shift. Economic statecraft – through the use of sanctions, export controls, and retaliatory measures – has become a defining feature of international relations. Financial institutions now operate in a world in which sanctions exposure is not only broader but also more volatile, as extraterritorial reach, real-time designations, and cross-regime contradictions reshape compliance expectations.

No longer confined to frozen asset lists or simple name-based blacklists, modern sanctions regimes target entire sectors, supply chains, and digital ecosystems. Dual-use technology restrictions and indirect ownership rules further complicate risk identification. Enforcement has intensified across major jurisdictions, and regulators increasingly expect institutions to demonstrate contextual awareness, proactive controls, and real-time responsiveness. In this climate, traditional screening setups – built around static lists and deterministic rule sets – are struggling to keep up. Financial institutions are increasingly turning to AI-powered solutions to modernize their sanctions-screening capabilities, reduce operational strain, and improve regulatory resilience.

#### 12.4.2.4.1 Starting position & specific challenges

Financial institutions face several interconnected challenges as sanctions regimes become more fragmented and enforcement-driven:

- Explosion in Volume and Legal Complexity: Sanctions designations have expanded significantly, both in scope and legal depth. They now include thousands of individuals, legal entities, vessels, and categories of goods and services – ranging from luxury products to digital asset infrastructure such as sanctioned wallets, mixing services, and blockchain addresses – many governed by jurisdiction-specific qualifiers. This requires systems capable of parsing and adapting to frequent regulatory changes.
- Geopolitical Fragmentation and Regulatory Divergence: A growing rift between U.S., EU, and Chinese sanctions regimes places institutions in a difficult position. A customer or transaction deemed permissible under one regime may simultaneously violate another – especially where extraterritorial reach and dual-use controls apply.
- Operational Inefficiencies: Legacy screening systems generate vast volumes of alerts, most of which are false positives. Investigators spend a disproportionate amount of time reviewing low-risk matches, delaying a true-hit resolution and creating an audit exposure.
- Circumvention Risks: Sanctioned actors increasingly rely on complex ownership structures, cross-border intermediaries, and digital loopholes to mask beneficial ownership or transaction intent. Traditional systems are often not equipped to detect these evolving typologies.
- Slow Policy Implementation: Compliance teams often rely on manual efforts to translate new regulatory frameworks into internal controls. This lag in policy integration delays frontline adaptation, undermines risk mitigation, and frustrates regulators expecting a timely execution.

In combination, these challenges create a compliance environment that is resource-intensive, slow to adapt, and increasingly misaligned with the pace and complexity of modern sanctions risk.

## 12.4.2.4.2 Solution: AI-augmented sanctions screening framework

To address these structural limitations, leading financial institutions are deploying AI-powered screening frameworks that combine the strengths of GenAI and ML. These technologies serve complementary roles: GenAI accelerates regulatory adaptation and operational agility, while ML enhances match accuracy, contextual analysis, and risk-based decision-making. Both technologies can also be applied in the context of trade finance, where document-heavy processes and indirect risk exposures create unique challenges for sanctions compliance

### Using GenAI to quickly process new sanctions rules

As the pace of regulatory change accelerates, financial institutions need the ability to integrate new sanctions requirements into operational policies almost in real time. GenAI enables them to ingest raw guidance and automatically draft-updated compliance policies, internal playbooks, client advisories, and staff communications into their system. This reduces the length of update cycles from weeks to mere days, allowing compliance professionals to shift from writing to quality-assuring AI-generated content, thereby improving speed without compromising control.

GenAI also supports policy harmonization across jurisdictions and departments, helping institutions maintain a consistent and auditable compliance posture. Additional use cases include updating control libraries in response to enhanced restrictions, drafting internal training materials and FAQs, and generating multilingual client notices or regulatory responses. In some cases, institutions are also applying GenAI to board reporting, regulatory correspondence, and internal audit documentation – domains that prioritize speed, accuracy, and traceability. This reduces the burden of manual legal interpretation and drafting, enabling compliance teams to focus more on strategic risk management. The ability to generate tailored content at scale is especially beneficial for global institutions operating across multiple jurisdictions, each with distinct supervisory expectations and often overlapping rule sets.

### Using Machine Learning to improve transaction screening

Modern sanctions screening systems must go beyond string matching. ML-based screening engines to generate confidence scores, learn from investigator feedback, and incorporate contextual metadata – such as the transaction type, jurisdiction, or counterparty profile – to assess risk with greater nuance. This enables institutions to reduce the number of false positives by deprioritizing low-relevance alerts, accelerating the resolution of high-confidence false matches, and prioritizing true risks for human escalation. Over time, these models can be retrained using historical case outcomes, enabling both a continuous performance improvement and adaptation to evolving typologies. ML is also increasingly used to model ownership and control networks, helping financial institutions identify entities indirectly tied to sanctioned actors. These models analyze entity hierarchies, offshore registries, and payment patterns, revealing circumvention attempts that static systems are likely to miss. When integrated with network analysis tools, ML can detect clusters of suspicious activity and map high-risk transaction flows – providing investigators with deeper insights into behavioral patterns and structural risk indicators.

Some institutions also deploy GenAI-powered copilots in the alert-handling process. These tools assist investigators by summarizing alerts with contextual risk factors, recalling prior decisions for similar cases, and drafting case narratives or SAR justifications. In more advanced use cases, copilots can suggest appropriate next steps in line with internal escalation procedures – such as whether an alert should be closed, reviewed by a senior investigator, or referred to compliance leadership – based on the case's nature and severity as well as past handling patterns. This shifts the human analysts' role from repetitive screening to strategic oversight, improving both investigative effectiveness and staff satisfaction while supporting a more defensible, risk-based decision-making.

#### Leveraging AI in trade finance screening

Trade finance remains a persistent blind spot in sanctions compliance, given its reliance on unstructured documentation and complex, cross-border counterparties. Traditional screening systems struggle to detect risks when key information – such as product types, ports of loading, or counterparties – is embedded in free-text documents like invoices, bills of lading, or customs declarations. This creates an opening for sanctioned actors to exploit document ambiguity, indirect routing, and opaque ownership structures. AI can help address these gaps with a combination of GenAI and ML models. The former are capable of parsing and summarizing unstructured trade documents, extracting key risk-relevant fields (e.g., commodity descriptions, vessel names, countries of origin) for downstream processing. These extracted data points can then be evaluated by the latter trained to identify typical circumvention patterns, such as transshipment through known intermediary hubs, unusual trade routes, or inconsistencies between declared goods and counterparties. In more advanced setups, AI tools can flag documentary discrepancies in real time, trigger escalation workflows, or suggest enhanced due diligence based on past case learnings. This creates a more dynamic, intelligence-driven control environment – one that aligns with the evolving expectations of global regulators and reduces reliance on manual document review.

### 12.4.2.4.3 Benefits for financial institutions

The integration of AI into sanctions screening delivers a range of benefits across compliance, operations, and governance:

- Faster Regulatory Response and Policy Adaptation: GenAI shortens the time needed to translate new rules into action, reducing compliance lag and improving readiness.
- Higher Accuracy, Fewer False Positives: ML-based matching improves precision, reduces alert fatigue, and enables better allocation of investigator resources.
- Improved Auditability and Regulatory Confidence: AI-driven systems generate transparent risk scores, explanations, and documentations that support regulatory expectations for oversight and traceability.

- Stronger Detection of Evasion and Indirect Risk: AI enhances detection of hidden relationships and circumvention patterns by using graph-based analysis and dynamic modeling.
- Operational Efficiency and Scalability: Automation reduces the manual workload and enables compliance functions to scale with growing alert volumes and complexity – especially relevant for high-velocity payment environments.

In sum, AI-driven sanctions screening empowers financial institutions to transition from static compliance checklists to a dynamic, risk-based compliance posture – critical for navigating today's unpredictable and politically charged global environment.

## 12.5 Responsible AI: addressing key challenges in AI deployment

As the adoption of AI accelerates in non-financial risk (NFR) management, financial institutions face a growing pressure to ensure that AI-enabled systems are not only effective but also transparent, accountable, and aligned with ethical and regulatory expectations. Responsible AI (RAI) has emerged as a guiding principle to help organizations develop and deploy AI technologies in a way that enhances trust, reduces risk, and supports long-term value creation.

### 12.5.1 Responsible AI frameworks

A robust RAI framework is not limited to a single function or business unit – it should apply to all AI applications across the institution, from customer service and credit scoring to fraud detection and risk management. As such, it must be developed at a strategic enterprise-wide level to then be tailored to reflect the specific requirements and risks of individual use cases, including those of NFR management.

Importantly, building an RAI framework should not be seen as a barrier to innovation. Quite the opposite: By establishing clarity on roles, responsibilities, and standards from the outset, a strong RAI framework helps institutions move faster and more confidently from experimentation to scaled deployment. It creates the foundations for safe and responsible innovations, giving both internal stakeholders and regulators the assurance needed to support AI adoption at scale. While AI offers transformative potential, it also introduces new challenges, including issues with data quality, explainability gaps, model drift, algorithmic bias, and ethical concerns. Addressing these risks proactively is essential to safeguarding trust, meeting regulatory expectations, and unlocking AI's full value in NFR contexts.

We propose an RAI framework built around six core pillars:

1. Responsible AI Strategy: Align AI initiatives with the organization's mission, risk appetite, and values. Define strategic goals and use cases that are not only technologically feasible but also ethically and socially responsible.

2. Governance: Establish clear structures for AI oversight, including roles and responsibilities, AI ethics committees, and documented policies. Governance should ensure accountability across the entire AI lifecycle.

3. AI Risk Management (see deep dive below): Integrate AI-specific risk management practices into enterprise risk frameworks. This includes model validation, performance monitoring, bias detection, and stress testing. Risk controls should reflect the criticality of the AI application, particularly when replacing any human decision-making.

4. Key Processes: Operationalize responsible AI principles throughout the AI lifecycle, from design and development to deployment and retirement. This includes regular impact assessments, audit trails, and mechanisms for human-in-the-loop (HITL) reviews.

5. Technology and Tools (see deep dive below): Ensure the use of tools and platforms that support transparency, interpretability, and resilience. Examples include explainability libraries that help clarify how an AI model arrived at a decision, making the results easier to interpret and validate; adversarial robustness testing frameworks that simulate hostile inputs to evaluate model stability under stress; and automated monitoring dashboards that provide real-time insights into model performance, drift detection, and incident alerts. These tools help institutions maintain control, ensure compliance, and support an informed decision-making process throughout the AI lifecycle.

6. Culture: Foster an organizational culture that promotes ethical awareness, open dialogue, and cross-functional collaboration. Encourage responsible innovation and equip employees with training on AI ethics and risk.

### 12.5.2 Deep dive: implementing effective AI risk management

As AI adoption accelerates in non-financial risk management, institutions must ensure that the AI-driven decision-making remains transparent, explainable, and aligned with both regulatory and ethical standards. The complexity of AI models introduces governance, bias mitigation, and performance monitoring to new challenges, thus requiring a structured approach to AI risk management. This section explores the key components of AI risk management, while focusing on model governance, bias detection, and stress testing to ensure that AI models remain fair, robust, and adaptable to evolving regulatory expectations. The approach to AI Risk Management is an integral element of the Responsible AI (RAI) framework described above.

#### 12.5.2.1 Managing AI model risk

AI models (in non-financial risk management) must operate reliably, predictably, and in compliance with regulatory frameworks. Without proper governance, AI systems can suffer from concept drift, unexplainable decisions, and bias, leading to regulatory scrutiny, reputational damage, and financial risks.

##### 12.5.2.1.1 Governing AI models to ensure reliability and compliance

AI governance involves the establishment of clear policies, accountability structures, and oversight mechanisms to manage AI-driven risk assessments. Thus, financial institutions must ensure that AI models:

- align with existing internal risk governance frameworks, integrating seamlessly into enterprise-wide risk management;
- adhere to regulatory requirements, such as the EU AI Act, U.S. regulatory guidelines, and sector-specific compliance mandates;
- are explainable and auditable, ensuring that risk decisions can be understood, traced, and justified.

Without robust governance, AI models may generate opaque decisions that financial institutions cannot fully validate, leading to a regulatory pushback and loss of stakeholder trust.

##### 12.5.2.1.2 Approach to managing AI model risks

To manage AI model risks effectively, institutions must implement a governance framework that ensures transparency, accountability, and compliance. This includes:

- Explainability Standards: AI models should be interpretable, with clear reasoning behind predictions and risk scores. Explainability techniques help ensure that AI decisions are auditable and can be justified in regulatory reviews. The most widely used techniques include: *SHAP values* (Shapley Additive Explanations; a game-theoretic approach that assigns a contribution value to each feature in a model, showing how much each input variable influenced the final decision; this helps, e.g., compliance teams understand why an AI model flagged a transaction as high-risk), *Counterfactual explanations* (a method that determines the minimal changes needed to alter an AI model's decision, for example, if a loan application is rejected, counterfactual explanations show what specific changes, e.g., income, credit score, would have led to an approval instead), and *Surrogate models* (simpler, interpretable models, such as decision trees or linear regressions, that approximate complex AI models to provide human-readable explanations of their decision-making logic; these are used when deep learning or ensemble models are too complex to be interpreted directly).

- Regulatory Compliance Measures: AI systems must align with global and sector-specific AI regulations, requiring a continuous documentation, validation, and external audits to ensure adherence to compliance mandates.
- AI Risk Committees: Establishing cross-functional governance teams, including compliance officers, data scientists, and legal experts, ensures that the AI model deployment aligns with ethical standards, regulatory requirements, and institutional risk policies.

AI models require an ongoing performance monitoring to detect concept drift, data inconsistencies, and evolving risk patterns. Continuous validation ensures that models remain accurate and reliable at all times. Key elements of AI model monitoring include:

- Automated Drift Detection: AI systems should track data distribution shifts and flag models that require retraining or recalibration.
- Real-Time Risk Evaluation: Institutions should establish continuous monitoring dashboards that assess AI performance against key risk indicators (KRIs).
- Periodic Model Retraining & Validation: AI models should undergo scheduled stress testing and benchmarking against historical risk cases to ensure a long-term reliability.

#### 12.5.2.2 Bias detection and fairness monitoring

AI models must ensure a fair, unbiased, and non-discriminatory decision-making. Bias can lead to unfair treatment of certain customer segments, exposing financial institutions to legal, reputational, and regulatory risks.

##### 12.5.2.2.1 Preventing discriminatory AI-driven decisions

Bias in AI models can happen due to historical data imbalances, algorithmic design flaws, or systemic biases. To prevent discrimination, institutions must:

- identify and mitigate biases in model training data and feature selection;
- ensure demographic fairness, e.g., in fraud detection and risk-scoring algorithms;
- comply with anti-discrimination regulations, such as fair lending laws in the U.S. and ethical AI guidelines in the EU.

### 12.5.2.2.2 Approach to bias detection and fairness monitoring

Bias detection requires a systematic approach that includes:

- Bias Audits: Regular testing to identify disparate impact and discriminatory patterns in AI-driven risk decisions.
- AI Fairness Testing: Methods such as equalized odds (ensuring that false positives and false negatives are consistent across different demographic groups, preventing certain parts of a population from being unfairly flagged as being high-risk), demographic parity (requiring that the likelihood of receiving a positive outcome, e.g., loan approval or passing a fraud check is similar across groups), and adversarial debiasing (minimizing bias by introducing a secondary AI system designed to detect and counteract discriminatory patterns in the primary model's decisions) help ensure that AI models treat all individuals equitably.
- Human Oversight & Intervention: AI models should incorporate HITL processes, in which compliance officers review AI-driven decisions before final actions are being taken.

Institutions must embed bias mitigation strategies into model development, ensuring that AI-driven compliance and fraud detection systems do not reinforce existing disparities.

### 12.5.2.3 Scenario stress testing and AI model validation

AI models must remain resilient during extreme scenarios, ensuring that they perform reliably under different risk conditions. Financial institutions must stress-test AI-driven risk models to confirm their stability, reliability, and compliance with regulatory expectations.

### 12.5.2.3.1 Ensuring AI models perform under varying market conditions

Risk landscapes are highly dynamic, requiring AI models to adapt to changing economic conditions, fraud trends, and regulatory shifts. A failure to stress-test AI models can result in:

- AI-driven over-reliance on outdated patterns, leading to inaccurate risk predictions,
- failure to adapt to crisis events, such as financial downturns or emerging fraud techniques, and
- regulatory penalties for AI models that fail to meet risk governance requirements.

#### 12.5.2.3.2 Approach to AI stress testing and AI model validation

Financial institutions should integrate stress testing and model validation with different scenarios into AI governance processes. Key elements include:

- Scenario-Based Simulations: AI models should be tested under extreme market conditions (e.g., economic crises, cyberattacks, geopolitical instability).
- Regulatory Audit Readiness: Institutions should maintain AI model audit trails, validation reports, and regulatory compliance documentation to ensure accountability.
- AI Model Benchmarking: Regularly benchmarking AI models against, e.g., historical financial crime cases and real-world fraud patterns helps validate their effectiveness.

By implementing robust AI stress testing and model validation protocols, financial institutions ensure that their AI models remain resilient, adaptable, and fully aligned with regulatory and business risk objectives.

### 12.5.3 Deep dive: sovereign AI and infrastructure – control, compliance, and capability

As financial institutions scale AI adoption across critical non-financial risk domains, infrastructure choices are becoming a strategic backbone of responsible AI governance. One central question is whether to deploy models in self-hosted, institution-controlled environments or to rely on externally hosted, API-based solutions offered by commercial providers. While externally hosted models offer speed, scalability, and ease of use, they often present significant challenges in terms of model transparency, data governance, and regulatory compliance. Institutions may have only a limited insight into how these models are trained, updated, or audited – and little control over where their data is processed or stored. These constraints can become problematic under evolving regulatory frameworks such as the EU AI Act, DORA, and GDPR, all of which emphasize explainability, traceability, and data sovereignty.[14]

A self-hosted AI approach – typically based on open-source models deployed on-premises or in EU-compliant private cloud environments – can offer a full control over infrastructure, model behavior, and data handling. Thus, institutions can align AI deployment closely with their internal governance frameworks and regulatory obligations. However, this strategy requires a significant investment in infrastructure, specialized talent, and technical tooling. Institutions must maintain a high-performance computing capacity,

[14] European Union Artificial Intelligence Act, Digital Operational Resilience Act, General Data Protection Regulation,

build and manage the full model lifecycle, and they must develop robust processes for model training, deployment, monitoring, and version control.

A growing number of financial institutions are opting for a hybrid model:

- For high-risk or regulated applications (e.g., risk scoring, compliance decisions), they use internally hosted or tightly controlled sovereign AI platforms.
- For lower-risk, efficiency-focused use cases (e.g. productivity tools, internal knowledge assistants), they leverage enterprise-grade services which offer regional data residency, access control, and contractual guarantees around data usage and model behavior.

Ultimately, an AI infrastructure strategy is no longer a technical afterthought but a governance-critical decision – with implications for regulatory alignment, operational resilience, and long-term trust in an AI-assisted decision-making process. The ability to demonstrate control, explainability, and localization of both models and data will become a key differentiator for financial institutions operating in a globally fragmented regulatory environment.

## 12.6 Conclusions and key takeaways

AI is transforming non-financial risk management, enabling financial institutions to enhance their risk detection, automate their compliance, and strengthen their risk intelligence. However, AI adoption must be accompanied by strong governance, regulatory alignment, and continuous model oversight to ensure both reliability and fairness. The following key takeaways summarize the most critical considerations for AI-driven non-financial risk management:

- AI is no longer optional in risk management: As financial crime and other non-financial risk threats become more sophisticated, AI adoption is critical to maintaining competitiveness, regulatory compliance, and operational efficiency.
- Regulatory expectations for AI are expanding: The introductions of the EU AI Act, and China's AI governance framework highlight the increasing focus on AI transparency, fairness, and accountability. Institutions must ensure AI-driven decision-making aligns with evolving compliance requirements and regulatory scrutiny.
- Data quality and governance define AI success: The accuracy and effectiveness of AI models depend on high-quality, well-governed data. Financial institutions must invest in automated data cleansing, continuous validation, and bias detection to ensure AI models remain reliable, explainable, and fair.

- AI risk governance and model oversight are critical: As AI adoption grows, institutions must implement robust governance frameworks to mitigate risks such as bias, model drift, and explainability challenges. Continuous stress testing, independent audits, and human oversight are essential to ensuring AI remains trustworthy and aligned with business objectives.
- AI must be scalable and interoperable for long-term success: AI-driven risk management must seamlessly integrate with existing risk frameworks while remaining scalable and adaptable. Financial institutions must build flexible AI infrastructures that support cross-functional collaboration and continuous improvement.

# 13 Enhancing the Cyber Resilience of Financial Institutions

*Anna Streuli, Dr. Roman Schnalle, Felix Hildebrand, Dr. Georg Lienke*

## 13.1 Introduction

The financial sector faces an unprecedented rise in cyber threats, driven not only by rapid digitalization, increasing reliance on third-party providers, and the growing sophistication of cybercriminals but also by escalating geopolitical tensions that manifest in cyber warfare. State-sponsored actors and politically motivated groups are increasingly targeting critical financial infrastructure as part of broader strategic conflicts, blurring the lines between cybercrime and national security. Cyberattacks are no longer solely the domain of individuals seeking financial gain; many are carried out to advance political objectives, destabilize adversaries, or exert strategic pressure. Financial institutions are prime targets for attacks due to the high value of financial data and complex digital infrastructures. Cyber resilience – the ability to anticipate, withstand, recover from, and adapt to cyber threats – is no longer an optional security measure but a fundamental requirement for financial stability. A single cyber incident can disrupt operations, lead to severe financial losses, trigger regulatory penalties, and damage reputations. In its 2023 "Global Risks Report", the World Economic Forum ranked "widespread cybercrime and cyber insecurity" as a top global risk both in the short and the long run.[1]

### 13.1.1 Focus of this chapter

While digital resilience encompasses a broad range of risks related to IT infrastructure, operational technology, data integrity, and business continuity, cyber resilience specifically focuses on an institution's ability to prevent, detect, respond to, and recover from cyber threats. Digital resilience includes broader IT disruptions such as system failures, cloud outages, and software malfunctions, whereas cyber resilience is centered on cybersecurity risks such as data breaches, ransomware attacks, and phishing schemes that directly target financial institutions. This chapter will focus on cyber resilience, including the risks associated with third-party dependencies, which have become a critical vulnerability in financial services.

[1] World Economic Forum 2023.

### 13.1.2 Magnitude of the cyber threat

The scale of cybercrime continues to grow, with financial losses and attack volumes reaching record levels. The total cost of damages incurred by cybercrime is expected to reach $10.5 trillion by 2025, highlighting the financial burden associated with security breaches, data theft, and operational disruptions. In 2023, 53% of businesses reported experiencing at least one cyberattack, with a significant portion of affected firms acknowledging that the attack posed an existential threat to their operations. Data breaches have also become increasingly costly, with the global average cost per breach reaching $4.88 million. The increasing reliance on digital services has also driven demand for cybersecurity professionals, with a worldwide workforce gap of four million experts, underscoring the challenges organizations face in defending themselves against cyber threats.[2]

### 13.1.3 Urgency of the issue: digital transformation, cyber threats, and third-party risks

Several factors amplify the urgency for financial institutions to strengthen their cyber resilience. The rapid pace of digital transformation is expanding the financial sector's attack surface, as institutions increasingly rely on cloud computing, AI-driven analytics, and real-time payment systems. While these technologies enhance efficiency, they also introduce new vulnerabilities that require continuous security oversight. At the same time, cyber threats are becoming more sophisticated and frequent, with attackers leveraging automation, AI-generated phishing campaigns, and ransomware-as-a-service models to target financial institutions at an unprecedented scale.

A third major risk driver is the growing dependence on third-party service providers, including cloud vendors, fintech partners, and outsourced IT providers. Supply chain attacks and third-party vulnerabilities have become a major concern, as a single breach within a critical service provider can have a cascading effect on multiple institutions. Recognizing these challenges, the European Central Bank (ECB) has made operational resilience, digital transformation, and risk management enhancement key supervisory priorities for 2024–2026. The ECB emphasizes that banks must not only strengthen their defenses against cyber risks but also enhance their ability to recover from attacks and disruptions to ensure financial stability across the sector.[3]

---

[2] St. John 2024.

[3] See Priority 3 in ECB 2023.

### 13.1.4 Impact on financial institutions

Cyber incidents can have severe operational, financial, and reputational consequences for financial institutions. From an operational standpoint, disruptions to critical banking systems, payment infrastructure, and digital services can lead to widespread customer impacts and financial losses. Cyberattacks that target core banking functions can halt transactions, disrupt online banking, and prevent access to essential financial services, affecting both retail and corporate customers. Financially, the costs associated with cyber incidents extend far beyond immediate recovery expenses. Institutions face remediation costs, legal fees, regulatory fines, and potential litigation from affected customers. The financial impact is particularly significant in ransomware attacks, where institutions may be forced to pay multimillion-dollar ransom demands or invest heavily in restoring compromised systems. Furthermore, regulatory penalties for failing to protect customer data can be substantial, with authorities increasingly holding financial institutions accountable for cybersecurity lapses.

The reputational risks associated with cyber incidents are equally damaging. A high-profile data breach or service disruption can erode customer trust, damage investor confidence, and reduce market valuation. As consumers demand stronger data protection measures, financial institutions must not only ensure that their cyber resilience strategies are robust, but also that these strategies are fully integrated into the organization's overall operations – particularly into business continuity management, crisis response planning, and enterprise risk management. Only a holistic and embedded approach can maintain credibility and stakeholder confidence in an increasingly digital and threat-prone environment.

## 13.2 Regulatory requirements and oversight: strengthening cyber resilience

In the realm of financial services, robust regulatory frameworks and oversight are essential to the strengthening of cyber resilience.

### 13.2.1 Regulatory frameworks

This section examines key regulations across the European Union (EU), the United States, and exemplary major Asia-Pacific markets, namely Singapore and Hong Kong. The maturity and scope of these frameworks increasingly diverge across regions, reflecting differing regulatory priorities, institutional capacities, and approaches to enforcement. This growing fragmentation poses challenges for globally active financial institutions, which must navigate inconsistent expectations while maintaining a coherent and resilient cybersecurity posture.

### 13.2.1.1 European Union: Digital Operational Resilience Act (DORA) and NIS2

The EU's Digital Operational Resilience Act (DORA)[4] aims to enhance the digital operational resilience of financial entities. With compliance required since January 2025, DORA establishes a unified regulatory framework to ensure that financial institutions can withstand, respond to, and recover from various ICT-related disruptions and threats. Cybersecurity is an important subset of DORA, but digital resilience under DORA also covers broader domains such as operational continuity, governance, third-party management, and regulatory compliance. The regulation applies to a broad spectrum of financial entities, including banks, payment institutions, and investment firms, as well as their critical third-party ICT service providers. Key requirements under DORA encompass the implementation of comprehensive ICT risk management frameworks, mandatory reporting of significant ICT-related incidents, digital operational resilience testing, and stringent oversight of third-party ICT service providers. By overriding conflicting national rules in its scope of application, DORA seeks to harmonize requirements and achieve cross-border consistency in the regulation of ICT and cyber risks.

Complementing the DORA framework, the European Banking Authority has updated its Guidelines on ICT and Security Risk Management to align with the regulation's objectives.[5] These guidelines reinforce expectations around governance structures, risk assessment processes, and incident response mechanisms. Financial institutions are now required to integrate ICT risk considerations into their overall risk management frameworks, ensure clear roles and responsibilities at the board as well as the senior management level, and maintain robust capabilities for ICT monitoring, detection, and recovery. The revised guidelines also emphasize the importance of business continuity planning and regular security testing as part of a proactive resilience strategy.

The European Securities and Markets Authority has issued "Guidelines on Outsourcing to Cloud Service Providers", which provide detailed expectations for cloud risk governance.[6] These include rigorous pre-outsourcing assessments, clear contractual provisions, effective exit strategies, and ongoing performance monitoring. Institutions must ensure that cloud arrangements do not compromise data confidentiality, integrity, or availability, and that supervisory authorities retain full access rights. Together with DORA, these

4 EUR-Lex 2022a.

5 EBA 2025a.

6 ESMA 2021.

guidelines aim to bolster third-party risk oversight in an increasingly digital and interconnected financial ecosystem.

Additionally, the Network and Information Security Directive 2 (NIS2) complements DORA by setting broader cybersecurity standards across various sectors, including finance, thereby strengthening the overall cyber resilience within the EU.[7]

#### 13.2.1.2 United States: New York Department of Financial Services Cybersecurity Regulation and U.S. SEC Cybersecurity Disclosure Rule

In the United States, the New York Department of Financial Services (NYDFS) implemented a pioneering Cybersecurity Regulation in 2017, specifically targeting financial institutions under its jurisdiction. The regulation mandates the establishment of comprehensive cybersecurity programs designed to protect consumers and ensure the safety and soundness of the financial services industry. Key requirements include conducting regular risk assessments, implementing robust cybersecurity policies approved by senior management, establishing incident response plans, and submitting annual certifications of continuous compliance throughout the preceding calendar year.[8]

Complementing state-level regulations, the U.S. Securities and Exchange Commission introduced the Cybersecurity Disclosure Rule in 2023, which applies to all publicly listed companies, including financial institutions.[9] The rule requires the disclosure of material cybersecurity incidents within four business days, along with annual reports detailing cybersecurity risk management practices, governance structures, and the role of leadership in overseeing cyber risks. This regulation significantly enhances transparency and accountability, reinforcing the integration of cybersecurity into corporate governance and investor communications.

In addition, the Office of the Comptroller of the Currency has reinforced its supervisory expectations around cybersecurity through the publication of its Cybersecurity Supervision Work Program (CSW) in 2023. The CSW provides examiners with a structured, risk-based framework to assess how well banks identify, protect against, detect, respond to, and recover from cyber threats.[10]

[7] EUR-Lex 2022b.
[8] NYDFS 2017.
[9] SEC 2023c.
[10] OCC s.a., Cybersecurity.

### 13.2.1.3 Asia-Pacific: Singapore's Cybersecurity Act and Hong Kong's Cybersecurity Measures

Singapore has established a "Cybersecurity Act", which came into effect in 2018 and was amended in 2024.[11] This legislation provides a legal framework for the oversight and maintenance of national cybersecurity, focusing on the protection of Critical Information Infrastructure (CII) across various sectors, including banking and finance. The Act imposes obligations on CII owners to establish robust cybersecurity measures, conduct regular risk assessments, and report cybersecurity incidents promptly. It also grants the Cyber Security Agency of Singapore authority to prevent and respond to cybersecurity threats and incidents, thereby ensuring the resilience of essential services.

In parallel, the Monetary Authority of Singapore has issued its comprehensive "Guidelines on Risk Management Practices – Technology Risk", which apply to all regulated financial institutions, regardless of CII designation. Updated most recently in 2021, these "Technology Risk Management (TRM) Guidelines" set out supervisory expectations for the governance and management of technology and cyber risks. Key focus areas include board-level oversight, secure software development practices, effective incident response mechanisms, and rigorous third-party risk management. The guidelines are designed to promote operational resilience by ensuring that financial institutions maintain robust cyber hygiene, continuously monitor their IT environments, and adopt a risk-based approach to managing emerging digital threats.[12]

In Hong Kong, financial institutions become subject to obligations under the Protection of Critical Infrastructures (Computer Systems) Ordinance, effective January 2026, only if they are formally designated as Critical Infrastructure Operators.[13] The designation process is coordinated in collaboration with sectoral regulators, notably the Hong Kong Monetary Authority for the financial sector. Institutions considered systemically important or operationally critical – such as major banks, clearing systems, or payment providers – are the most likely to be designated as such. Once notified, designated financial institutions must comply with a range of requirements, including the establishment of internal cybersecurity governance structures, annual risk assessments, independent audits, and mandatory reporting of significant cyber incidents. This designation-based approach ensures a risk-sensitive application of the law while reinforcing Hong Kong's financial sector's resilience against cyber threats.

[11] Parliament of Singapore 2024.

[12] MAS 2021a.

[13] GLD 2025.

### 13.2.2 Regulatory oversight

To ensure the cyber resilience of financial institutions, regulators have established a comprehensive oversight framework that mandates continuous supervision, incident reporting, enforcement mechanisms, third-party risk management, and resilience testing. The following requirements under DORA outline how financial authorities monitor compliance and enforce cybersecurity standards across the financial sector.

#### 13.2.2.1 Supervision and enforcement

EU regulators continuously oversee financial entities to ensure ongoing compliance with DORA standards. This involves regular assessments, reviews, and audits to evaluate cybersecurity practices and operational resilience. A risk-based supervision approach allows regulators to focus more intensively on institutions that pose greater risks to financial stability due to their size, function, or interconnectedness. Regulators have the authority to enforce compliance with DORA through various measures, including fines, mandated improvements, and other sanctions. Legal powers enable regulators to conduct investigations, issue corrective actions, and, when necessary, take enforcement steps against non-compliant institutions to ensure adherence to cybersecurity and resilience requirements.[14]

#### 13.2.2.2 Incident reporting and management

Articles 19 and 20 DORA mandate that financial institutions report significant cyber incidents to the respective competent authorities within specified timeframes. This ensures a timely regulatory response and helps mitigate broader systemic risks. Regulators maintain a database of reported incidents, allowing them to analyze trends, share intelligence, and enhance sector-wide cyber resilience.

#### 13.2.2.3 Third-party provider oversight

Under DORA, regulatory supervision extends to critical third-party providers, including cloud service providers, to ensure they meet resilience and reporting requirements. Article 28 mandates that financial institutions manage ICT third-party risks by maintaining a register of information and integrating security and risk management provisions

[14] Under Article 46 a) DORA oversight responsibilities are shared between the European Central Bank and National Competent Authorities (NCA) within EU member states. The ECB directly supervises significant financial institutions under the Single Supervisory Mechanism (SSM) in accordance with Regulation (EU) No. 1024/2013, while the NCAs retain supervisory authority for institutions not subject to ECB supervision.

into contracts. Article 30 strengthens oversight by requiring contracts to include audit, access, and inspection rights.

Article 32 introduces a Lead Overseer, a designated regulatory authority responsible for the direct supervision of most critical ICT third-party service providers that support multiple financial institutions. The Lead Overseer is tasked with assessing compliance, conducting audits, and ensuring these providers implement robust security measures to minimize systemic risk. By establishing centralized oversight, DORA aims to prevent vulnerabilities in key infrastructure providers from cascading across the financial sector. These provisions ensure that third-party providers meet strict resilience standards, reinforcing the financial sector's overall cyber resilience.

### 13.2.2.4 Stress testing and audits

Article 26 DORA requires financial institutions to conduct regular digital operational resilience testing, including advanced threat-led penetration testing (TLPT),[15] to assess the ability of their ICT tools, systems, and processes to withstand cyber threats and operational disruptions. These kinds of stress tests help identify vulnerabilities and ensure that financial institutions maintain robust defenses against evolving cyber risks. Additionally, upon completion of the TLPT, financial institutions are required to provide a summary of the relevant findings, remediation plans, and documentation demonstrating compliance with the testing requirements to the designated authority. The authority then issues an attestation confirming that the test was performed in accordance with the regulatory standards, facilitating mutual recognition of TLPTs between competent authorities.

## 13.3 Industry frameworks for cyber resilience

Financial institutions operate in an increasingly complex cyber threat landscape, requiring structured frameworks to ensure comprehensive risk management, governance, and regulatory compliance. Several well-established frameworks provide guidance for securing IT systems and maintaining resilience against cyber threats. Among the most widely

[15] Advanced Threat-Led Penetration Testing (TLPT) is a controlled cybersecurity assessment where ethical hackers simulate real-world cyberattacks to evaluate an organization's defensive capabilities, threat detection, and incident response mechanisms. Unlike standard penetration tests, TLPT is designed to mimic the tactics, techniques, and procedures of actual threat actors, providing a more realistic and dynamic security assessment.

adopted are the NIST Cybersecurity Framework 2.0 (NIST CSF; focus of this chapter), and ISO/IEC 27001,[16] each offering unique strengths based on their scope and focus.

### 13.3.1 Overview of NIST CSF and ISO/IEC 27001

NIST CSF was developed by the National Institute of Standards and Technology, a U.S. government agency. It provides a structured approach to managing cybersecurity risks and is widely used across industries, particularly in critical infrastructure sectors, including financial services. The ISO/IEC 27001 standard, developed by the International Organization for Standardization (ISO) and the International Electrotechnical Commission (IEC), is an internationally recognized benchmark for information security management systems. It provides a structured methodology for establishing, implementing, maintaining, and continuously improving information security controls. Many organizations use ISO/IEC 27001 to demonstrate compliance with regulatory security requirements.

### 13.3.2 Comparison of NIST CSF and ISO/IEC 27001

Each of these frameworks plays a distinct role in cybersecurity resilience and IT governance, with variations in scope, implementation approach, and typical use cases.

#### 13.3.2.1 Scope and focus

NIST CSF is designed for cybersecurity risk management and operational resilience, providing a flexible, risk-based framework that can be adapted across industries. It is particularly well-suited for financial institutions managing critical infrastructure risks, as it allows organizations to tailor security controls to their specific operational needs. ISO/IEC 27001 focuses strictly on information security management, offering a structured methodology to ensure confidentiality, integrity, and availability of sensitive data. It is widely adopted by organizations that require a formalized approach to security risk management and regulatory compliance.

#### 13.3.2.2 Implementation approach

NIST CSF provides a flexible and scalable framework that allows organizations to customize cybersecurity measures based on risk exposure, industry needs, and regulatory requirements. It integrates core cybersecurity functions – Identify, Protect, Detect, Re-

[16] NIST CSF = National Institute of Standards and Technology Cybersecurity Framework; ISO = International Organization for Standardization; IEC = International Electrotechnical Commission.

spond, and Recover – into enterprise-wide risk management strategies, which makes it an adaptable tool for financial institutions. ISO/IEC 27001 follows a structured implementation model, requiring organizations to define a risk-based information security management system (ISMS). This involves formalized risk assessments, security controls, documentation, and continuous improvement cycles to align with regulatory expectations.

### 13.3.2.3 Typical use cases

NIST CSF is widely used by organizations in critical infrastructure sectors, including financial services, where cyber resilience and adaptability to evolving threats are key priorities. It is often adopted by institutions seeking to strengthen security controls without rigid compliance mandates. ISO/IEC 27001 is preferred by organizations that require a formalized security management system, particularly in industries with strict regulatory and compliance requirements, such as finance, healthcare, and government agencies. While ISO/IEC 27001 is often viewed as a foundation for establishing baseline cybersecurity hygiene, organizations aiming to mature and optimize their cyber capabilities typically leverage NIST CSF instead.

## 13.4 The six functions of NIST CSF

The NIST Cybersecurity Framework provides a structured approach for organizations to manage and reduce cybersecurity risks while ensuring operational resilience. It consists of six key functions – Govern, Identify, Protect, Detect, Respond, and Recover –, each of which represents a critical aspect of a comprehensive cybersecurity strategy. This section explores each function in detail, outlining their focus areas, key requirements, and relevance to financial institutions.

Figure 1: NIST Cybersecurity Framework

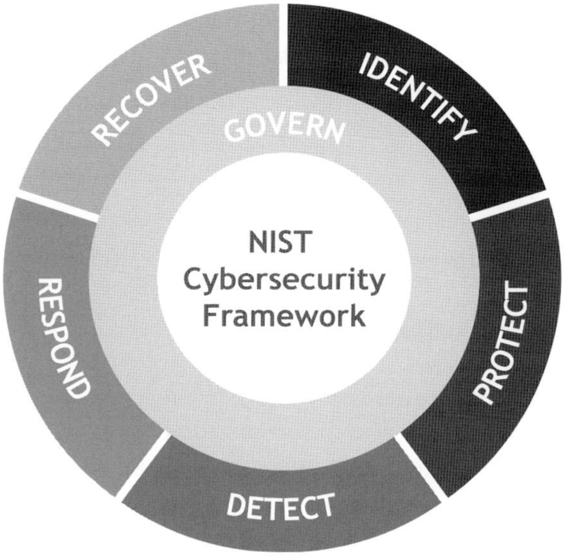


### 13.4.1 Function 1: Govern

The Govern function establishes the foundational policies, oversight, and strategic direction for an organization's cybersecurity risk management. It ensures that cybersecurity is integrated into enterprise-wide governance and aligns with business objectives, regulatory requirements, and risk tolerance levels. This function informs and supports all other CSF functions – Identify, Protect, Detect, Respond, and Recover – by providing the necessary governance structures and policies and is structured along six categories.

#### 13.4.1.1 Organizational context

Effective cybersecurity governance requires a comprehensive understanding of the organization's mission, stakeholder expectations, legal obligations, and operational dependencies. Financial institutions must identify critical business objectives, capabilities, and external dependencies that could impact cybersecurity risk management. A clear understanding of legal, regulatory, and contractual cybersecurity obligations is essential to ensuring compliance with data privacy laws and industry standards. Organizations must also maintain open communication with external stakeholders, including regulatory bodies and third-party service providers, to make sure that cybersecurity expectations are aligned with compliance requirements, industry standards, and operational risk management strategies.

### 13.4.1.2 Risk management strategy

A well-defined cybersecurity risk management strategy provides a structured approach to assessing, mitigating, and prioritizing cyber threats. Financial institutions must document, communicate, and regularly update their risk appetite and tolerance levels, in line with changing threat landscapes and evolving regulatory requirements. Cyber risk management must be integrated into incident response strategies, business continuity planning, and operational risk management. To stay ahead of evolving threats, institutions must establish standardized methods for assessing cybersecurity risks, incorporating both qualitative and quantitative risk analysis for a better decision-making process.

### 13.4.1.3 Roles, responsibilities, and authorities

Clear governance structures are necessary to assign cybersecurity roles, responsibilities, and decision-making authority across the organization's first, second, and third lines of defence of the organization. Leadership teams must take accountability for cybersecurity risks, ensuring that cybersecurity policies are consistently implemented and supported with the necessary resources. Organizations must also establish workforce training programs and ensure that employees understand their role in maintaining cyber resilience. By integrating cybersecurity awareness into corporate culture, institutions can reinforce proactive security practices and foster a shared responsibility for mitigating risks.

### 13.4.1.4 Policy

A strong cybersecurity policy framework defines the organization's risk management approach, security controls, and compliance requirements. Cybersecurity policies must align with industry regulations, organizational objectives, and operational needs. Policies should cover a broad range of cybersecurity topics, including IT supply chain management, access controls, information protection in close coordination with data protection, third-party risk management, incident response, and reporting requirements – both internally to executive leadership and, where applicable, externally to regulatory and supervisory authorities. To remain effective, cybersecurity policies must be regularly reviewed and updated in response to technological advancements, regulatory changes, and emerging cyber threats.

### 13.4.1.5 Oversight

Continuous oversight is necessary to evaluate the effectiveness of an organization's cybersecurity governance practices and risk management strategies. Senior management and board-level committees must conduct periodic reviews of cybersecurity performance metrics and assess whether risk mitigation strategies (still) align with evolving threats.

Adjustments to risk management strategies should be based on insights from cybersecurity assessments, industry benchmarks, and lessons learned from previous security incidents. Strong oversight ensures that organizations remain agile in their cybersecurity approach while maintaining compliance with regulatory requirements.

### Deep dive: measuring cyber resilience based on cybersecurity performance metrics

Cyber resilience is best measured through quantifiable cybersecurity performance metrics that assess an institution's ability to prevent, detect, respond to, and recover from cyber threats. These metrics provide actionable insights into security effectiveness, operational efficiency, and regulatory compliance, allowing financial institutions to continuously enhance their cyber defenses. A data-driven approach, which relies on the systematic collection and analysis of security-related data rather than assumptions or subjective evaluations, ensures that organizations can identify weaknesses, improve security strategies, and meet regulatory expectations.

Security incident metrics help organizations track the number, type, and severity of security incidents over time. Monitoring successful breaches, detected attacks, and near misses provides a clear picture of an institution's exposure to cyber threats. A high volume of successful breaches may indicate vulnerabilities in security defenses, while an increase in detected attacks could suggest improved threat monitoring and detection capabilities. Categorizing incidents based on business impact, financial losses, and reputational damage helps align mitigation efforts with critical risks.

Time metrics, particularly 'mean time to detect' (MTTD) and 'mean time to respond' (MTTR), provide insight into organization's efficiency to identify and mitigate cyber threats. Shorter detection and response times typically indicate stronger threat intelligence, rapid incident escalation, and effective response coordination. Organizations that experience delays in detection and mitigation should evaluate their SOC (Security Operations Center) performance, automation capabilities, and incident escalation processes to enhance response readiness.

Compliance metrics measure how well financial institutions follow cybersecurity regulations and industry standards, ensuring that security policies and controls meet legal and regulatory expectations. These metrics track factors such as audit pass rates, the number of security policy violations, and the timeliness of regulatory filings. Institutions that fail to meet compliance requirements face fines from regulators, increased scrutiny from auditors, and potential reputational damage. By continuously monitoring compliance metrics, organizations can ensure accurate reporting, improved audit outcomes, and stronger alignment with cybersecurity regulations, thus reducing the risk of regulatory penalties and reputational harm.

User behavior metrics provide insights into potential insider threats and security awareness gaps by tracking anomalous login attempts, unusual data access patterns, and unauthorized privilege escalations. Behavioral monitoring also evaluates the effectiveness of phishing awareness training, multifactor authentication adoption, and security policy adherence. If user anomalies increase, organizations should reinforce cyber hygiene programs, improve access controls, and ensure continuous security education.

Patch management metrics assess how efficiently organizations apply security updates to mitigate vulnerabilities. Tracking the average time to deploy security patches helps institutions evaluate their vulnerability management effectiveness. Metrics such as patching frequency, deployment speed for critical updates, and compliance with security best practices provide insights into an organization's ability to address known cyber risks in time. Ensuring that critical patches are prioritized minimizes exposure to security threats and reduces the risk of system compromise.

#### 13.4.1.6 Cybersecurity supply chain risk management

Managing cybersecurity risks associated with outsourcing to third-party vendors, suppliers, and service providers is critical for digital resilience. Organizations must establish a formal cybersecurity third-party risk management program that assesses vendor risks and integrates third-party risk considerations into their overall cybersecurity framework. Contracts with third-party service providers must include cybersecurity requirements, due diligence obligations, and continuous monitoring provisions to mitigate supply chain vulnerabilities. Financial institutions must also evaluate the security posture of their external partners, ensuring that suppliers adhere to the industry's best practices and regulatory standards to prevent cascading cybersecurity failures.

##### Deep dive: outsourcing models in cybersecurity operations

Financial institutions increasingly adopt outsourcing models to manage cybersecurity operations, balancing internal expertise with external capabilities. There are three primary outsourcing approaches: limited outsourcing, partial outsourcing, and full outsourcing.

In limited outsourcing, institutions retain internal control over core cybersecurity operations while selectively engaging external service providers for specialized tasks. This model is typically used for complex forensic analyses, a local service coverage, or interim support, ensuring the in-house teams' operational oversight. Organizations that opt for this model often have high cybersecurity budgets and prioritize internal skill development over external reliance.

Partial outsourcing focuses on high-volume, low-complexity functions such as 24/7 monitoring, alerting support, and penetration testing, while retaining critical cybersecurity competencies internally. Managed Security Service Providers (MSSPs) play a key role in this model, helping institutions optimize resource allocation without losing control over strategic security functions. With this model, institutions define standardized security technologies and operational playbooks to ensure external providers adhere to strict compliance and security standards.

In contrast, full outsourcing involves delegating the entire security perimeter management to an external provider. This approach is common among smaller financial institutions and fintech firms that lack the resources to develop robust in-house cybersecurity capabilities. It allows them to rapidly deploy advanced security solutions without the time and cost of building a full-scale Cyber Security Operations Center (SOC). However, institutions that fully outsource cybersecurity functions must establish strong contractual agreements and audit mechanisms to ensure their third-party providers maintain high levels of security and compliance.

### Deep dive: strategic reasons for outsourcing cybersecurity functions

Outsourcing cybersecurity operations is often a strategic decision driven by several key factors. One of which is the specialized expertise offered by third-party providers. Given the rapid evolution of cyber threats, financial institutions often struggle to maintain in-house expertise in niche areas such as threat intelligence, digital forensics, and advanced penetration testing. By outsourcing these aspects, institutions can leverage specialized cybersecurity talent without the challenges of recruitment and internal training. Cost efficiency is another major factor. The high cost of acquiring and implementing cybersecurity platforms, combined with the ongoing expenses of maintaining an in-house security team, makes outsourcing an attractive alternative. Service-based outsourcing models provide predictable operational costs, reducing the financial burden of large upfront investments in security infrastructure.

Operational scalability is another important benefit. Third-party providers offer 24/7 security monitoring, ensuring uninterrupted protection across multiple geographies. Financial institutions operating in global markets face human resource constraints, making it difficult to staff cybersecurity teams around the clock. Outsourcing to specialized providers allows institutions to scale their security capabilities efficiently, ensuring continuous monitoring and rapid incident response across different time zones.

Lastly, regulatory compliance and data localization requirements influence outsourcing decisions. Some financial regulators mandate that security operations, particularly their incident responses and forensic analyses, be handled by domestically based service providers to ensure compliance with data sovereignty laws. In regions where financial institutions face strict localization requirements, outsourcing to pre-approved cybersecurity vendors becomes a necessary strategy for maintaining compliance.

### 13.4.2 Function 2: Identify

The Identify function in NIST CSF 2.0 ensures that an organization understands its cybersecurity risks, critical assets, and areas requiring improvement. By establishing a clear risk baseline, organizations can prioritize security investments, align cybersecurity measures with business objectives, and comply with regulatory requirements.

#### 13.4.2.1 Asset management

Organizations must identify, categorize, and maintain an inventory of all assets critical to their cybersecurity operations. This includes hardware, software, data repositories, cloud services, and physical IT infrastructure. Effective asset management ensures that all systems are monitored, classified based on risk exposure, and protected according to their criticality. Maintaining updated asset inventories helps reduce blind spots in cybersecurity operations and allows for a more effective incident response and resilience planning.

#### 13.4.2.2 Risk assessment

Organizations must regularly identify, assess, and document cybersecurity risks to systems, data, and operations. This includes analyzing internal and external cyber threats, vulnerabilities, and potential business impacts. Risk assessments should be conducted using both quantitative and qualitative methodologies to provide a comprehensive view of cybersecurity risks. Quantitative assessments assign numerical values to risks, such as estimated financial losses from a cyber incident or the probability of a system failure, allowing organizations to prioritize threats based on measurable impact. Qualitative assessments, on the other hand, rely on expert judgment, scenario analysis, and regulatory requirements to evaluate risks that may be difficult to quantify, such as reputational damage or emerging threat landscapes. By integrating both approaches along with threat intelligence and compliance considerations, financial institutions can make informed decisions, proactively address vulnerabilities, and continuously adjust their cybersecurity strategies to stay ahead of evolving threats.

#### 13.4.2.3 Improvement

Cybersecurity risk management is a continuous process, requiring organizations to identify, document, and implement improvements across all cybersecurity functions. Thus, institutions should regularly evaluate their cybersecurity programs, response strategies, and operational processes to enhance resilience. Lessons learned from security incidents, penetration testing, and security audits should inform strategic updates to cybersecurity policies and infrastructure. Ongoing improvements ensure that organizations remain proactive in mitigating risks and optimizing their security performance.

### 13.4.3 Function 3: Protect

The Protect function focuses on implementing safeguards to ensure the security, integrity, and availability of critical assets, data, and operational processes. It establishes proactive defense measures to mitigate risks found with the Identify function, ensuring that financial institutions can prevent and limit the impact of cybersecurity incidents.

#### 13.4.3.1 Identity management, authentication, and access control

Making sure that only authorized users and systems have access to critical data and infrastructure is a cornerstone of cybersecurity. Organizations must establish robust authentication mechanisms, such as a multi-factor authentication,[17] least privilege access controls,[18] and role-based access policies. Access control mechanisms should be continuously reviewed to prevent unauthorized access, insider threats, and privilege misuse.

#### 13.4.3.2 Awareness and training

Cybersecurity awareness is essential for building a strong security culture within an organization. Financial institutions must conduct regular training programs tailored to different roles, ensuring employees understand cyber hygiene, phishing awareness, and secure handling of sensitive information. Specialized training should be provided for frontline staff, IT and security teams, executives, and third-party service providers to maintain a high level of vigilance against evolving cyber threats.

---

17 Security mechanism that requires users to verify their identity using two or more authentication factors, such as a password, fingerprint or facial recognition, or a one-time passcode sent to their phone or via email.

18 Security principle that ensures users, applications, and systems have only the minimum level of access necessary to perform their tasks.

## Deep dive: enhancing cyber threat awareness through targeted training

Building a strong cybersecurity culture within financial institutions requires a well-structured awareness and training program. Employees, executives, and third-party stakeholders must understand cybersecurity risks, follow best practices, and actively contribute to the organization's resilience. Frontline employees, such as customer service representatives and payment processors, are frequent targets of phishing,[19] social engineering,[20] and fraud attempts. Training should focus on recognizing suspicious activities, securely verifying customer identities, and escalating security concerns. Phishing simulations and real-world fraud scenarios reinforce best practices, ensuring frontline staff remain vigilant against evolving cyber threats. IT and cybersecurity professionals need specialized training in threat detection, vulnerability management, and incident response. Hands-on penetration testing, red team/blue team simulations,[21] and exposure to real-world attack scenarios are essential. Training should also cover AI-driven security tools, regulatory compliance, and evolving threat intelligence to keep teams prepared for emerging risks. Concurrently, regulatory expectations increasingly require active Board-level engagement in cybersecurity oversight. Board members are expected to receive regular training to understand cyber risks, guide strategic decisions, and fulfill their fiduciary responsibilities under evolving governance standards.

Senior leadership plays a crucial role in setting the organization's cybersecurity strategy and risk tolerance. Executives should be trained in crisis management, cyber risk governance, and regulatory compliance requirements. Tabletop exercises[22] and cyber risk workshops prepare people in leadership roles to respond to cyber incidents effectively and enable them to make informed security decisions.

19 Phishing is a cyberattack technique where attackers impersonate trusted entities (such as banks, colleagues, or service providers) to trick individuals into revealing sensitive information like passwords, financial details, or login credentials.

20 Social engineering is a deceptive tactic used by cybercriminals to manipulate individuals into revealing sensitive information, granting unauthorized access, or performing actions that compromise security.

21 Red team/blue team simulations are cybersecurity exercises in which a red team (attackers) simulates real-world cyberattacks to test an organization's defenses, while a blue team (defenders) works to detect, respond to, and mitigate the threats. These simulations help financial institutions identify vulnerabilities, improve incident responses, and strengthen the overall cyber resilience by exposing security gaps in a controlled environment.

22 In cybersecurity, tabletop exercises are used to simulate cyber incidents, such as ransomware attacks or data breaches, to assess an organization's response capabilities. The goal of a tabletop exercise is to evaluate decision-making, coordination, and preparedness in a controlled, discussion-based setting.

Finally, financial institutions rely on third-party vendors, cloud providers, and service partners, making external cybersecurity awareness critical. Vendors should also undergo security training, access control enforcement, and periodic cybersecurity audits. Given the rise of supply chain attacks, institutions must ensure that third-party stakeholders align with their risk management frameworks and security policies.

#### 13.4.3.3 Data security

Protecting sensitive data from unauthorized access, corruption, and loss is critical. Organizations should implement encryption, tokenization,[23] and secure data storage measures to ensure data confidentiality, integrity, and availability. Regular data classification, backup procedures, and secure disposal methods must be maintained to prevent exposure of sensitive financial and customer information.

#### 13.4.3.4 Platform security

Ensuring that IT infrastructure, software, and cloud environments are configured securely minimizes the risk of cyber threats exploiting vulnerabilities. Organizations must adopt secure system configurations, endpoint protection, and continuous patch/software update management to safeguard against malware and exploit attacks. Security monitoring tools should be deployed to detect unauthorized system modifications, misconfigurations, and potential threats in real time.

#### 13.4.3.5 Technology infrastructure resilience

Building a resilient cybersecurity infrastructure ensures that organizations can continue operations despite attempted attacks. This includes implementing redundant systems, network segmentation, endpoint detection and response, and distributed denial-of-service (DDoS) protection measures.[24] Organizations must also conduct resilience testing and tabletop exercises to assess their ability to maintain business continuity under cyber stress conditions.

[23] Tokenization is a data security technique that replaces sensitive information (such as credit card numbers, personal identification numbers, or financial data) with a unique, randomly generated token that has no exploitable value.

[24] A Distributed Denial-of-Service (DDoS) attack is a cyberattack that floods a network, server, or website with an overwhelming amount of traffic, rendering it slow or completely unavailable to legitimate users.

### 13.4.4 Function 4: Detect

The Detect function focuses on identifying cybersecurity threats, anomalous activities, and potential security incidents in real time. By implementing continuous monitoring and anomaly detection mechanisms, financial institutions can quickly identify deviations from normal behavior, enabling both a rapid response and mitigation. This function plays a critical role in early threat detection, ensuring that organizations can respond proactively before an incident escalates.

#### 13.4.4.1 Continuous security monitoring

Continuous security monitoring involves ongoing surveillance of networks, systems, and applications to identify suspicious activities, vulnerabilities, and cyber threats. Organizations must establish real-time security monitoring capabilities that provide continuous visibility into network traffic, endpoint activity, and application behavior. Financial institutions typically leverage Security Information and Event Management (SIEM) systems,[25] automated log analyses, and behavioral analytics to detect early indicators of compromise. To maintain effective monitoring, institutions must regularly update their detection rules, aligning them with the latest threat intelligence feeds and regulatory requirements. Continuous monitoring goes beyond just internal networks, instead, incorporating cloud security monitoring, third-party risk assessments, and anomaly detection in digital transactions. A well-implemented continuous monitoring program allows financial institutions to identify potential cyber threats before they evolve into full-scale security incidents.

#### 13.4.4.2 Anomalies and events

Anomalies and events refer to the detection of deviations from expected system behavior that could indicate unauthorized access, fraud, or cyberattacks. Organizations must define baseline behavioral patterns for critical systems and user activities, allowing security teams to detect and investigate unusual activity. AI-driven anomaly detection tools can analyze vast amounts of transactional, network, and endpoint data, identifying subtle deviations that traditional rule-based systems might miss. Financial institutions must also implement automated alerting mechanisms that trigger real-time notifications when anomalies exceed predefined risk thresholds. Detection processes should include automated correlation of security events, allowing analysts to prioritize high-risk anomalies based on their potential impact. By continuously refining anomaly detection models with

[25] SIEM systems are centralized security solutions that collect, analyze, and correlate log data from various sources to detect, investigate, and respond to cybersecurity threats in real time.

machine learning and real-time analytics, financial institutions can enhance their ability to detect sophisticated cyber threats, fraud schemes, and insider risks.

#### Deep dive: use of AI-driven anomaly detection tools

Traditional cybersecurity monitoring relies on rule-based detection, which often struggles to identify new, sophisticated cyber threats. AI-driven anomaly detection tools provide a more adaptive approach by using machine learning and behavioral analytics to identify unusual patterns that may indicate a cyberattack, fraud attempt, or insider threat. AI-driven anomaly detection continuously learns normal behavior across networks, endpoints, and user activity. Instead of relying solely on predefined rules, these tools repetitively analyze vast amounts of data to establish baselines of expected behavior. When deviations occur – such as unexpected login attempts, unauthorized data access, or irregular transaction flows – the AI system flags them as potential threats. In financial institutions, AI-driven detection tools enhance security by identifying subtle anomalies that would otherwise go unnoticed, such as low-frequency fraud schemes or emerging attack patterns. These systems can correlate anomalies across multiple data points, allowing cybersecurity teams to prioritize high-risk threats while reducing false positives.

### 13.4.5 Function 5: Respond

The Respond function focuses on ensuring that organizations take appropriate action in a timely fashion (immediately, if necessary) when cybersecurity incidents occur. By establishing structured incident response capabilities, organizations can contain, analyze, report, and mitigate cyber threats effectively, thus minimizing operational disruptions and financial losses. A well-defined response function is essential for regulatory compliance, operational continuity, and stakeholder confidence.

#### 13.4.5.1 Incident management

A swift and effective incident management strategy is essential to the containment and control of cybersecurity incidents before their escalation. Organizations must have predefined response protocols, automated containment measures, and real-time security controls to prevent further damage. Incident management efforts must ensure that compromised systems are isolated, malicious activity is blocked, and security controls are activated to prevent the lateral spread of threats. Affected assets should be assessed and prioritized based on business impact to prevent disruptions of critical financial services. To enhance their timely and effective response capabilities, financial institutions must integrate real-time monitoring, forensic analysis, and automated threat containment technologies.

### 13.4.5.2 Incident analysis

Thorough incident analysis is critical for an understanding of an attack's scope, root cause, and potential impact. Organizations must establish forensic investigation processes to collect and analyze security logs, network traffic, endpoint activity, and affected systems. AI-driven analytics tools can correlate attack indicators, automate the detection of related incidents, and provide deeper visibility into whether an attack is isolated or part of a broader threat campaign. A structured incident classification framework helps determine severity levels and response priorities, ensuring that high-risk incidents receive immediate attention. Lessons learned from the analysis phase also inform future prevention, detection, and security policy enhancements, allowing organizations to continuously improve their cybersecurity posture.

### 13.4.5.3 Incident response reporting and communication

Effective incident response communication is critical for the coordination of response efforts, the maintenance of transparency, and compliance with regulatory reporting requirements. Organizations must implement formal communication plans to keep internal teams, regulatory authorities, customers, and other external stakeholders (incl. shareholders and investors) informed as necessary. Incident response teams should work closely with executive leadership, IT security teams, legal departments, and public relations teams to ensure a consistent, controlled, and transparent message throughout the crisis. Incident notification policies should clearly define when and how security breaches must be reported to whom. Financial institutions operating in regulated environments must ensure compliance with frameworks such as DORA, GDPR,[26] and sector-specific cyber reporting obligations, which require institutions to notify authorities within specified timeframes following a security incident. Failure to meet these requirements can result in regulatory sanctions, financial penalties, and reputational damage.

### 13.4.5.4 Incident mitigation

Cybersecurity incident response is an iterative process, requiring a continuous evaluation, refinement, and adaptation. Organizations must conduct post-incident reviews, debriefings, and forensic analyses to assess what worked well and identify areas for improvement. Lessons learned from past incidents should be used to update response playbooks, security policies, threat detection mechanisms, and, last but not least, training materials. To stay ahead of emerging threats, financial institutions should participate in threat intelligence sharing initiatives and collaborate with industry-wide cybersecurity

[26] EUR-Lex 2016.

networks. Regularly testing response plans with tabletop exercises and red team/blue team simulations ensures that security teams remain prepared, responsive, and resilient against evolving cyber threats. A structured continuous improvement process strengthens an organization's ability to respond more effectively to future cyber incidents while ensuring ongoing compliance with regulatory expectations.

### 13.4.6 Function 6: Recover

The Recover function focuses on restoring systems, services, and operations after a cybersecurity incident. It ensures that financial institutions can resume normal activities while minimizing disruptions, financial losses, and reputational damage. A well-structured recovery strategy includes the execution of recovery plans, a clear communication, and a continuous improvement of response capabilities.

#### 13.4.6.1 Incident recovery plan execution

A structured incident recovery plan is essential for quickly and efficiently restoring affected systems and services. Financial institutions must maintain predefined recovery procedures that include data restoration, system reconfiguration, and infrastructure rebuilding. Effective recovery planning ensures that organizations can resume normal operations while mitigating long-term damage from cyber incidents. Recovery plans should align with business continuity and disaster recovery strategies, integrating both automated and manual restoration processes. Organizations must also define recovery time objectives and recovery point objectives to establish acceptable downtime limits and data restoration thresholds.[27] Post-incident evaluations should be conducted to identify weaknesses in recovery processes and inform future improvements. Regular testing of recovery plans through cyber resilience exercises and tabletop drills ensures that organizations remain prepared for real-world cybersecurity disruptions.

#### 13.4.6.2 Incident recovery communication

Effective communication during and after recovery is critical to transparency and trust among internal teams, regulators, customers, and business partners. Organizations must implement a clear recovery communication strategy that includes an internal coordina-

[27] Recovery Time Objective defines the maximum acceptable downtime after a cybersecurity incident or system failure before business operations must be restored. It determines how quickly systems need to be recovered to minimize any disruption and financial loss. Recovery Point Objective specifies the maximum acceptable data loss measured in time, indicating how much data an organization can afford to lose during an incident. It helps determine the frequency of backups and ensures that critical data is preserved.

tion effort among IT teams, security leadership, and senior executives. External communication must be carefully managed to inform regulators, shareholders, and affected customers while ensuring compliance with mandatory reporting obligations. Recovery communication should follow a structured escalation framework, ensuring that updates are provided at key milestones throughout the recovery process. Institutions must also coordinate with third-party vendors, incl. cloud service providers and law enforcement agencies when necessary. Lessons learned from past incidents should be documented and shared internally to strengthen future resilience efforts. A well-executed communication plan fosters trust, regulatory compliance, and stakeholder confidence during the recovery phase.

## 13.5 Emerging challenges and adaptation strategies in cyber resilience

As cyber threats continue to evolve, financial institutions must stay ahead of emerging risks by adapting to new technologies, strengthening resilience strategies, and fostering a proactive cybersecurity culture.

### 13.5.1 Emerging technologies: impact on cybersecurity

As financial institutions continue their digital transformation, emerging technologies are reshaping both cybersecurity defenses and attack methods. While innovations such as AI, cloud and API security, digital identity solutions, and quantum computing bring significant advancements, they also introduce new cybersecurity risks that institutions must proactively address to maintain resilience.

#### 13.5.1.1 Artificial Intelligence (AI): enhancing security and enabling sophisticated attacks

AI is revolutionizing cybersecurity by enhancing threat detection, automating security operations, and accelerating incident responses.[28] However, AI is also empowering cybercriminals to launch highly sophisticated attacks. AI-generated phishing campaigns, deepfake fraud, and automated malware developments enable attackers to bypass traditional defenses. Adversarial AI techniques can manipulate machine learning models, evade detection systems, and exploit AI-driven security controls. Financial institutions must balance AI-driven cybersecurity benefits with robust defenses against AI-powered threats, ensuring human oversight and explainable AI in critical security functions.

[28] See chapter 12 for details on the deployment of AI in non-financial risk management.

### 13.5.1.2 Cloud and API security: securing financial infrastructure in a digital world

The rapid adoption of cloud banking,[29] fintech integrations, and open banking APIs[30] has expanded the attack surface for financial institutions. Cloud environments store vast amounts of sensitive financial data, making them prime targets for data breaches, misconfigurations, and insider threats. Meanwhile, the growing reliance on third-party APIs for the facilitation of digital transactions and financial services introduces new attack vectors such as API hijacking, credential stuffing, and data exposure. Securing cloud and API ecosystems requires strong and advanced access controls, continuous security monitoring, and robust encryption mechanisms. Financial institutions must implement zero-trust architectures,[31] multi-factor authentication, and API security gateways to prevent unauthorized access and protect financial transactions from being exploited. Given the increasing regulatory scrutiny around third-party cloud service providers, organizations must also ensure compliance with industry security frameworks while enforcing rigorous cloud governance policies.

### 13.5.1.3 Digital identity and authentication security: strengthening fraud prevention

Identity security is a growing concern as cybercriminals exploit stolen credentials, deepfake technology, and synthetic identities to bypass authentication measures. Traditional password-based security is no longer sufficient, with financial institutions increasingly adopting biometric authentication, decentralized identity solutions, and behavioral analytics for an enhanced security.

Biometric security solutions, such as facial recognition, fingerprint authentication, and voice biometrics, provide a stronger identity verification while reducing reliance on easily compromised passwords. Decentralized identity models leverage blockchain and cryp-

[29] Cloud banking refers to the use of cloud computing technology to deliver banking services, infrastructure, and applications via the internet. Instead of relying on traditional, on-premises IT infrastructure, financial institutions leverage public, private, or hybrid cloud environments to enhance their scalability, security, and operational efficiency.

[30] Open Banking APIs (Application Programming Interfaces) are secure, standardized interfaces that allow financial institutions to share customer data and banking services with third-party providers (TPPs), such as fintech companies, payment service providers, and other financial institutions. These APIs enable seamless, real-time access to banking functionalities, fostering innovation, competition, and enhanced customer experiences in the financial sector.

[31] Zero-Trust Architecture (ZTA) is a cybersecurity framework that operates under the principle of "never trust, always verify." Unlike traditional security models that assume trust within a corporate network, ZTA continuously validates every user, device, and application attempting to access network resources – regardless of location or prior authentication.

tographic techniques to offer secure, tamper-proof identity verification without relying on centralized databases. Behavioral biometrics analyze keystroke dynamics, mouse movement, and transaction patterns to detect anomalous activity in real time. As cybercriminals adopt AI-driven fraud techniques, financial institutions must enhance their identity security measures to prevent account takeovers, unauthorized transactions, and synthetic identity fraud.

#### 13.5.1.4 Quantum computing: a future threat to encryption standards

Quantum computing poses a long-term but significant cybersecurity risk, particularly in the realm of encryption and cryptographic security.[32] While still in its developmental stages, quantum computing has the potential to break widely used encryption protocols, making financial transactions and sensitive data vulnerable to decryption by quantum-powered attacks. To prepare for the post-quantum security era, financial institutions must begin their transition to quantum-resistant encryption algorithms and adopt cryptographic agility strategies. Organizations must closely follow advancements in post-quantum cryptography standards and work toward integrating quantum-safe encryption techniques before quantum computing becomes a mainstream threat. Regulatory bodies and cybersecurity agencies are already advising financial institutions to assess their cryptographic dependencies and develop migration plans to ensure long-term data protection.

### 13.5.2 Adaptation strategies: adapting to evolving cyber threats

As cyber threats grow more complex, financial institutions must continuously evolve their security strategies to stay resilient. This requires a proactive approach focused on the following key elements:

- *Continuous Learning* ensures organizations stay ahead of evolving threats by investing in cybersecurity training, real-time threat intelligence, and advanced testing methods such as penetration testing and cyber range exercises.[33]
- *Industry Collaboration* strengthens cyber resilience through, e.g., intelligence-sharing platforms, public-private partnerships, and coordinated incident response initiatives, allowing financial institutions to anticipate and respond to threats more effectively.

---

[32] Quantum computing is an advanced computing model that leverages quantum mechanics to perform calculations exponentially faster than classical computers. By utilizing qubits, superposition, and entanglement, quantum computers can solve complex problems more efficiently, posing both opportunities and risks for cybersecurity, particularly in breaking traditional encryption methods.

[33] Cyber range exercises are simulated cybersecurity training environments where security teams can practice their responses to real-world cyber threats in a controlled setting.

- *Regulatory Compliance* is essential. Institutions must integrate compliance monitoring, risk assessments, and security-by-design principles to meet regulatory expectations and reduce exposure to financial and operational risks.
- *Cybersecurity Culture* must be embedded at all levels, ensuring employees, executives, and third-party providers understand security risks, follow best practices, and contribute to a zero-trust environment to minimize human-related security vulnerabilities.

## 13.6 Four strategic recommendations for strengthening cyber resilience

Financial institutions must adopt a proactive, multi-layered cybersecurity strategy to stay ahead of evolving threats, technological advancements, and regulatory expectations. A well-integrated cybersecurity framework enhances threat detection, incident response, and overall resilience, ensuring institutions can protect critical assets while maintaining operational continuity.

### 13.6.1 Strengthen cybersecurity governance and leadership

Cyber resilience must be driven by strong governance structures and executive leadership that align cybersecurity priorities with business objectives. Financial institutions should establish dedicated cybersecurity governance committees that oversee risk management, compliance, and strategic cybersecurity initiatives. Leadership must actively engage in cyber risk assessments, policy development, and regulatory alignment for a proactive security posture. Implementing clear roles, responsibilities, and accountability mechanisms at all organizational levels fosters a culture of cybersecurity awareness and preparedness. Board members and executives should receive regular cybersecurity briefings and trainings to ensure an informed decision-making process in response to evolving threats.

### 13.6.2 Implement comprehensive cybersecurity

Cybersecurity must be embedded into every aspect of an organization's operations, from infrastructure protection to risk management. A strong cybersecurity strategy involves identifying key assets, assessing risks, and implementing layered defense mechanisms that account for external threats, insider risks, and third-party vulnerabilities. Effective cyber resilience requires institutions to develop incident response capabilities, ensure business continuity, and integrate cybersecurity into overall risk management frameworks. Financial institutions should also focus on best practices in cyber hygiene, continuous workforce training, and active monitoring of the evolving threat landscape to stay ahead of emerging risks.

### 13.6.3 Perform rigorous third-party oversight

Third-party service providers introduce significant cybersecurity risks. Financial institutions must enforce comprehensive third-party risk management frameworks, ensuring that vendors meet stringent security, resilience, and regulatory compliance requirements. Conducting regular security audits, enforcing contractual cybersecurity clauses, and implementing continuous monitoring mechanisms ensures that external partners do not become weak links in an institution's cybersecurity defenses. Given the increasing number of supply chain attacks, financial institutions must establish real-time threat intelligence sharing with third-party providers, ensuring collaborative risk mitigation strategies.

### 13.6.4 Strategic technology adoption

The rapid evolution of cyber threats requires financial institutions to carefully evaluate and integrate new security technologies that enhance resilience. AI-powered cybersecurity tools improve threat intelligence, anomaly detection, and fraud prevention, while cloud security frameworks ensure secure infrastructure for digital banking services. Organizations must adopt a risk-based approach to technology investment, prioritizing interoperable, scalable, and compliant security solutions that support their evolving cybersecurity needs.

# 14 Core Elements of Conduct and Ethics in the Context of Non-Financial Risk

*Dr. Barbara Roth, Dr. Erasmus Faber, Dr. Julia Gebhardt, Dr. Katharina Hefter, Constanze Westwood*

## 14.1 Conduct risk: definitions, characteristics and regulatory landscape

### 14.1.1 Conduct and compliance, ethics versus integrity

#### 14.1.1.1 Finding common ground: definition of key terms

While researchers agree that ethics are crucial in today's business world, the concept lacks a precise definition.[1] This is particularly true for the financial industry. As Geddes asserts, the "importance of business ethics is a fact that cannot be overshadowed by the vague details that seem to escape an organisation that embraces the need for it."[2] Others argue that business ethics remain controversial and elude any attempts at universal application, as no single philosophy will fit all organisations.[3] In this chapter, we attempt to establish a common definition for ethics by borrowing Roberts' definition of ethics as "the structuring of principles," built on the foundation of reflective choices and standards of right and wrong.[4] We describe the subtle interplay between ethics, conduct and integrity in the context of the financial industry and outline the implications for managers who must learn to navigate today's complex regulatory landscape.[5]

To grasp the subtleties of the definition, we further explore the origin of our sense of ethical decision-making. As Geddes argues, our sense of right and wrong stems from our exposure to the concept during early childhood. This becomes part of our individual

---

1 In our definition, ethics is interchangeable with "morality." The term "ethics" comes from the ancient Greek word "ethikos," which is derived from "ethos" – custom or habit. Roman politician and philosopher Cicero coined the term "moralis" as a Latin equivalent of "ethikos." From both a historical and linguistic perspective, the two terms are identical, one is a translation of the other. As such, we will not make a distinction between the two terms in this chapter and will use the term "ethics" due to its prevalence in business literature.

2 Geddes 2017.

3 Onyebuchi 2011.

4 Roberts 2009.

5 Geddes 2017.

makeup as we become adults and we realise that this makeup instructs decisions based on alternative action choices.[6] Our realisation has become ever more present in today's world, where "stories of ethical violations are just a mouse click away."[7] Ethics and the dilemma that ethics bring to our lives are not only faced by individuals but also spill over into organisational behaviour as an ever-increasing portion of businesses establish ethical codes and ethics trainings. A study of US businesses showed that in 1994 only 13% of businesses had ethical codes and 7% provided ethical training; by 2017 this had increased to 75% for ethical codes and 40% for ethical training.[8] By 2020, ethical documentation and training have become mandatory for certain regulated industries in the financial sectors. In the US, this requirement is enforceable by regulators. Since 2020, these requirements have continued to evolve, with increased regulatory and stakeholder expectations not only around formal policies and training but also around the demonstration of ethical culture and behavioural outcomes. Ethical considerations now extend to areas such as digital conduct, sustainability responsibilities, and the governance of emerging technologies, including AI. Regulators have expanded their focus to include how firms promote psychological safety, support speak-up cultures, and measure conduct beyond compliance.

Before describing the interplay between integrity and conduct in financial institutions, we must look at two concepts that are derived from ethics and establish a common definition for each. According to the *Oxford English Dictionary*, "conduct" stems from the Latin root of "bringing together" and denotes a manner in which a person behaves. While the definition of conduct is fairly straightforward and generally agreed upon, the same cannot be said about "integrity." According to the *Oxford English Dictionary*, the meaning of integrity – from the Latin root of "intact," is a *personal quality of moral consistency, wholeness and honesty.* However, as Hartman suggests, integrity "is a lot of things to a lot of people and organisations, but its basic premise is based on honesty."[9] And while the precise meaning of integrity is "seldom agreed on and sometimes even contradictory in nature,"[10] we select the most fundamental approach to integrity, which involves a sense of honesty and adherence to a set of personal values in "all situations regardless of how adversarial an encounter may become."[11] Moreover, in the context of business ethics, these values should also elicit trust and esteem, as Treviño and Nelson suggest.[12] In today's business environment, integrity is increasingly viewed not only as a personal virtue but as a strategic and regulatory imperative – especially in sectors like financial services

6 Ibid.
7 Ibid.
8 Ibid.
9 Hartman 2000.
10 Tullberg 2012.
11 Geddes 2017.
12 Treviño/Nelson 2017.

where lapses in integrity can erode market confidence and lead to systemic consequences. In summary, we will define the term integrity for this discussion as an individual's or an organisation's values, which represent honesty, trust, and the adherence to a set of personal standards.

#### 14.1.1.2 Conduct-based versus integrity-based ethics

What is the relationship between ethics, conduct, compliance and integrity?[13] Once again, it is not clearly defined and is often open to interpretation. However, most business ethicists agree that, in general, the ethical taxonomy in financial institutions could be divided into two key categories: conduct-/compliance-based ethics and integrity-based ethics.

Conduct-based ethics are typically based on rules and codes derived from governmental regulations. By penalising the violation of norms and providing incentives for certain forms of desired behaviour, the legal framework plays an important role in treating conduct risk. Compliance programmes primarily aim at preventing conduct risk, e.g., in the form of fraud, money laundering, bribery, insider trading, cartel agreements, data protection breaches (including those related to emerging technologies such as artificial intelligence and automated decision-making systems) and many other violations of relevant laws. Legal compliance requirements typically require management and compliance officers to prevent risks of non-compliance as far as possible, to detect cases of non-compliance and to adequately respond to them. As Paine pointed out in her much-discussed article "Managing for Organisational Integrity," the goal of compliance-based ethics programmes is to prevent, detect and punish legal violations, whereas an integrity-based approach to ethics management combines a concern for the law with an emphasis on managerial responsibility for ethical behaviour.[14]

This compliance-based ethical system came into being as a result of illegal practices committed by businesses that were rewarded government contracts in the 1990s.[15] In the face of corporate fraud scandals of unprecedented proportions in the early 2000s, (such as the collapse of Enron in 2001 and WorldCom in 2002), the US Congress moved swiftly to pass the Sarbanes-Oxley Act of 2002. This aimed to curtail such events and establish ethical boundaries for corporations and, following the 2007 subprime crisis, for the overall financial industry. Underpinned by legal obligations, conduct-based ethics establish rules and penalties for disobedience. Fear seems to be the key motivator in the adherence of conduct-based ethics and, as Geddes describes, "the repercussions of non-compliance

13 Please note that this term is interchangeable with the term "compliance-based ethics," which is also commonly used.

14 Paine 1994.

15 Roberts 2009.

keep employees in line."[16] In conduct-based ethics, employees are driven by "fear of consequence" or by some "ethical compass."[17] Ethical programmes rooted in better conduct are often adopted by organisations that do not wish to face government fines.[18]

Where does integrity stand in the context of business ethics? While conduct-/compliance-based ethics constitute principles and codes born from government regulations, integrity-based ethical programmes are based on the establishment of core principles to which all employees are asked to adhere and govern themselves accordingly.[19] In the case of integrity-based programmes, financial institutions often provide guiding principles, not rules, according to which employees can self-govern. Employees comprehend the importance of such principles to the mission and the organisation's continued success. This understanding is derived from a top-down management approach of installing a clear and precise mission statement that employees will acknowledge.[20]

#### 14.1.1.3 An integrative approach for synthesising conduct-/compliance-based and integrity-based ethics

While compliant (lawful) behaviour will in many cases be regarded as a minimum requirement of ethical conduct, several prominent cases of non-compliance show that just "playing by the rules" may not be enough. A pure conduct-/compliance-based strategy for managing conduct risk is limited for several reasons. First, a complete regulation of (mis)conduct, for example, by a code of conduct or by compliance guidelines, seems impossible due to some typical limits of rulemaking and regulation.[21] Rather, experience shows that rules cannot cover all cases. This applies in particular to those issues that are not fully covered by existing rules. Second, even those cases covered by existing rules may require some form of interpretation to apply them to individual cases. In this context, it seems impossible to completely avoid grey areas.[22] Third, the possibility of creative circumvention of legal rules cannot be completely avoided.

In summary, a conduct-/compliance-based strategy can provide a useful framework but will not suffice to handle conduct risk. However, like conduct(compliance)-based ethics, neither are integrity-based ethical programmes without certain drawbacks. Hartman assesses that "an integrity-based system can be neutral and allow too much debate

[16] Geddes 2017.
[17] Bandsuch et al. 2008.
[18] Lager 2010.
[19] Geddes 2017.
[20] Hartman 2000.
[21] Schulz 2021.
[22] Ibid.

without providing clear direction for employees."[23] In this system, sanctions are difficult to impose as there are no clear rules for how to deal with transgressions. The legal principle of *nulla poena sine lege* – no penalty without law – is relevant here and translates into national labour laws.

Without a strong link to relevant rules and compliance guidelines, a purely integrity-based approach may be considered as some kind of philosophy to be voluntarily adapted by each individual. Moreover, significant training is required to educate employees at financial institutions in applying integrity-based ethics versus simply applying a set of rules as in conduct-based programmes. Finally, it is challenging for employees to consider competing courses of action instead of applying a set of rules to their own individual circumstance.[24] These challenges have become more pronounced as financial institutions face increasingly complex ethical questions, including those related to digital platforms, algorithmic decision-making, and social responsibility.

Therefore, in line with several commentators upon the ongoing discussion on compliance-based and integrity-based strategies, we think that both strategies can be seen as two sides of the same coin and should complement each other.[25] As Geddes summarised his view, integrating the best of both methods leads to the determination that firms must be able to synthesise the two theories.[26] Combining a conduct-/compliance-based strategy with a value-based integrity approach may then serve as an effective compass for the organisation's stakeholders, providing guidance and orientation for proper conduct and serving as a sound framework for managing conduct risk.[27] This synthesis now represents a best-practice standard in the financial industry and reflects an increasing pressure from regulators, investors, and society for firms to demonstrate both formal compliance and authentic ethical culture.[28]

A truly effective ethical programme at a forward-looking financial institution should thus attempt to synthesise conduct-/compliance strategies with an integrity approach. As Eliason notes, "ethical behaviour is not solely good laws or good people but a combination of both."[29] To establish a holistic ethical approach, any financial institution would benefit from adopting conduct-based codes of compliance and a value-based corporate culture.[30] As described above, the two philosophies of conduct/compliance and integrity

[23] Hartman 2000.

[24] Lager 2010.

[25] Geddes 2017; Thielemann 2005, 31–45.

[26] Geddes 2017.

[27] Schulz 2021.

[28] IOSCO 2017.

[29] Eliason 1999.

are at opposite ends of a continuum but should be united in harmony. We argue that an effective risk-based approach that combines both strategies to manage conduct risk should be adopted by organisations in the financial industry. Organisations that combine both conduct-based/compliance-based ethics with integrity-based ethics could significantly mitigate conduct risk. By 2025, such integration is not only considered best practice but has become central to how regulators, investors, and boards assess whether an organisation's ethical culture is truly embedded and effective. This is a topic which we will discuss in chapter 15.

Figure 1: Definitions of key terms[31]

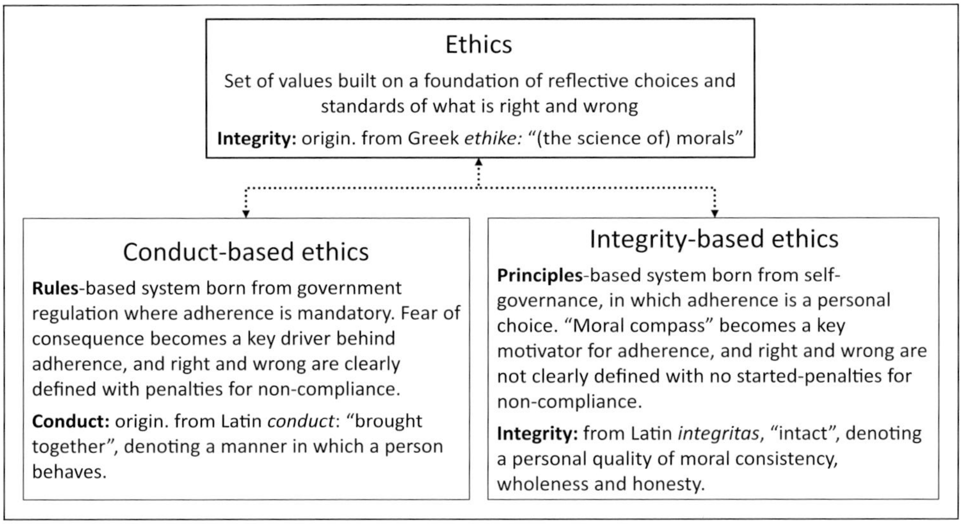


## 14.1.2 What is meant when we talk about conduct risk?

### 14.1.2.1 No universal definition

Going forward, we shall expand the definition of "conduct" as merely rules stemming from legal norms and regulations towards a more expansive definition by *Merriam-Webster* of conduct "as a manner, in which a person acts." As Copley asserts, there is no universal definition of either conduct risk, that is the risk stemming from a person's actions, or what good conduct means in practice.[32] While multiple, sometimes contradicting,

[30] Ibid.

[31] Geddes 2017.

[32] Copley 2016.

definitions of conduct risk exist, we shall settle on the Central Bank of Ireland's definition published in its "Guide to Consumer Protection Management": conduct risk "is the risk a financial services firm poses to its customers from its direct interaction with them."[33] This definition of conduct risk is in contrast to the EBA's definition, which limits conduct risk to the risks relevant if harm to a banking institution emerges. Interestingly, while poor conduct can generally be identified more easily (and be denounced by the public), the line between good and bad conduct is still fairly blurred and good conduct is rarely formalised or rewarded, despite growing regulatory interest in doing so.[34] Ethical culture is viewed as a continuum. Whereas bad culture and poor conduct are regarded as clear issues that can be addressed and disclosed, good culture and conduct are rarely acknowledged and rewarded, as Stark argues.[35]

We shall first describe the fundamental origin of conduct risk: the repetitive nature of behavioural patterns among financial institution stakeholders. The same behavioural patterns have been observed to occur across jurisdictions, geographies and different asset classes, as described in the Fixed Income, Currencies and Commodities (FICC) Markets Standard Board's (FMSB) "Behavioural Cluster Analysis of Misconduct in Financial Markets".[36] While stakeholders often adapt to new technologies and market structures, the repetitive nature of their behaviours allows us to categorise conduct risk into three groups: misconduct against the market's integrity, misconduct against clients' interest and misconduct from employees. Such categorisation stands at the core of the European Insurance and Occupational Pensions Authority's (EIOPA) regulatory framework, and we use it as a springboard for our discussion of conduct risk.[37] These three key types of conduct risk (market conduct risk, client conduct risk and employee conduct risk) will be explored further in the next chapter.

### 14.1.2.2 Three key topics: market, client and employee conduct risk

First, market conduct risk can be defined as the risk of the integrity and transparency of the market being harmed by unfair or abusive behaviour towards fellow market participants. FMSB outlines seven client misconduct patterns observable in the market:

1. price manipulation (spoofing/layering, new issue/M&A price support, ramping, squeezing/cornering, bull/bear raids);
2. inside information (insider dealing, soundings, research);

[33] Central Bank of Ireland 2017, 7.

[34] FCA 2020b.

[35] Stark 1993.

[36] FMSB 2018a.

[37] EIOPA 2019.

3. circular trading (wash trades, matched trades, money pass & compensation trades, stop losses & limits);
4. reference price influence (benchmarks, closing prices, reference prices, portfolio trades, barriers);
5. conclusion and information sharing (pools, information disclosure);
6. improper order handling (front running, cherry picking & partial fills, stop losses & limits);
7. misleading (guarantees, window dressing, misrepresentation).[38]

While the above analysis is not entirely original, and a number of different authorities and reviews – most recently the "Fair and Effective Markets Review" (FEMR) by the Bank of England in 2015 – have recognised the importance of focusing on the behavioural patterns underlying market misconduct, in 2018 the FMSB became the first standard-setting body to collate, analyse and publish these behavioural patterns of market conduct risk as a single reference point for market participants.[39] This work remains foundational for market conduct monitoring in 2025, especially in algorithmic and high-frequency trading contexts.

The second conduct risk category – client conduct risk – can be defined as the risk of harm to clients by resolving conflicts of interests to their disadvantage, causing them financial loss or other detriment. There are seven key client misconduct patterns observable in the market, which form the basis of the conduct risk definition in the European Banking Authority (EBA) guidelines on common procedure and methodology for the Supervisory Review and Evaluation Process (SREP)[40]:

1. mis-selling of products, in both retail and wholesale markets;
2. pushed cross-selling of products to retail customers, such as packaged bank accounts or add-on products customers do not need;
3. conflicts of interest in conducting business;
4. barriers to switching financial products during their lifetime and/or to switching financial service providers;
5. poorly designed distribution channels that may enable conflicts of interest with false incentives;
6. automatic renewals of products or exit penalties;
7. unfair processing of customer complaints.

---

[38] FMSB 2018b.

[39] Bank of England/HM Treasury 2015.

[40] EBA 2014, 97–98.

Together with the FMSB's report, the EBA's guidelines serve as an exhaustive list of key conduct risk subcategories. While individual entities and institutions have adopted their own taxonomies, the above categories have served as the backbone for several conduct risk analyses. In recent years, the rise of digital distribution channels and algorithmically driven product placements has introduced new forms of client conduct risk, prompting regulators to examine the role of customer data, profiling, and product suitability in more detail.

The third conduct risk category – employee conduct risk – can be defined as the risk of harm to the organisation by employees engaging conflicts of interests or violations of the code of conduct. The European Union defines conflict of interest as a situation in which

> *"the 'impartial and objective exercise of the functions of a financial actor or other person' involved in budget implementation 'is compromised for reasons involving family, emotional life, political or national affinity, economic interest or any other direct or indirect personal interest.'"*[41]

According to the U.S. Securities and Exchange Commission (SEC), organisations need to integrate the conflict of interest risk into their three lines of defence (LoD) structure and should consider conflict of interest throughout their key business processes including strategic planning, capital allocation, performance monitoring as well as evaluation of business units and individual business leaders.[42]

Beyond formal conflicts of interest, regulators and boards are increasingly concerned with how cultural factors, such as speak-up environments, retaliation risks and behavioural norms, affect employee conduct and ethical decision-making. This includes growing awareness of how mental health, psychological safety, and overall well-being influence ethical behaviour and long-term conduct outcomes.[43]

### 14.1.3 Conduct risk in the NFR taxonomy

NFR risk class (see Figure 2 in Chapter 2 on page 21), in general, consists of eleven key risk categories, which include conduct risk (grouped together with financial crime risk and regulatory compliance risk).[44]

---

[41] EUR-Lex 2021.

[42] SEC 2012.

[43] FCA 2020b, 1.

[44] Please, note that "client tax evasion" also falls under the tax department's responsibility (in addition to that of the compliance department).

Where does conduct risk fall within the overall taxonomy of NFR? Financial institutions employ their own NFR Risk Taxonomy rubrics to organise specialist teams. The remits and chains of command of conduct teams, in particular, tend to overlap with other NFR teams, such as compliance and ethics, or they fall within the same category. Moreover, additional NFR frameworks are often created without considerations for existing taxonomies. Lack of a clearly defined NFR taxonomy often leads to serious inefficiencies and might further exacerbate potential conduct risk rather than alleviate it.

## 14.2 Regulatory landscape

After the 2007–08 financial crisis, the need to ramp up legal efforts to build a more ethical market became apparent. Regulatory oversight has increased significantly as a result. This increase has occurred both on a global level, with new guiding standards imposed, and on a national level, with emergence of more complex legal frameworks. Global principles and codes often started as non-legally binding but have had regulatory impact as national governments employed such codes in drafting binding legislations. "Principles for Sound Compensation Practices" and "Global FX Code" published by the Financial Stability Board (FSB), an international body that includes all G20 major economies, serve as early examples of codes that have had ramifications well beyond their non-binding nature.

As a direct result of the crisis, the „Principles for Sound Compensation Practices“ introduced several recommendations in 2009 to align compensation with prudent risk-taking.[45] Other measures by the FSB also focused particularly on how incentive systems can aid in preventing and responding to conduct incidents.[46] It is important to note that the FSB's recommendations complemented other elements of its misconduct action plan and came as part of "broader measures to restore public trust in the financial system."[47] Interestingly, FSB's toolkit focused significantly on identifying conduct risks and emphasised 19 tools that FI stakeholders could employ to address three key misconduct issues, namely:

1. alleviating cultural drivers of misconduct,
2. reinforcing individual responsibility and accountability, and
3. addressing the "rolling bad apples" phenomenon referring to individuals who change firms or roles within a firm without disclosing previous misconduct.[48]

---

45 FSB 2009, 2.

46 FSB 2018.

47 Ibid.

48 Addressing "rolling bad apples" phenomenon included tools to improve interview processes and onboarding of new employees and for regular updates to background checks to avoid hiring an individual with a history of misconduct.

Another global committee, the Foreign Exchange Working Group (FXWG), was established in 2015 by 21 central banks in collaboration with market participants to develop a global perspective on conduct in the wholesale foreign exchange market. The resulting "Global FX code" contained a set of good-practice principles that aimed to set the tone for the whole market.[49] The code was developed to provide a common set of guidelines to promote the integrity and effective functioning of the market, in which FXWG members were involved.[50] Its intention to promote a robust, fair, liquid, open and appropriately transparent marketplace was also based on recommendations rather than laws. While the code was developed through a partnership between central banks and market participants from 16 jurisdictions around the globe, it clearly emphasised its non-binding nature ("no legal or regulatory obligations"[51]). Instead, the code was meant to supplement any local laws, rules and regulations by highlighting good practices and processes.[52] Although it was not legally binding, it has influenced regulatory endeavours. For instance, Singapore's "Guide to Conduct & Market Practices for the Wholesale Financial Markets" references the code as its global counterpart.[53]

As these committees continue to push for global standards, regulators have increased their efforts to translate these recommendations into nationally binding guidelines and directives. Three major trends have been looming in this regulatory landscape:

1. *from penalising to preventing* while in the past, regulators primarily sanctioned poor conduct once it occurred, in recent years they have incorporated preventive measures into their requirements, demanding firms to actively tackle the cultural and organisational inadequacies enabling misconduct in the first place;

2. *from case-by-case to systemic:* while both legal investigations and the public used to focus on isolated cases, often struggling to reconstruct responsibilities, more recent regulations have extended individual liability to senior management regimes in an effort to establish a more systemic approach;

3. *from box-ticking to outcome-driven:* instead of refining directives to cover ever-emerging loopholes, regulators are now beginning to frame expectations of good conduct in the shape of open questions, leaving companies to resolve the practicalities on their own.

49 GFEC 2018, 1.

50 Ibid.

51 Ibid.

52 Ibid.

53 SFEMC 2018.

Figure 2: Timeline and trends in the conduct risk regulatory landscape

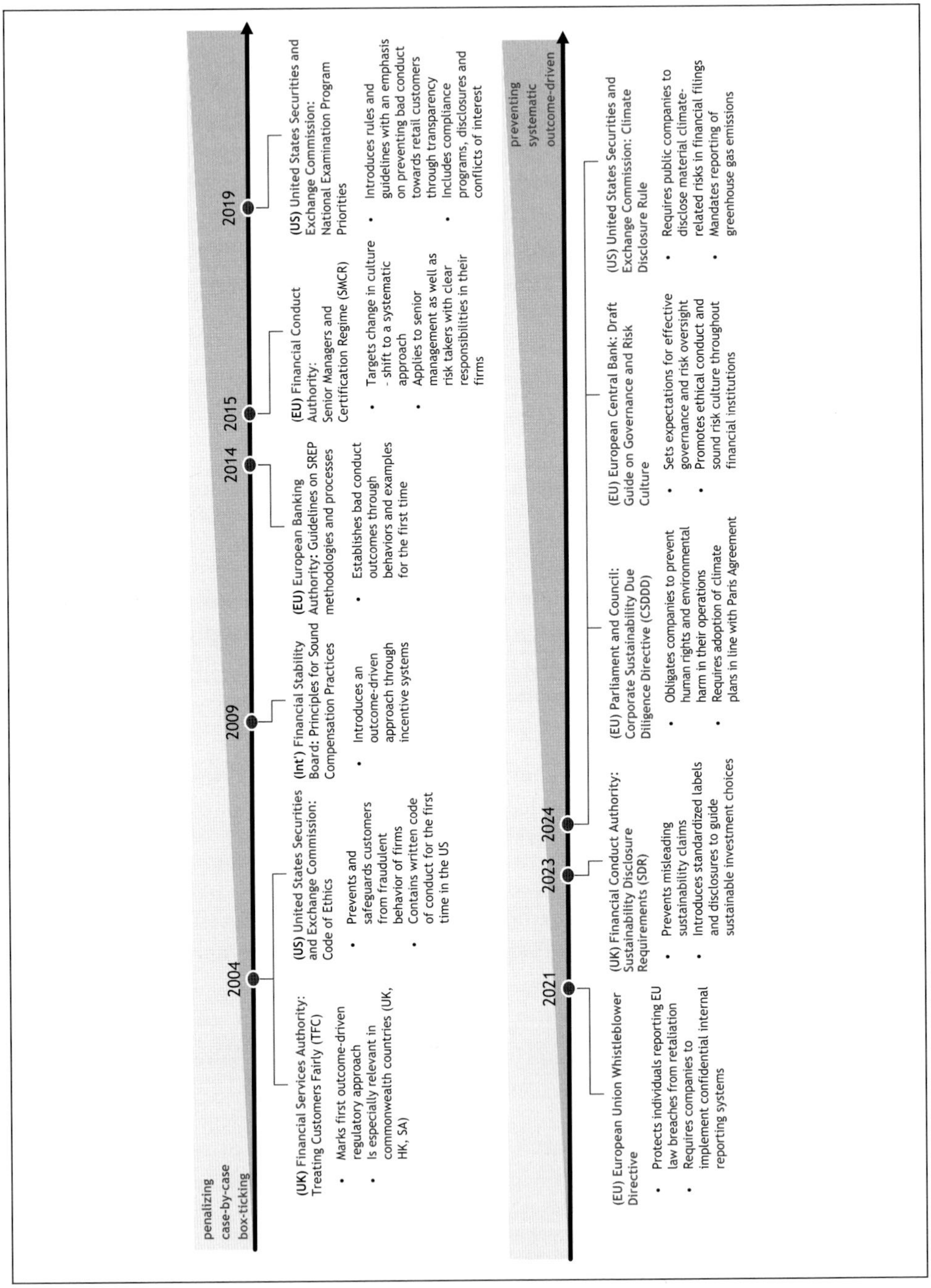

While the above developments have often been of a global nature, with a high level of collaboration and intertwined partnerships between financial institution stakeholders in different countries, important regional and national approaches to conduct risk have emerged. The following chapters discuss regional and national tactics with a particular focus on EU/UK, US and Asia-Pacific perspectives.

### 14.2.1 European perspective

#### 14.2.1.1 European/UK regulators

UK regulators, in particular the Financial Services Authority (FSA), now the Financial Conduct Authority (FCA), have been at the forefront of shaping the European perspective since the early 2000s. In 2004, the FSA published a report on "Treating Customers Fairly" (TCF). This report was followed by a 2006 paper, which provided a list of key outcomes and addressed the further need for action among regulated players in the financial services market.[54] Besides publishing six specific outcomes of good conduct the FSA went on to emphasise that in order to ensure such outcomes were attained it was insufficient to simply implement a set of rules.[55] Instead, financial institution stakeholders were asked to continuously embed the program in their corporate cultures.[56] To do so, as the FSA suggested, companies must consider the entire product life cycle as well as its value chain, from product design, market targeting, marketing, sales and after-sales through to complaint handling.[57]

In the early 2010s, EU regulators built on a series of rules published via MiFID I to continue their focus on conduct risk, refining a set of definitions and rules for good versus bad conduct. In 2014, the European Securities and Markets Authority (ESMA) published

[54] FSA 2006.

[55] Outcome 1: consumers can be confident they are dealing with firms where the fair treatment of customers is central to the corporate culture.
Outcome 2: products and services marketed and sold in the retail market are designed to meet the needs of identified consumer groups and are targeted accordingly.
Outcome 3: consumers are provided with clear information and are kept appropriately informed before, during and after the point of sale.
Outcome 4: where consumers receive advice, the advice is suitable and takes account of their circumstances.
Outcome 5: consumers are provided with products that perform as firms have led them to expect, and the associated service is of an acceptable standard and as they have been led to expect.
Outcome 6: consumers do not face unreasonable post-sale barriers imposed by firms to change product, switch provider, submit a claim or make a complaint.

[56] FSA 2006, 2–4.

[57] Ibid., 6.

regulations to enhance customer and investor protection, including a definition of good and bad practices for product governance arrangements. In the same year, the EBA published "Guidelines on SREP methodologies and processes," which contained specific references to conduct risk, including definitions and a list of both conduct risk categories and examples of behaviours associated with bad conduct.[58] The EBA guidelines were directed at national authorities and recommended regulatory measures focusing on the elimination of individual misconduct by identifying dominant positions and misguided incentives, as well as by overseeing sanctions against institutions exhibiting misconduct. It also urged relevant authorities to "apply a forward-looking approach," considering the impact of EU-wide financial developments as well as overall strategies to protect consumers in general.[59]

Two years later, in 2016, the FCA's handbook "Code of Conduct (COCON)" laid down explicit rules for individual conduct committing players in banking to act with integrity, due skill, care, diligence, transparency and fairness.[60] Moreover, in addition to the above, the FCA included specific rules for senior management, highlighting management's responsibility in taking "reasonable steps" to ensure "good conduct" standards are met.[61] One of the "reasonable steps" that the FCA expected was detailed "appropriate" disclosure of any information "of which the FCA or Prudential Regulation Authority (PRA) would reasonably expect to notice."[62] In doing so, the regulators had placed the burden of responsibility on the shoulders of senior management – not just for the fair treatment of customers but also for the disclosure of any relevant information to the authorities.

Senior management has, in fact, become the core focus throughout the late 2010s. These new regimes have significantly expanded upon the above-mentioned rules and responsibilities. In 2015, the FCA first introduced the "Senior Managers and Certification Regime" (SM&CR), which further elaborated on roles, responsibilities, and the need for expanded accountability among senior management.[63] Ultimately, this regime pushed for the systematisation of liability at the level of an individual employee, as shown by the increase in the proportion of cases against individuals. Between 2015 and 2019, the share of cases against individuals doubled from 40% to 80%. This trend will likely continue. In 2020, 73% of practitioners surveyed believed that regulatory focus on culture and

58 EBA 2014, 97–98.

59 Ibid., 98.

60 FCA 2020a.

61 Ibid.

62 Ibid.

63 The SMCR was last updated in 2019; FCA 2019d.

conduct risk would increase the personal liability of senior managers.[64] Subsequent developments, including the adoption of the EU Corporate Sustainability Due Diligence Directive,[65] have reinforced this trajectory, expanding board-level accountability and embedding individual responsibility for organisational conduct and risk governance.

What trends and developments will shape the future of the European conduct risk regulatory landscape? Increasing focus on outcomes with conduct risk frameworks that are specifically tailored to each company's needs will serve as key drivers for the future of conduct risk legislation. In 2015, the FCA launched this trend by publishing its "5 Conduct Questions" (5CQ) program for wholesale banks. This stood at the forefront of initiating a more outcome-oriented approach to conduct regulations and a cultural change. The five questions asked by the FCA were[66]:

1. *What proactive steps do you take as a firm to identify the conduct risks inherent within your business?*
2. *How do you encourage the individuals who work in front, middle, back office, control and support functions to feel and be responsible for managing the conduct of their business?*
3. *What support (broadly defined) does the firm put in place to enable those who work for it to improve the conduct of their business or function?*
4. *How does the Board and ExCo (or appropriate senior management) gain oversight of the conduct of business within their organisation and, equally importantly, how does the Board or ExCo consider the conduct implications of the strategic decisions that they make?*
6. *Has the firm assessed whether there are any other activities that it undertakes that could undermine strategies put in place to improve conduct?*

The FCA provided a manual to help firms answer the above questions. In it, the FCA suggested that instead of simply complying with a fixed set of rules, firms were expected to develop their own definitions of conduct risk and recommended four key considerations: purpose, leadership, people and governance.[67] The manual also explained that while early initiatives concentrated on "problematic aspects of process flows and bad behaviour," firms should now start paying more attention to developing and safeguarding

[64] Thomson Reuters 2020, 22.
[65] EUR-Lex 2024a.
[66] FCA 2019c, 4.
[67] Ibid.

positive behaviour in their own right.[68] In doing so, the FCA launched an important shift away from identifying "bad conduct" towards developing "good conduct" and embedding it in a firm's DNA. In fact, they went as far as to assert that firms must recognise that "good conduct" was "part of the corporate engine driving growth" and a potential "differentiating factor in competition for customers."[69] Understanding conduct risk thus changes significantly – away from preventing "bad conduct" towards encouraging the development of good conduct as a competitive edge. In this spirit, the FCA finalised its Sustainability Disclosure Requirements (SDR) and anti-greenwashing rules between 2023 and 2024. These measures are intended to ensure that firms market sustainable investment products transparently and align product labelling with actual investment characteristics.[70]

By 2019, the FCA noticed that non-financial misconduct was a significantly larger problem that required more energy from senior management and staff at all levels. The approach that the FCA took to further address the issues of misconduct lie in improving a more generalised "speak-up culture" and specific whistleblowing channels.[71] Establishing a well-functioning whistleblowing channel became a regulatory requirement for firms in 2016. Three years later, the FCA re-emphasised the importance of whistleblowing systems in its 5CQ report by stressing the critical importance of "speak-up" channels to ensure that "staff members feel that they can use [them] without fear of reprisal, embarrassment or other problems arising."[72] Furthermore, in 2019 the EU Whistleblower Directive was adopted, which was due to be transposed into national law by the EU member states by 17 December 2021.[73] According to the Directive, companies with more than 250 employees will have to implement whistleblowing systems, introduce protective measures for whistleblowers and inform employees about available reporting lines.[74] This directive has since come into force, embedding transparency and protection of internal reporters into the EU's broader risk governance framework.[75]

In addition to whistleblowing, the follow-up report pushed for a company-specific code of conduct to reflect the company's inherent business model and its stakeholders. In doing so, the FCA's definition of conduct risk began to encompass the entire value chain of products. To illustrate this point, the FCA asserted that it would investigate whether

68 Ibid.
69 Ibid.
70 FCA 2023, 1.
71 Ibid., 24.
72 Ibid.
73 EUR-Lex 2019a.
74 Ibid.
75 EUR-Lex 2019c, 17–56.

the board of a firm examines high return products and services and whether these products and services are being sold to the markets for which they had been designed.[76]

The embedding of product governance within a firm's conduct risk framework has become ever more apparent and important with changes brought in by the "Markets in Financial Instruments Directive II" (MiFID II) regime.[77] This EU directive regulates the market for financial instruments and products, establishing a uniform legal framework for banks, brokerage houses and other brokerage operations in the European Economic Area (EEA). MiFID II introduces rigorous obligations for financial institutions with respect to customer conduct based on the overarching principles of fairness, honesty, professionalism and client interest. Key elements under MiFID II with regards to reducing conduct risk within financial markets are rules on:

1. product governance,
2. information disclosure and transparency,
3. enhanced suitability and appropriateness,
4. conflicts of interest management,
5. best execution, and
6. complaints handling.[78]

The regulatory impetus towards code of conduct frameworks that better reflect inherent business models and the entire value chain of products has been led by one body in particular: the EIOPA. This organisation took a firm lead in the regulatory space when, in February 2019, it published a framework for assessing conduct risk throughout insurance product life cycles.[79] The EIOPA framework launched a common starting point for what DAC Beachcroft described as "more practical supervision" of certain products, services or market segments.[80] The framework concentrated on the exploration of conduct risk throughout all stages of product life cycles, from the point before a contract enters into force to the point at which contract obligations have been completed.[81] The framework identified four key conduct risk areas across the product value chain: business model and management risks, manufacturing risks, delivery risks and product management risks.

[76] Perry et al. 2017, 2.

[77] 2014/65/EU came into force on 3 January 2018.

[78] ESMA 2020, 1–3.

[79] Groundwork set in 2016 by Insurance Distribution Directive 2016/97/EU; DAC Beachcroft 2019b, 2.

[80] Ibid.

[81] Ibid., 4.

In recent years, European regulators have become particularly active in addressing conduct risk as part of their regulatory effort to limit instances of market abuse and increase transparency. Rules designed to prevent market abuse and insider trading came into force in 2014.[82] This presented a significant shift towards a better aligned European approach, as such rules became harmonised for the first time. In 2017, the focus on increasing transparency (as part of the directive targeting stakeholder transparency) arrived through emphasis on codes of conduct. Proxy advisers were asked to publicly disclose a reference to a code of conduct used or explain why they lacked one.[83] Such attempts to make a code of conduct more prevalent among advisers were closely related to the emergence of sustainability topics, which will be discussed in greater detail later in this chapter.

In 2024, the EU adopted the Corporate Sustainability Due Diligence Directive (CSDDD)[84], introducing legally binding obligations for large companies to identify, mitigate, and disclose human rights and environmental risks across their value chains. The directive formally assigns board-level accountability for these issues, reinforcing the link between sustainability governance and corporate conduct obligations.

Looking ahead, European regulators are beginning to address conduct risks associated with digital product design, algorithmic targeting, and the use of artificial intelligence in customer interactions. These developments demonstrate the growing influence of behavioural science and technology ethics on regulatory expectations around fair treatment, informed consent, and cultural resilience. These concerns have also been reflected in the EU's broader digital strategy[85] and recent regulatory initiatives including the AI Act.[86]

Most recently, in late 2024, the European Central Bank (ECB) published a guide draft on governance and risk culture. While not yet finalised, the guide outlines supervisory expectations for significant institutions under its remit, focusing on the integration of behavioural risk factors, board accountability, and effective oversight mechanisms. It underscores the ECB's growing emphasis on proactive risk governance, aligning with a broader European shift toward outcome-oriented supervision and the embedding of ethical culture within internal control frameworks.[87]

---

82 Market Abuse Directive 2014/57/EU together with the Market Abuse Regulation 596/2014 which directly applies in all EU member states since 2 July 2016; EUR-Lex 2017.

83 Ibid.

84 EUR-Lex 2024a, 1.

85 European Commission 2020, 1.

86 EUR-Lex 2024b.

87 ECB 2024.

Overall, the UK and European regulators have broadened their understanding and handling of conduct risk by establishing specific outcomes of good conduct during the last years, by creating a speak-up culture in the senior management regimes and by expanding conduct risk regulation throughout all stages of product life cycles.

### 14.2.1.2 Other European countries

Although the conduct risk regulatory landscape in Europe has been largely driven by either UK or EU authorities, several European national governments have begun to translate global or regional recommendations into their own directives, often employing their own perspectives and approaches. In the following paragraphs, we shall discuss how Germany, Switzerland, the Netherlands and Ireland approach conduct risk and conduct-risk regulation.

Germany's Federal Financial Supervisory Authority (BaFin) published its rather conservative "Minimum Requirements for the Compliance Function and Additional Requirements Governing Rules of Conduct, Organisation and Transparency" (MaComp) in 2010, providing rules and guidance including selected measures to mitigate conduct risk.[88] This document has been amended and updated several times.[89] Moreover, based on the German Banking Act (KWG), BaFin supervises in the "Remuneration Regulation for Institutions" ("InstitutsVergV") appointments, renumerations and rules for risk takers in a firm, also involving organisational requirements on behalf of the firm.[90] The German approach to mitigating conduct risk mirrored global trends at the time, in particular the shift towards customer-centricity. In describing potential conflicts of interests, BaFin emphasised that the interests of clients "must, as a matter of principle, take precedence over those of the investment service enterprise."[91] Interestingly, BaFin also mentions several specific instances of misconduct behaviours, such as cold calling, which it prohibits.[92] Moreover, BaFin orders firms to separate their functions into individual units to prevent potential misconduct, such as separation of trading, settlement and control. It also carries out annual checks or "special inspections" to verify whether the rules set out are being observed. Furthermore, in September 2020, BaFin published a guidance notice on dealing with sustainability risks, expecting entities supervised by BaFin to ensure that the relevant sustainability risks are being adequately considered.[93] In 2023, BaFin formalised these expectations through the 7$^{th}$ amendment to its Minimum Requirements for

[88] BaFin 2011.
[89] BaFin 2020.
[90] BMJ 2018.
[91] BaFin 2016.
[92] Ibid.
[93] BaFin 2019.

Risk Management (MaRisk), requiring institutions to integrate sustainability risks into their governance and risk frameworks. This includes explicit responsibilities for management to ensure that environmental and social risks are considered in the internal controls, conduct, and strategic decision-making.[94]

Switzerland's Financial Market Supervisory Authority (FINMA) named the suitability of products and services for clients as well as market integrity among cross-border business conduct and AML as key principles of conduct supervision in the form of a fact sheet. For these areas, a conduct risk assessment guide including tools such as benchmarking was provided.[95] FINMA highlighted several tools in its conduct risk supervisory arsenal, of which the most prominent was "benchmarking." FINMA described its benchmarking supervisory approach as the audit of identical processes across an array of financial services providers to directly compare stakeholders' levels of compliance.[96] This approach was meant to highlight any potential shortcomings, and as a result led to FINMA's closer monitoring of a firm's compliance framework. One FINMA-specific element is the direct mentioning of external parties, to which FINMA outsources some of its watchdog responsibilities. The goal of these audit firms was to act on FINMA's behalf in reviewing conduct rules at firms.[97] In recent years, FINMA has increasingly linked conduct risk to reputational damage, board accountability, and cultural weaknesses, with greater scrutiny of escalation channels, governance failures, and tone from the top.[98]

The two Dutch supervisory units – the Dutch Authority of Financial Markets (AFM) and the Dutch Central Bank (DNB) – highlight the cultural aspects of conduct, suggesting a set of rules might be insufficient to foster change. While the Dutch Financial Supervisory Act (WFT) provides a high-level legal base for conduct – highlighting specifically the role of governance –, the DNB has published a comprehensive book with a more practical perspective.[99] Similarly, the AFM provided brochures and case studies.[100] It is worth mentioning that the Dutch perspective is fairly unique in its emphasis on what AFM identifies as "unwritten rules, behaviour and culture at financial organisations."[101] The AFM further argues that as a result of its review of a firm's culture it could gain better "insight into what drives people to put the customer's interest or public interest first."[102]

---

94 BaFin 2023.
95 FINMA 2018, 1–2.
96 Ibid.
97 Ibid.
98 FINMA 2024.
99 DNB 2015.
100 AFM s.a.
101 Ibid.
102 Ibid.

As such, these insights into the unwritten are meant to identify high-risk practices before any harm is done. Last but not least, it is important to mention that, emulating the UK's and EU's regulators, the Dutch authorities also place the responsibility for developing a culture of good conduct and compliance on the shoulders of each organisation.[103]

Two additional Dutch regulatory efforts are worth mentioning: the Banker's Oath and the Systematic Integrity Risk Assessment (SIRA). First, Dutch regulators began requiring a large number of financial services employees to take the Banker's Oath, which included concrete references to conduct issues. This has serious legal ramifications, since breaking an oath can result in legal disciplinary actions. Moreover, the Dutch Central Bank introduced the Systematic Integrity Risk Assessment as part of its push for a more documented approach to integrity risk identification by businesses. SIRA requires an explicit definition of a market participant's risk appetite and clear outline of both inherent and residual risks. These two examples illustrate a significant cultural shift in the Netherlands, from a low-touch regulation environment to one of the most stringently regulated countries.

Ireland both adopted global recommendations and provided reinterpretations of its own. The Central Bank of Ireland published a "Guide to consumer protection risk assessment" in 2017, requiring firms to implement Customer Protection Risk management frameworks. Moreover, the guide contained instructions on how such a risk-based and evidence-based framework can be developed, providing major topics firms need to address and a consideration of both design and operative effectiveness of governance and controls, people and culture as well as the complete product life cycle.[104] The CPRA divided its efforts into five specific modules, each of which covered different aspects of conduct risk and recommended a specific conduct risk setup to ensure the maintenance of the "good nature" of products and services.[105] Building on this foundation, the Central Bank of Ireland has since introduced additional supervisory measures. In 2022, the Individual Accountability Framework (IAF) was enacted, establishing a Senior Executive Accountability Regime (SEAR) to reinforce personal responsibility and internal governance standards.[106] The Central Bank of Ireland has also issued a series of *Dear CEO letters* and thematic reviews highlighting expectations around incentive frameworks, conduct-related risk culture, and broader governance structures.[107]

---

103 Ibid.

104 Central Bank of Ireland 2017, 8.

105 Ibid.

106 ISB 2023.

107 Central Bank of Ireland 2024, 2020.

### 14.2.2 US perspective

US regulators anticipated their European counterparts in codifying codes of conduct. While the concept of a written code of conduct has been a fairly recent phenomenon in Europe, the Securities and Exchange Commission (SEC) first introduced a written code of ethics in 2004. The "Code of Federal Regulations" in Part 270, 275 and 279 of Title XVII required investment advisors to establish a code of ethics tailored to their business needs and required that all employees commit to it. The law came as a result of rising prevalence of violations of fiduciary obligations and was meant to further prevent associated fraud.[108] The SEC strove to ensure that firms sought compliance from employees by instituting a rule that required all advisers to obtain and keep written acknowledgement from each person s/he had supervised. Such acknowledgement is meant to confirm that each employee had received a copy of the firm's code of ethics and any amendments to it.[109] Nonetheless, while the SEC proposal included some provisions, it had left advisers with a large degree of freedom when designing individualised codes.

It was not until the late 2000s that the US code of conduct landscape changed significantly. The shift happened during and after the global financial crisis. In 2010 (adapted in 2016), the US Congress passed the Dodd-Frank Wall Street Reform and Consumer Protection Act as a legislative response to the perceived causes of the financial crisis.[110] The act contained references to conduct risk in Section 731 of Title VII, which prohibits "fraudulent, deceptive, and manipulative acts or practices [...] based on good faith compliance with policies and procedures."[111] It is worth mentioning that US regulators have leveraged strong political momentum to pass other legislation focused on protecting consumers, in addition to regulating financial instruments. In establishing the Consumer Financial Protection Bureau (CFPB), US regulators launched an important supervisory authority with far-reaching oversight powers, although its direction and intensity of enforcement may shift under the current administration.

Alongside the CFPB, the Financial Industry Regulatory Authority (FINRA) has played a pivotal role in overseeing conduct standards within the US financial industry. Established in 2007 as a self-regulatory organisation under SEC oversight, FINRA is responsible for regulating broker-dealers and has become an essential actor in promoting ethical behaviour and investor protection, particularly in the brokerage sector. FINRA may impose fines against firms and individual people in case of misconduct. In 2009, FINRA published two guidelines addressing market conduct risk, namely manipulation and the

108 SEC 2004.

109 SEC s.a.

110 United States Congress 2010.

111 CFTC 2012, 1.

misuse of information.[112] It was at this time that FINRA began to provide a risk ranking for every financial adviser it regulates.[113]

Just as the EBA did, the FINRA began to provide concrete categories and examples of customer misconduct in 2017.[114] A total of 13 categories encompassed a range of fairly specific misconduct behaviours from "switching a customer from one mutual fund to another when there is no legitimate investment purpose" through "trading ahead, which involves placing an order for the firm's account before entering a customer's limit order."[115] In describing instances of misconduct in detail, FINRA might have reached the peak of its regulatory attempts to outline examples of misconduct in as specific terms as possible for as general an audience as possible. Following this report, FINRA began to steer towards an approach emphasizing the tailoring of code of conduct to individual business needs while placing the responsibility of developing such codes on the shoulders of firms. In other words, the regulatory approach towards conduct risk changed from prescriptive to customer centric.

In 2013 and 2014, FINRA released a series of customer-oriented guidelines, which focused on and defined standards to be met by financial advisers. Marketing rules were introduced for the first time, in particular with respect to cold calling. The SEC might have left some room for interpretation by asserting that a financial adviser must have a "reasonable basis" to think that his/her recommended transaction or strategy is suitable for the customers obtained via "reasonable diligence."[116] The regulators were, however, more specific in describing the facets of a customer's profile that the advisers must take into account when undertaking their due diligence: age, other investments, financial situation and needs, tax status, investment objectives, investment experience, investment time horizon, liquidity needs, risk tolerance and "any other information the customer may disclose."[117]

Despite the similarities in defining and regulating misconduct, the SEC and FINRA have become known for the harshness of their sentences and large fines often significantly exceeding rulings by their European counterparts.[118] Nevertheless, US regulators, too, have come to understand that hard laws fail to cover all loopholes and have started to intro-

112 FINRA 2009a, 2009b.

113 FINRA 2009a.

114 FINRA 2017.

115 Ibid.

116 FINRA 2013, 2020.

117 Ibid.

118 Citigroup, for instance, settled for $285 million and Goldman Sachs for $550 million for misleading investors.

duce soft laws that place responsibility on the firms themselves. A shift in mindset began to take shape in 2019 with the Office of Compliance Inspections and Examinations (OCIE), now called the Division of Examinations, introduction of a number of rules and guidelines that placed the emphasis on transparency towards retail customers and included descriptions of compliance programs, disclosures and conflicts of interest.[119] These efforts have remained an active part of supervisory practice, with a continued emphasis on firm-level responsibility and customer outcomes, despite potential changes in enforcement tone at the federal level.[120]

In recent years, US regulators have continued to evolve the conduct risk framework through several high-impact initiatives. The SEC's Regulation Best Interest[121] and the Form CRS requirement[122], both effective since June 2020, introduced a more stringent best interest standard and enhanced transparency for retail clients. Meanwhile, the SEC and CFTC have imposed over $2.5 billion in fines since 2021 for failures to preserve off-channel communications, such as business-related messages on WhatsApp[123], framing these breaches as firm-wide governance and conduct failures under Exchange Act Rule 17a-4.[124] In parallel, regulators have broadened their conduct oversight to include sustainability-related disclosures[125] and the use of AI-driven advisory tools, which may raise risks of bias, manipulation, or insufficient transparency.[126] These developments reflect a growing emphasis on aligning technology, culture, and disclosure with core conduct expectations.

### 14.2.3 Asia-Pacific perspective

Asia-Pacific regulators have, over the past few years, developed and implemented their own national conduct risk guidelines, often building on global standards such as the Foreign Exchange (FX) Global Code. The focus reflects both global trends but also a rising sense of urgency among senior managers in the region. When asked whether they perceive that the regulatory focus on conduct will increase senior managers' personal liability, 77% of Asia-Pacific respondents responded that it would, a 10% increase from the year before.[127] More recent surveys suggest that this sentiment has persisted, with reg-

[119] SEC 2019a, 8–22, 2019b, 1–7.
[120] SEC 2023a, 1.
[121] SEC 2020b, 1.
[122] Ibid., 2.
[123] CFTC 2023, 1.
[124] SEC 2020a, 3.
[125] SEC 2024, 1.
[126] SEC 2023b, 2.
[127] Thomson Reuters 2018, 5.

ulators in the region continuing to emphasise individual accountability and cultural oversight.[128]

In its "Guidelines on Risk Management Practices" for a financial institution's internal control environment, the Monetary Authority of Singapore (MAS) emphasises that customer interaction should be "conducted in good faith" and in a "manner that promotes public confidence in the integrity of the market."[129] Further, the "Singapore Guide to Conduct & Market Practices for the Wholesale Financial Markets," published in 2018, outlines "global code principles" regarding wholesale financial markets and gives guidance to institutions in adopting them, aiming to complement the FX Global Code on a national level.[130] Forty-nine principles in total encompass roles and responsibilities of "market participants" and are in line with similar principles in Europe and the US. In addition, MAS's 2020 Guidelines on Individual Accountability and Conduct (IAC) have become a central pillar of conduct supervision, with increasing regulatory focus on implementation, feedback mechanisms, and the alignment of governance structures with conduct expectations.[131]

The customer-centric approach to conduct risk, as first developed by European and US regulators, was quickly adopted by Australian watchdogs. In 2019, the Australia Royal Commission published a detailed report on "Misconduct in the Banking, Superannuation and Financial Services," laying out principles and rules for conduct built on a customer-centric approach. The guiding principle established by the report is for companies to "obey the law, not to mislead or deceive, act fairly, provide services that are fit for purpose, deliver services with reasonable care and skill, and when acting for another, act in the best interests of that other."[132] Moreover, the Australian report dived into the motives of misconduct and identified four key topics: misguided incentive schemes, an imbalance of information, conflicts of interest between customer, intermediary and provider, as well as missing deterrence and sanctions.[133] Beyond that, detailed recommendations were provided on remuneration systems, organisational culture and governance arrangements. Systems culture and governance are seen as strongly correlated with conduct risk and, therefore, must be tackled at the same time to effectively reduce future misconduct.[134] The report identifies the source of responsibility for the firm's conduct culture and includes relevant case studies. The responsibility accordingly lies primarily with the firms to take

128 Herbert Smith Freehills 2024, 1.
129 MAS 2014, 10.
130 SFEMC 2018.
131 MAS 2020b, 1.
132 Australia Royal Commission 2019, 5.
133 Ibid., 1–4.
134 Ibid., 388–393.

respective measures. The report also warns market participants that supervisory efforts in the future will go far beyond financial risks.[135] A collection of case studies gives both advisers and regulators concrete examples and recommendations, asking them to go beyond merely complying with the law. These recommendations have since been embedded in regulation through the Financial Accountability Regime (FAR), which replaced the Banking Executive Accountability Regime (BEAR). FAR came into effect for banks in March 2024 and will apply to insurers and superannuation trustees from March 2025, significantly broadening the scope of personal accountability in the Australian financial sector.[136]

How did the Hong Kong Monetary Authority (HKMA), one of the key regulating bodies in Asia-Pacific, deal with conduct risk? Besides a brief mention in the HKMA's "Supervisory Policy Manual" that a financial institution's code of conduct must contain a "set of ethical values,"[137] the HKMA published five principles for the fair treatment of customers in 2013 and continued its focus on conduct risk in following years by also publishing a number of conduct guidelines. In 2015, the HKMA introduced a non-statutory "Code of the Banking Practice" which addressed topics such as the treatment of customers, disclosure and transparency, and complaints handling.[138] The effort continued with guidelines on a "Bank Culture Reform." These guidelines highlighted necessary governance in order to adopt a culture that supports prudent risk management by proposing three pillars: governance, incentive systems as well as assessment and feedback mechanisms.[139] In December 2017, the HKMA added another module on "Competence and ethical behaviour" to its "Supervisory Policy Manual," where it highlighted the responsibility of an authorised institution to ensure staff competence and ethical behaviour. The standard set for ethical behaviour included a commitment to high standards of business conduct and integrity, the integration of those values into the corporate culture and the monitoring and penalising of misbehaviour.[140] In addition to these guidelines, the HKMA launched a detailed website, highlighting topics such as consumer protection, financial inclusion, bank culture, director empowerment, complaints handling and redress mechanisms, accompanied by an overview of enforcement actions conducted by the HKMA to ensure good conduct in all of the fields.[141] Since 2023, the HKMA has further strengthened its conduct supervision by conducting thematic reviews on how banks assess cultural effectiveness and by encouraging internal audit functions to evaluate cultural

135 Ibid., 412.

136 Commonwealth Numbered Acts 2023.

137 HKMA 2002, 6.

138 HKMA 2015, 1–2.

139 HKMA 2017c, 1–3.

140 HKMA 2017d, 14–16.

141 HKMA 2019.

alignment. These steps mark a shift from principle-setting to actively measuring conduct outcomes, aligning with international trends in outcome-based supervision.[142]

As Asia-Pacific regulators began to incorporate global standards into national guidelines, outcome-focused senior management regimes began taking off in the region. In 2017, Hong Kong's Securities and Futures Commission (SFC) launched its "Manager-In-Charge Regime," which applies to senior managers at licensed corporations, mandating companies to review their organisation, roles, responsibilities and reporting methods.[143] The MAS followed suit a year later and initiated efforts to promote accountability in its own jurisdiction by publishing "Guidelines on Individual Accountability and Conduct" (IAC).[144] In 2018, the Australian Banking Executive Accountability Regime (BEAR) classified accountable persons, required their registration and an accountability statement at the Australian Prudential Regulation Authority (APRA) and laid out further notification obligations, potential disqualifications and civil penalties.[145] Asia-Pacific guidelines largely mirrored similar efforts in Europe and the US.

In summary, while national and regional regulations might contain specific points, overall global standards have become more prevalent. Across all regions, efforts to identify, specify and regulate conduct risk have increased significantly and three key global trends have emerged. First, prevention has increased in importance. While investigations and sanctions remain core tasks for regulators, a rising number of regulatory bodies have taken on the challenge to prevent crimes. Second, regulators have begun to require market participants to adopt a systemic approach for their conduct risk policies. To really tackle the root of the problem, it has become apparent that singular measures are not enough. Regulators have, therefore, begun to mandate firms to tackle the root of the problem from within their own ranks by transforming the culture of a firm to one where good conduct is recognised and celebrated, while bad conduct is identified and punished early on. Last but not least, a shift toward outcome-focused supervision has emerged among key regulating bodies. Instead of defining what is prohibited, regulators have begun to focus on the outcome, asking firms to take on responsibility for creating a business of good conduct themselves in order to avoid ever-increasing loopholes.

As a result of the above trends, three specific regulatory forms have begun to take shape. First, soft laws have begun to replace hard laws. Open questions and guidelines have emerged, which encourage companies to go beyond mere compliance with the law and rather act in its spirit, while formal rulemaking and enforcement continue to play a key

142 HKMA 2024.

143 Bogardi/Chau 2017.

144 MAS 2019; Pattwell et al. 2019, 1–5.

145 APRA 2018, 8–10.

role in reinforcing accountability. Second, regulators have begun to promote senior management regimes, whose goal is to increase individual liability not only among C-level executives but also across all senior managers and employees with relevant roles. Third, conduct risk frameworks have emerged with greater frequency. Such frameworks aim to help companies develop and implement respective measures, offering pragmatic advice and guidance on how companies can nurture a culture of good conduct in the workplace.

With three key trends and three specific new regulatory forms, conduct risk policies are clearly moving further up on the agendas of financial institutions. Companies must not just seek to transform conduct risk systems to avoid significant repercussions stemming from non-compliance but also view conduct as a driver of trust, resilience, and competitive advantage. Increasingly, this also includes emerging risks related to AI, predictive analytics, and digital client engagement, which regulators are now integrating into the conduct oversight agenda. While recent political and economic shifts have sparked calls to streamline or rebalance some regulatory initiatives, the emphasis on ethical culture and individual accountability remains largely intact across global financial centres. It is fair to expect that scrutiny and emphasis on good conduct will continue to intensify in the years ahead, even as regulatory strategies evolve.

## 14.3 Why conduct risk matters

### 14.3.1 Increased regulatory scrutiny

#### 14.3.1.1 Focus on regulatory oversight

Besides the above-mentioned key trends and new regulatory forms, three major areas have emerged as key focuses for regulatory oversight: expansion of the circle of stakeholders, elimination of "rolling bad apples" and greater cross-border collaboration. First, key regulators began to move away from only sanctioning firms that harmed customers, towards expanding the circle of relevant stakeholders. In the past, misconduct was sanctioned only once it demonstrably harmed customers. Recently, however, regulators began to sanction incidents of misconduct towards investors (for example Wells Fargo) and/or employees (for example the whistleblower scandal at Barclays).[146] Supervisory bodies now expect companies to behave ethically and maintain a strong focus on good conduct, not just towards their customers but towards all stakeholders, including internal staff, shareholders, and the wider public.

[146] SEC 2020c; Bank of England 2018.

Second, regulatory oversight, following the FSB recommendation, has begun to focus on eliminating so-called "rolling bad apples." This trend has led regulators to take decisive action against individuals, in the hope that a focus on individual responsibility and accountability will deter all employees from potential misconduct. This is closely related to regulators' increasing attention on corporate culture and the introduction of soft laws, which grant regulators the flexibility to take action against misconduct in whatever form it occurs. Recent enforcement waves, particularly around off-channel communications using WhatsApp or Signal, have highlighted how personal behaviour and recordkeeping failures are now being treated as conduct governance issues.[147] As a result, a rising number of CEOs have been seen packing their bags after neglecting to introduce reasonable measures to establish or restore a culture of good conduct.

Third, as companies take their business abroad, supervisors have also begun to look across borders. For instance, the SEC has been seen to take forceful action against foreign companies in recent years, and regulators across various countries have begun to cooperate when investigating and prosecuting multinationals.[148] This cross-border alignment now extends to areas like AI oversight, digital conduct analytics, and crypto-related enforcement.[149] The Global Financial Innovation Network, an international group of financial regulators launched in 2019 and led by the FCA, has grown from a few dozen members to over 50 participating entities, showing regulators are growing much more interested in sharing lessons learned and seeking to benefit from one another's experiences.[150] Despite some political and economic headwinds, this cross-border collaboration remains a critical force in elevating global conduct standards.

#### 14.3.1.2 Frequency of regulatory actions

The financial crisis of 2008 made it apparent that misconduct not only occurred at a few institutions but seemed to be prevalent through the entire financial industry. This realisation led to a significant ramp-up in regulatory actions. As of 2016, the SEC had charged over 200 entities and individuals with penalties, disgorgements and other monetary reliefs. Approximately $3.76 billion in fines due to misconduct during the financial crisis have been levied. There were 93 C-level executives charged in these misconduct cases, 54 of which received either bans or suspensions from the industry.[151] Financial and reputational losses faced by firms were immense. Public shock at the scale of misconduct among

[147] DOJ 2024a.

[148] Other prominent examples include, DOJ prosecution within FCPA framework, Financial Sanctions, AML (Banking Secrecy).

[149] IOSCO 2021.

[150] FCA 2019b.

[151] SEC 2016.

market participants resulted in widespread mistrust of the financial industry, amplified by an outcry from the international media.

Penalties for misconduct remain high. Over the past 15 years (2010–2024), conduct-related penalties have globally amounted to approximately $280 billion. The peak years were 2012 to 2014 and 2016, each recording annual fines of over $30 billion. Since 2018, penalty volumes have declined significantly, with yearly totals under $5 billion[152], but regulatory scrutiny remains high and individual fines can be significant. The large fines reflect the significant efforts by key regulatory bodies to discourage future misconduct and to restore public trust in the financial industry. The frequency of regulatory actions seems to have reached a steady level. In 2015/16, 784 actions were taken by the SEC. This number dropped slightly to 754 in 2016/17 but jumped by almost 9% to 821 in 2017/18.[153] We expect that this trend of increased regulatory scrutiny of conduct will continue.

## 14.3.2 Supervisory and legal actions

### 14.3.2.1 Actions against firms

The following examples of recent misconduct risk serve to illustrate above-described trends and regulatory frameworks: Citibank, Danske Bank, Wells Fargo and Barclays.

*Citibank:* In 2015, Citibank, N.A. and its subsidiaries were charged with damages in the amount of $700 million by the Consumer Financial Protection Bureau (CFPB) for illegal credit card add-on products and services in combination with deceptive marketing, billing and handling to around seven million customers. Moreover, there was a civil penalty of $35 million due to expedited payment fees on 1.8 million accounts, collected during collection calls.[154]

*Danske Bank:* In addition to a scandal of money laundering, in which several countries investigated the bank's misconduct, the Danish Financial Supervisory Authority (DFSA) accused Danske Bank of facilitating systematic wash trades between 2016 and 2019, and filed a respective lawsuit over violations of market abuse regulations.[155]

*Wells Fargo:* In January 2020, Wells Fargo agreed to civil penalties of $500 million after the SEC had found out it had opened millions of fake, unused or even unauthorised

[152] Internal BCG analysis.

[153] DAC Beachcroft 2019a, 3.

[154] CFPB 2015, 1.

[155] Skydsgaard 2020.

accounts with the intention of systematically misleading investors about its success in cross-selling products.[156]

*Barclays:* In 2018, the New York State Department of Financial Services (NYSDFS) investigated Barclays after the bank's CEO tried to identify a whistleblower who had anonymously issued complaints against a senior manager via the company's whistleblowing system. The NYSDFS fined the bank $15 million, claiming deficiencies in governance, controls and culture.[157]

*Allianz Structured Alpha*: In 2022, Allianz Global Investors agreed to pay over $6 billion in restitution and penalties after the SEC and DOJ found that portfolio managers had misled institutional investors about the risk profile of its Structured Alpha funds and concealed losses during the 2020 market crash. Fund managers pleaded guilty to securities fraud, and the case highlighted severe deficiencies in internal controls and risk disclosure.[158]

*Credit Suisse:* Between 2021 and 2023, Credit Suisse faced multiple conduct-related scandals, for example the collapse of Archegos Capital and Greensill Capital, exposing serious failures in risk oversight, governance, and due diligence. The firm incurred losses exceeding $5.5 billion, faced regulatory investigations in several jurisdictions, and ultimately underwent a forced takeover by UBS, marking one of the most high-profile collapses linked to, not only, but also repeated conduct failings.[159]

### 14.3.2.2 Actions against individuals

According to a study by Reuters, the main reason for CEO turnover in 2019 was legal actions, exemplified by the examples of Barclays, Wells Fargo and several others (Westpac, National Australia Bank, HSBC, Credit Suisse).[160] Actions against Barclays' CEO and Wells Fargo executives serve to illustrate the increasing regulatory focus on individual actions. Barclays' CEO only narrowly escaped an occupational ban and had to pay roughly £1.1 million of his own money for his personal misconduct in the whistleblower case in 2018 – half of it was charged by the FCA and PRA as a result of a legal prosecution while the remainder was retained from his bonus by the bank.[161]

156 SEC 2020c.
157 Loconte 2018.
158 SEC 2022, 1.
159 FINMA 2023, 1.
160 Starling 2020, 11.
161 Fletcher 2018; Loconte 2018.

Moreover, the example of Wells Fargo was one of the most severe instances of misconduct, and regulators took relevant actions to punish individuals responsible for the scandal. In order to meet their overambitious goals, employees testified to being pressurised by management into cheating. Following a combined settlement of $3 billion, split between the SEC, the US Department of Justice and the bank, a former CEO was charged with a record fine of $17.5 million in addition to a lifetime ban from the banking industry. Seven of his former colleagues, also executives, received fines totalling $40 million and further work restrictions.[162] The increase in frequency of prosecution cases and in the harshness of fines against individuals shows regulators' mounting efforts to increase emphasis on personal liability through senior management regimes.[163]

More recently, the 2024 conviction of FTX founder Sam Bankman-Fried, who was sentenced to 25 years in prison for securities fraud and misappropriation of customer funds[164], illustrates how individual accountability has extended beyond traditional financial institutions into the digital asset space. Regulators and prosecutors have made it clear that leadership failures – regardless of industry – can trigger severe personal consequences.

Considering the above, CEOs are continuing to elevate conduct compliance on their agendas, establishing roles for dedicated compliance executives, rejecting potential business opportunities that might risk non-compliance, expanding responsibilities and ramping up training efforts. First, companies have increasingly hired dedicated executives responsible for compliance and culture, a trend that gained traction in the mid-2010s and has since become a governance norm in many jurisdictions. Second, conduct risk has become a material factor in strategic decision-making with firms more willing to walk away from profitable opportunities when ethical or reputational risks are too high. In 2018, for example, CEOs rejected 28% of business propositions due to conduct or culture concerns.[165] This risk-sensitive lens has only sharpened in recent years as regulatory expectations and stakeholder scrutiny have intensified.

Third, even though the C-level and compliance functions are identified as the senior personnel responsible, awareness for personal accountability has expanded. Surveys of global systemically important financial institutions (G-SIFIs) continue to indicate that personal liability is a growing concern among senior leaders reinforcing the importance of clearly defined responsibilities and oversight structures. Evidently, the "ownership" of conduct risk in an organisation is being expanded.

[162] Tappe 2020.
[163] Starling 2020, 11.
[164] DOJ 2024b, 1.
[165] Ibid., 5.

Finally, firms are ramping up their training efforts to ensure employees are well aware of the risks associated with non-compliance. In recent years, many institutions have expanded company-wide training programmes and reinforced their importance by linking them to performance evaluations and incentive structures. In some firms, completion of mandatory training has become a precondition for bonus eligibility, signalling the integration of ethical expectations into broader employee engagement and reward systems. The enterprise-wide approach reflects a growing recognition that good conduct is not confined to the top but must be consistently reinforced across all levels of the organisation.

# 15 Managing Conduct Risk: Framework and Perspectives

*Prof. Dr. Martin Schulz, Dr. Julia Gebhardt, Dr. Katharina Hefter, Constanze Westwood*

## 15.1 Trends and perspectives in respect of conduct risk in the regulatory context

This chapter will drill down into two key elements in the regulation of conduct risk: "Treating Customers Fairly" (TFC) and the "Senior Managers and Certification Regime" (SM&CR), which are both milestones in the regulatory landscape. In addition, it investigates differences in the adoption of these regulations across countries and discusses conduct risk management as an integral part of sustainability.

### 15.1.1 Treating Customers Fairly (TCF)

TCF presents an outcomes-based regulatory approach, the goal of which is to ensure that regulated financial institutions deliver fair outcomes for their customers. Under the TCF approach, institutions must demonstrate delivery of fair outcomes through the entire product life cycle, from design through advice, service, complaints and claims handling. It has become a unique regulatory perspective as it partially shifts responsibility for protecting the consumers from the regulator to the financial services provider. The approach was implemented in the UK through the Financial Conduct Authority (FCA) and was soon adopted by relevant financial authorities in Hong Kong and South Africa. In 2023, the UK extended the TCF framework with the introduction of the Consumer Duty. This new regulation places an even greater emphasis on firms proactively "delivering good outcomes" to retail customers. This includes ensuring that products and services meet customer needs, provide fair value, and support informed decision-making. Particular attention is given to protecting vulnerable consumers and making outcomes both measurable and transparent.[1]

Institutions under the governance of the FCA must abide by 11 key principles of business. The sixth principle, customers' interests, states that "a firm must pay due regard to the interests of its customers and treat them fairly."[2] The FCA's principle of "treating customers fairly" requires that all firms show consistently that "fair treatment of customers

[1] FCA 2022, 3.
[2] FSA 2006, 4.

is at the heart of their business model."[3] Furthermore, the FCA enumerates six consumer outcomes that firms should follow to ensure fair treatment of customers (Figure 1):

Figure 1: TCF's six consumer outcomes

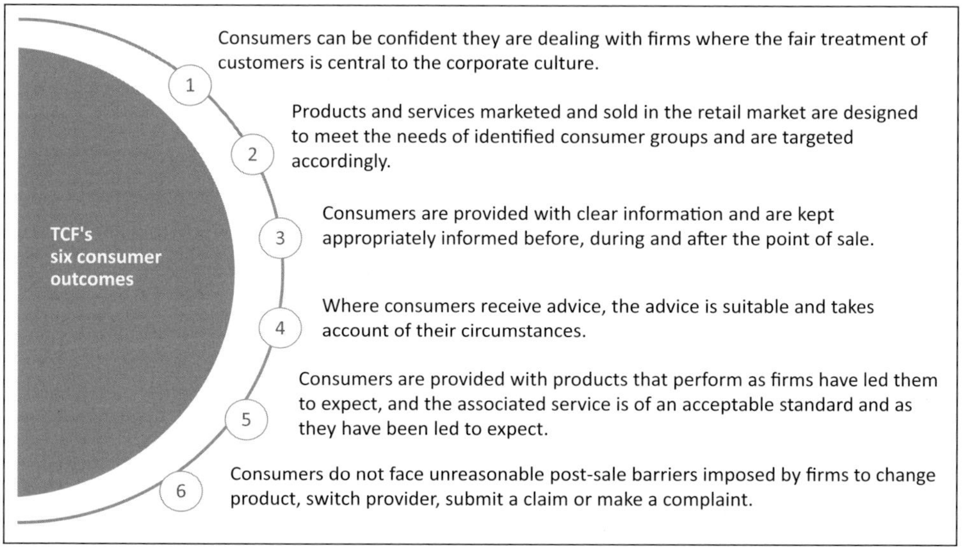


With the introduction of the Consumer Duty in 2023, an additional $12^{th}$ principle now applies: 'A firm must act to deliver good outcomes for retail customers.' While the six original TCF outcomes remain relevant, the Duty raises expectations through four updated outcomes focused on product value, governance, communication, and support.[4]

Beyond the UK, the idea of treating customers fairly as the standard for good conduct has made its way into financial regulatory frameworks all over the globe. Particularly countries of the former British Empire with a strong financial sector are using this framework to protect consumers from misconduct. The UK's Financial Services Authority (FSA), the predecessor to the FCA, paved the way in 2004 with its report on TFC and the call for financial institutions to deliver six desired consumer outcomes. The culture of treating customers fairly has to be ingrained throughout the product life cycle, including product design and governance, marketing practices, the sales process, information and customer support after the point of sale as well as complaint handling.[5] This culture-

[3] Ibid., 11.

[4] FCA 2022, 4–5.

[5] FSA 2006, 6.

based view of customer protection continues to evolve globally, often under broader "purpose-led" governance agendas.

In the aftermath of the 2007/08 financial crisis, the Hong Kong Monetary Authority (HKMA) developed five principles for retail banks with its *Treat Customer Fairly Charter* in 2013, which was derived from the TCF's six consumer outcomes.[6] These principles offered concrete examples to help banks install a culture focused on the fair treatment of consumers.[7] Distinct from the UK's TCF from 2006, the "Treat Customer Fairly Charter" put a special emphasis on the needs of vulnerable customers, as outlined in the charter's fifth principle. The fair treatment of customers has remained a core element in Hong Kong's regulatory landscape, with the "Code of Banking Practice" in 2015 and the "Bank Culture Reform" in 2017 both further stressing this aspect. As of 2025, this focus has continued, with growing pressure on banks to demonstrate how they identify and protect vulnerable customers through design, communication, and decision – an approach reinforced by HKMA's 2022 guidance on fair treatment and data protection practices.[8]

In South Africa, the Financial Sector Conduct Authority (FSCA) implemented its version of TCF in 2014.[9] The six customer outcomes are identical to those of the UK's TCF. A detailed roadmap was published by the Financial Service Board of South Africa, outlining the framework, implementation, incentives and deterrence system as well as support structures.[10] Furthermore, the Financial Service Board also provides self-assessment and benchmarking tools for firms to use for the comparison of their level of success in achieving the TCF outcomes.[11]

### 15.1.2 Senior management regimes as emerging global trends in conduct risk

One of the overarching trends across all regions has been the shift away from a case-by-case approach towards treating conduct risk as a systemic phenomenon. The creation of elaborate senior accountability frameworks is part of this move. As such, recent regulations have focused on extending the individual liability through elaborate senior management regimes, the chief goal of which is a more systemic approach to liability by increasing individual liability not only to the C-level but also to senior management and other relevant roles. The following chapter will offer four deep dives into regulatory landscapes that embraced senior management regimes as a key tool for regulating conduct risk.

6 Berry et al. 2013, 2.

7 HKMA 2014, 1–6.

8 HKMA 2022a.

9 National Treasury, department of South Africa 2014, 10.

10 Ibid., 1–2.

11 Ibid., 32.

#### 15.1.2.1 UK

The UK's SM&CR entered into force in 2016 and applies to all senior management functions as well as other risk-takers who have to be assessed and equipped with clear responsibilities by their firms.[12] The SM&CR was intended to support a change in the British banking and insurance sectors. The legislation was rolled out to banks in 2016 and was extended to insurers two years later. The SM&CR contained four key elements:

(1) the *Senior Managers Regime*, which stipulated that senior managers should be assessed as "fit and proper," exercise clearly defined responsibilities and be subject to conduct requirements;

(2) a *Certification Regime*, which required firms to certify annually that key risk-taking employees below the top tier are fit to undertake their roles;

(3) *regulatory references*, which set rules for the hiring process for senior decision-makers and key risk-taking employees; and

(4) *Conduct Rules*, establishing minimum conduct standards, requiring, among other things, that all financial services staff act with "integrity and due skill, care and diligence."[13]

The first aspect of note regarding the SM&CR is the legislation's emphasis on the approval process for senior staff appointments. Individuals must seek approval before taking up any position that is designated by the Prudential Regulation Authority (PRA) as a senior management function. Moreover, for firms regulated by both PRA and FCA, the PRA was designed to lead the assessment of applications, but both the PRA and FCA must grant the approval after a review that concludes that an applicant meets the relevant regulatory standards as laid out in the Financial Services and Markets Act 2000 (FSMA). The SM&CR emphasised that severe repercussions would follow non-compliance. Failure to receive approval before taking up a role may lead to action against the firm and/or individual, with liability falling on both the institution and future employee.[14]

Moreover, the Certification Regime extended liability beyond senior management to junior employees in roles that could potentially allow them to cause significant harm either to the firm or its customers.[15] Groups of such employees were called "certification functions." The appointment of these employees does not need to be approved by the FCA or PRA. The firms, however, must do proper checks and certify that employees in

[12] Bank of England 2020, 1–3.

[13] Ibid.

[14] Ibid.

[15] FCA 2019d.

"certification functions" are "fit and proper to perform their role" and such certification must take place at least once a year.[16]

Last, the regime required that every senior management has "a statement of responsibilities" to clearly specify the range of responsibilities owned by each individual manager. However, the firms were not given complete freedom in defining their own statement of responsibilities, as the regime also designated certain specific responsibilities that the firms need to give to their senior managers. These responsibilities were referred to as "prescribed responsibilities" and their goal was to ensure that a senior manager is "accountable for the SM&CR and key conduct and prudential risks."[17] Furthermore, each senior manager became responsible (in addition to the prescribed responsibilities) for each of the firm's business functions and activities. These responsibilities were called "overall responsibilities."[18]

Since its implementation, the SM&CR has become a cornerstone of UK regulatory supervision, with regulators using it to promote personal accountability, assess culture, and evaluate leadership behaviours, including in cases involving non-financial misconduct such as bullying or harassment.[19]

### 15.1.2.2 Hong Kong and Singapore

Hong Kong's Securities and Futures Commission (SFC) took similar steps towards establishing a senior management regime by introducing the "Manager-In-Charge Regime" (MIR) regulation in 2017. When MIR came into effect, firms were asked to provide the following information: (1) clearly laid-out corporate governance and reporting structures with relevant roles, and (2) a review of insurances for relevant roles to cover potential claims resulting from misconduct.[20] Since its introduction, the MIR framework has become a central tool for defining individual accountability and improving corporate governance expectations across licensed corporations.[21]

The HKMA attempted to address the issue of "rolling bad apples" by publishing a consultation paper in May 2020. The goal of the paper was to establish a reference-checking framework to increase chances of early detection of potential misconduct risk by requiring

16 Ibid.

17 Ibid.

18 Ibid.

19 Ibid.

20 Ng 2018, 12.

21 Bogardi/Chau 2017, 1.

employees to disclose employment records for the previous 10 years.[22] Moreover, the HKMA also proposed that firms maintain the employment records of their employees for at least 10 years after their departure.

Likewise, the Monetary Authority of Singapore (MAS) has recently announced an adoption of a Senior Management Regime similar to those of other financial regulators around the world. The MAS' Individual Accountability and Conduct Guideline establishes five outcomes that each market participant must achieve, of which the most important is that senior managers are personally accountable for the conduct of business and the actions of employees under their areas of responsibility. Announced in October 2020, the MAS required all affected institutions to achieve the above five outcomes by September 2021.[23] Since then, the regime has become embedded in Singapore's supervisory approach, with a growing focus on how firms integrate conduct accountability into leadership development, risk culture, and succession planning.[24]

### 15.1.2.3 Malaysia

In December 2019, the Central Bank of Malaysia, Bank Negara Malaysia (BNM), issued an exposure draft of a "Responsibility Mapping Framework" to delineate the responsibilities and accountabilities of individuals in leadership positions working in financial institutions.[25] The BNM's goal was to promote an organisational culture that "reinforces ethical, prudent and professional behaviour" and to encourage individuals with leadership responsibilities to take "greater ownership" of their respective areas.[26] Subsequently, on 29 December 2023, Bank Negara Malaysia released the final Policy Document on Responsibility Mapping, which is scheduled to come into effect on 1 January 2026. While the policy has not yet been implemented, its anticipated impact has already led many financial institutions to begin aligning their internal governance structures and accountability frameworks with the forthcoming requirements.[27]

### 15.1.2.4 Australia

Australia's senior regime came into force as part of a series of reforms to the country's financial system, which represented "the most significant overhaul of Australian Pruden-

22 HKMA 2020b, 1–20.
23 MAS 2019.
24 MAS 2021, 1.
25 Regulation Asia 2019.
26 BNM 2019, 1.
27 BNM 2023, 1.

tial Regulation Authority's (APRA) powers since its creation."[28] The Banking Executive Accountability Regime (BEAR) classifies accountable persons, requires their registration and an accountability statement at the APRA, and lays out further notification obligations and potential disqualifications and civil penalties.[29] Interestingly, BEAR makes mention of variable remuneration for authorised deposit-taking institutions (ADI). Variable remuneration was set to be deferred for at least four years with APRA's assuming stronger powers to require ADIs to review and adjust their remuneration policies.[30] In 2023, BEAR was replaced by the *Financial Accountability Regime* (FAR), which extends personal accountability beyond banks to a broader set of institutions, including insurers and superannuation funds. The FAR also strengthened the connection between accountability, risk governance, remuneration and organisational culture.[31]

In summary, the credit crisis of 2008/09, with its multiple revelations of misconduct and lack of care for the welfare of clients throughout financial institutions, caused a sea-change in regulatory practice and perspective around conduct risk. Firstly, the fair treatment of customers was expected to become a fundamental principle at all regulated institutions and one that should be embodied throughout the life cycle of any financial product. Secondly, regulators required managers throughout these institutions to become not only personally responsible for good conduct but also liable for breaches thereof. These changes originated in the anglophone world, but they have now become entrenched in many areas of the globe. Regulatory action is only expected to intensify and widen to many more jurisdictions in future years.

## 15.2 Conduct risk management as an integral part of sustainability

### 15.2.1 Governance and conduct in a sustainability context

A company's sustainability policies and approach have become major concerns for investors, many of whom now consider these factors when assessing their investments. The growing emphasis on sustainability is driven by both social and regulatory factors. Pressure from the public and from institutional investors have pushed financial institutions to provide transparent information about their impacts, which recently expanded to include social and governance risks. Although interest in sustainable investing has recently

[28] Morrison 2017, 2.
[29] APRA 2018, 3.
[30] Ng 2018, 16.
[31] APRA 2024, 1.

slowed, particularly in the US, where regulatory uncertainty has made some firms more cautious, sustainability remains a significant consideration as of May 2025.

In 2020, BlackRock, the world's largest asset manager, announced plans to double the size of its sustainable exchange traded fund (ETF) strategies, increasing the cash in its sustainability-focused mandates from $90 billion to $1 trillion within a decade. By late 2024, BlackRock reported that it had surpassed this goal, with sustainable investments exceeding $1 trillion in assets under management.[32] At the time, the firm evaluated sustainability "with the same rigor as traditional measures such as liquidity and credit risk."[33] However, recent developments have led a more cautious public stance. In response to mounting pressures, BlackRock has rebranded some sustainability funds and exited the Net Zero Asset Managers Initiative, although it continues to manage over 500 sustainable strategies.[34]

### 15.2.2 New legislative focus and recent regulatory developments

Regulatory attention on sustainability has intensified in recent years, especially as environmental and human rights concerns intersect more directly with global business practices. We can generally distinguish between two types of human rights-related legislation. The first type imposes general due diligence obligations on companies, requiring them to map, assess, and manage sustainability risks in their supply chains. The second type is more targeted and outcomes-focused, banning or restricting products linked to a specific harm.

The first type of legislation is characterised by high-level, process-driven requirements, and has raised concerns about the legal complexity and administrative burden. The most notable example is the EU Corporate Sustainability Due Diligence Directive (CSDDD), formally known as Directive (EU) 2024/1760, adopted on 13 June 2024.[35] It establishes mandatory human rights and environmental due diligence obligations for large companies operating within the EU and aims to ensure that companies identify, prevent, mitigate, and account for adverse human rights and environmental impacts in their own operations, subsidiaries, and value chains.[36] The directive reflects the EU's recognition that voluntary measures alone have not delivered sufficient due diligence across global supply chains, and that binding legal obligations are necessary to ensure accountability and sustainability throughout value chains.[37]

---

[32] BlackRock 2024, 1.

[33] BlackRock 2020.

[34] BlackRock 2025.

[35] EUR-Lex 2024a, 1.

[36] Ibid.

[37] Ibid., sub. I.1., 6.

Germany's Supply Chain Act (Lieferkettensorgfaltspflichtengesetz, LkSG), which came into force in 2023[38], was a precursor to the EU directive. However, in 2025, the recently elected German government announced its intention to repeal the law and replace it with a streamlined national implementation of the EU CSDDD, aiming to avoid duplication and reduce bureaucracy for companies.[39]

Nonetheless, the question of the repeal of the LkSG remains unresolved, and if it does occur, its form is yet to be determined. It is clear that any new legislative proposal or amendment to an existing supply chain regulation would have to pass through the required parliamentary proceedings with the necessary majorities. A closer review of the new German government's coalition agreement suggests that the LkSG is not intended to be fully replaced. Instead, the agreement proposes the abolition of reporting requirements.[40] Furthermore, in line with the coalition agreement, the imposition of sanctions for infringements of supply chain due diligence obligations (excluding reporting requirements) is to be avoided, except in cases of so-called "massive human rights violations".[41] For this category of violation, supply chain obligations are expected to remain in force. In the absence of a clear definition of said "massive human rights violations" and given the ambiguity surrounding the notion of "no sanctions", companies are well advised to maintain their focus on supply chain compliance. To that end, firms must still perform thorough supply chain risk analyses to identify any potential "massive human rights violations" and implement appropriate risk management measures whenever necessary. Moreover, maintaining and refining existing supply chain compliance efforts can serve as a useful step toward preparing for the implementation of the CSDDD into national law.

Other national initiatives include France's vigilance law, the Dutch Child Labour Due Diligence Act, and the EU directive on conflict minerals. In parallel, financial supervisors have begun integrating sustainability risks into governance expectations. In Germany, BaFin has continued to integrate sustainability into financial supervisions, including expectations for climate-related risk disclosures and internal risk management frameworks.[42] Finally, in April 2021, the European Central Bank adopted an initiative to amend MiFID II so that financial institutions must begin to take sustainability preferences into account in the product oversight and governance processes. This requirement came into effect under delegated regulations in August 2022, and firms must now gather and incorporate clients' sustainability preferences as part of their suitability assess-

[38] MAS 2021, 1.

[39] Tagesschau 2025.

[40] Bundesregierung 2025.

[41] Ibid.

[42] BaFIN 2023.

ments.[43] In the United Kingdom, the Financial Conduct Authority introduced new Sustainability Disclosure Requirements (SDR) and investment labelling rules in 2023, which aim to combat greenwashing and enhance transparency in sustainable investment offerings.[44]

The second type of legislation takes a stricter approach, directly prohibiting certain products or practices. In the US, the Uyghur Forced Labor Prevention Act (UFLPA) bans imports linked to forced labour in China's Xinjiang region[45], while the EU Deforestation Regulation, adopted in 2023, prohibits the sale of products sourced from recently deforested land.[46] These rules have immediate compliance implications and are increasingly shaping procurement, disclosure, and trade policy decisions.

Conduct risk has emerged as a key issue in the evolving sustainability regulatory landscape because it directly intersects with both types of legislation outlined above. On the one hand, process-based due diligence rules, such as the CSDDD or national supply chain laws, require firms to implement robust governance, risk management, and internal control systems. Failure to do so, or to document them transparently, can constitute a conduct breach. On the other hand, outcome-focused rules, like the UFLPA or the EU Deforestation Regulation, create immediate compliance obligations where false claims or lack of oversight can lead to regulatory and reputational consequences.

One of the clearest ways conduct risk materialises is in how firms communicate sustainability information to investors and consumers. Misleading investors about the sustainability characteristics of products – whether by omission, overstatement, or poor documentation – can violate both conduct and sustainability standards. A firm's misrepresentation of a product's carbon footprint, for example, not only undermines investor trust but also creates regulatory exposure under conduct frameworks. Conduct risk is expected to grow alongside new sustainable investment pathways. Even firms with limited sustainability exposure are increasingly required to consider clients' sustainability preferences in product design and distribution. This expansion brings new risks, particularly around greenwashing. The UK's FCA has already identified numerous conduct breaches in the labelling of "sustainable" funds and intensified enforcement in 2023 and 2024.[47] In parallel, the EU's proposed Green Claims Directive seeks to ban unsubstantiated environmental claims, requiring firms to use verified data before communicating

[43] ESMA 2022, 1.

[44] FCA 2023, 1.

[45] U.S. Department of Homeland Security 2022.

[46] European Commission 2023a.

[47] FCA 2024, 1; ESAs 2024, 1.

green features.[48] If adopted, it will extend conduct obligations beyond financial products into broader marketing, labelling, and disclosure practices. As of May 2025, the directive remains under trilogue negotiations between the European Parliament, Commission, and Council, with adoption expected later in 2025.

## 15.3 Managing conduct risk

### 15.3.1 The Conduct Risk House

Figure 2: Conduct Risk House

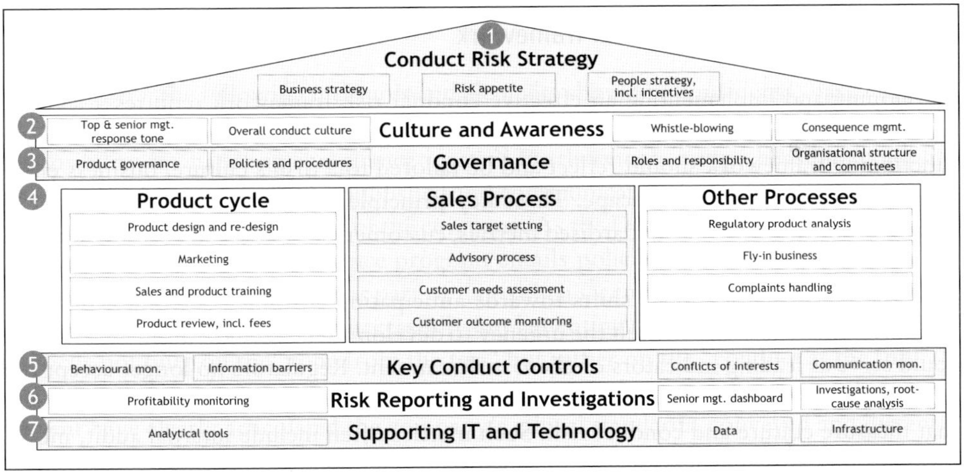


As market participants begin to wake up to the notion that strict compliance with regulatory requirements is only a piece of the overall puzzle, they also begin to realise that developing a culture of good conduct includes the right employees, processes and systems as well as a holistic conduct risk framework. Such a framework must clearly set up a vision that strives to attain good conduct and align all stakeholders around that vision. The right framework identifies and manages risks, rewards ethical behaviour and establishes a clear set of consequences following misconduct.

The Conduct Risk House is founded upon seven key pillars, each of which is required to support a culture of ethical conduct.[49] A comprehensive conduct risk strategy stands at the top of the house and this can further be subdivided into three categories: business

[48] European Commission 2023b.

[49] BCG.

the business model and/or the regulatory landscape.[58] This includes the ability to adapt to emerging digital conduct risks, such as misuse of AI, data governance failures, or algorithmic bias in customer treatment.

While what constitutes "good" conduct should be well-delineated in the organisation's taxonomy, the working scope should not be too narrow. Limiting the definition of conduct would restrict potential and likely necessary definitions of conduct risk and its outcomes. On the other end of the spectrum, firms should spend equal effort in defining "poor" conduct. The twofold approach – defining both "good" and "poor" conduct – would serve as guidance for firms that are building their own conduct risk frameworks.

Once a firm has developed its own conduct risk framework (using the above three guiding principles), it should stress test its effectiveness and applicability. To do so, we recommend a structured health check with three tangible deliverables. For this, three questions should be asked to determine whether a conduct risk framework will stand the test of time:

1. Has the firm undertaken a thorough, detailed description of the status quo, including maturity assessments and quantitative benchmarking results, structured according to its target operating model?

2. Based on the firm's risk profile, has an integrated conduct/compliance and ethics-based strategy been developed?

3. Has a high-level roadmap of the delineation of tasks been developed, employing in-depth reviews of major interfaces with business units?

4. Has an effective compliance and ethics programme been implemented and also communicated?

5. Does the framework effectively track progress of measures towards identified recommendations, such as a high-level compliance heat map?

In conclusion, attention paid by regulators and the public to institutional good conduct is unlikely to diminish. Indeed, the opposite is more likely. Corporations need to devote renewed energies and increased investment to the development of a robust conduct risk and compliance framework. While the intricacies of each framework will be specific to the firm in question, there are general principles that apply to all. Senior management must not only ensure these are in place but also that their behaviour and messaging is consistent with them. Failure to do so may result in calamitous consequences.

58 Ibid., 14: "One hallmark of an effective compliance program is its capacity to improve and evolve."

# 16 A Holistic Approach to Sustainability Risk Management in Financial Institutions – A Global Perspective

*Oliver Engels, Jannik Leiendecker*[1], *Larissa Pilz, Aytech Pseunokov, Benedetta Testino, Anita Varshney*

## 16.1 Introduction

In recent years, sustainability has become an increasingly important consideration for policymakers, businesses, and financial institutions. Climate change is now widely seen not only as an environmental issue but also as a relevant risk with implications for long-term economic performance and financial stability. This includes both physical risks – such as those from extreme weather events and gradual environmental changes – and transition risks linked to the shift toward a low-carbon economy. These developments are informed by a growing awareness of environmental constraints and risks, including those related to climate change, biodiversity, and water and resource use. The international community, through efforts such as the Paris Agreement, has set clear targets to guide the global transition – most notably the objective of limiting the rise in global average temperatures to well below 2°C, while pursuing efforts to stay below 1.5°C. Achieving these goals will require coordinated actions and structural changes across economies, including the redirection of capital flows, adaptation of business models, and incorporation of climate resilience into investment and lending decisions.

In this context, financial institutions – defined as entities engaged in financial intermediation activities such as lending, insurance, investing, and asset management – occupy a uniquely dual role. On the one hand, they are significantly exposed to sustainability-related risks through their balance sheets, investment portfolios, and client relationships; on the other hand, they are key transition enablers, capable of reallocating capital towards sustainable activities and accelerating decarbonization in the real economy. However, this role is fraught with complexity. The transition to a net-zero economy introduces a new suite of financial risks stemming from policy changes (e.g., carbon pricing, regulatory reforms), technological disruptions, market shifts away from high-emission sectors, and evolving stakeholder expectations.

Sustainability typically encompasses a broad set of Environmental, Social, and Governance topics that are increasingly relevant to financial institutions. While these elements are often discussed individually, supervisory authorities have emphasized that sustaina-

[1] Views articulated do not necessarily represent official EFRAG positions.

bility should not be viewed as a separate or standalone risk category. Instead, sustainability factors are to be understood as forward-looking and cross-cutting risk drivers that influence and amplify traditional risk types – such as credit, market and operational risks. For example, environmental events like floods or wildfires can impair collateral values, while social and governance shortcomings may lead to legal liabilities or reputational damage. Recognizing sustainability in this integrated way supports a more comprehensive approach to risk identification, measurement, and management – one that reflects the evolving expectations of regulators, investors, and society at large.

Sustainability risk drivers manifest in multiple forms, each requiring targeted risk management strategies:

- Increased climate-related and environmental risk drivers, which cut across traditional risk types and can be differentiated into:
  - Physical risks, such as extreme weather events (hurricanes, droughts, floods) and resource depletion, which could directly impact asset values, e.g., by reducing the collateral value of loans, or increasing operational risks, such as infrastructure damage from those extreme events.
  - Transition risks that arise from shifts to a low-carbon economy, including regulatory changes (carbon pricing, emission caps) and market shifts away from carbon-intensive industries, e.g., leading to stranded assets. The financial sector is particularly exposed due to its lending and investment activities in industries undergoing a structural transformation.
- Increased social risk drivers stemming from corporate actions affecting employees, communities, and customers. Key risk drivers include:
  - Poor labor conditions or human rights violations, which can result in regulatory penalties, reputational damage, and loss of investor confidence.
  - Consumer protection concerns, such as unfair lending practices or lack of product transparency, can trigger regulatory scrutiny and public backlash.
- Increased governance risk drivers – while governance failures have long been embedded in corporate risk management, sustainability regulation has heightened expectations for ethical conduct and transparency:
  - Corruption, financial crime, and non-compliance with sustainability regulations have substantial financial, legal, and reputational consequences.
  - Sustainability-washing and -hushing, a growing concern, occurs when companies misrepresent their sustainability efforts, misleading investors and consumers. Consequently, these sustainability risk drivers must be integrated not as a peripheral concern but as a core component of financial institutions' enterprise risk management.

While the theoretical understanding of sustainability-related risk drivers has advanced in recent years, spurred by scientific consensus, regulatory initiatives, and investor pressure, the practical integration of these insights into comprehensive sustainability risk management frameworks within financial institutions remains a work in progress. Many financial institutions are in the process of building the professional structures and capabilities needed to embed sustainability across governance, risk assessment, and decision-making systems. Progress is often hindered by the forward-looking, non-linear, and uncertain nature of sustainability risks, which contrast with the backward-looking and data-rich approaches typically used in financial risk modelling. Challenges such as the absence of standardized taxonomies, data inconsistencies, and evolving methodological guidance continue to complicate the attribution of sustainability factors to existing risk categories. However, the increasing clarity of regulatory expectations – along with industry collaboration – offers an important catalyst for raising the bar on consistency, comparability, and strategic coherence in sustainability risk management.

This chapter aims to help bridge that gap by outlining a pragmatic and structured approach to sustainability risk management within financial institutions. Based on a detailed analysis of the commonalities and differences across leading regulatory regimes, we have identified a target operating model (TOM) for sustainability risk management. By mapping the components of this target operating model, we provide a practical tool for aligning with regulatory expectations and guiding implementation. By conceptualizing sustainability not as a standalone domain but as a transversal set of risk drivers that reshape the financial risk landscape, the article offers a pathway for institutions to navigate the change with greater clarity, accountability, and resilience. The intention is to equip decision-makers with a practical blueprint that aligns sustainability imperatives with financial soundness, enabling institutions not only to mitigate risks but to actively support the global transition toward a more sustainable economic system.

To lay the foundation for a structured approach, we will briefly summarize the most relevant global sustainability risk management frameworks and regulatory initiatives impacting financial institutions. This includes a comparative view in Section 16.2 of five key regulatory regimes that shape the sustainability compliance and risk landscape across jurisdictions. Section 16.3 outlines the implementation challenges financial institutions face in operationalizing sustainability risk management across traditional risk types and functions, identifying the key barriers and enablers for effective integration. Building on this regulatory foundation, we introduce a TOM for sustainability risk management that reflects both supervisory expectations and practical implementation needs. The model is structured along four key dimensions – strategy, governance and organization, steering, and enabling factors – and provides a comprehensive framework to institutionalize sustainability integration across financial institutions. We map the selected regulations against the sub-categories of this model to illustrate areas of convergence and divergence, as well as to identify implementation gaps. Section 16.4 will describe this target operating model in detail, highlighting its design logic, alignment with global regulatory developments, and practical suitability for enhancing sustainability risk resilience across financial institutions.

## 16.2 Regulatory frameworks in selected key jurisdictions

The regulatory landscape for sustainability management is evolving rapidly, with jurisdictions around the world taking different approaches in terms of scope, timing, and enforcement. This chapter provides an overview of selected regulatory frameworks that are shaping expectations for financial institutions. The focus lies neither on delivering an exhaustive overview of all global sustainability-related regulations nor a detailed discussion of the specific requirements but rather on highlighting a representative set of regulations from key financial markets.[2]

### 16.2.1 EBA Guidelines on ESG Risk Management (EU – Banks)

In January 2025, the European Banking Authority (EBA) published its "Final Report: Guidelines on the management of ESG risks", under the CRD6 mandate.[3] Binding across the EU, these guidelines apply from 2026 for large banks and 2027 for smaller institutions, setting clear expectations for integrating sustainability risks into core banking activities.

The EBA Guidelines set minimum standards for integrating sustainability factors into risk strategy, governance, steering and internal controls. Banks are required to develop credible transition plans aligned with the EU's 2050 climate goals, with interim targets integrated into business strategy, capital planning, and risk appetite. Sustainability risk drivers must be embedded into traditional risk types – credit, market, liquidity, and operational – supported by revised models, limits, and internal policies.

Governance expectations entail clear board and senior management responsibility for sustainability risks, and engagement with clients on their sustainability strategies. Supervisors expect proactive client engagement on sustainability matters – rather than reliance on external disclosures. The guidelines also introduce process requirements across risk identification, scenario analysis, internal standards, training, controls, and reporting.

2 This overview of regulation is based solely on publicly available documents and is intended for informational purposes only. It does not constitute legal or regulatory advice.

3 EBA 2025b.

Though without prescribing specific capital charges, sustainability risk management will feature prominently in the Supervisory Review and Evaluation Process (SREP). Weaknesses may result in supervisory findings, capital add-ons, or other measures.

### 16.2.2 OCC/Federal Reserve/FDIC Climate Risk Management Principles (US – Banks)

U.S. federal bank regulators have moved more cautiously but have set clear expectations for large banks on climate-related financial risks with the Climate Risk Management Principles. In October 2023, the Federal Reserve, Office of the Comptroller of the Currency (OCC), and FDIC jointly finalized high-level Principles for Climate-Related Financial Risk Management for banks over $100 billion in assets.[4]

Though issued as guidance rather than regulation, the principles are supervisory in nature and will inform examination processes. They set out six core areas: strategic planning, governance, scenario analysis, policies and procedures, risk management, as well as data and reporting. Boards and senior executives are expected to oversee the integration of climate risks into institutional risk appetite and long-term business strategies. This includes the identification and measurement of exposures to both physical and transition risks across all major risk types – credit, market, liquidity, operational, legal, and reputational.

Institutions are expected to enhance their internal frameworks to account for emerging climate-related risk drivers. This involves setting internal standards, improving data capture and analysis capabilities, and using scenario analyses to test climate risk vulnerabilities – although these exercises are not yet formalized as regulatory stress tests.

While the principles avoid prescribing industry-specific credit guidance, supervisors have made it clear that deficiencies in climate risk management may result in examination findings or lower management ratings. Banks must now invest in governance structures, data infrastructure, and specialist capabilities to demonstrate that climate risk is being managed prudently as part of a safe and sound banking system. Although the guidance currently applies to larger institutions, smaller banks are also expected to manage material climate risks in a manner proportionate to their risk profile and operational complexity.

### 16.2.3 PRA Supervisory Statement on Climate Risk (UK – Banks & Insurers)

The UK Prudential Regulation Authority (PRA) has been at the forefront of integrating climate risk into prudential supervision. It issued Supervisory Statement SS3/19 "Enhancing

[4] Board of Governors et al. 2023.

banks' and insurers' approaches to managing the financial risks from climate change."[5] This binding guidance applies to all UK banks and insurance companies (regulated by the PRA) and set explicit expectations in four key areas: governance, risk management, scenario analysis, and disclosure.

Boards are expected to understand and oversee climate-related financial risks, embedding them into the firm's overall business strategy and risk appetite. Senior managers must be assigned responsibility for climate risk and supported by sufficient resources and expertise to carry out this mandate effectively.

Firms are required to incorporate climate considerations into their existing risk management structures. This means assessing how climate risk drivers impact credit, market, insurance underwriting, and operational risks, as well as including these in internal risk assessments and capital adequacy processes where material.

Scenario analysis is a central expectation. Firms must assess the resilience of their business models to a range of climate outcomes – including disorderly transitions or no further policy action – and use these insights to inform long-term strategic decisions. Initially, the PRA adopted a developmental approach, but it set a clear deadline: full compliance was expected by the end of 2021.

Since then, the PRA has intensified its supervisory stance. In 2022, it identified progress in governance but noted gaps in quantification and data. By 2025, it signaled plans to update SS3/19, and in communications with firms, called for faster progress in fully embedding climate risk capabilities. Supervisory tools include firm-specific findings and, where warranted, Pillar 2 capital adjustments for inadequately managed material risks. The PRA's approach, though principle-based, embeds climate risk into the core of prudential expectations – requiring institutions to demonstrate credible, board-level ownership and robust internal frameworks for climate resilience.

### 16.2.4 MAS Environmental Risk Management Guidelines (Singapore – Banks, Insurers, Asset Managers)

In December 2020, the Monetary Authority of Singapore (MAS) issued comprehensive "Guidelines on Environmental Risk Management"[6] for banks, insurers, and asset managers – tailored to the specific activities of each sector. Although not legally binding, these guidelines represent clear supervisory expectations. Financial institutions regulated

[5] Bank of England 2024.

[6] MAS 2020a.

by MAS are expected to adopt them as part of sound risk governance and prudent practice.

Across all sectors, the guidelines require institutions to establish robust governance over environmental risks, with board and senior management accountable for oversight. Environmental factors, including climate-related risks, must be integrated into risk management frameworks, internal controls, and business decision-making. Institutions are expected to identify material risk drivers, assess exposures, and adapt risk appetites accordingly.

For banks, this includes embedding environmental risks into credit assessments, loan origination, and portfolio monitoring – particularly in sectors vulnerable to climate transition or environmental degradation. Asset managers are expected to integrate these risks into investment research and portfolio construction, supported by active stewardship of investee companies. Insurers are required to consider environmental impacts in underwriting and reserving.

Scenario analysis and stress testing are encouraged to evaluate long-term resilience under different environmental pathways. Disclosure is also a key focus: firms are expected to publish their environmental risk management practices and align their reporting with international frameworks such as TCFD.

While MAS has not imposed hard rules or penalties, it monitors implementation through thematic reviews and climate risk assessments. In 2022, it conducted industry surveys and pilot stress tests, highlighting varying levels of maturity. MAS has indicated that persistent gaps may be addressed through supervisory actions, including enhanced expectations or adjustments to risk assessments. Together with mandatory sustainability reporting under SGX rules, the MAS guidelines have firmly positioned environmental risk management as a core prudential expectation in Singapore's financial sector.

### 16.2.5 HKMA Supervisory Policy Manual GS-1 Climate Risk Management (Hong Kong – Authorized Institutions)

The Hong Kong Monetary Authority (HKMA) has established a structured and supervisory-led approach to embedding climate-related risks within the banking sector. In December 2021, it issued Supervisory Policy Manual module "GS-1: Climate Risk Management",[7] applicable to all authorized institutions operating in Hong Kong. The guidance is organized around four pillars – strategy, governance, risk management, and

[7] HKMA 2021b.

disclosure – closely aligned with the recommendations of the Task Force on Climate-related Financial Disclosures (TCFD).

Boards and senior management are expected to exercise clear oversight of climate risk, ensuring that climate-related considerations are embedded in business strategies, risk appetite statements, and governance frameworks. "GS-1" emphasizes that climate risk should be treated as a cross-cutting driver within existing risk categories – credit, market, operational, and liquidity – requiring banks to adapt internal processes, controls, and methodologies accordingly.

The HKMA encourages the use of forward-looking tools such as scenario analyses and stress tests to assess the resilience of business models under varying climate pathways. Institutions are expected to develop these capabilities in a proportionate manner, reflecting the nature, scale, and complexity of their operations.

Implementation is being supervised through a phased approach: starting with baseline self-assessments, followed by more detailed implementation reviews and thematic examinations. Alongside these requirements, the HKMA supports sector-wide capability building through training initiatives and its leadership role in the Green and Sustainable Finance Cross-Agency Steering Group.

"GS-1" forms a cornerstone of Hong Kong's green banking agenda, embedding climate risk management into prudential expectations and reinforcing the shift toward a more resilient and sustainability-conscious financial system.

## 16.3 Sustainability risk management: upcoming challenges for FIs

From a risk management perspective, financial institutions are increasingly confronted with sustainability-related risks that are difficult to isolate, quantify, or fully integrate into traditional frameworks. While the regulatory landscape continues to mature, the practical challenge lies not in conceptually recognizing sustainability risks but in operationalizing them within risk identification, control, and mitigation processes. Institutions are confronted with fragmented and evolving regulatory expectations, the forward-looking and often long-term nature (requiring data beyond traditional risk management cycles) of sustainability risk drivers, and the difficulty of attributing sustainability impacts to traditional risk categories like credit, market, and operational risk. Sustainability risks are inherently cross-cutting – climate change can affect asset quality and collateral values; social risks can result in litigation or reputational loss; and governance failures can trigger systemic breakdowns (Figure 1).

Figure 1: ESG risk drivers' impact on traditional risk types (BCG analysis based on EBA 2025b)

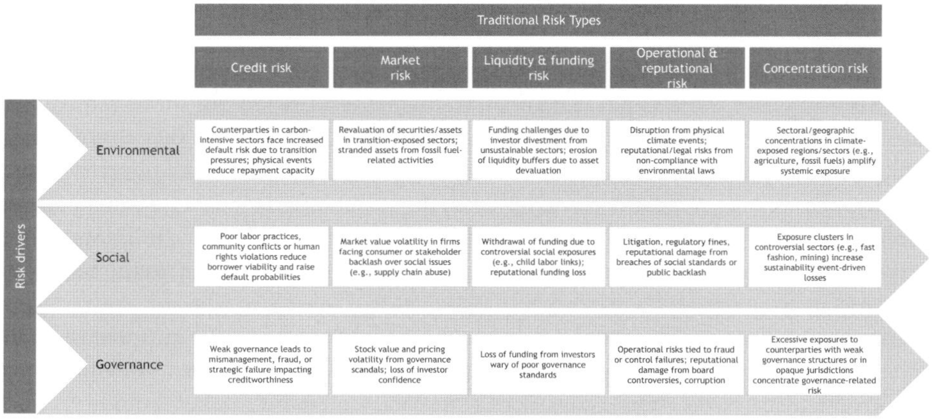


Source: EBA 2025b ("Final Guidelines on the management of ESG risks")

Mitigation requires a systematic integration of sustainability factors into the core risk management cycle – starting with materiality assessments, continued with embedding sustainability considerations into risk taxonomies, and ensuring alignment of risk appetite frameworks, limits, and controls. A holistic governance model is critical, with clearly defined ownership and accountability for sustainability risks, not limited to sustainability functions but fully integrated into first and second lines of defense. Moreover, sustainability risk drivers need to be mapped to internal risk types and monitored over time using both quantitative tools – such as scenario analysis and early warning indicators – and qualitative assessments, particularly for risks with long-dated or uncertain horizons. In the absence of historical data, institutions must rely on proxies, stress tests, and judgment-based escalation paths. In short, the path forward is not about building a parallel sustainability system but about adapting existing risk infrastructures to coherently, consistently, and proportionately incorporate sustainability risks. The following section outlines how this can be achieved in practice through a target operating model that addresses the key structural enablers of sustainability risk management.

## 16.4 Target picture: effective management of sustainability risk drivers

As an enhancement to a traditional risk target operating model (TOM) which is structured vertically along risk types (e.g., credit risk or market risks), the multi-dimensional and cross-operational nature of sustainability issues requires a TOM that cuts across all traditional risks and embeds sustainability risk drivers (climate, social, governance factors) into the core logic of risk decisions. Thus, the sustainability TOM (see an illustrative example in Figure 2), is embedded within the traditional risk TOM as a horizontal, integrative layer instead of a standalone silo of a specific risk type. It enhances the traditional TOM by ensuring sustainability drivers are considered wherever relevant. As horizontal risk drivers, institutions should assess how these factors cut across traditional risk categories (2) and implement a sound sustainability TOM. With regards to environmental risk drivers, institutions should consider the impacts on credit, market, liquidity, operational and reputational risk. Specific sectoral concentrations in climate-exposed regions could amplify a systemic exposure. There is also a cross-cutting impact across E, S, and G dimensions, affecting multiple traditional risk types at the same time.

Figure 2: Sustainability risk management Target Operating Model (illustrative)

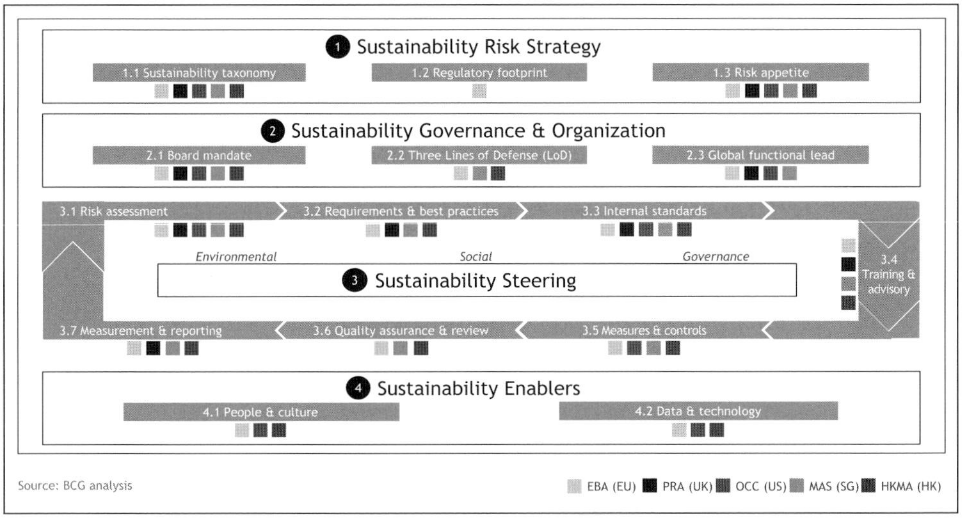

### 16.4.1 Sustainability strategy

The operating model's main building block is a structured sustainability risk strategy, developed across three interdependent pillars: *sustainability taxonomy, regulatory footprint,* and *risk appetite*. Together, they form the strategic core through which financial institutions can identify, evaluate, and manage sustainability-related risk drivers.

The *sustainability taxonomy* forms the analytical foundation by defining a comprehensive set of sustainability factors that are most material to the institution. A proper taxonomy helps determine which risk drivers to monitor and assess across business lines and jurisdictions. This step is critical for prioritization and aligning risk management efforts with strategic objectives.[8] To ensure continued relevance, the taxonomy should be reviewed and updated on a regular basis, ideally in alignment with the institution's existing review cycles for risk and compliance processes.

The *regulatory footprint* involves assessing the institution's legal structure and business model to derive a map of applicable sustainability risk regulations across relevant jurisdictions. This should include active monitoring of emerging requirements and supervisory expectations. Given the heterogeneity and fluidity of the sustainability regulatory landscape, such a footprint allows institutions to anticipate and respond to jurisdiction-specific obligations with agility.[9] It also reinforces the need for a well-defined and regularly updated sustainability taxonomy, ensuring that identified regulatory drivers are consistently mapped to the institution's material sustainability risk factors.

The *risk appetite* dimension defines the overall entity's appetite toward sustainability risks. This includes setting clear thresholds for environmental, social, and governance exposures and ensuring that all group entities and business lines understand and implement this framework consistently. Ambition levels should be measurable (e.g., financed emissions thresholds) and go beyond compliance minimums, supporting long-term strategic positioning and resilience.[10] In addition, institutions are expected to develop or assess credible transition plans at the client level, particularly for clients operating in carbon-intensive or sustainability-critical sectors. These client transition plans should be aligned with the institution's overall sustainability risk appetite.

[8] EBA 2025b, 6; Bank of England 2024, 1; Board of Governors et al. 2023, 5–7; HKMA 2021b, 18–19.

[9] EBA 2025b, 8.

[10] Ibid., 18; Bank of England 2024, 7; MAS 2020, 6.

## 16.4.2 Sustainability governance and organization

A robust sustainability strategy must be supported by effective *governance and organizational structures*, structured around three core enablers: *board mandate, three Lines of Defence (3LoD)*, and a *global functional lead.*

The *board mandate* formalizes individual and collective sustainability risk responsibilities at the board level, often supported by a dedicated sustainability or risk committee. This governance setup reinforces accountability, ensures board awareness of sustainability developments, and provides the authority required to implement sustainability risk measures.[11] Thereby, the board sets a clear tone from the top and underlines the strategic relevance of sustainability across the institution to ensure alignment across legal entities and business units, sustainability-related decisions with group-wide relevance should be anchored in a clear committee structure.

The *three Lines of Defence (3LoD)* model must be explicitly adapted to include sustainability risk responsibilities. The *1st LoD* (e.g., client-facing business units) are risk owners and responsible for incorporating sustainability materiality and proportionality into key activities such as onboarding, credit decisions, and client reviews. The *2nd LoD*, which includes risk management and compliance, must independently monitor sustainability risks, assess regulatory alignment, and ensure effectiveness of controls. The *3rd LoD*, or internal audit, plays a vital role in evaluating the sustainability control environment and validating the performance of both the 1st and 2nd LoDs.[12] This requires cross-functional coordination across Finance, Risk, Sustainability, and Compliance teams to ensure sustainability responsibilities are embedded holistically instead of addressed in functional silos.

The *global functional lead* ensures that sustainability governance and reporting are streamlined across all legal entities and operations. Maintaining a register of regulated entities and tracking jurisdictional sustainability obligations helps create consistency, eliminate blind spots, and allow for efficient reporting and oversight across the group.[13] To support implementation, sustainability staff in regional entities or business units operate under a dual reporting line – formally reporting to their respective Shared Operations Center (SOC) or business leadership, while being functionally aligned with the global sustainability lead. This structure ensures consistent two-way communication between local and global levels.

11 EBA 2025b, 39; Bank of England 2024, 7; Board of Governors et al. 2023, 5.

12 EBA 2025b, 30–31; MAS 2020, 7; HKMA 2021b, 19.

13 Bank of England 2024, 8; Board of Governors et al. 2023, 6.

### 16.4.3 Sustainability risk steering

The sustainability risk steering function acts as the operational engine room of sustainability risk management, comprising seven interconnected sub-components:

*Risk Assessment* – Institutions must conduct regular (monthly or quarterly) sustainability risk exposure checks. These assessments should evaluate control quality, analyze residual risk, compare results to the defined risk appetite, and run scenario analyses to identify and address potential weaknesses.[14]

*Requirements & Best Practices* – A central team should continuously scan the external landscape (regulators, industry initiatives, peers) to identify relevant requirements and best practices. The function should translate findings into actionable tasks and direct them to the appropriate roles, escalating when unclear.[15]

*Internal Standards* – These external requirements must then be implemented into internal standards, ensuring they are current, complete, and embedded in organizational procedures (e.g., onboarding processes, investment review).[16]

*Training & Advisory* – Delivered by the 2nd LoD, sustainability training programs ensure that staff understand risk expectations and have the capabilities to detect and manage sustainability risk factors in their day-to-day responsibilities.[17] The training content should differentiate between sustainability aspects relevant to the institution's own operations – such as internal governance, procurement, or facility management – and those applicable to downstream activities, particularly in client-facing roles such as relationship managers who must be equipped to assess client transition plans and align onboarding or advisory processes with sustainability standards.

*Measures & Controls* – Sustainability-specific control mechanisms should be developed and implemented, enabling the 1st LoD to act when risk levels become excessive. These should be linked to the institution's ambition level and appetite.[18] Controls should reflect the specific context of different functions – for example, front-office staff may require controls embedded in direct interaction with clients, meaning for example in client onboarding or advisory, whereas non-front roles may focus on internal policies, supply chain screening, or operational practices.

---

[14] EBA 2025b, 26; MAS 2020a, 9; HKMA 2021b, 23.

[15] EBA 2025b, 30; HKMA 2021b, 19.

[16] Bank of England 2024, 8; Board of Governors et al. 2023, 5; MAS 2020, 6.

[17] EBA 2025b, 29; MAS 2020a, 7; HKMA 2021b, 17.

[18] Board of Governors et al. 2023, 6; HKMA 2021b, 28.

*Quality Assurance & Review* – The 2nd LoD must regularly review 1st LoD actions to confirm completeness and effectiveness, generating feedback loops to continuously improve sustainability risk mitigation.[19] These reviews should account for the differing roles of front- and non-front functions – ensuring that client-facing activities align with sustainability standards, and that internal processes like procurement and risk controls are effectively monitored.

*Measurement & Reporting* – Institutions must track the implementation status of regulatory frameworks and prioritize based on materiality, regulatory relevance, and residual risk.[20]

**DEEP DIVE: Leveraging GenAI for sustainability washing risk controls**

With increasing regulatory scrutiny and stakeholder demand for transparency, sustainability-washing – misleading sustainability claims – has become a critical risk driver for reputational, business, and regulatory risk. Sustainability washing extends beyond greenwashing to include social and governance misrepresentations. Traditional risk management frameworks often fail to effectively capture and mitigate these risks. A structured sustainability washing risk management framework aligns with traditional risk processes, covering four key steps: first, *risk identification* through regular, second-level control functions scanning public sustainability claims made by the institution across various sources, similarly as described in the TOM section *risk assessment*. Second, *assessing the effectiveness of first-level controls* and procedures in mitigating sustainability washing, as assessed in the *measures & controls* dimension of the TOM. Third, *new monitoring controls,* as described in *quality assurance & review,* need to be introduced if necessary to address the sustainability washing accusations. Last, once the controls are executed and discussed with the relevant business owners, the findings are aggregated and reported to the appropriate *internal committees* (see also the section regarding the *board mandate*). Given the routine, intensive, and evolving nature of sustainability-washing risk management, GenAI enhances efficiency by supporting risk identification, measurement, and monitoring:

1. Risk identification: automated identification of sustainability claims

   Sustainability claims are often dispersed around multiple channels, including corporate websites, social media posts, press releases, and other public sources, making it challenging to maintain an up-to-date list of claims. This challenge is even greater for large organizations with multiple subsidiaries, where sustainability claims may be inconsistently communicated. GenAI usage through web scraping can help accelerate data collection and increase clarity over corporate claims to streamline communication across various channels.

19 EBA 2025b, 30; MAS 2020, 5.

20 Bank of England 2024, 10–11; MAS 2020, 11–12.

2. Risk measurement: risk-based prioritization of sustainability commitments

   One key challenge for implementing an effective sustainability-control framework is the prioritization of sustainability claims based on their potential impact. Many companies lack a structured approach to monitoring sustainability commitments, making it especially challenging for financial institutions with diverse investment portfolios to identify where sustainability washing risks could materialize. GenAI can assist in risk prioritization scores based on public information, such as recent litigation cases or market sentiment. As self-learning AI models continuously refine their analyses based on new data, risk assessments become more accurate and adaptive over time.

3. Risk monitoring: assessment of control adequacy

   Once the relevant sustainability claims have been identified and prioritized, GenAI can help map and assess existing controls. Natural Language Processing (NLP) and AI-driven pattern recognition assess sustainability controls by scanning bond prospectuses, investment mandates, and disclosures for inconsistencies. Automated look-through analyses ensure compliance with sustainability commitments by verifying fund-level and security-level sustainability characteristics.

4. Risk monitoring: enhancement of risk controls

   GenAI can help design new controls to minimize sustainability risks. Predictive modelling can forecast potential greenwashing risks based on historical sustainability controversies and evolving regulatory expectations. By embedding GenAI into sustainability risk control frameworks, companies can transition from a reactive, compliance-driven sustainability assessment to a proactive, risk-based approach. GenAI can help enhance the efficiency, accuracy, and clarity of sustainability risk management as well as strengthen stakeholder trust and regulatory confidence. As regulatory bodies increase oversight of sustainability washing risks, AI-driven sustainability control mechanisms will increasingly become the industry standard for financial institutions.

### 16.4.4 Identification of enabling factors

The TOM's final layer focuses on *sustainability enablers* – the underlying drivers that allow sustainability risk management to function effectively at scale. These are structured across two critical categories: *people & culture* and *data & technology*.

*People & Culture* – Institutions must foster a culture of sustainability awareness from the top down, with a clear tone from the top, which is playing a critical role in setting expectations and embedding sustainability into the broader risk culture. Empowerment begins with clear role definitions across the 1$^{st}$ and 2$^{nd}$ LoD and is reinforced through targeted trainings, communication, and cross-functional collaboration. This includes establishing a common baseline of sustainability knowledge across all functions and levels, ensuring that both front- and non-front staff understand their specific roles in managing sustainability risks. Training should go beyond compliance and enable a long-term, cross-functional perspective that reflects the strategic relevance of sustainability. Sustainability risk management must therefore be recognized as a shared and enduring responsibility.[21]

*Data & Technology* – Institutions must ensure access to complete, accurate, and timely sustainability data. This includes defining the relevant data points, building efficient pipelines, and implementing systems capable of systematically analyzing and reporting sustainability risks. Centralized, automated solutions such as control towers and sustainability data platforms are increasingly essential to maintaining traceability, meeting regulatory expectations, and informing business decisions.[22] For effective scenario planning and long-term risk assessment, institutions should leverage long-term data series – such as those provided by reinsurance companies. To ensure consistency and reduce fragmentation, a single point of truth in the form of a sustainability data warehouse is essential, serving as the centralized backbone for all risk, disclosure and steering processes. An adequate selection of the tool should ensure that both regulatory disclosure obligations and internal sustainability steering requirements are comprehensively supported through integrated reporting and analytics functionalities.

## 16.5 Conclusion

The evolving sustainability landscape has transformed sustainability risk from a niche concern into a fundamental driver of financial and non-financial risks. While regulatory dynamics remain fragmented and politically sensitive, the direction is clear: institutions are expected to manage sustainability risks with the same rigor as traditional risk types. The unique characteristics of sustainability – its cross-cutting nature, forward-looking time horizon, and data complexity – require financial institutions to move beyond reactive compliance toward a structured, proactive, and integrated approach. A dedicated sustainability TOM, anchored in clear governance, coordinated steering, and strong enablers, such as data, culture, and technology, provides the necessary framework. This target picture is not intended as a fixed end state from the beginning but rather as a framework that institutions can progressively build up. A stepwise approach allows for preparatory work and incremental enhancements over time, enabling organizations to align ambition and resources while gradually converging toward the full model.

[21] EBA 2025, 30; Board of Governors et al. 2023, 6.

[22] EBA 2025b, 21; HKMA 2021b, 17.

Companies may take a path along the following three phases to fully implement and establish a target picture:

1. the status quo assessment, including a comprehensive check of sustainability compliance with the target operating model;
2. the development of a target picture and its implementation plan; and
3. the actual implementation of the target picture.

The *status quo assessment* should consider internal and external aspects regarding sustainability compliance. Ideally, the assessment should be based on multiple sources, including current policies, definitions of roles and responsibilities, control processes, as well as questionnaires and interviews. Particularly important is the analysis of the regulatory footprint and the key sustainability risk exposures of the business across all locations.

In the second phase, a detailed *target picture* should be established, starting with the definition of sustainability ambitions based on strategic goals and regulatory requirements. To meet defined ambitions, the target picture should be detailed with short- and long-term plans, including plans for the establishment of roles and decision structures in the organization. Companies should consider a step-by-step implementation plan, starting with fundamental elements and allowing for continuous enhancement. Aligning the developed target picture and implementation plan with affected units will increase acceptance and support for the implementation phase.

In the third and final phase, the *target picture should be implemented*, including organizational adjustments to incorporate sustainability compliance and a sustainability steering cycle for all sustainability factors. The build-up of supporting data and software structures will be a fundamental aspect of efficient and comprehensive compliance monitoring and reporting, allowing for continuous and transparent steering of business operations towards the target picture. Insights gained from monitoring should be used to build up sustainability topic expertise and, if necessary, derive business process adjustments, changes to the implementation plan and other measures for improved compliance.

Australian Prudential Regulation Authority [APRA] (2017), Prudential Standard CPS 231 – Outsourcing, https://www.apra.gov.au/sites/default/files/Prudential-Standard-CPS-231-Outsourcing-%28July-2017%29.pdf, accessed: 17 February 2022.

Australian Prudential Regulation Authority [APRA] (2018), Information Paper – Implementing the Banking Executive Accountability Regime, https://www.apra.gov.au/sites/default/files/information_paper_implementing_the_bear.pdf, accessed: 26 February 2022.

Australian Prudential Regulation Authority [APRA] (2019), Information Paper – Transforming governance, culture, remuneration and accountability: APRA's approach, https://www.apra.gov.au/sites/default/files/Transforming%20governance%2C%20culture%2C%20remuneration%20and%20accountability%20-%20APRA%E2%80%99s%20approach.pdf, accessed: 16 February 2022.

Australian Prudential Regulation Authority [APRA] (2024), Financial Accountability Regime: Information for Accountable Entities, https://www.apra.gov.au/financial-accountability-regime-information-for-accountable-entities, accessed: 13 May 2025.

Australia Royal Commission (2019), Final Report – Royal Commission into Misconduct in the Banking, Superannuation and Financial Services Industry, https://www.royalcommission.gov.au/sites/default/files/2019-02/fsrc-volume-1-final-report.pdf, accessed: 26 February 2022.

Autoriteit Financiële Markten [AFM] (s.a.), Behaviour and culture, https://www.afm.nl/en/professionals/onderwerpen/gedrag-cultuur, accessed: 26 February 2022.

Bandsuch, Mark/Pate, Larry/Thies, Jeff (2008), Rebuilding Stakeholder Trust in Business – An Examination of Principle-Centred Leadership and Organisational Transparency in Corporate Governance, in: Business & Society Review 113, 99–127.

Bank for International Settlements [BIS] (1998), Framework for internal control systems in Banking organisations, https://www.bis.org/publ/bcbs40.pdf, accessed: 25 February 2022.

Bank for International Settlements [BIS] (2009), Issues in the Governance of Central Banks, https://www.bis.org/publ/othp04.pdf, accessed: 21 March 2025.

Bank for International Settlements [BIS] (2010), Basel Committee on Banking Supervision – Principles for enhancing corporate governance, https://www.bis.org/publ/bcbs176.pdf, accessed: 21 February 2022.

Bank Negara Malaysia [BNM] (2019), Responsibility Mapping – Exposure Draft, https://www.bnm.gov.my/index.php?ch=57&pg=144&ac=886&bb=file, accessed: 26 February 2022.

Bank Negara Malaysia [BNM] (2023), Responsibility Mapping, issued 29 December 2023, effective 1 January 2026, https://www.bnm.gov.my/documents/20124/938039/pd-Responsibility-Mapping-Dec2023.pdf, accessed: 13 May 2025.

Bank of England (2018), FCA and PRA jointly fine Mr James Staley £642,430 and announce special requirements regarding whistleblowing systems and controls at Barclays, https://www.bankofengland.co.uk/news/2018/may/fca-and-pra-jointly-fine-mr-james-staley-and-announce-special-requirements-at-barclays, accessed: 26 February 2022.

Bank of England (2019a), Outsourcing and third party risk management, https://www.bankofengland.co.uk/-/media/boe/files/prudential-regulation/consultation-paper/2021/march/ps721.pdf?la=en&hash=6C70BEE48B89D7965D43894DB848F-C41CD5EC6C0, accessed: 17 February 2022.

Bank of England (2019b), Supervisory Statement SS3/19 Enhancing banks' and insurers' approaches to managing the financial risks from climate change, https://www.bankofengland.co.uk/-/media/boe/files/prudential-regulation/supervisory-statement/2024/ss319-november-2024-update.pdf, accessed: 15 November 2024.

Bank of England (2020), Joint FCA and PRA statement Senior Managers and Certification Regime (SM&CR) and coronavirus (Covid-19): our expectations of dualregulated firms, London, https://www.bankofengland.co.uk/prudential-regulation/publication/2020/smcr-and-covid-19-pra-and-fca-expectations-of-firms, accessed: 26 February 2022.

Bank of England (2021), Policy Statement PS7/21 Outsourcing and third party risk management, https://www.bankofengland.co.uk/-/media/boe/files/prudential-regulation/consultation-paper/2021/march/ps721.pdf?la=en&hash=6C70-BEE48B89D7965D43894DB848FC41CD5EC6C0, accessed: 16 February 2022.

Bank of England (2024), Update: Enhancing banks' and insurers' approaches to managing the financial risks from climate change, https://www.bankofengland.co.uk/-/media/boe/files/prudential-regulation/supervisory-statement/2024/ss319-november-2024-update.pdf, accessed: 16 July 2025.

Bank of England/HM Treasury (2015), Fair and Effective Markets Review Final Report, https://www.bankofengland.co.uk/-/media/boe/files/report/2015/fair-and-effective-markets-review-final-report.pdf?la=en&hash=1985B00AA2221D81606668501E01EB0B0412403A, accessed: 16 February 2022.

Basel Committee on Banking Supervision [BCBS] (s.a.), Basel II, https://www.bis.org/publ/bcbsca.htm, accessed: 16 February 2022.

Basel Committee on Banking Supervision [BCBS] (s.a.), History of the Basel Committee, https://www.bis.org/bcbs/history.htm, accessed: 15 February 2022.

Basel Committee on Banking Supervision [BCBS] (2000), Principles for the management of credit risk, https://www.bis.org/publ/bcbs75.pdf, accessed: 22 February 2022.

Basel Committee for Banking Supervision [BCBS] (2001), QIS 2 – operational loss data, https://www.bis.org/bcbs/qisoprisknote.pdf, accessed: 16 February 2022.

Basel Committee on Banking Supervision [BCBS] (2004), International Convergence of Capital Measurement and Capital Standards, https://www.bis.org/publ/bcbs107.pdf, accessed: 15 February 2022.

Basel Committee on Banking Supervision [BCBS] (2008), Principles for sound liquidity risk management and supervision, https://www.bis.org/publ/bcbs144.htm, accessed: 16 February 2022.

Basel Committee on Banking Supervision [BCBS] (2012), Core Principles for Effective Banking Supervision, https://www.bis.org/publ/bcbs230.pdf, accessed: 15 February 2022.

Basel Committee on Banking Supervision [BCBS] (2017), Basel III – Finalizing post-crisis reforms, https://www.bis.org/basel_framework/chapter/OPE/10.htm?inforce=20230101&published=20240705, accessed: 16 February 2022.

Basel Committee on Banking Supervision [BCBS] (2019), MAR10 – Definition and application for market risk, https://www.bis.org/basel_framework/chapter/MAR/10.htm, accessed: 16 February 2022.

Basel Committee of Banking Supervision [BCBS] (2020 [2014]), Sound management of risks related to money laundering and financing of terrorism, https://www.bis.org/bcbs/publ/d505.htm, accessed: 16 February 2022.

Basel Committee on Banking Supervision [BCBS] (2021a), Principles for Operational Resilience, https://www.bis.org/bcbs/publ/d516.htm, accessed: 17 February 2022.

Basel Committee on Banking Supervision [BCBS] (2021b), Revision to the Principles for the Sound Management of Operational Risk, https://www.bis.org/bcbs/publ/d515.pdf, accessed: 15 February 2022.

Berry, Simon/Liu, Michael/Powell, Simon/Yeung, Cathy/Guo, Carmen (2013), Hong Kong Banks Pledge to Treat Customers Fairly, Latham & Watkins, https://m.lw.com/thoughtLeadership/lw-hong-kong-tcf-principles, accessed: 26 February 2022.

Bicker, Eike/Steinle, Christian/Skoupil, Christoph (2021), Principles and Guidelines for Internal Investigations in Germany, in: Seddon, Judith et al. (eds.), The Practitioner's Guide to Global Investigations, 5th ed., Law Business Research, London, 234–254.

BlackRock (2020), Sustainability as BlackRock's New Standard for Investing, https://www.blackrock.com/ch/individual/en/blackrock-client-letter, accessed: 26 February 2022.

BlackRock (2024), 2024 Climate Report, https://www.blackrock.com/corporate/literature/continuous-disclosure-and-important-information/climate-report-blkinc.pdf, accessed: 13 May 2025.

BlackRock (2025), BlackRock's decision to leave NZAM, 10 January 2025, https://www.blackrock.com/corporate/newsroom/announcement/blackrock-withdraws-from-nzam, accessed 19 May 2025.

Board of Governors of the Federal Reserve System (1995), Policy letter SR 95-51 (SUP), https://www.federalreserve.gov/boarddocs/srletters/1995/sr9551.htm, accessed: 20 March 2025.

Board of Governors of the Federal Reserve System (2013), Guidance on managing outsourcing risk, https://www.federalreserve.gov/supervisionreg/topics/legal_risk.htm, accessed: 17 February 2022.

Board of Governors of the Federal Reserve System (2019), Supervision and Regulation Report, https://www.federalreserve.gov/publications/2019-november-supervision-and-regulation-report.htm, accessed: 16 February 2022.

Board of Governors of the Federal Reserve System (2020), Sound Practices to Strengthen Operational Resilience, the Office of the Comptroller of the Currency, and the Federal Deposit Insurance Corporation, https://www.occ.gov/news-issuances/news-releases/2020/nr-occ-2020-144a.pdf, accessed: 17 February 2022.

Board of Governors of the Federal Reserve System (2021a), Supervisory Policy and Guideline topics, Legal/Reputational risk, https://www.federalreserve.gov/supervisionreg/topics/legal_risk.htm, accessed: 17 February 2022.

Board of Governors of the Federal Reserve System (2021b [2008]), SR 08-8/CA 08-11, https://www.federalreserve.gov/boarddocs/srletters/2008/sr0808.htm, accessed: 5 June 2025.

Board of Governors of the Federal Reserve System/Federal Deposit Insurance Corporation/Office of the Comptroller of the Currency (2023), Principles for Climate-Related Financial Risk Management for Large Financial Institutions, 24 October 2023, https://www.federalreserve.gov/supervisionreg/srletters/SR2309a1.pdf, accessed: 16 July 2025.

Bogardi, Etelka/Chau, Lillian (2017), Hong Kong – Manager-In-Charge regime comes into force, Norton Rose Fulbright, https://www.regulationtomorrow.com/asia/regulation-and-compliance-asia/hong-kong-manager-in-charge-regime-comes-into-force/, accessed: 13 May 2025.

Boston Consulting Group [BCG] (2024), Global ESG, Compliance, and Risk Report 2024: New ways to combat rising complexity and costs, https://web-assets.bcg.com/4f/1e/f15654d44628a6b2d8e5d4a5aacd/bcg-global-esg-compliance-and-risk-report-2024-nov-2024.pdf, accessed: 27 March 2025.

Boston Consulting Group [BCG] (2025), Fine Whines: Six Factors That Can Protect Banks From Compliance Sanctions, https://media-publications.bcg.com/Fine-Whines-Six-Factors-That-Can-Protect-Banks.pdf, accessed: 27 March 2025.

Bruce, Eric/Cendan, Daniel/Marcu, Aaron/Radin, Olivia/Siegel, Adam/Zelnick, Kimberley (2022), What to expect from US enforcement agencies in 2022, https://riskandcompliance.freshfields.com/post/102hgj9/what-to-expect-from-us-enforcement-agencies-in-2022, accessed: 25 February 2022.

Bundesanstalt für Finanzdienstleistungsaufsicht [BaFin] (2011), Circular 4/2010 (WA) – Minimum Requirements for the Compliance Function and Additional Requirements Governing Rules of Conduct, Organisation and Transparency, Frankfurt am Main, https://www.bafin.de/SharedDocs/Veroeffentlichungen/EN/Rundschreiben/rs_1004_wa_macomp_en.html?nn=7857902#doc7856464bodyText4, accessed: 26 February 2022.

Bundesanstalt für Finanzdienstleistungsaufsicht [BaFin] (2016), Rules of conduct, https://www.bafin.de/dok/7857902, accessed: 26 February 2022.

Bundesanstalt für Finanzdienstleistungsaufsicht [BaFin] (2021), MaRisk, BAIT und ZAIT: BaFin veröffentlicht Novellen von MaRisk und BAIT und neues Rundschreiben ZAIT, https://www.bafin.de/SharedDocs/Veroeffentlichungen/DE/Meldung/2021/meldung_2021_08_16_RS_MaRisk_BAIT_ZAiT.html, accessed: 25 February 2022.

Bundesanstalt für Finanzdienstleistungsaufsicht [BaFin] (2023), Circular 05/2023 (BA) – Minimum Requirements for Risk Management (MaRisk), https://www.bafin.de/SharedDocs/Downloads/EN/Rundschreiben/dl_rs_0523_marisk_ba_en.html, accessed: 13 May 2025.

Bundesministerium der Justiz [BMJ] (2018), Gesetz über das Kreditwesen (Kreditwesengesetz – KWG), http://www.gesetze-im-internet.de/kredwg/__25a.html, accessed: 26 February 2022.

Bundesministerium der Justiz [BMJ] (2020), Gesetzesentwurf der Bundesregierung: Entwurf eines Gesetzes zur Stärkung der Integrität in der Wirtschaft (VerSanG) vom 16.06.2020, https://www.bmj.de/SharedDocs/Gesetzgebungsverfahren/Dokumente/RegE_Staerkung_Integritaet_Wirtschaft.pdf;jsessionid=E74712F27005CD722D386A1EA7DEEAEC.1_cid324?__blob=publicationFile&v=2, accessed: 24 February 2022.

Bundesregierung (2021), Koalitionsvertrag 2021–2025 zwischen der Sozialdemokratischen Partei Deutschlands (SPD), BÜNDNIS 90/DIE GRÜNEN und den Freien Demokraten (FDP), https://www.bundesregierung.de/resource/blob/974430/1990812/04221173eef9a6720059cc353d759a2b/2021-12-10-koav2021-data.pdf?download=1, accessed: 24 February 2022.

Bundesregierung (2025), Koalitionsvertrag 2025 – Verantwortung für Deutschland zwischen der Christlich Demokratischen Union Deutschlands (CDU), Christlich-Sozialen Union in Bayern (CSU) und der Sozialdemokratischen Partei Deutschlands (SPD), https://www.koalitionsvertrag2025.de/, accessed: 27 May 2025.

Central Bank of Bahrain (s.a.), CBB rule book, intra-group outsourcing, https://cbben.thomsonreuters.com/rulebook/intra-group-outsourcing-0, accessed: 17 February 2022.

Central Bank of Ireland (s.a.), Introduction to financial sanctions, https://www.centralbank.ie/regulation/how-we-regulate/international-financial-sanctions, accessed: 16 February 2022.

Central Bank of Ireland (2017), A Guide to Consumer Protection Risk Assessment, https://www.centralbank.ie/docs/default-source/regulation/consumer-protection/compliance-monitoring/reviews-and-research/a-guide-to-consumer-protection-risk-assessment.pdf?sfvrsn=4, accessed: 16 February 2022.

Central Bank of Ireland [CBI] (2020), Dear CEO Letter: Securities Markets Conduct Risk – January 2020 Industry Communication, https://www.centralbank.ie/docs/default-source/regulation/industry-market-sectors/securities-markets/wholesale-markets/securities-market-conduct-risk---dear-ceo-letter.pdf?sfvrsn=7, accessed: 13 May 2025.

Central Bank of Ireland [CBI] (2024), Guidance on the Individual Accountability Framework, https://www.centralbank.ie/docs/default-source/publications/consultation-papers/cp153/appendix-2-to-the-feedback-statement-to-cp153-guidance-on-the-iaf.pdf, accessed: 13 May 2025.

Committee of Sponsoring Organizations of the Treadway Commission [COSO] (2004), Enterprise Risk Management – Integrated Framework, https://www.coso.org/guidance-erm, accessed: 21 March 2025.

Committee of Sponsoring Organizations of the Treadway Commission [COSO] (2016), Fraud Risk Management Guide, https://www.acfe.com/-/media/files/acfe/pdfs/fraud-risk-tools/coso-fraud-risk-management-guide-second-edition-executive-summary.pdf, accessed: 16 February 2022.

Commodity Futures Trading Commission [CFTC] (2012), Final Rules Regarding Business Conduct Standards for Swap Dealers and Major Swap Participants Dealing with Counterparties, https://www.cftc.gov/sites/default/files/idc/groups/public/@newsroom/documents/file/bcs_factsheet_final.pdf, accessed: 26 February 2022.

Commodity Futures Trading Commission [CFTC] (2023), Statement of Commissioner Christy Goldsmith Romero In Support of Holding Banks Accountable For Widespread Use of Personal Text Messaging and/or WhatsApp to Evade Regulatory Oversight, https://www.cftc.gov/PressRoom/SpeechesTestimony/romerostatement080823, accessed: 30 June 2025.

Commonwealth Numbered Acts (2023), Financial Accountability Regime Act 2023 (No. 67, 2023), austlii.edu.au/cgi-bin/viewdb/au/legis/cth/num_act/fara2023273/, accessed: 13 May 2025.

Consumer Financial Protection Bureau [CFPB] (2015), CFPB Orders Citibank to Pay $700 Million in Consumer Relief for Illegal Credit Card Practices, https://www.consumerfinance.gov/about-us/newsroom/cfpb-orders-citibank-to-pay-700-million-in-consumer-relief-for-illegal-credit-card-practices/, accessed: 26 February 2022.

Copley, Rebecca (2016), Making Sense of Conduct Risk, in: The Oath 51, 28–29.

Cornell Law School, Legal Information Institute (s.a.), Credit Card Fraud, https://www.law.cornell.edu/wex/credit_card_fraud, accessed: 16 February 2022.

Corporate Finance Institute (s.a.), Business risk, https://corporatefinanceinstitute.com/resources/knowledge/finance/business-risk/, accessed: 17 February 2022.

Cravath, Swaine & Moore LLP (2020), Universal Issues in Global Investigations – Client Briefing.

DAC Beachcroft (2019a), Regulators shift focus to conduct risk, https://insurance.dacbeachcroft.com/thought-leadership/regulators-shift-their-focus-to-conduct-risk/, accessed: 26 February 2022.

DAC Beachcroft (2019b), Thought Leadership 2019/20 – Regulators shift their focus to conduct risk, https://insurance.dacbeachcroft.com/media/yswln0hi/regulators-shift-their-focus-to-conduct-risk.pdf, accessed: 26 February 2022.

De Nederlandsche Bank [DNB] (2015), Supervision of Behaviour and Culture – Foundations practice & future developments, https://www.dnb.nl/en/binaries/Book%20Supervision%20of%20Behaviour%20and%20Culture_tcm47-380398.pdf, accessed: 26 February 2022.

Deutsche Bundesbank (2021), Financial sanctions, https://www.bundesbank.de/en/service/financial-sanctions/financial-sanctions-619000, accessed: 16 Februar 2022.

Deutsches Institut für Menschenrechte (2016), Assessing Human Rights Risks and Impacts, https://www.institut-fuer-menschenrechte.de/fileadmin/Redaktion/Publikationen/HRIA_Assessing_Human_Rights_Risks_and_Impacts_Perspectives_from_corporate_practice.pdf, accessed: 17 February 2022.

Donaldson, William H. (2003), Testimony Concerning Implementation of the Sarbanes-Oxley Act of 2002, https://www.sec.gov/news/testimony/090903tswhd.htm, accessed: 25 February 2022.

EIOPA (2019), EIOPA sets out framework for identifying conduct risks, https://www.eiopa.europa.eu/content/eiopa-sets-out-framework-identifying-conduct-risks-0_en, accessed: 26 February 2022.

Eliason, Michael J. (1999), Compliance plus Integrity, in: The Internal Auditor 56, 30–33.

EUR-Lex (2015), DIRECTIVE (EU) 2015/849 of the European Parliament and of the Council of 20 May 2015 on the prevention of the use of the financial system for the purposes of money laundering or terrorist financing, amending Regulation (EU) No 648/2012 of the European Parliament and of the Council, and repealing Directive 2005/60/EC of the European Parliament and of the Council and Commission Directive 2006/70/EC, https://eur-lex.europa.eu/legal-content/EN/TXT/PDF/?uri=CELEX:32015L0849&from=DE, accessed: 20 March 2025.

EUR-Lex (2016), General Data Protection Regulation – Regulation (EU) 2016/679 of the European Parliament and of the Council, https://eur-lex.europa.eu/legal-content/DE/TXT/?uri=CELEX%3A02016R0679-20160504, accessed: 17 February 2022.

EUR-Lex (2017), Directive (EU) 2017/828 of the European Parliament and of the the Council of 17 May 2017 amending Directive 2007/36/EC as regards the encouragement of long-term shareholder engagement, https://eur-lex.europa.eu/legal-content/EN/TXT/HTML/?uri=CELEX:32017L0828&from=DE, accessed: 26 February 2022.

EUR-Lex (2019a), Directive of the European Parliament and of the council on the Protection of Persons who Report Breaches of Union, https://eur-lex.europa.eu/legal-content/EN/TXT/PDF/?uri=CONSIL:PE_78_2019_REV_1&from=EN, accessed: 26 February 2022.

EUR-Lex (2019b), Regulation (EU) 2019/2088 of the European Parliament and of the Council of 27 November 2019 on sustainability-related disclosures in the financial services sector, https://eur-lex.europa.eu/legal-content/EN/TXT/?uri=celex%3A32019R2088, accessed: 14 March 2022.

EUR-Lex (2019c), Directive (EU) 2019/1937 of the European Parliament and of the Council of 23 October 2019 on the protection of persons who report breaches of Union law, L 305, 26 November 2019, https://eur-lex.europa.eu/eli/dir/2019/1937/oj/eng, accessed: 30 June 2025.

EUR-Lex (2021), Guidance on the avoidance and management of conflicts of interest under the Financial Regulation, https://eur-lex.europa.eu/legal-content/EN/TXT/PDF/?uri=CELEX:52021XC0409(01)&from=EN, accessed: 26 February 2022.

EUR-Lex (2022a), Regulation (EU) 2022/2554 of the European Parliament and of the Council of 14 December 2022 on digital operational resilience for the financial sector and amending Regulations (EC) No 1060/2009, (EU) No 648/2012, (EU) No 600/2014, (EU) No 909/2014 and (EU) 2016/1011, https://eur-lex.europa.eu/legal-content/EN/TXT/PDF/?uri=CELEX:32022R2554, accessed: 14 July 2025.

EUR-Lex (2022b), Directive (EU) 2022/2555 of the European Parliament and of the Council of 14 December 2022 on measures for a high common level of cybersecurity across the Union, amending Regulation (EU) No 910/2014 and Directive (EU) 2018/1972, and repealing Directive (EU) 2016/1148 (NIS 2 Directive), https://eur-lex.europa.eu/eli/dir/2022/2555/oj/eng, accessed: 17 July 2025.

EUR-Lex (2024a), Directive (EU) 2024/1760 of the European Parliament and of the Council of 13 June 2024 on corporate sustainability due diligence and amending Directive (EU) 2019/1937 and Regulation (EU) 2023/2859, L series, https://eur-lex.europa.eu/eli/dir/2024/1760/oj/eng, accessed: 5 July 2024.

EUR-Lex (2024b), Regulation (EU) 2024/1689 of the European Parliament and of the Council of 13 June 2024 laying down harmonised rules on artificial intelligence (Artificial Intelligence Act) and amending Regulations (EC) No 300/2008, (EU) No 167/2013, (EU) No 168/2013, (EU) 2018/858, (EU) 2018/1139 and (EU) 2019/2144 and Directives 2014/90/EU, (EU) 2016/797 and (EU) 2020/1828 (Artificial Intelligence Act), L 2024/1689, 12 July 2024, https://eur-lex.europa.eu/eli/reg/2024/1689/oj/eng, accessed: 30 June 2025.

European Banking Authority [EBA] (2014), Guidelines on common procedures and methodologies for the supervisory review and evaluation process (SREP), https://www.eba.europa.eu/sites/default/files/documents/10180/935249/4b842c7e-3294-4947-94cd-ad7f94405d66/EBA-GL-2014-13%20%28Guidelines%20on%20SREP%20methodologies%20and%20processes%29.pdf, accessed: 21 March 2025.

European Banking Authority [EBA] (2017), Final Report: Guidelines on internal governance under Directive 2013/36/EU, https://www.eba.europa.eu/sites/default/files/document_library/Publications/Guidelines/2021/1016721/Final%20report%20on%20Guidelines%20on%20internal%20governance%20under%20CRD.pdf, accessed: 5 June 2025.

European Banking Authority [EBA] (2018), EBA guidelines on common procedures and methodologies for the supervisory review and evaluation process (SREP) and supervisory stress testing, https://www.eba.europa.eu/sites/default/files/document_library/Publications/Guidelines/2022/EBA-GL-2022-03%20Revised%20SREP%20Guidelines/1028500/Final%20Report%20on%20Guidelines%20on%20common%20procedures%20and%20methodologies%20for%20SREP%20and%20supervisory%20stress%20testing.pdf, accessed: 17 February 2022.

European Banking Authority [EBA] (2019a), EBA Guidelines on outsourcing arrangements, https://www.eba.europa.eu/sites/default/files/documents/10180/2551996/38c80601-f5d7-4855-8ba3-702423665479/EBA%20revised%20Guidelines%20on%20outsourcing%20arrangements.pdf, accessed: 5 June 2025.

European Banking Authority [EBA] (2019b), EBA publishes guidelines on ICT and security risk management, https://www.eba.europa.eu/sites/default/files/2025-02/23684f95-f669-4852-94a0-dac6c2ae67ad/Final%20report%20on%20amending%20GLs%20on%20ICT%20risk%20and%20security.pdf, accessed: 5 June 2025.

European Banking Authority [EBA] (2020), Consultation Paper – Guidelines on internal governance, https://www.bankingsupervision.europa.eu/ecb/pub/pdf/ssm.202011finalguideonclimate-relatedandenvironmentalrisks~58213f6564.en.pdf, accessed: 21 February 2022.

European Banking Authority [EBA] (2021a), EBA publishes its report on management and supervision of ESG risks for credit institutions and investment firms, https://www.eba.europa.eu/eba-publishes-its-report-management-and-supervision-esg-risks-credit-institutions-and-investment, accessed: 17 February 2022.

European Banking Authority [EBA] (2021b), Final Report – Guidelines on customer due diligence and the factors credit and financial institutions should consider when assessing the money laundering and terrorist financing risk associated with individual business relationships and occasional transactions, https://www.eba.europa.eu/sites/default/files/2024-01/a3e89f4f-fbf3-4bd6-9e07-35f3243555b3/Final%20Amending%20%20Guidelines%20on%20MLTF%20Risk%20Factors.pdf, accessed: 19 March 2025.

European Banking Authority [EBA] (2021c), Final Report – Guidelines on internal governance under Directive 2013/36/EU, https://www.eba.europa.eu/sites/default/documents/files/document_library/Publications/Guidelines/2021/1016721/Final%20report%20on%20Guidelines%20on%20internal%20governance%20under%20CRD.pdf, accessed: 5 June 2025.

European Banking Authority [EBA] (2022), Final Report – Guidelines on the role, tasks and responsibilities AML/CFT compliance officers, https://www.eba.europa.eu/sites/default/files/document_library/Publications/Guidelines/2022/EBA-GL-2022-05%20GLs%20on%20AML%20compliance%20officers/1035126/Guidelines%20on%20AMLCFT%20compliance%20officers.pdf, accessed: 19 March 2025.

European Banking Authority [EBA] (2024), EBA Guidelines on internal policies, procedures and controls to ensure the implementation of Union and national restrictive measures (EBA/GL/2024/14):, https://www.eba.europa.eu/sites/default/files/2024-11/eaeae49d-81a5-4154-8af9-5014f6ee8881/Final%20Report%20Guidelines%20restrictive%20measures%20.pdf, accessed: 20 March 2025.

European Banking Authority [EBA] (2025), Guidelines amending Guidelines EBA/2019/04 on ICT and security risk management, https://www.eba.europa.eu/sites/default/files/2025-02/23684f95-f669-4852-94a0-dac6c2ae67ad/Final%20report%20on%20amending%20GLs%20on%20ICT%20risk%20and%20security.pdf, accessed: 14 July 2025.

European Banking Authority [EBA] (2025b), Final Report: Guidelines on the management of environmental, social and governance (ESG) risks, https://www.eba.europa.eu/sites/default/files/2025-01/fb22982a-d69d-42cc-9d62-1023497ad58a/Final%20Guidelines%20on%20the%20management%20of%20ESG%20risks.pdf, accessed: 16 July 2025.

European Central Bank [ECB] (2018a), Risk appetite frameworks: good progress but still room for improvement, Speech by Danièle Nouy, Chair of ECB Supervisory Board, https://www.bankingsupervision.europa.eu/press/speeches/date/2018/html/ssm.sp180410.en.html, accessed: 21 February 2022.

European Central Bank [ECB] (2018b), Guide to the internal capital adequacy assessment process, https://www.bankingsupervision.europa.eu/ecb/pub/pdf/ssm.icaap_guide_201811.en.pdf, accessed: 24 March 2025.

European Central Bank [ECB] (2020a), Guide on climate-related and environmental risks – Supervisory expectations relating to risk management and disclosure, https://www.bankingsupervision.europa.eu/ecb/pub/pdf/ssm.202011finalguideonclimate-relatedandenvironmentalrisks~58213f6564.en.pdf, accessed: 17 February 2022.

European Central Bank [ECB] (2020b), Strengthening banks' compliance frameworks, https://www.bankingsupervision.europa.eu/press/publications/newsletter/2020/html/ssm.nl200212_1.en.html, accessed: 24 March 2025.

European Central Bank [ECB] (2021), Annual report on the outcome of the 2024 SREP IT Risk questionnaire, https://www.bankingsupervision.europa.eu/activities/srep/2024/html/ssm.srep202412_aggregatedresults2024.en.html, accessed: 9 July 2025.

European Central Bank [ECB] (2023), ECB Banking Supervision: SSM supervisory priorities for 2024–2026, https://www.bankingsupervision.europa.eu/framework/priorities/html/ssm.supervisory_priorities202312~a15d5d36ab.en.html, accessed: 14 July 2025.

European Central Bank [ECB] (2024), Draft Guide on Governance and Risk Culture, https://www.bankingsupervision.europa.eu/framework/legal-framework/public-consultations/pdf/ssm.pubcon202407_draftguide.en.pdf, accessed: 13 May 2025.

European Central Bank [ECB]/Financial Stability Review (2024), "The rise of artificial intel-ligence: Benefits and risks for financial stability", https://www.ecb.europa.eu/press/financial-stability-publications/fsr/special/html/ecb.fsr-art202405_02~58c3ce5246.en.html, accessed: 26 June 2025.

European Commission (s.a.), Taxation and customs union, Time to get the missing part back, https://taxation-customs.ec.europa.eu/taxation/vat/fight-against-vat-fraud_en, accessed: 16 February 2022.

European Commission (2020), Shaping Europe's Digital Future: Communication from the Commission to the European Parliament, the Council, the European Economic and Social Committee and the Committee of the Regions, https://eufordigital.eu/wp-content/uploads/2020/04/communication-shaping-europes-digital-future-feb2020_en_4.pdf, accessed: 13 May 2025.

European Commission (2021a), Commission delegated regulation (EU) 2021/1256 of 21 April 2021 amending Delegated Regulation (EU) 2015/35 as regards the integration of sustainability risks in the governance of insurance and reinsurance undertakings, https://eur-lex.europa.eu/legal-content/EN/TXT/HTML/?uri=CELEX:32021R1256&qid=1705988017764, accessed: 26 June 2025.

European Commission (2021b), EU Sustainable Finance – April Package, https://ec.europa.eu/info/sites/default/files/business_economy_euro/banking_and_finance/documents/sustainable-finance-communication-factsheet_en.pdf, accessed: 14 March 2022.

European Commission (2023a), Regulation (EU) 2023/1115 on the making available on the Union market and the export from the Union of certain commodities and products associated with deforestation and forest degradation, https://environment.ec.europa.eu/topics/forests/deforestation/regulation-deforestation-free-products_en, accessed: 27 May 2025.

European Commission (2023b), Proposal for a Directive of the European Parliament and of the Council on the Substantiation and Communication of Explicit Environmental Claims (Green Claims Directive), COM/2023/166 final, https://eur-lex.europa.eu/legal-content/EN/TXT/?uri=CELEX%3A52023PC0166, accessed: 13 May 2025.

European Commission (2024), Sustainability-related disclosure in the financial services sector, https://finance.ec.europa.eu/sustainable-finance/disclosures/sustainability-related-disclosure-financial-services-sector_en, accessed: 26 June 2025.

European Parliament (2020), Committee on Economic and Monetary Affairs, 2020/0266 (COD), https://eur-lex.europa.eu/eli/reg/2022/2554/oj/eng, accessed: 17 February 2022.

European Parliament (2025), EU AI Act: first regulation on artificial intelligence, https://www.europarl.europa.eu/topics/en/article/20230601STO93804/eu-ai-act-first-regulation-on-artificial-intelligence, accessed: 9 July 2025.

European Securities and Markets Authority [ESMA] (s.a.), MIFID II, https://www.esma.europa.eu/policy-rules/mifid-ii-and-mifir, accessed: 15 February 2022.

European Securities and Markets Authority [ESMA] (2021), Guidelines on Outsourcing to Cloud Service Providers, https://www.esma.europa.eu/document/guidelines-outsourcing-cloud-service-providers, accessed: 14 July 2025.

European Securities and Markets Authority [ESMA] (2022), Final Report – Guidelines on certain aspects of the MiFID II suitability requirements, https://www.esma.europa.eu/sites/default/files/library/esma35-43-3172_final_report_on_mifid_ii_guidelines_on_suitability.pdf, accessed: 13 May 2025.

European Securities and Markets Authority [ESMA] (2023), Artificial intelligence in EU securities markets, February 2023, https://www.esma.europa.eu/sites/default/files/library/ESMA50-164-6247-AI_in_securities_markets.pdf, accessed: 26 June 2025.

European Supervisory Authorities [ESAs] (2024), Final Report on Greenwashing, June 2024, https://www.esma.europa.eu/sites/default/files/2024-06/ESMA36-287652198-2699_Final_Report_on_Greenwashing.pdf, accessed: 13 May 2025.

European Union (s.a.), Antitrust Overview, https://ec.europa.eu/competition-policy/antitrust/antitrust-overview_en, accessed: 16 February 2022.

European Union (s.a.), Comprehensive approach on personal data protection in the European Union, https://edps.europa.eu/data-protection/our-work/publications/opinions/comprehensive-approach-personal-data-protection_en, accessed: 15 February 2022.

European Union (s.a.), Data Protection Directive, https://eur-lex.europa.eu/legal-content/EN/TXT/?uri=celex%3A31995L0046, accessed: 15 February 2022.

European Union (s.a.), General Data Protection Regulation, https://eur-lex.europa.eu/eli/reg/2016/679/oj, accessed: 15 February 2022.

European Union (2021), Conflict of Interest, https://eur-lex.europa.eu/legal-content/EN/TXT/PDF/?uri=CELEX:52021XC0409(01)&from=EN, accessed: 16 February 2022.

Europol (2017), From suspicion to action: Converting financial intelligence into greater operational impact, Publications Office of the European Union, https://www.europol.europa.eu/publications-events/publications/suspicion-to-action-converting-financial-intelligence-greater-operational-impact, accessed: 24 February 2022.

Europol (2021), Cyber Scams 2.0 – New Tips to Help Boost Your Cyber Skills, https://www.europol.europa.eu/newsroom/news/cyber-scams-20-%E2%80%93-new-tips-to-help-boost-your-cyber-skills, accessed: 15 February 2022.

Executive office of the U.S. president (2025), Removing barriers to American leadership in artificial intelligence, 23 January 2025, https://www.whitehouse.gov/presidential-actions/2025/01/removing-barriers-to-american-leadership-in-artificial-intelligence/, accessed: 26 June 2025.

Federal Bureau of Investigation (s.a.), White-Collar Crime, https://www.fbi.gov/investigate/white-collar-crime, accessed: 15 February 2022.

Federal Deposit Insurance Corporation [FDIC] (s.a.), Supervisory guidance on model risk management, https://www.fdic.gov/news/news/financial/2017/fil17022a.pdf, accessed: 17 February 2022.

Federal Deposit Insurance Corporation [FDIC] (2008), Guidance for Managing Third Party Risk, https://www.fdic.gov/bank-examinations/third-party-arrangements-elevating-risk-awareness, accessed: 16 February 2022.

Federal Financial Institutions Examination Council [FFIEC] (2014), BSA/AML Examination Manual, https://bsaaml.ffiec.gov/manual, accessed: 19 March 2025.

FICC Markets Standards Board [FMSB] (2018a), Behavioural Cluster Analysis – Misconduct Patterns in Financial Markets, London, https://fmsb.com/wp-content/uploads/2018/07/BCA_v32_1.pdf, accessed: 26 February 2022.

FICC Markets Standards Board [FMSB] (2018b), Updated analysis published on misconduct in global financial markets, https://fmsb.com/updated-analysis-published-on-misconduct-in-global-financial-markets/, accessed: 16 February 2022.

Financial Action Task Force [FATF] (s.a.), FAQ, Money Laundering, https://www.fatf-gafi.org/faq/moneylaundering/, accessed: 16 February 2022.

Financial Action Task Force [FATF] (s.a.), Glossary, https://www.fatf-gafi.org/en/pages/fatf-glossary.html, accessed: 16 February 2022.

Financial Action Task Force [FATF] (2016), Report to G20 on Counter-Terrorist Financing, Information Sharing, Transparency and Beneficial Ownership, https://www.fatf-gafi.org/media/fatf/documents/reports/G20-Beneficial-Ownership-Sept-2016.pdf, accessed: 25 February 2022.

Financial Action Task Force [FATF] (2019), Terrorist Financing Risk Assessment Guidance, https://www.fatf-gafi.org/media/fatf/documents/reports/Terrorist-Financing-Risk-Assessment-Guidance.pdf, accessed: 16 February 2022.

Financial Action Task Force [FATF] (2020), Objectives for the FATF during the German Presidency (2020–2022), https://www.fatf-gafi.org/media/fatf/documents/German-Presidency-Priorities.pdf, accessed: 25 February 2022.

Financial Conduct Authority [FCA] (s.a.), FCA handbook, Glossary, operational risk, https://www.handbook.fca.org.uk/handbook/glossary/G2210.html, accessed: 16 February 2022.

Financial Conduct Authority [FCA] (2019a), Building operational resilience: Feedback to CP19/32 and final rules, https://www.fca.org.uk/publication/policy/ps21-3-operational-resilience.pdf, accessed: 16 February 2022.

Financial Conduct Authority [FCA] (2019b), Global Financial Innovation Network (GFIN), https://www.fca.org.uk/firms/innovation/global-financial-innovation-network, accessed: 16 February 2022.

Financial Conduct Authority [FCA] (2019c), Progress and challenges – 5 Conduct Questions, London, https://www.fca.org.uk/publication/market-studies/5-conduct-questions-industry-feedback-2018-19.pdf, accessed: 26 February 2022.

Financial Conduct Authority [FCA] (2019d), Senior Managers and Certification Regime – dual-regulated firms, https://www.fca.org.uk/firms/senior-managers-certification-regime/dual-regulated-firms, accessed: 26 February 2022.

Financial Conduct Authority [FCA] (2020a), Code of Conduct (COCON), London, 53rd edition, https://www.handbook.fca.org.uk/handbook/COCON.pdf, accessed: 26 February 2022.

Financial Conduct Authority [FCA] (2020b), Transforming Culture in Financial Services – Driving Purposeful Cultures, http://www.fca.org.uk/publication/discussion/dp20-1.pdf, accessed: 13 May 2025.

Financial Conduct Authority [FCA] (2022), PS22/9: A new Consumer Duty, https://www.fca.org.uk/publications/policy-statements/ps22-9-new-consumer-duty, accessed: 13 May 2025.

Financial Conduct Authority [FCA] (2023), PS23/16: Sustainability Disclosure Requirements (SDR) and investment labels, https://www.fca.org.uk/publication/policy/ps23-16.pdf, accessed: 13 May 2025.

Financial Conduct Authority [FCA] (2024), FG24/3: Finalised Non-Handbook Guidance on the Anti-Greenwashing Rule, Financial Conduct Authority, April 2024, https://www.fca.org.uk/publication/finalised-guidance/fg24-3.pdf, accessed: 13 May 2025.

Financial Crimes Enforcement Network [FinCEN] (2020), FinCEN Director emphasizes the importance of information sharing among financial institutions, https://www.fincen.gov/news/news-releases/fincen-director-emphasizes-importance-information-sharing-among-financial, accessed: 25 February 2022.

Financial Industry Regulatory Authority [FINRA] (2009a), Anti-Intimidation/Coordination, https://www.finra.org/rules-guidance/rulebooks/finra-rules/5240, accessed: 26 February 2022.

Financial Industry Regulatory Authority [FINRA] (2009b), Trading Ahead of Research Reports, https://www.finra.org/rules-guidance/rulebooks/finra-rules/5280, accessed: 26 February 2022.

Financial Industry Regulatory Authority [FINRA] (2013), Telemarketing, https://www.finra.org/rules-guidance/rulebooks/finra-rules/3230, accessed: 26 February 2022.

Financial Industry Regulatory Authority [FINRA] (2017), Prohibited Conduct, https://www.finra.org/investors/learn-to-invest/choosing-investment-professional/prohibited-conduct, accessed: 26 February 2022.

Financial Industry Regulatory Authority [FINRA] (2020), Suitability, https://www.finra.org/rules-guidance/rulebooks/finra-rules/2111, accessed: 26 February 2022.

Financial Service Authority [FSA] (2006), Treating customers fairly – towards fair outcomes for consumers, https://www.fca.org.uk/publication/archive/fsa-tcf-towards.pdf, accessed: 26 February 2022.

Financial Stability Board [FSB] (2009), FSF Principles for Sound Compensation Practices, https://www.fsb.org/wp-content/uploads/r_0904b.pdf, accessed: 26 February 2022.

Financial Stability Board [FSB] (2013a), Principles for An Effective Risk Appetite Framework, https://www.fsb.org/wp-content/uploads/r_131118.pdf, accessed: 21 February 2022.

Financial Stability Board [FSB] (2013b), Thematic Review on Risk Governance, https://www.fsb.org/wp-content/uploads/r_130212.pdf, accessed: 21 February 2022.

Financial Stability Board [FSB] (2018), The Chair – to G20 Leaders, https://www.fsb.org/wp-content/uploads/P271118.pdf, accessed: 26 February 2022.

Financial Stability Institute/Bank of International Settlements (2024), "Regulating AI in the financial sector: recent developments and main challenges (December 2024)", https://www.bis.org/fsi/publ/insights63.pdf, accessed: 26 June 2025.

Finansinspektionen Sweden [FFFS] (2017), Regulations and general guidelines regarding measures against money laundering and terrorist financing, https://www.fi.se/contentassets/423320243f35401f97aa85d5562df59c/fs1711_engn.pdf, accessed: 19 March 2025.

Finansinspektionen Sweden [FFFS] (2024), Regulations amending Finansinspektionen's regulations (FFFS 2017:11) regarding measures against money laundering and terrorist financing, Regulations amending Finansinspektionen's regulations (FFFS 2017:11) regarding measures against money laundering and terrorist financing: https://www.fi.se/en/our-registers/fffs/search-fffs/2017/201711/20244/, accessed: 5 June 2025.

Finanzmarktaufsicht [FINMA] (2018), Aufsicht über das Geschäftsverhalten (Conduct), https://www.finma.ch/de/~/media/finma/dokumente/dokumentencenter/myfinma/faktenblaetter/faktenblatt-conduct.pdf?la=de, accessed: 26 February 2022.

Finanzmarktaufsicht [FINMA] (2023), Archegos: FINMA concludes proceedings against Credit Suisse, https://www.finma.ch/en/news/2023/07/20230724-mm-archegos/, accessed: 13 May 2025.

Finanzmarktaufsicht [FINMA] (2024), FINMA's strategic goals 2025–2028, https://www.finma.ch/en/~/media/finma/dokumente/dokumentencenter/myfinma/finma-publikationen/strategische-ziele/20241113-strategische_ziele_der_finma_2025-2028.pdf?sc_lang=en&hash=BDB18DC12C553860E7088FD6607E2CA7, accessed: 13 May 2025.

Findling, Jean-Francois/Schmitt, Torsten (s.a.), Corporate liability in Luxembourg, https://www.globalcompliancenews.com/white-collar-crime/corporate-liability-in-luxembourg/, accessed: 25 February 2022.

Fletcher, Nick (2018), Barclays boss Jes Staley fined £642,000 over whistleblower scandal, The Guardian, https://www.theguardian.com/business/2018/may/11/barclays-jes-staley-fined-whistleblower-fca, accessed: 26 February 2022.

Gartner (s.a.), Glossary, Vendor Risk Management, https://www.gartner.com/en/information-technology/glossary/vendor-risk-management, accessed: 17 February 2022.

Gautier, Rudolphe (s.a.), Corporate Liability in Switzerland, https://www.globalcompliancenews.com/white-collar-crime/corporate-liability-in-switzerland/, accessed: 25 February 2022.

Geddes, Bruce (2017), Integrity or Compliance Based Ethics – Which Is Better for Today's Business?, in: Open Journal of Business and Management 5, 420–429.

Gittfried, Norbert/Lenhard, Erik/Bohmayr, Walter/Helbing, Claus (2017), When Agile Meets Regulatory Compliance, https://www.bcg.com/de-de/publications/2017/financial-institutions-technology-digital-when-agile-meets-regulatory-compliance, accessed: 25 February 2022.

Global Foreign Exchange Committee [GFEC] (2018), FX Global Code – A set of global principles of good practice in the foreign exchange market, London, https://www.globalfxc.org/docs/fx_global.pdf, accessed: 26 February 2022.

Government Logistics Department [GLD] (2025), Protection of Critical Infrastructures (Computer Systems) Ordinance (Ordinance No. 4 of 2025), https://www.gld.gov.hk/egazette/english/gazette/file.php?year=2025&vol=29&no=13&extra=0&type=1&number=4, accessed: 15 July 2025.

Gutermann, Arne/De Winter, Koen (s.a.), Corporate Liability in Belgium, https://www.globalcompliancenews.com/white-collar-crime/corporate-liability-in-belgium/, accessed: 25 February 2022.

Hartman, Laura (2000), Compliance versus Integrity – The Process of Ethics Integration, in: Journal of Employment Discrimination Law 2, 157–159.

Harvard Law School Forum (2016), On Corporate Governance: Calculating SEC Civil Money Penalties, https://corpgov.law.harvard.edu/2016/01/24/calculating-sec-civil-money-penalties/, accessed: 25 February 2022.

Hedwall, Mattias (s.a.), Corporate Liability in Sweden, https://www.globalcompliancenews.com/white-collar-crime/corporate-liability-in-sweden/, accessed: 25 February 2022.

Herbert Smith Freehills (2024), The Evolution of Individual Accountability Regimes, FSR Outlook 2024, https://www.herbertsmithfreehills.com/insights/reports/fsr-outlook-2024/the-evolution-of-individual-accountability-regimes, accessed: 13 May 2025.

Hillson, D. (2000), Project risks: identifying causes, risks, and effects, PM Network, 14(9), 48–51.

Hong Kong Monetary Authority [HKMA] (2002), Supervisory Policy Manual – CG3 – Code of Conduct, Hong Kong, https://www.hkma.gov.hk/media/eng/doc/key-functions/banking-stability/supervisory-policy-manual/CG-3.pdf, accessed: 26 February 2022.

Hong Kong Monetary Authority [HKMA] (2014), Treat Customers Fairly Charter, Hong Kong, https://www.hkma.gov.hk/media/eng/doc/key-information/guidelines-and-circular/2014/20140328e1.pdf, accessed: 26 February 2022.

Hong Kong Monetary Authority [HKMA] (2015), Code of Banking Practice, https://www.hkma.gov.hk/media/eng/doc/code_eng.pdf, accessed: 26 February 2022.

Hong Kong Monetary Authority [HKMA] (2017a), Supervisory Policy Manual – IC 1 – Risk Management Framework, 2.1.3, https://www.hkma.gov.hk/media/eng/doc/key-functions/banking-stability/supervisory-policy-manual/IC-1.pdf, accessed: 5 June 2025.

Hong Kong Monetary Authority [HKMA] (2017b), Supervisory Policy Manual, CG-1, Corporate governance of locally incorporated authorized institutions, 9.1.1, https://www.hkma.gov.hk/media/eng/doc/key-functions/banking-stability/supervisory-policy-manual/CG-1.pdf, accessed: 20 March 2025.

Hong Kong Monetary Authority [HKMA] (2017c), Bank Culture Reform, Hong Kong, https://www.hkma.gov.hk/media/eng/doc/key-information/guidelines-and-circular/2017/20170302e2.pdf, accessed: 26 February 2022.

Hong Kong Monetary Authority [HKMA] (2017d), Supervisory Policy Manual – CG-6 – Competence and Ethical Behaviour, https://www.hkma.gov.hk/media/eng/doc/key-functions/banking-stability/supervisory-policy-manual/CG-6.pdf, accessed: 26 February 2022.

Hong Kong Monetary Authority [HKMA] (2019), High-level Principles on Artificial Intelligence, https://www.hkma.gov.hk/media/eng/doc/key-information/guidelines-and-circular/2019/20191101e1.pdf, accessed: 25 February 2022.

Hong Kong Monetary Authority [HKMA] (2020a), Artificial Intelligence in Banking: The Changing Landscape in Compliance and Supervision, https://www.hkma.gov.hk/eng/news-and-media/press-releases/2020/08/20200821-3/, accessed: 25 February 2022.

Hong Kong Monetary Authority [HKMA] (2020b), Consultation Paper on Implementation of Mandatory Reference Checking Scheme to Address the "Rolling Bad Apples" Phenomenon, Hong Kong, https://www.hkma.gov.hk/media/eng/regulatory-resources/consultations/Enclosure_20200508.pdf, accessed: 26 February 2022.

Hong Kong Monetary Authority [HKMA] (2021a), Technology Risk Management, https://www.hkma.gov.hk/eng/regulatory-resources/regulatory-guides/by-subject-current/technology-risk-management/, accessed: 25 February 2022.

Hong Kong Monetary Authority [HKMA] (2021b), Supervisory Policy Manual: GS-1 Climate Risk Management, https://www.hkma.gov.hk/media/eng/doc/key-functions/banking-stability/supervisory-policy-manual/GS-1_for_consultation_20Jul2021.pdf, accessed: 14 March 2022.

Hong Kong Monetary Authority [HKMA] (2022a), Circular on Treat Customers Fairly – Sound Practices for Customer Data Protection, 4 April 2022, https://brdr.hkma.gov.hk/eng/doc-ldg/docId/getPdf/20220404-1-EN/20220404-1-EN.pdf, accessed 19 May 2025.

Hong Kong Monetary Authority [HKMA] (2022b), Supervisory Policy Manual, OR-1, Operational risk management, https://www.hkma.gov.hk/media/eng/doc/key-functions/banking-stability/supervisory-policy-manual/OR-1.pdf, accessed: 24 March 2025.

Hong Kong Monetary Authority [HKMA] (2023), Guideline on Anti-Money Laundering and Counter Financing of Terrorism, https://www.hkma.gov.hk/media/eng/doc/key-information/guidelines-and-circular/guideline/Guideline_on_AML-CFT_(for_AIs)_eng_May%202023.pdf, accessed: 5 June 2025.

Hong Kong Monetary Authority [HKMA] (2024), Banking Conduct and Enforcement, https://www.hkma.gov.hk/eng/key-functions/banking/banking-conduct-supervision/, accessed: 13 May 2025.

Hungerford, Jason/Lev, Ori/Soliman, Tamer/Ford, James/Lee, Timothy (2021), Issues Arising for Financial Institutions and Regulated Entities, in: The Guide to Sanctions, https://globalinvestigationsreview.com/guide/the-guide-sanctions/second-edition/article/issues-arising-financial-institutions-and-regulated-entities, accessed: 25 February 2022.

Institute of Internal Auditors [IIA] (2013), Position Paper: The Three-Lines-of-defense in effective risk management and control, https://theiia.fi/wp-content/uploads/2017/01/pp-the-three-lines-of-defense-in-effective-risk-management-and-control.pdf, accessed: 22 February 2022.

Institute of Risk Management [IRM] (s.a.), Competition Law Risk, https://www.theirm.org/what-we-say/thought-leadership/competition-law-risk/, accessed: 17 February 2022.

International Chamber of Commerce (s.a.), Antitrust & competition, https://iccwbo.org/global-insights/global-trade/competitive-markets/, accessed: 16 February 2022.

International Compliance Association [ICA] (s.a.), What Is Crime?, https://www.int-comp.org/careers/your-career-in-financial-crime-prevention/what-is-financial-crime/, accessed: 16 February 2022.

International Monetary Fund [IMF] (2025), Power Hungry: How AI Will Drive Energy De-mand, April 2025, https://www.imf.org/en/Publications/WP/Issues/2025/04/21/Power-Hungry-How-AI-Will-Drive-Energy-Demand-566304, accessed: 26 June 2025.

International Organization of Securities Commissions [IOSCO] (2017), IOSCO Task Force Report on Wholesale Conduct, https://www.iosco.org/library/pubdocs/pdf/IOSCOPD563.pdf, accessed: 13 May 2025.

International Organization of Securities Commissions [IOSCO] (2021), The use of artificial intelligence and machine learning by market intermediaries and asset managers, https://www.iosco.org/library/pubdocs/pdf/IOSCOPD684.pdf, accessed: 13 May 2025.

Investopedia (2021a), Definition: Embezzlement, https://www.investopedia.com/terms/e/embezzlement.asp, accessed: 16 February 2022.

Investopedia (2021b), Definition: What is Financial Risk?, https://www.investopedia.com/terms/f/financialrisk.asp, accessed: 22 February 2022.

Irish Statute Book [ISB] (2023), Central Bank (Individual Accountability Framework) Act 2023, https://www.irishstatutebook.ie/eli/2023/act/5/enacted/en/html, accessed: 13 May 2025.

IRS (s.a.), Worksheet solutions – the difference between tax avoidance and tax evasion, https://apps.irs.gov/app/understandingTaxes/whys/thm01/les03/media/ws_ans_thm01_les03.pdf, accessed: 16 February 2022.

ISO (2020), Draft: Compliance management systems – Requirements with guidance for use, ISO/DIS 37301:2020(E).

Lager, James M. (2010), Governments Demand Compliance, Ethics Demands Leadership, in: Journal of Public Affairs 10, 216–224.

Lasry, Eric/Koski, Sara/Guyot-Rechard (s.a.), Clotilde Anti-Corruption in France, Global Compliance News, https://www.globalcompliancenews.com/anti-corruption/handbook/anti-corruption-in-france/, accessed: 25 February 2022.

Loconte, Richard (2018), DFS Fines Barclays Bank PLC and New York branch $15 Million Following Whistleblower Investigation, New York State Department of Financial Services, https://www.dfs.ny.gov/reports_and_publications/press_releases/pr1812181, accessed: 26 February 2022.

Masters, Brooke (2011), Financial Groups Hit by Flood of New Rules, *Financial Times*, https://www.ft.com/content/158171f6-218e-11e1-a19f-00144feabdc0, accessed: 25 February 2022.

Meyer, Laurence H. (2000), Why risk management is important for global financial institutions, in: BIS Review 68, 1, https://www.bis.org/review/r000904b.pdf, accessed: 15 February 2022.

Missal, Michael J./Lambrakopoulos, Stavroula E./Kowalk, Curtis S. (2010), Conducting Internal Investigations, K&L GATES LLP, Washington, D.C., https://files.klgates.com/files/publication/9c8c688d-f33b-4e00-befd-067ccd918740/presentation/publicationattachment/08668f67-5813-4c92-ac28-121554cc82a2/conducting_internal_tinvestigations.pdf, accessed: 25 February 2022.

Mondaq (2024), Dutch Public Prosecution Office Publishes Rules On Self-Disclosure, Cooperation And Self-Investigation – Policy With Incentives In Case Of Irregularities, 16 December 2024, https://www.mondaq.com/white-collar-crime-anti-corruption-fraud/1557412/the-dpps-instruction-on-self-reporting-cooperation-and-investigation-policy-with-incentives-in-case-of-irregularities, accessed: 19 May 2025.

Monetary Authority of Singapore [MAS] (2013), Board and senior management, https://www.mas.gov.sg/-/media/MAS/Regulations-and-Financial-Stability/Regulatory-and-Supervisory-Framework/Risk-Management/Board-and-Senior-Mgmt_1-Apr-2013.pdf, accessed: 20 March 2025.

Monetary Authority of Singapore [MAS] (2014), Guidelines on risk management practices – internal controls, https://www.mas.gov.sg/-/media/MAS/Regulations-and-Financial-Stability/Regulatory-and-Supervisory-Framework/Risk-Management/Internal-Control.pdf, accessed: 23 February 2022.

Monetary Authority of Singapore [MAS] (2018a [2016]), Guidelines on Outsourcing, https://www.mas.gov.sg/regulation/guidelines/guidelines-on-outsourcing, accessed: 17 February 2022.

Monetary Authority of Singapore [MAS] (2018b), FATF Guidance on Private Sector Information Sharing and Revised INR.18, https://www.mas.gov.sg/regulation/external-publications/fatf-guidance-on-private-sector-information-sharing-and-revised-inr18, accessed: 25 February 2022.

Monetary Authority of Singapore [MAS] (2019), Proposed Guidelines on Individual Accountability and Conduct, https://www.mas.gov.sg/-/media/Response-to-Feedback-Received_Proposed-Guidelines-on-Individual-Accountability-and-Conduct.pdf, accessed: 26 February 2022.

Monetary Authority of Singapore [MAS] (2020a), Guidelines on Environmental Risk management (Banks), https://www.mas.gov.sg/-/media/MAS/Regulations-and-Financial-Stability/Regulations-Guidance-and-Licensing/Commercial-Banks/Regulations-Guidance-and-Licensing/Guidelines/Guidelines-on-Environmental-Risk---Banks/Guidelines-on-Environmental-Risk-Management-for-Banks.pdf, accessed: 14 March 2022.

Monetary Authority of Singapore [MAS] (2020b), Guidelines on Individual Accountability and Conduct, https://www.mas.gov.sg/-/media/mas/mpi/guidelines/guidelines-on-individual-accountability-and-conduct.pdf, accessed: 30 June 2025.

Monetary Authority of Singapore [MAS] (2021a), Guidelines on Risk Management Practices – Board and senior management, 2.3.1, https://www.mas.gov.sg/-/media/MAS/Regulations-and-Financial-Stability/Regulatory-and-Supervisory-Framework/Risk-Management/Board-and-Senior-Mgmt_01-Jul-2021.pdf, accessed: 5 June 2025.

Monetary Authority of Singapore [MAS] (2021b), Notice 626 – Prevention of money laundering and countering the financing of terrorism, https://www.mas.gov.sg/-/media/mas-media-library/regulation/notices/amld/notice-626/mas-notice-626-dated-28-march-2024.pdf, accessed: 19 March 2025.

Monetary Authority of Singapore [MAS] (2024a), Guidelines on risk management practices – internal controls, https://www.mas.gov.sg/-/media/mas/regulations-and-financial-stability/regulatory-and-supervisory-framework/risk-management/guidelines-on-risk-management-practices--internal-controls-july-2024.pdf, accessed: 24 March 2025.

Monetary Authority of Singapore [MAS] (2024b), MAS Notice 637, Risk-based capital requirements for banks incorporated in Singapore, https://www.mas.gov.sg/-/media/mas-media-library/regulation/notices/ppd/notice-637/mas-notice-637-effective-1-january-2025.pdf, accessed: 24 March 2025.

Monetary Authority of Singapore [MAS]/The association of Banks in Singapore [ABS] (2021), Risk management and operational resilience in a remote working environment, https://www.mas.gov.sg/-/media/MAS/News-and-Publications/Monographs-and-Information-Papers/Risk-Management-and-Operational-Resilience-in-a-Remote-Working-Environment.pdf, accessed: 17 February 2022.

Morrison, Scott (2017), House of Representatives – Official Hansard – 19 October 2017 – Second Reading, https://www.aph.gov.au/Parliamentary_Business/Hansard?wc=19/10/2017, accessed: 26 February 2022.

National Institute of Standards and Technology [NIST] (s.a.), Cyber Risk, Glossary, Computer Security Resource Center, https://csrc.nist.gov/glossary/term/cyber_risk, accessed: 17 February 2022.

National Institute of Standards and Technology [NIST] (s.a.), Data Confidentiality, Glossary, Computer Security Resource Center, https://www.nccoe.nist.gov/data-confidentiality-identifying-and-protecting-assets-against-data-breaches, accessed: 17 February 2022.

National Treasury, department of South Africa (2014), Treating Customers Fairly in the Financial Sector: A Draft Market Conduct Policy Framework for South Africa, http://www.treasury.gov.za/public%20comments/fsr2014/Treating%20Customers%20Fairly%20in%20the%20Financial%20Sector%20Draft%20MCP%20Framework%20Amended%20Jan2015%20WithAp6.pdf, accessed: 21 March 2022.

New York Department of Financial Services [NYDFS] (2017), 23 NYCRR 500: Cybersecurity Requirements for Financial Services Companies, https://www.dfs.ny.gov/system/files/documents/2023/03/23NYCRR500_0.pdf, accessed: 14 July 2025.

Ng, Lena (2018), Senior Manager Responsibility – UK Senior Managers Regime and HK Manager-in-Charge Regime, Clifford Chance, http://www.imas.org.sg/public/media/2020/01/06/1796_Clifford_Chance_-_Senior_Manager_Regimes.pdf, accessed: 26 February 2022.

Oesterreichische Nationalbank [OeNB]/Financial Market Authority [FMA] (2006), Guidelines on Operational Risk Management, https://www.oenb.at/dam/jcr:04766cfa-aed3-4461-b393-da903359f08a/operational_risk_screen_tcm16-49652.pdf, accessed: 15 February 2022.

Office of Foreign Assets Control [OFAC] (2019), A Framework for OFAC Compliance Commitments, https://home.treasury.gov/system/files/126/framework_ofac_cc.pdf, accessed: 9 March 2022.

Office of the Comptroller of the Currency [OCC] (s.a.), Financial Crime, https://www.occ.treas.gov/topics/supervision-and-examination/bank-operations/financial-crime/index-financial-crime.html, accessed: 16 February 2022.

Office of the Comptroller of the Currency [OCC] (s.a.), Cybersecurity Supervision Work Program Overview, https://www.occ.gov/topics/supervision-and-examination/bank-operations/bit/cybersecurity-supervision-work-program-overview.html, accessed: 14 July 2025.

Office of the Comptroller of the Currency [OCC] (1996), Categories of Risk, https://www.occ.treas.gov/publications-and-resources/publications/comptrollers-handbook/files/corporate-risk-governance/pub-ch-corporate-risk.pdf, accessed: 17 February 2022.

Office of the Comptroller of the Currency [OCC] (2014), OCC Guidelines Establishing Heightened Standards for Certain Large Insured National Banks, Insured Federal Savings Associations, and Insured Federal Branches; Integration of Regulations, https://www.federalregister.gov/documents/2014/09/11/2014-21224/occ-guidelines-establishing-heightened-standards-for-certain-large-insured-national-banks-insured, accessed: 5 June 2025.

Office of the Comptroller of the Currency [OCC] (2018), Handbook, Capital and Dividends, https://www.occ.treas.gov/publications-and-resources/publications/comptrollers-handbook/files/capital-dividends/pub-ch-capital-and-dividends.pdf, accessed: 24 March 2025.

Office of the Comptroller of the Currency [OCC] (2019a), Operational risk: Fraud risk management principles, OCC Bulletin 2019-37, https://www.occ.treas.gov/news-issuances/bulletins/2019/bulletin-2019-37.html, accessed: 16 February 2022.

Office of the Comptroller of the Currency [OCC] (2019b), Handbook: Corporate and Risk Governance, https://www.occ.gov/publications-and-resources/publications/comptrollers-handbook/files/corporate-risk-governance/pub-ch-corporate-risk.pdf, accessed: 19 March 2025.

Office of the Comptroller of the Currency [OCC] (2021), Bank secrecy Act (BSA), https://www.occ.treas.gov/topics/supervision-and-examination/bsa/index-bsa.html, accessed: 19 March 2025.

Office of the Superintendent of Financial Institutions [OSFI] (2021a), Enhancing banks' and insurers' approaches to managing the financial risks from climate change, https://www.osfi-bsif.gc.ca/en/print/pdf/node/571, accessed: 17 February 2022.

Office of the Superintendent of Financial Institutions [OSFI] (2021b), Technology and Cyber Risk Management, https://www.osfi-bsif.gc.ca/Eng/fi-if/rg-ro/gdn-ort/gl-ld/Pages/b13.aspx, accessed: 17 February 2022.

Onyebuchi, Vincent N. (2011), Ethics in Accounting, in: International Journal of Business and Social Science 2, 275–276.

Open Risk Manual (s.a.), Business Execution, https://www.openriskmanual.org/wiki/Business_Execution#:~:text=6%20External%20Links-,Definition,execution%20of%20regular%20business%20tasks, accessed: 17 February 2022.

Paine, Lynn S. (1994), Managing for Organizational Integrity, in: Harvard Business Review, https://hbr.org/1994/03/managing-for-organizational-integrity, accessed: 26 February 2022.

Parliament of Singapore (2024), Cybersecurity (Amendment) Bill, Bill No. 15/2024, https://www.parliament.gov.sg/docs/default-source/bills-introduced/cybersecurity-(amendment)-bill-15-2024.pdf?sfvrsn=1bb05508_1, accessed: 17 July 2025.

Pattwell, Jennifer/Lim, Denise/Maheshwari, Raksha (2019), MAS' latest updates on "Guidelines on Individual Accountability and Conduct", PwC, https://www.pwc.com/sg/en/risk-assurance/assets/mas-updates-guidelines-on-individual-accountability-and-conduct-062019.pdf, accessed: 26 February 2022.

Perry, James/Capps, David/Green, Jake/Johnston, Lorraine (2017), Conduct Risk framework – a guide for firms, https://www.ashurst.com/en/news-and-insights/legal-updates/conduct-risk-framework-a-guide-for-firms/, accessed: 26 February 2022.

Rechtsinformationssystem des Bundes [RIS] (2005), Bundesgesetz über die Verantwortlichkeit von Verbänden für Straftaten (Verbandsverantwortlichkeitsgesetz – VbVG), https://www.ris.bka.gv.at/Dokumente/BgblAuth/BGBLA_2005_I_151/BGBLA_2005_I_151.pdfsig, accessed: 25 February 2022.

Regulation Asia (2019), BNM Issues Draft Responsibility Mapping Framework for FIs, https://www.regulationasia.com/bnm-issues-draft-responsibility-mapping-framework-for-fis/, accessed: 26 February 2022.

Roberts, Robert (2009), The Rise of Compliance-Based Ethics Management, in: Public Integrity 11, 261–277.

Roos, Philipp/Merali, Zara/Nicholas, Geoff/Zelnick, Kimperly/Nolte, Norbert (2022), Global Enforcement Outlook: Critical data management issues in investigations, Freshfields Bruckhaus Deringer, https://riskandcompliance.freshfields.com/post/102hhf6/global-enforcement-outlook-critical-data-management-issues-in-investigations, accessed: 9 March 2022.

Schulz, Martin R. (2021), Compliance Management – Grundlagen, Orientierungshilfen und Erfolgsfaktoren, in: Schulz, Martin R. (ed.), Compliance Management im Unternehmen: Erfolgsfaktoren und praktische Umsetzung, 2nd edition, Fachmedien Recht und Wirtschaft, Frankfurt, 1–55.

Schürrle, Thomas/Popp, Friedrich/Deschins, Jennifer (2020), Attorney-client privilege according to German law, in: GIR Privilege Know-how 2020 – Germany, Association of Corporate Counsel, https://www.acc.com/resource-library/gir-privilege-know-how-2020-germany, accessed: 25 February 2022.

Securities and Futures Commission Hong Kong [SFC] (2003), Management, Supervision and Internal Control Guidelines, https://www.sfc.hk/-/media/EN/assets/components/codes/files-current/web/guidelines/management-supervision-and-internal-control-gu/management-supervision-and-internal-control-guidelines-for-persons-licensed.pdf, accessed: 25 February 2022.

Security and Exchange Commission [SEC] (2004), Investment Adviser Codes of Ethics, https://www.sec.gov/rules/final/ia-2256.htm, accessed: 26 February 2022.

Security and Exchange Commission [SEC] (2012), Conflicts of Interest and Risk Governance, https://www.sec.gov/news/speech/2012-spch103112cvdhtm, accessed: 16 February 2022.

Security and Exchange Commission [SEC] (2016), SEC Enforcement Actions – Addressing Misconduct That Led To or Arose From the Financial Crisis, https://www.sec.gov/spotlight/enf-actions-fc.shtml, accessed: 26 February 2022.

Security and Exchange Commission [SEC] (2019a), Examination Priorities – Office of Compliance Inspections and Examinations, https://www.sec.gov/about/offices/ocie/national-examination-program-priorities-2020.pdf, accessed: 26 February 2022.

Security and Exchange Commission [SEC] (2019b), Observations from Examinations of Investment Advisers – Compliance, Supervision, and Disclosure of Conflicts of Interest, https://www.sec.gov/files/OCIE%20Risk%20Alert%20-%20Supervision%20Initiative.pdf, accessed: 26 February 2022.

Securities and Exchange Commission [SEC] (2020a), Exchange Act Rule 17a-4: Records to Be Preserved by Certain Exchange Members, Brokers and Dealers, 17 CFR § 240.17a-4, https://www.ecfr.gov/current/title-17/chapter-II/part-240/section-240.17a-4, accessed: 30 June 2025.

Securities and Exchange Commission [SEC] (2020b), Regulation Best Interest: The Broker-Dealer Standard of Conduct, 17 CFR § 240.15l-1, https://www.ecfr.gov/current/title-17/chapter-II/part-240/section-240.15l-1, accessed: 30 June 2025.

Securities and Exchange Commission [SEC] (2022), SEC Charges Allianz Global Investors and Three Former Senior Portfolio Managers with Multibillion Dollar Securities Fraud, https://www.sec.gov/news/press-release/2022-84, accessed: 13 May 2025.

Securities and Exchange Commission [SEC] (2023a), Division of Examinations: 2023 Examination Priorities, https://www.sec.gov/files/2023-exam-priorities.pdf, accessed: 13 May 2025.

Securities and Exchange Commission [SEC] (2023b), SEC Proposes New Requirements to Address Risks to Investors From Conflicts of Interest Associated With the Use of Predictive Data Analytics by Broker-Dealers and Investment Advisers, https://www.sec.gov/newsroom/press-releases/2023-140, accessed: 30 June 2025.

Security and Exchange Commission [SEC] (2023c), 17 CFR Parts 229, 232, 239, 240, and 249, https://public-inspection.federalregister.gov/2023-16194.pdf?1691070880, accessed: 14 July 2025.

Securities and Exchange Commission [SEC] (2024), SEC Adopts Rules to Enhance and Standardize Climate-Related Disclosures for Investors, https://www.sec.gov/newsroom/press-releases/2024-31, accessed: 30 June 2025.

St. John, Mariah (2024), Cybersecurity Stats, Facts And Figures You Should Know, 28 August 2024, Forbes, https://www.forbes.com/advisor/education/it-and-tech/cybersecurity-statistics/#16, accessed: 14 July 2025.

Security and Exchange Commission [SEC] (2020c), Wells Fargo to Pay $500 Million for Misleading Investors About the Success of Its Largest Business Unit, https://www.sec.gov/news/press-release/2020-281, accessed: 26 February 2022.

Security and Exchange Commission [SEC] (2021), SEC Announces Enforcement Task Force Focused on Climate and ESG Issues, https://www.sec.gov/news/press-release/2021-42, accessed: 14 March 2022.Senior Supervisors Group [SSG] (2009), Risk Management Lessons from the Global Banking Crisis of 2008, https://www.fsb.org/wp-content/uploads/r_0910a.pdf?page_moved=1, accessed: 21 February 2022.

Senior Supervisors Group [SSG] (2010), Observation on developments in RAF and IT infrastructure, https://www.newyorkfed.org/medialibrary/media/newsevents/news/banking/2010/an101223.pdf, accessed: 21 February 2022.

Singapore Foreign Exchange Market Committee [SFEMC] (2018), The Singapore Guide to Conduct and Market Practices for the Wholesale Financial Markets, http://www.sfemc.org/pdf/Blue%20Book_FINAL.pdf, accessed: 26 February 2022.

Single Supervisory Mechanism (2016), SSM supervisory statement on governance and risk appetite, https://www.bankingsupervision.europa.eu/ecb/pub/pdf/ssm_supervisory_statement_on_governance_and_risk_appetite_201606.en.pdf, accessed: 21 February 2022.

Skydsgaard, Nikolaj (2020), FSA reports Danske Bank to police over market abuse, Reuters, https://www.reuters.com/article/us-danske-bank-regulations/fsa-reports-danske-bank-to-police-over-market-abuse-idUSKBN23H1RR, accessed: 26 February 2022.

Sliger, Nicole/Wong, Pei Li/Weinberg, Linda/Howard, Roscoe C, Jr. (2020), The Role of Forensics in Sanctions Investigations, https://globalinvestigationsreview.com/guide/the-guide-sanctions/first-edition/article/the-role-of-forensics-in-sanctions-investigations, accessed: 25 February 2022.

Stark, Andrew (1993), What's the Matter with Business Ethics?, in: Harvard Business Review 71, 38–48.

Starling (2020), Culture & Conduct Risk in the Banking Sector, https://starlingtrust.com/the-starling-compendium/, accessed: 26 February 2022.

State of California, Department of Justice (s. a.), California Consumer Privacy Act (CCPA), https://oag.ca.gov/privacy/ccpa#:~:text=The%20California%20Consumer%20Privacy%20Act,how%20to%20implement%20the%20law.&text=The%20right%20to%20opt%2Dout,of%20their%20personal%20information%3B%20and, accessed: 22 February 2022.

Storage Networking Industry Association [SNIA] (s. a.),What is data privacy?, https://www.snia.org/education/what-is-data-privacy, accessed: 17 February 2022.

Studio Legale Pisano (s. a.), Government Investigations in Italy, https://www.lexology.com/library/detail.aspx?g=2dd27402-5489-4f7f-9747-c1e0c4838aa8, accessed: 25 February 2022.

Tagesschau (2025), Neuer Streit über die Lieferkettenrichtlinie?, 14 May 2025, https://www.tagesschau.de/wirtschaft/weltwirtschaft/lieferketten-reform-koalition-100.html, accessed: 2 July 2025.

Tappe, Anneken (2020), Former Wells Fargo CEO banned from banking industry and fined $17.5 million, CNN, https://edition.cnn.com/2020/01/23/investing/wells-fargo-executives-regulator/index.html, accessed: 26 February 2022.

Task Force on Climate-Related Disclosures [TFCD] (2021), 2021 Status Report, https://www.fsb.org/wp-content/uploads/P141021-1.pdf, accessed: 14 March 2022.

The Wolfsberg Group (2019), Wolfsberg Guidance on Sanctions Screening, https://db.wolfsberg-group.org/assets/4b6c2db6-696d-492e-bdd5-c51552708597/Wolfsberg%20Guidance%20on%20Sanctions%20Screening.pdf, accessed: 16 February 2022.

Thielemann, Ulrich (2005), Compliance und Integrity – zwei Seiten ethisch integrierter Unternehmenssteuerung: Lektionen aus dem Compliance-Management einer Großbank, in: Zeitschrift für Wirtschafts- und Unternehmensethik, 6(1), 31–45, https://nbn-resolving.org/urn:nbn:de:0168-ssoar-347214.

Thomson Reuters (2018), Culture and conduct risk survey – How do you compare?, New York, https://legal.thomsonreuters.com/en/insights/articles/culture-and-conduct-risk-survey-2018, accessed: 26 February 2022.

Thomson Reuters (2020), Cost of Compliance Report 2020, https://corporate.thomsonreuters.com/Cost-of-Compliance-2020, accessed: 26 February 2022.

Transparency International (s.a.), Global Anti-Bribery Guidance https://www.antibriberyguidance.org/guidance/5-what-bribery/guidance#:~:text=TI%20defines%20bribery%20as%3A%20the,donations%2C%20favours%20etc, accessed: 22 February 2022.

Transparency International (s.a.), Tax Evasion, Corruptionary, https://www.transparency.org/en/corruptionary/tax-evasion, accessed: 16 February 2022.

Treviño, Linda K./Nelson, Katherina A. (2017), Managing Business Ethics – Straight Talk about How to Do It Right, Hoboken, 7th edition.

Tullberg, Jan (2012), Integrity-Clarifying and Upgrading an Important Concept for Business Ethics, in: Business & Society Review 117, 89–121.

United Nations Environment Programme [UNEP] (2014), Finance Initiative, Human Rights Guidance tool, https://www.unepfi.org/humanrightstoolkit/, accessed: 17 February 2022.

United States Congress (2021), H.R.3948 – GSIB Act of 2021, https://www.congress.gov/bill/117th-congress/house-bill/3948/text, accessed: 14 March 2022.

U.S. Department of Commerce/National Institute of Standards and Technology (2012), Guide for conducting risk assessments, https://nvlpubs.nist.gov/nistpubs/Legacy/SP/nistspecialpublication800-30r1.pdf, accessed: 15 February 2022.

U.S. Department of Homeland Security (2022), Uyghur Forced Labor Prevention Act (UFLPA), https://www.dhs.gov/uflpa, accessed: 27 May 2025.

U.S. Department of Justice Criminal Division [DOJ] (2020), Evaluation of Corporate Compliance Programs https://www.justice.gov/criminal-fraud/page/file/937501/download, accessed: 24 February 2022.

U.S. Department of Justice [DOJ] (2024a), Evaluation of Corporate Compliance Programs in Criminal Antitrust Investigations, https://www.justice.gov/d9/2024-11/DOJ%20Antitrust%20Division%20ECCP%20-%20November%202024%20Updates%20-%20FINAL.pdf, accessed: 20 May 2025.

U.S. Department of Justice [DOJ] (2024b), Samuel Bankman-Fried Sentenced to 25 Years for His Orchestration of Multiple Fraudulent Schemes, https://www.justice.gov/archives/opa/pr/samuel-bankman-fried-sentenced-25-years-his-orchestration-multiple-fraudulent-schemes#:~:text=Samuel%20Bankman%2DFried%2C%20also%20known, orchestration%20of%20multiple%20fraudulent%20schemes., accessed: 13 May 2025.

U.S. Department of Justice [DOJ] (2024c), Evaluation of Corporate Compliance Programs (Updated September 2024), Criminal Division, https://www.justice.gov/criminal/criminal-fraud/page/file/937501/dl?inline=, accessed: 13 May 2025.

U.S. Department of Justice/Procurement Collusion Strike Force (2021), A Whole-of-Government Approach to Combating a Whole-of-Government Problem, https://www.justice.gov/atr/procurement-collusion-strike-force, accessed: 16 February 2022.

van den Berg, Valérie (s. a.), Corporate Liability in the Netherlands, https://www.globalcompliancenews.com/white-collar-crime/corporate-liability-in-the-netherlands/, accessed: 25 February 2022.

Wass, Sanne (2020), Banks use privacy – enhancing tech to tackle money laundering as regulation lags, https://www.spglobal.com/marketintelligence/en/news-insights/latest-news-headlines/banks-use-privacy-enhancing-tech-to-tackle-money-laundering-as-regulation-lags-61074568, accessed: 25 February 2022.

World Economic Forum (2023), The Global RisksReport 2023, 18th Edition, Insight Report, 11 January 2023, https://www3.weforum.org/docs/WEF_Global_Risks_Report_2023.pdf, accessed: 14 July 2025.

Your Europe (2021), Data protection under GDPR, https://europa.eu/youreurope/business/dealing-with-customers/data-protection/data-protection-gdpr/index_en.htm, accessed: 25 February 2022.